Fighting for
Our Health

*The Epic Battle to Make Health
Care a Right in the United States*

The author at a Health Care for America Now rally on Capitol Hill, June 25, 2009

Photo by Jocelyn Augustino

Fighting for Our Health

*The Epic Battle to Make Health
Care a Right in the United States*

Richard Kirsch

The Rockefeller Institute Press
Albany, New York

The Rockefeller Institute Press, Albany, New York 12203-1003
© 2011 by the Rockefeller Institute Press
All rights reserved.
Printed in the United States of America

The Rockefeller Institute Press
The Nelson Rockefeller of Institute of Government
The University at Albany
411 State Street
Albany, New York 12203-1003

Library of Congress Cataloging-in-Publication Data

Kirsch, Richard.
  Fighting for our health : the epic battle to make health care a right in the United States / Richard Kirsch.
    p. ; cm.
  Includes bibliographical references and index.
  ISBN 978-1-930912-24-3 (alk. paper)
  I. Title.
  [DNLM: 1. United States. Patient Protection and Affordable Care Act. 2. Insurance, Health—legislation & jurisprudence—United States. 3. Legislation as Topic—history—United States. 4. Health Care Reform—history—United States. 5. Health Care Reform—legislation & jurisprudence—United States. 6. History, 21st Century—United States. 7. Politics—United States. W 32.5 AA1]

  362.10973—dc23
                                    2011036496

ISBN: 978-1-930912-24-3

For

Claudia, Jocelyn, Evan, Lindsay,
Noah, Abby, and Bob

and

Lisa and all our sisters and brothers
in our fight for economic justice.

Table of Contents

Website: www.FightingforOurHealth.com is designed as an accompaniment to *Fighting for Our Health*. Readers will find pictures of the people discussed in the book, pictures and video of many of the events, video of HCAN advertisements and ads run by other groups, copies of key documents, and links to other documents. The website is organized to correspond with the chapters of *Fighting for Our Health*.

Foreword

F*ighting for Our Health* is an unusual book for the Rockefeller Institute Press to publish. Most of our authors are academicians or former government officials. Richard Kirsch, however, has spent nearly his entire professional career outside of government advocating for policy change. Most of our books focus on issues affecting state and local governments. But *Fighting for Our Health* deals with one of the most important *national* policy changes in recent decades. Finally, the Institute strives to provide neutral analyses of state and local policy issues. Yet there's nothing dispassionate in Kirsch's exciting, insider account of the tortuous process by which the Affordable Care Act of 2010 (ACA) became law, or in his perspective as the national campaign manager of the fascinating coalition he helped to create, Health Care for American Now (HCAN).

Still, in many ways, this book deals with core concerns of the Institute, as the ACA has now passed much of the responsibility down to the states for making health care reform work. And as that happens, a critical question is how political advocates on all sides of the reform issue adjust to the much larger, fifty-state decision-making arena, where many policy, administrative, and budgetary choices are still to be made and eventually re-made many times over. From that perspective, it's important to understand how the national coalition around health care reform was constructed. By seeing the strategies and capacities of the organizations involved in the national struggle over reform, we will have a clearer sense of whether the political balance of power is likely to shift markedly as policy choices move down the federal system and stretch out over time.

Richard Kirsch offers a vivid, first-person account of how health care reform came to be — and he brings to light many points about the political struggle that are not found in other descriptions of these momentous events. For instance, most accounts of the politics of the Affordable Care Act stressed the battles between the parties and between the White House and the Congress. These fights and relationships were obviously important, but *Fighting for Our Health* also shows just how hard a slog it was to bring the Democrats on board — and not just the Democrats at the extreme conservative and liberal ends of ideological spectrum, but mainstream Democrats as well.

Kirsch also corrects the widespread perception that nearly all of the grassroots activities were on the right — lined up primarily against national Democrats. Press coverage may have given this impression. When the Pew Research Forum looked at topics covered by the press relating to health care reform, the only citizen activities making the top subjects were the tea party activists, who were overwhelmingly opposed to the legislation and the Obama Administration. But as Kirsch points out, there were many, often quite large, citizen rallies in support of health care reform — and though they may not have gotten the broad public attention that the conservative activities received, they often got noticed by their intended targets, Democratic Members of Congress.

Kirsch also checks a popular view of lobbying, as primarily an "inside the beltway" activity, involving campaign contributions, meetings with legislators, policy briefings, and other direct communications with politicians. Certainly, some groups still restrict their activities to "inside" lobbying. But Kirsch's account of a large-scale campaign shows not only how crucial "outside-the-beltway lobbying" was (as one anonymous reviewer of the book put it) but also how community-based organizing could be closely coordinated with what HCAN and other pro-reform organizations were doing back in Washington for maximum effect.

Fighting for Our Health also touches on many other issues of interest to students of U.S. politics as well as to readers with a special interest in health care. Kirsch gives a detailed "nuts-and-bolts" account of how a big advocacy organization gets started, including the role of major foundations and the importance of longstanding personal ties in building a team. He shows that citizen groups don't just work with the Congress but also deal directly with the White House. And he shows that citizen groups can be just as sophisticated as any large political campaign, as he describes how he worked with polling organizations, focus groups, and consultants in devising a political strategy for the organization.

What does this mean for the future of health care policies? This rich, fascinating account offers many possible interpretations. On the one hand, HCAN revealed a deft capacity to move across national, state, and local levels — a capacity that may suggest that it (and perhaps some other pro-reform advocacy groups) can continue to play an important role in shaping health policy as the decisions move to the states. On the other, it's not clear whether all the factors that helped make HCAN effective — its foundation support, broad agreement on principles among the component organizations, passionate participation at the grass roots, and its skilled leadership — will continue at a level strong enough to make it an effective force well into the future.

What is clear is that effective advocacy in the U.S. is increasingly demanding, as national policies fail to resolve many issues and devolve many issues to lower levels of government. Twenty-seven years ago, Jack Walker, Mark Peterson, and I wrote about the erosion of closed sub-governments in national politics, the growing complexity and uncertainty in policymaking, and how interest group advocacy both affects and is affected by these developments. The complexity is much greater now, as new national laws like the ACA serve largely to launch ongoing fights across many governments over what is to be done within a controversial policy area. A big question is whether our federal system is too vast and complicated for any broad new purpose to be put into effect. For an answer to that question, we'll have to wait and watch — or get into the trenches, as Richard Kirsch has long done.

Thomas L. Gais
Director
The Nelson A. Rockefeller
Institute of Government

Acknowledgments

The Campaign: The hardest thing about writing *Fighting for Our Health* has been having to leave out, or barely mention, most of the people who contributed to Health Care for America Now's campaign and the allied effort to pass comprehensive health reform. The book could have been 1,000 pages and I still wouldn't have done justice to the extraordinary contribution of so many people and organizations to making history. My hope in writing the book is that everyone who played a part will see their contribution, if not their name, in the stories I tell.

I do want to thank by name many of the key people and organizations that played a leading role in HCAN, starting with the Steering Committee, which was made up by the following organizations: AFSCME, SEIU, USAction, ACORN, AFL-CIO, Americans United for Change, American Federation of Teachers, Campaign for America's Future, Campaign for Community Change/NWFCO, Communications Workers of America, Campaign for American Progress, MoveOn, NAACP, National Council of La Raza, National Education Association, National Women's Law Center, United Auto Workers, United Food and Commercial Workers, and Working America. These groups were represented by staff members who demonstrated their deep commitment to the goal of making affordable health care a right: Alan Reuther, Barbara Coufal, Barbara Gilbert-Chen, Ben Waxman, Bill Dailey, Bill Raabe, Bob Creamer, Bruce Colburn, Caren Benjamin, Carol York, Carolyn Malone, Cassandra McKee, Craig Robbins, Diane Archer, Gerry Shea, Ilyse Hogue, Jeff Blum, Jennifer Ng'andu, Joel Solomon, Jotaka Eady, Judy Waxman, Karen Davenport, Kat Barr, Katie Gjertson, Khalid Pitts, Kim Fellner, La Quita Honeysucker, LeeAnn Hall, Lisa Codispoti, Louise Novotny, Maggie Priebe, Mary Dailey, Mary Lassen, Mary Leyman MacDonald, Mike

xiii

Podhorzer, Roger Hickey, Shavon Arline, Steve Kest, and Steve Kreisberg.

Many other staff of HCAN member groups made big contributions through their work on HCAN's committees. While I can't name them all, I do want to acknowledge the following people: Al Campo, Alex Lawson, Allison Buist, Bill Cunningham, Bill Samuels, Chuck Loveless, Desiree Hoffman, Farheen Qurashi, Garlin Gilcrest, Jessica Kutch, JoAnne Volk, Josh Nassar, Karin Feldman, Kate Kahan, Lori Lodes, Marvin Silver, Michelle Nawar, Sabrina Corlette, Suzanne Haviland and Sylvia Johnson.

When I write "We did..." or "HCAN" did, that collective action was led by HCAN staff, who put their hearts and souls and talent into a splendid campaign. In a short time we built a great team, whose members included: Avram Goldstein, Darren Fenwick, Dave Mason, Doneg McDonough, Esther Garcia, Ethan Rome, Jacki Schechner, Jason Rosenbaum, Justin Anderson, Karlyn Barker, James Davis, Katie Wagenblass, Kerry Greeley, Levana Layendecker, Margarida Jorge, Melinda Gibson, Nathan Riding, Ricky Battle, Shadia Garrison, Tara Straw, Tom Swan, and Vanessa Marlin Weisbrod. We also received invaluable staff help and strategic guidance from three consultants, Bob Brandon, Carla Ohringer Engle, and Mike Lux.

Many other people made key contributions to the HCAN campaign through their work for their firms assisting with our earned and paid communications and our events, including: Saul Shorr, Andi Johnson, Adam Magnus, Marty Sonnenberg, Erin MacGillivray Hart, Neil Sonnenberg, Matt Reilly, Tess Wald, Jennifer Lindenauer, Jonathan Cranin, Doug Gordon, Will Robinson Tierney Hunt, Jonathan Rosen, Blake Zeff, Scott Goodstein, Keegan Goudiss, Celinda Lake, David Mermin, Rick Johnson, John Anzalone, Jeff Liszt, David Smith, Alison Betty, Andrew Boyd, John Sellers, Marco Ceglie, and Nadine Bloch.

In addition to the campaign staff, we had a wonderful team of field managers who made the crucial connection between D.C. and grassroots America: Brenda Barron, Carin Schiewe, Cate Poe, Cynthia Ward Wikstrom, Danisha Christian, David

Desiderato, Deirdra Reed, Evelyn Miks, Gerald Smith, Jeff Ordower, Jennifer Kern, Jill Reese, Julie Sampson, Katy Heins, Kimberly Olsen, Matthew Henderson, Pat McCoy, Paul Getsos, Ryan Canney, Sam Blair, and Steve Bradbury.

We entrusted the HCAN field partner groups with carrying out the heart of our campaign, outside the Beltway. Organizers and other key staff at these groups devoted a huge amount of time and energy into bringing the campaign alive in the minds and hearts of Americans around the country: Arkansas Community Organizations, Health Access (California), California Partnership, Colorado Progressive Action, Californians for Community, Connecticut Citizen Action Group, Organize Now (Florida), Florida Consumer Action Network, Georgia Rural Urban Summit, FACE (Hawaii), Idaho Community Action Network, Citizen Action/Illinois, Central Indiana Jobs with Justice, Iowa Citizen Action Network, Sunflower (Kansas), Maine People's Alliance, Progressive Maryland, MOSES (Michigan), Michigan Citizen Action, Take Action Minnesota, ISAIAH (Minnesota), Missouri Progressive Vote Coalition, Grass Roots Organizing (MO), Nebraska Appleseed, NH Citizens Alliance for Action, Granite State Organizing Project, New Jersey Citizen Action, New Jersey Partnership for Working Families, Organizing in the Land of Enchantment, Citizen Action of New York, New Yorkers For Fiscal Fairness, North Carolina Fair Share, Action North Carolina, North Dakota People's Alliance, Ohio Organizing Collaborative, Progress Ohio, Philadelphia Unemployment Project, PennAction, Ocean State Action, Texas Organizing Project, Vermont PIRG, Virginia Organizing Project, ACORN (Arizona; Delaware; Indiana; Louisiana; Michigan; Missouri; Ohio), Alliance for a Just Society (Montana; Oregon), and Campaign for Community Change (Tennessee). In a handful of states, HCAN hired local organizers who did an outstanding job of coordinating the activities of our state partners: Candis Collins, Cate Poe, Gregg Potter, Jesse Ramirez, Karen Krause, Marc Stier, Renee Lapeyrolerie, and Theresa Navarro.

Finally, a note of thanks to the staff of our key funding partners who regularly checked in with us and lent the advantage of their own considerable experience and wisdom: Antha Williams, Bill Roberts, Matt Hollamby, Robert Phillips, Stuart Schear, and Michael Vachon.

The Book: During the campaign people would ask me if I planned to write a book when it was over. I always said, "No, I don't have a book in me." So it was with real surprise that I found in February of 2010, during my morning meditations, that entire chapters of a book were pouring into my head. My wife is a writer and she often talks about the muse that dictates to her. Now a muse was dictating to me. But I wouldn't have had the opportunity to listen to that muse is it weren't for Gara LaMarche of The Atlantic Philanthropies, who generously awarded me a fellowship to spend the time after the campaign ended to write that book. My thanks also to Andy Rich at the Roosevelt Institute for inviting me to become a Senior Fellow at the Four Freedoms Center and to Lynn Parramore, editor of New Deal 2.0, who gave me a place to voice my thoughts during the past year.

Most of the stories that I tell in *Fighting for Our Health* were shared with me by the 118 people who graced me with interviews in which they shared their memories and insights. I learned a huge amount about what HCAN did around the country from these interviews and in some sense they, too, are authors of this book. I also received important assistance from Emilee Durand, my research assistant, who watched hours of video of local organizing events and provided me with very observant summaries and transcripts, highlighting the drama of the grassroots campaign.

I found writing *Fighting for Our Health* to be a joy and so was relieved when my first group of readers also agreed that the "book was a good read," while giving me the benefit of many sharp suggestions for ways that it could be strengthened. Thanks to Andy LaCoppola and Marti Rosenberg, who not only gave me good feedback but also voluntarily copy-edited the first manuscript! And to Anthony Wright, Dan Beauchamp, Debbie Curtis, John Atlas, John Gaudette, Joan Mandle, Michael Miller, and Pat Rotondo for their insights and helpful challenges. My appreciation also to Ethan Rome who read the second manuscript and helped sharpen my focus in the book as he did during the campaign.

To get to a final manuscript I needed a good editor, who could tighten my writing without losing my voice and suggest what stories I could shorten or leave out. John Paine did a great job of doing both, sensitively and quickly, and made what I feared would be a difficult process into a breeze.

I owe a great deal to Tom Gais, director of the Rockefeller Institute of Government, who surprised me with his offer to publish *Fighting for Our Health*. Tom has made multiple, significant contributions throughout the process in his quiet, thoughtful way. I thank the two anonymous reviewers of the book, both of whom provided excellent suggestions and criticisms; and I thank Bob Ward, deputy director at the Rockefeller Institute for a final read of the manuscript, showing that a fresh eye is always helpful. Mike Cooper, who is the director of publications at the Rockefeller Institute, shepherded the book from manuscript to final publication, with grace and good humor. And as I write this, I look forward to the assistance of Rockefeller Institute staff Joe Chamberlin, Zack Block, and Claire Hughes in helping to publicize the book.

Finally, thanks to the woman who has been my muse for thirty-five years. Claudia Ricci — herself a highly accomplished journalist and a powerful novelist — taught me how to conduct interviews, provide detailed editing on a big chunk of the book, and, most important, was totally confident in my ability to pull this off. Her faith and support kept me chugging along.

I conclude, as do all authors, with the humble and scary realization that I am solely responsible for what you read here. If nothing else, I hope you find it a good read.

Richard Kirsch
August 2011

Acronyms

1199SEIU	Service Employees International Union, District 1199
ACA	Affordable Care Act
ACORN	Association of Community Organizations for Reform Now
AFL-CIO	American Federation of Labor and Congress of Industrial Organizations
AFSCME	American Federation of State County and Municipal Employees
AFT	American Federation of Teachers
AHA	American Hospital Association
AHIP	America's Health Insurance Plans
AMA	American Medical Association
AMSA	American Medical Students Association
AUPSS	Americans United to Protect Social Security
BRT	Business Roundtable
CAF	Campaign for America's Future
CALPIRG	California Public Interest Research Group
CANY	Citizen Action of New York
CAP	Center for American Progress
CCAG	Connecticut Citizen Action Group
CCC	Center for Community Change
CHD	Campaign for Human Development
CLEC	Citizen Labor Energy Coalition
CPC	Colorado Progressive Coalition
CTW	Change That Works
CWA	Communications Workers of America
DFA	Democracy for America
EPI	Economic Policy Institute
FEHBP	Federal Employees Health Benefits Plan
HCAN	Health Care for American Now
HELP	Health, Education, Labor and Pensions Committee

HHS	Department of Health and Human Services
HIAA	Health Insurance Association of America
ICAN	Iowa Citizen Action Network
IPAC	Illinois Public Action Council
MichUHCAN	Michigan Universal Health Care Access Network
MPA	Maine People's Alliance
MSA	Main Street Alliance
NAACP	National Association for the Advancement of Colored People
NCLR	National Council of La Raza
NEA	National Education Association
NFIB	National Federation of Independent Business
NJCA	New Jersey Citizen Action
NPA	National Physicians Alliance
NPR	National Public Radio
NWFCO	Northwest Federation of Community Organizations
NWLC	National Women's Law Center
OFA	Organizing for America
OSI	Open Society Institute
PCCC	Progressive Change Campaign Committee
PhRMA	Pharmaceutical Research and Manufacturers of America
PICO	Pacific Institute for Community Organization
PIRGs	Public Interest Research Groups
PLAN	Progressive Leadership Alliance of Nevada
PPFA	Planned Parenthood Federation of America
SCHIP	State Child Health Insurance Plan
SEIU	Service Employees International Union
SPAN	Single Payer Action Network
TCE	The California Endowment
TPM	Talking Points Memo
UFCW	United Food and Commercial Workers
UMWA	United Mine Workers of America
VOP	Virginia Organizing Project
WASHPIRG	Washington State Public Interest Research Group

WCAN	Washington Community Action Network
WFP	Working Families Party
YWCA USA	Young Women's Christian Association USA

Introduction
The Great Quest

There's nothing like getting your hopes crushed to pieces. I rushed into Ethan's office to get on the phone with Saul Shorr, a brilliant bulldog of an ad man who had created our TV ads for the past five months. This was a conversation that I'd been looking forward to for more than a year. We were going to discuss the final ad campaign to help push the health care bill through Congress. The bill had survived the nasty tea party attacks in August, tens of millions of dollars in negative ads aimed at vulnerable Democrats up for reelection, and multiple Republican filibusters in the Senate. The press had written the health care bill's obituary over and over again. Now the President and Congressional leadership were only a few days from completing negotiations on a final agreement.

Shorr put a halt to the discussion before we had even begun.

"I hate to throw water on this whole thing, but I wouldn't count on having a deal after Tuesday."

"What are you talking about?" I asked.

"Massachusetts," Shorr said. "It looks terrible. I don't think Coakley can win."

I hadn't been thinking at all about the Massachusetts special election for U.S. Senate, set for January 19, 2010. We'd heard that the Democratic candidate, Attorney General Martha Coakley, had made some blunders, but this was Massachusetts, the state that had mourned Edward Kennedy's passing just a few short months before.

Shorr's firm had been hired to run ads attacking Scott Brown, the Republican candidate for Senate. Shorr had reviewed the polling and assessed the dynamics of the campaign. The picture wasn't pretty. Nor was a turnaround likely in the final few days. Blunders by Coakley, like putting down Brown for shaking hands outside Fenway Park and a misspelling of Massachusetts on a campaign ad, had come to symbolize her botched campaign. Worse, Coakley had lost the narrative. The press was throwing fuel on the fire, reveling as they always do in bad news for those in power. Brown was picking up momentum and the Dems didn't have enough time to reverse the tide.

I didn't want to believe Saul. I'm an optimist. You have to be in my business. But I knew in my gut that Saul was right. I was sick to my stomach for several hours. Could health care reform really all slip away? Ever since we had beaten back the tea party in August I'd been confident of the outcome. But Election Day is what most matters to elected officials. A defeat at the ballot box is the most powerful rebuke, capable of snatching defeat from the jaws of victory.

By Tuesday the election's outcome was a foregone conclusion. At the weekly meeting White House staff held with progressive groups in Washington, the Administration assured us that we'd find a way forward, but they didn't sound convinced.

The obstacles thrown up by Brown's victory were both symbolic and real. A candidate who opposed the health reform bill had won the U.S. Senate seat held for decades by the champion of health reform, Ted Kennedy. If Massachusetts' voters could spurn his heir apparent, then no Democrat in the entire country was safe. That's the story the press was telling. In more practical terms, Democrats no longer had the sixty votes they needed to break a Republican filibuster and pass the bill. Even if Democrats braved the political storm, how could they approve the bill in the Senate? Not a single Republican had voted for it in December.

We saw little to hope for in what happened publicly in the next few days. The President, always eager to appear open to compromise, gave a TV interview in which he seemed willing to scale back the bill. That's not how I read his remarks, but then I knew by now that Obama liked to look like a conciliator, to appear to give some room, as he probed for a way to move forward. The White House denied that Obama meant to shrink from his ambitious agenda for comprehensive reform. But the press raised a huge cry because of Obama's apparent retreat.

Democrats in the House also believed that the President had given them a signal to step back from a comprehensive bill. Some, including a few stalwart supporters of reform, started to say publicly that maybe partial reform was the only option. Unbeknownst to me, or to my fellow foot soldiers in the fight for reform, White House Chief of Staff Rahm Emanuel was advocating a scaled-back bill that would provide universal coverage only to children.

Ten days after the Massachusetts election, my Blackberry buzzed with a call from 991, an international area code. "Hello, Richard, is that you? Are you OK?" my father asked, with real concern in his voice. My parents were taking a long-planned cruise to the Pacific. "It's hard to get much news on the ship, but it sounds tough."

Given what my dad had been reading in the papers, his concern for my spirits was entirely justified. But the papers never told the whole story.

By that point I was feeling like we were back in the game — not quite with the confidence I had held all fall: a 90 percent sure bet. But I felt the odds were 60 percent and not just because I wear rose-colored glasses.

The White House staff told reform supporters privately that they were not going to retreat. Obama had given the House Democrats a pep talk, reiterating his determination to move forward. In the Senate, two key senators were publicly supporting passage of reform through a process that would circumvent any Republican filibusters.

On the House side, the initial panic was easing. Support for passing a watered-down bill was drying up. Democrats understood that it was impossible to deliver on the key promises of reform, including stopping insurance companies from denying coverage for preexisting conditions, unless they passed comprehensive reform.

Plus, we had an ace in the hole in the House: Speaker Nancy Pelosi. She had made it clear to the Democratic caucus that she wasn't giving up. A week after the Massachusetts election, Pelosi told the press: "You go through the gate. If the gate's closed, you go over the fence. If the fence is too high, we'll pole-vault in. If that doesn't work, we'll parachute in. But we're going to get health care reform passed for the American people."[1]

Pelosi backed up her passion with extraordinary political acumen. She had already proven herself to be the most effective speaker in years. She knew how to align her caucus, slowly, carefully giving her members the time and political space to find a way forward. Now she was declaring that retreat was not an option, while giving Democrats the time to find a way over that fence.

"It's going to be OK," I told my father. "Don't believe what you read in the papers or see on Fox," which was the only TV news they could get on ship. "There's a lot going on behind the scenes. It's tough, but we're going to get this done."

"I'm glad to hear that. We'll call again soon." But his tone was more like he was offering condolences to someone who was in denial after being diagnosed with a terminal illness. He clearly loved me and wanted to protect me from being hurt.

There's one more reason that I was optimistic. Almost three years ago to the day of Scott Brown's election, in January 2007, I'd had the first conversation with colleagues about creating a campaign to pass comprehensive health reform, anticipating the election of a Democrat as president in 2008. For the past fifteen months Health Care for America Now — HCAN for short — had been organizing Americans around the country, so that we would be ready for these kinds of moments. We knew that finally making health care a right in the United States would be a monumental struggle. It was our job to carry members of Congress through the darkest storm. I still believed we would win the prize that had eluded presidents and progressive activists for almost a century.

Fighting for Our Health

Fighting for Our Health is the story of the organized progressive campaign that fought for the health care reform bill of 2010. This story will not be found in conventional journalistic histories of efforts to enact reform, which focus on what the President and Congressional leaders did. The only outside forces described are major health industry players, such as the prescription drug and health insurance companies. The only grassroots actors are the tea party activists. In this version, health care was enacted because the President and Congress made smart deals with powerful interests, braving popular wrath. If progressive forces are included in the narrative, they appear on the sidelines.

The first reason I wrote this book is to tell a story of what really happened. When the health care narrative graduates from journalism to history, the historians will have a source that describes the crucial role played by the organized progressive campaign to win reform.

The campaign we built was many years in the making. It had its roots in a part of the American left that originated in the Vietnam War era. I have been working in that tradition, building community-labor coalitions to fight for economic justice issues, since 1980. The success of Health Care for America Now stemmed from lessons learned and relations built during thirty of the most conservative years in modern American politics.

That's the second reason I wrote *Fighting for Our Health* — to provide lessons to others trying to create a more just America. Health Care for America Now undertook several specific strategies that differentiated it from previous progressive campaigns. By explaining what we did in detail, I hope that the things we did right, the mistakes we made, and the tensions we faced will provide lessons to allies in other fights.

The fight for health care reform did not end with the President signing the bill into law. Its key provisions, those that will make affordable health coverage available to millions of uninsured and underinsured Americans, do not take effect until 2014. The responsibility for implementing those provisions is shared by the federal and state governments, and the states will play a central role. An aggressive campaign by Republicans and their supporters, like the United States Chamber of Commerce, aims to eviscerate the law in Congress. The Supreme Court will review challenges to the law's constitutionality. In each state, the health insurance industry will battle consumers about how the law's provisions will be implemented. I believe that the lessons we learned will inform and inspire the work needed to see that the promise of health care reform is fulfilled.

Universal health care has been the holy grail of the American left. Like any great quest, the struggles to achieve it are rich in history and drama. I invite you to ride along with me on this journey, which is why I've written this history as a personal memoir as well as a memoir of a movement.

I can do only scant justice to all the extraordinary people and organizations that worked to win passage of health care reform in 2010. *Fighting for Our Health* concentrates largely on the work done through the Health Care for America Now coalition. Many other groups poured everything they had into this fight as well. My hope is that in capturing a little of what so many did, that all of those who helped make history will see themselves on this quest. I hope that readers for whom the fight for health care reform was no more than newspaper headlines, cable-news theater or material for Comedy Central will also come to understand the role that ordinary people played — and can still play — in creating a better, more just America.

1

Thumb Out in Both Directions

I'd been standing on the same stretch of Highway 1, north of Big Sur, for three hours. The view behind me was spectacular: steep cliffs dropping to the deep blue of the Pacific. But by now the scenery was getting old. Oh, what the hell, I thought. I could just as well visit my friend Tim at Stanford as go hiking in the mountains east of Big Sur. I'd have to give up my dream of taking a two-month backpacking trip out West, but I'd seen hardly any cars coming in either direction.

I started crossing the road with my thumb out every time I saw a car coming. In a few minutes a small gray pickup pulled over. I hopped in the open bed and watched the coast whiz by as we headed north, away from Big Sur. An hour later we stopped in Carmel, and the driver, a guy in his early twenties, asked me where I was going. "I don't know," I said.

"That's why we picked you up. We thought that it was cool that you were hitching in both directions. Would you like to come to our place for dinner and spend the night?"

What does hitchhiking have to do with health care reform? I can trace back the whole history of my entire career as an activist to this one moment. The key was the letting go. In giving up my plan to go backpacking, I experienced the freedom from always being the driven, high-achieving, high expectations, got to always know what's coming next guy. It was the gull flying off the back of the boat and letting the wind take him.

Almost forty years later, on the night of March 21, 2010, I experienced another deep feeling of joy — a profound sense of peace, as I watched from Speaker Nancy Pelosi's box while the House enacted the Patient Protection and Affordable Care Act, finally making health care a right in the United States. If I hadn't hitched that ride north, I might never have ended up in the U.S. Capitol watching history being made.

I had a good time that night in Carmel. I had Mexican food for the first time ever, taco shells and all the fillings. In 1972, Mexican food hadn't made it back east yet, at least not to Chappaqua, New York, where I went to high school, or Providence, Rhode Island, where I was attending Brown University. The next morning I headed north, catching several rides over the redwood-lined roads that crossed from Santa Cruz into Palo Alto, before showing up at Tim's dorm at Stanford.

I walked onto the Stanford campus in the fall of 1972 and picked up a copy of the *Stanford Daily*. A front-page article began with a quote from Camus that read, "The opposite of love is not hate, it's apathy." The author of the newspaper article argued that the upcoming presidential election, less than five weeks away, was a referendum on the Vietnam War and that people had an obligation to get involved. With nothing else to do, my guilt got to me, and I decided I should volunteer on the campaign of democratic presidential candidate George McGovern.

Even though I started college in 1970, at the height of anti-war activism, I had not been involved in politics. However, I did submit an application for conscientious objector status when I applied for the draft. I knew that I would not serve in what was a clearly immoral war.

Where did my politics come from? My parents were liberals, although I don't remember any political conversations around the house. I took seriously what I was taught in synagogue and religious school about The Golden Rule. I was impressed by the prophets' admonishments to be just, railing at the people as they forsook God by leading evil, greedy, selfish lives.

Jews have a long history of being persecuted. In my case, that led to an empathy with those who are being persecuted, with victims of tyranny and prejudice. Jewish teachings meant showing compassion for those who are denied realizing their full God-given potential because of the family or circumstances into which they were born.

I'm far from alone in this. There's a long tradition of Jews leading campaigns for social justice. Many of my colleagues in the work I do are Jewish, including many of the people with whom I've worked most closely. Overall, Jews in the United States remain a reliably liberal voting bloc, despite having achieved a level of economic prosperity that would typically produce much more conservative politics.

I was taking the semester off that fall, and I joined the McGovern campaign in Seattle barely two weeks before Election Day, November 7, 1972. They put me to work looking up telephone numbers, long before the days of computer-generated lists. By Election Day I was running the phone bank, in charge of recruiting and instructing and deploying enough volunteers to keep sixty phones humming. That evening I watched the election returns roll in, as Richard Nixon won 61 percent of the vote, and McGovern carried only Massachusetts and D.C.

When I graduated from Brown in May 1974, I headed back to Seattle and volunteered to work on the reelection campaign of U.S. Senator Warren Magnuson. Magnuson was a powerhouse in Congress. He'd been elected to the House in 1937 and the Senate in 1944. In 1955 he became chair of the Senate Commerce Committee. By the late 1960s he had become a staunch ally of Ralph Nader, fighting for passage of the seminal consumer legislation that went through the Commerce Committee.

The Magnuson campaign was struggling to recruit volunteers. Pretty soon I was expanding volunteer phone banks. I figured out how to systematically keep track of volunteers and connect to them personally. In my volunteer book I'd keep track of each contact. When I called them back, I could ask if they were over that cold, or had a good vacation or some other personal detail that made them feel like I knew them. When they arrived at the office, I remembered their names, made them feel at home, and gave them enough training so that they felt comfortable on the phone. I learned to spot leaders whom I could train to recruit and train other volunteers.

My responsibility extended to the Election Day get-out-the-vote operation. I trained volunteers on how to keep track of who voted at each polling place and transmitting the information back to headquarters so that we could remind people to vote. The campaign provided great basic training in the field side of elections. It was also a great place to build camaraderie. When you work fourteen-hour days, seven days a week with a group of people, close friendships emerge in no time.

When the campaign ended it was time to look for a paying job. Again, good luck played its hand. My thirteen-year-old sister learned from a family friend that Ralph Nader was looking to hire a recent college grad to organize student public interest research groups — PIRGs — in California and Washington state. My Magnuson connection meant a lot to Nader, and a short time later I found myself at a college auditorium in northern Oregon, listening to Nader give a speech. I was pacing frenetically, too nervous to hear a word he was saying.

He was already a legend, as were "Nader's Raiders," the young lawyers who had joined in his campaign to win breakthrough legislation protecting consumers and the environment. The progressive era of the 1960s is most remembered for the historic civil-rights legislation, the passage of Medicare and Medicaid, and other Great Society programs. Continuing on into the 1970s, Ralph Nader and his organizations led the fight for the National Traffic and Motor Vehicle Safety Act, the Occupational Safety and Health Act, the Consumer Product Safety Act, the Clean Water Act, and the Clean Air Act.

After the speech I drove Nader to the airport in Portland; he interviewed me as I drove. Ralph immediately put me at ease, and by the time I left him I knew I had the job. He gave me a list of books written by some of the Raiders to begin my education. As he hopped out of the car, he asked me how much sleep I usually needed. When I told him eight hours, he smiled and said, "You won't be getting that much."

I was now a community organizer, part of a national movement for economic justice. It would prove to be an important step forward in learning all of the techniques and tactics that would be needed during the fight for health care reform.

Creating Power Out of Nothing

My work organizing PIRGs, from December 1974 until August 1977, was baptism by fire. I was on my own, 3,000 miles from the D.C. office, with little training and virtually no supervision. I wouldn't recommend this style of management; most of the PIRG organizers who were hired dropped out quickly. But I learned a tremendous amount by being forced to figure it out on my own.

I spent all of 1975 running up and down the coast, literally from the Mexican border (University of California San Diego) to the Canadian border (Western Washington State College in Bellingham). I rented an apartment with a college friend in Hayward, an industrial suburb in the South Bay, but I ended up sleeping there less than two weeks that year. The rest of the time I crashed with the students who were trying to organize PIRG chapters, mostly at three campuses in Washington state and three University of California campuses. It was a job that only a recent college graduate could love.

The PIRG idea was sweeping campuses around the country. Nader's consumer and environmental accomplishments inspired students to take on corporate power in concrete ways that improved people's lives. I would go to a campus where a student had written to Nader about starting a campus PIRG and see if I could help them organize a petition drive. The goal of the drive was to get half of the student body to request that the university administration collect a contribution for a PIRG through the fee system. The fees would finance a professional staff to work with students on issues that the students chose. The fees could only raise enough money if students were automatically charged, although a student was given the option to decline paying the fee. The idea of a college helping to fund a Nader group was controversial, and the "negative check-off" made it even a tougher sell. The impetus behind the petition drive was to demonstrate that a majority of students wanted to tax themselves, making this an exercise in democracy. Of course, that assumed that colleges cared about what their students thought.

The reality is that students have very little power at a college or university. They attend for only four years. Power is held by the administrators, active alumni who fund the college, the board of trustees, and to a lesser degree the faculty.

Organizing is the art of creating power out of little or nothing. This is the reality for most people in the United States and all over the world. Most people have few resources, particularly when they are demanding change from interests that have abundant resources and who run the government or have ready access to those in power.

The PIRG petition was a concrete way to create power out of nothing. First by having a majority of students say they wanted to be taxed. And then by asserting that the petition meant something, even though it had no legal standing. I learned that you have to assume you have power, even when you don't. Then you back that up with organized people to convince others that you indeed now have power.

During these years, I learned the joy and the frustrations of volunteer leadership. All popular movements have leaders who are totally devoted to their cause. Often they have been harmed directly by those in power. Sometimes they have a personal sense of mission, of wanting to make a better world. Their passion and commitment can lead them to climb mountains, but first they have to find the trail, and figure out what to pack for the trek. Their personal involvement and passion can also blind them to reality.

The PIRG student leaders were motivated by the idealism of youth and the vision that they could make a difference. They worked incredibly hard to organize other students, collect signatures, and negotiate with the university administrators. I have no idea how they managed to pass their classes, let alone get good grades, as most of them did.

But they needed help, advice, guidance, and strategy. That was my job, even though I was barely a year out of college myself and was making up the steps as I went along. I would spend a few days on a campus, organizing the students, and then I'd go on to the next school.

Often when I left, the effort fell apart. I'd check in with the student leaders while I was traveling, and nothing that we had planned was working. Sometimes this was the fault of the students. Other times they faced a conservative campus and a recalcitrant administration that opposed PIRG because it did not want to provide funding for a non-university group, controlled by students, working on "political" issues.

But sometimes, the students kept making progress. Finally, I realized that I had to focus my time on those campuses where the students had the ability to move ahead without me. This decision might seem counterintuitive, but the fact was that if the student leadership didn't have the ability to function on its own, I could never rescue them. And if the powers that were opposed were so dug in, a difficult task would become impossible.

It was tough emotionally too, to stop helping students who were doing their best but failing. I felt like I was abandoning them. But this was another lesson that I had to learn. You can't rescue people; you can only help them do their best.

Occasionally, I'd arrange for Nader to give a speech on campus as a way to recruit students. I was told that in D.C. he could be a bear to work with. But he would relax as we traveled from campus to campus around western Washington state, surrounded by the endless beauty of wheat fields, river valleys, and wave after wave of red cliffs.

Nader has a great sense of humor, fiercely ironic and fueled by passion, which was a trademark of his speeches. Once when I picked him up at the airport, the students had rented a car that didn't turn on unless the seat belts were buckled. He immediately quipped, "Whose fault is that?" making fun of his aggressive push for car safety.

Oftentimes students would ask him why he didn't run for president. He always answered that the way to make change was to organize outside the process, that the power for change had to come from people armed with facts and energy. It's too bad that twenty years later he got so frustrated with how corporations had come to dominate the Democratic and Republican parties that he forgot his own advice.

I gave speeches too. I would give a talk in order to raise some money for the local PIRG chapter, since I would collect a speaker's fee from the student government as a "Nader Raider." I would piece together facts from Nader books or newspaper articles, trying to emulate Nader but lacking any of his understanding of the issues or narrative power. I'd had no coaching and I was not a natural public speaker. Making the problem worse were the Young Americans for Freedom, the advance guard of the emerging conservative movement. They were usually easy to spot in the sparse crowd that came to hear me speak: short hair and neat buttoned-down shirts, at a time when long-hair and T-shirts were in fashion. They pretty much cleaned my clock with the questions they'd ask, because they knew much more about the issues than I did.

I learned one other really big lesson. Persistence counts. Despite all the challenges, we won PIRG contracts with the University of California and the University of Washington. Both organizations, CALPIRG and WASHPIRG, continue to work today on a host of issues, opposing corporate attacks on the environment and democracy and working to protect consumers.

As I thought about what I wanted to do beyond PIRG, I realized that I needed more education. I'd been thinking that I should go to law school, if only because that's what people who worked for Nader did. But a comment by a vice-chancellor at U.C. Berkeley changed my mind. As we were wrestling over how to implement the PIRG fee-collection agreement he commented, "Let's figure out how to make this work, and let the lawyers tell us why it won't."

That comment hit me right in the gut, and I realized that I had no desire to be a lawyer. Instead I decided to get an MBA, for two reasons. One was to learn economics, the foundation of every issue Nader discussed. The second was to get management training, so I could build organizations.

The choice of which business school to attend wasn't mine alone. In January 1976, I'd moved near the Berkeley campus. I shared a house with three other people, including a woman I knew from college named Claudia Ricci, who was getting her master's in journalism at Berkeley. Claudia and I became better and better friends over the next several months. Thirty-five years later, the oldest of our three children is married and three years older than when Claudia and I started sharing a house at the foot of the Oakland hills.

Claudia finished her degree at Berkeley and I left my job with Nader. We decided that rather than plunging right into the next career moves — a newspaper job for her and business school for me — we should take a year off. We worked for my parents' catering business in suburban Westchester County, New York, saving enough money for a two-month trip to Europe and Israel. While jogging across the Ponte Vecchio in Florence, we talked about marriage for the first time. Florence will do that to you. Staring at an ancient arch of golden Jerusalem stone against a cobalt blue sky, Claudia blurted out that if we ever had kids we should raise them as Jews. This from a woman who was raised as a Catholic, was not at all religious, and said she never wanted to have kids. Jerusalem will do that to you.

We headed back to California. I told Claudia that I'd go to business school wherever she could find a newspaper job. We wanted to stay in the Bay Area, but I'd also been accepted to MBA programs in Los Angeles, New York, and Chicago. While Claudia looked for a job, I began to work as a door-to-door canvasser and organizer for a small community group in Oakland that supported state legislation to protect nursing home patients. There's no better experience than canvassing. To be successful knocking on a stranger's door and asking for money, you have to overcome any shyness, continually project positive energy, learn to read people quickly, and, more than anything else, not give up. My first night out, a German shepherd lunged through a screen door and bit off a piece of my jeans.

I canvassed two days a week, and as I went door-to-door, I found people whose relatives had been mistreated in nursing homes. After two months the group of citizens I organized met with their state assemblyman to share their personal stories and ask him to support the nursing home legislation. It was another basic lesson in organizing for me, discovering the life experiences of ordinary people and then bringing these strangers together to share their stories with someone in power. It was also another example of how to create power with people who felt powerless.

Finding a first job as a journalist is tough, and Claudia was coming up empty in California and New York. But a friend of hers from journalism school said that Chicago was more promising, so a few days after getting married, we drove from the balmy Bay Area to the Windy City.

I was a fish out of water at the University of Chicago Graduate School of Business, which was a bastion of conservative economics, but I got what I wanted: a top-flight education in economics and an insight into the way that conservative economists view the world. To make money, I ran a large marketing study for the University of Chicago Hospital, gaining valuable experience in focus groups, polling, and statistics. Working with one of the two — yes two — liberal professors on the faculty, I published research on how public utilities used a tax loophole to permanently avoid billions of dollars of taxes that were supposed to be "deferred." I majored in public and non-profit management.

The most important lesson that I learned was in the first five minutes of a finance course. The professor opened the class by asking, "What is the purpose of the firm?" I was clearly the only person in the class who had no idea, as a sea of hands flew up to recite a catechism that was a new to me: "To maximize profits."

"For whom?" Professor Hamada asked. "For the shareholders," the class responded in unison.

"For who else?" Some hesitation here, but a few students offered, "For the management."

"Who else?" Silence. Long silence.

Finally Professor Hamada said, "The firm could aim to maximize profits for its workers. Or for the community. Or for society at large. The tools we will learn could be applied to benefit a variety of constituencies. But for our purposes, the purpose of the firm is to maximize profits for its shareholders." End of story.

By the time I completed my MBA, a first loop had been completed. I had used my hands-on experience in organizing to define what sort of professional training would further my goals. Now I needed to find a place to put what I'd learned to work.

Citizen Action

Just before graduating in the spring of 1980, I walked into Bob Creamer's downtown Chicago office. I had no idea that I was about to take a job that would define the entire course of my career. Actually, career is the wrong word. I was entering a movement, a family of friends and colleagues who shared a vision, a passion, and a common strategy for winning economic justice.

Creamer was and still is — he was a key part of the health care campaign — a brilliant strategist, with an incisive mind, a font of fresh ideas, and relentless optimism. However, he was a lousy financial manager, who took foolhardy risks to keep the organization afloat.

When I met him, Bob was the executive director of the Illinois Public Action Council (IPAC), a six-year-old coalition organization that brought together unions, community groups, senior citizens, and farmers to fight together on economic issues. Bob's administrative/financial director had just given notice, and from his perspective, a UChicago MBA looking for a job with a public interest group was a godsend. I took the job without asking a single question about the organization's finances.

In my day-to-day responsibilities, I learned how to manage canvasses, do foundation fund-raising, set up accounting systems, and constantly juggle cash flow when there was no money flowing. And from the rest of the staff, I learned how to build organizations that ran campaigns for economic justice.

Looking back on it, I'm still astonished by the extraordinary quality of the staff that Bob had assembled. The staff included a future member of the Democratic Congressional leadership, the future president of a leading progressive training academy, and five individuals who would go on to found or run key progressive groups.

I was a sponge at the weekly staff meetings, as I watched Creamer and his staff run statewide issue campaigns; organize marches, rallies, and conventions; and build a coalition that united and inspired an extraordinary diversity of Americans — black and white; young and old; poor and middle-class; machinists, autoworkers, farmers, teachers. I remember a white labor guy, after hearing an impassioned speech by a black Southside preacher, blurt out, "This is the greatest thing since sliced bread."

Ronald Reagan's election in 1980 was a wake-up call to progressive organizers who had shied away from electoral politics. Until then we had felt our job was to encourage politicians of all parties to do the right thing. We feared that if we backed a politician for office, we'd be forced to compromise our principles and would inevitably be disappointed by them. However, the election of a president who opposed everything we were fighting for made us rethink these assumptions.

Ed Nelson, an IPAC leader from Peoria, pointed the way forward. The expression "Will it play in Peoria?" means will something be accepted by mainstream America: white people, living behind white picket fences. Ed wasn't white; he was African American. And he didn't own his home; he was a leader of the Peoria tenants' association. Ed was proof that America included much more than what Ronald Reagan portrayed. Ed settled the debate on whether to become involved in elections with this observation: "It makes no sense to be involved in politics 364 days a year and stay home the one day that politicians care most about."

IPAC was one of five statewide organizations that had started independently in the 1970s, each with a similar mission. They recently had formed a new national organization named Citizen Action, and the executive directors of the groups met in Chicago several times a year. When Creamer couldn't go, he would send me. Because so many of his staff were super-qualified to go, he would have created tensions by picking one of them. I didn't meet that criterion, luckily.

Listening in on those meetings was an incredible learning experience. Each of the participants was an entrepreneur who had started his or her own statewide multi-issue organization to work on economic justice issues. Ira Arlook, who had founded the Ohio Public Interest Campaign, was also serving as the executive director of Citizen Action. Here's how Arlook put it:

> The organizations that came together to form Citizen Action did so out of a sense that working-class and poor people could find common ground on economic issues and thereby get beyond the divisive political and cultural conflicts of the '60s and early '70s. They also believed that whatever organizing strategies each of the founding groups preferred in their local work — building labor-community coalitions or direct organizing — they also had to create a way for people to address urgent problems that could only be solved nationally.

Another participant was Heather Booth, who headed up the newly formed Citizen Labor Energy Coalition, or CLEC. CLEC brought labor and community forces together to fight for affordable energy prices, including opposing a campaign by the oil industry to get Congress to deregulate the price of natural gas. Booth founded CLEC to address the divisions that had emerged after the movements of the sixties "between labor and the newer emerging forces for change — consumer, environmental and growing neighborhood organizing movements." Booth was to play a key role in the health care fights of 1994, and then go on to run a campaign that pushed the passage of the landmark financial reform legislation in the summer of 2010.

In the early 1980s Citizen Action was aggressively looking to form affiliates in new states. Claudia and I decided we wanted to move back East to be closer to our parents. Ira Arlook was looking for a co-director to start a new group in New Jersey. When Claudia was offered a job with *The Wall Street Journal*, we moved to northern New Jersey in July 1982.

On paper, I did not have enough experience to help run a statewide multi-issue organization. While I knew the financial end, I had never organized an issue campaign, built a coalition, or supervised staff. But I had watched others do it. Now it was my turn.

Co-director Jeanne Oterson and I began talking to labor, community, and constituency groups about forming New Jersey Citizen Action (NJCA). Our pitch was straightforward. In order to have an impact on state politics, particularly in an increasingly conservative political era, groups that shared a commitment to economic justice had to work together effectively. A wide variety of groups wanted policies that benefitted the great majority of New Jersey residents, rather than corporate interests or the wealthy.

I'm often told that coalitions are incredibly difficult to organize and keep together. Maybe because I saw the success of the coalition in Illinois, I was not daunted by the task. Putting the New Jersey coalition together didn't seem that much more complicated than any other organizing. We identified organizations that had a mutual interest because they held similar values. We listened to their frustrations about the current state of politics and talked about how a new united effort might be able to address the increasing power of corporate forces. We learned about each particular organization: what were its priorities, who were its members, how it made decisions. We also listened to what each group feared about joining a coalition: giving up its own identity; being forced to take positions it didn't agree with; having to give way to a few powerful groups. In this way, organizations are much like people, with their own organizational histories, identities, hopes, fears, and egos. Organizers are always listening to people and finding a common purpose. It's the same with building coalitions.

In many ways the first campaign I ran at NJCA is a good example of the successful ingredients for any issue campaign, including the 2009 health care campaign. The first ingredient is a political opportunity, an opening for change. In 1983 New Jersey was facing a budget deficit and needed to raise revenues. Republican Governor Thomas Kean wanted to raise the gas tax and hike tuition at state colleges, burdens that would have fallen on working families. The budget crisis created the opportunity to push for transforming the New Jersey income tax, which levied a flat rate of 1 percent on all incomes, into a progressive income tax with higher rates for people who made more money.

The second ingredient is a coalition of forces that will make the issue a priority. The Communications Workers of America (CWA) had won the right to represent public employees in New Jersey in 1981, making CWA overnight into one of the state's biggest unions. Larry Cohen, their lead organizer, saw that the income tax could be a great first test of NJCA's ability to mobilize a broad array of progressive forces.

Other key members of NJCA also readily embraced the progressive income tax campaign. Ronald Reagan had spent 1981 pushing tax breaks for the wealthy, and progressives were anxious to show that Reagan's approach could be challenged. Still, raising taxes is a tricky issue, not a propitious one for a new organization seeking to demonstrate that it is championing the interests of the average New Jersey family.

To turn an idea with a supporting coalition into a *campaign* — a strategically executed effort to build public support and make political change — takes resources. The most important resource is dedicated staff with the experience to develop and execute a campaign strategy. My principal job for the next several months would be to run a statewide campaign effort to pass the progressive income tax.

For advice on the vexing problem of how to run a popular campaign on raising taxes, I turned to Peter Sandman, a professor of communications at Rutgers University. Sandman tutored me on another crucial ingredient for a campaign, a message that most people could understand and support.

We came up with a device that met one other criterion of a successful campaign, a way to unite people around a common demand. We would ask a group, "How many of you earn $50,000 a year?" That was a lot of money in 1982, when the median family income was $22,433.[2]

We went on, "Raise your right hand and repeat after me. I am paying my fair share of New Jersey taxes to support my community. (Pause for crowd to repeat.) I pledge to continue to pay my fair share and, should my income be $60,000 (here people would laugh, not imagining they could ever earn that much), I will pay another $100 in New Jersey taxes to meet my community's needs. I support efforts in the New Jersey State Legislature to have all New Jerseyans pay their Fair Share through a graduated tax on high income."[3]

Actually, one person's hand *did* go up the first time we publicly unveiled the fair share tax pledge. It was Alan Karcher, the speaker of the New Jersey State General Assembly. Karcher, who was sitting on the podium, waiting to address the gathering of labor activists, had decided to support the progressive income tax proposal. Karcher's support was another key ingredient of a successful campaign: a politician with power willing to champion the effort. Most campaigns don't start with the politician in hand, but you need to find a supporter who has power if the proposal is going to be taken seriously by others in power and by the press.

A key tactic in the campaign was to have a broad variety of constituents directly lobby their state legislator. The Senate president was lobbied by a group that included the head of a local tenant organization, two teachers, a worker from Bell telephone, a senior citizen activist, and a legal services attorney — all from the Senator's district. Having his constituents demand that he support a tax increase was a new experience.

All these added up to a successful campaign with a typical conclusion: a compromise. After New Jersey Governor Tom Kean vetoed the progressive income tax passed by the legislature, an agreement was reached to raise the income tax by 1 percent on earnings over $50,000 and increase the sales tax by 1 percent, with exemptions for some basic necessities. The result was that the New Jersey tax system was more progressive and cuts in services were avoided.

* * * *

In October 1985 Claudia and I, along with our eleven-month-old daughter Jocelyn, moved to a 125-year-old farmhouse in the hamlet of Spencertown, New York, thirty miles southeast of Albany. We were fulfilling a long-held dream, to live in a rural area. I had taken a job as legislative director of Citizen Action of New York (CANY), which had been formed earlier in the year, opening their Albany office. Claudia took a part-time job at the State University of New York at Albany, working on publications and promotion for the newly formed School of Public Health.

I spent the next 23 years at CANY, becoming co-executive director with Karen Scharff in 1987. During two extraordinary decades Scharff and I built one of the largest and most respected statewide groups in the national network, which became USAction (from Citizen Action) in 1999. Over that period I had the opportunity to do a wide variety of work. I spent a good chunk of my time at CANY working on public financing of elections. In 2004 I coordinated a big grassroots effort aimed at defeating President George W. Bush's reelection. But most of that time I worked on health care, starting in the fall of 1986 with the first steps in the effort that culminated in the defeat of President Clinton's plan in 1994. That defeat in turn paved the way for President Obama's successful campaign fifteen years later.

2

The Solution Is the Problem

When I gave a speech about heath reform in the early 1990s, I usually began with this story:

> A wonderful senior citizen activist, and old friend, died recently. When she got to the Pearly Gates, St. Peter told her: "You've worked hard all your life to make health care affordable to everyone. For all your good work you get to ask the Lord one question." My friend stood up tall in front of the Lord and said, "I remember when FDR was about to propose national health care at the same time as Social Security, but the doctors were opposed and he was told that he might lose both if he pushed too hard, so he let it go. And I can still see Harry Truman, at the back of his train on a whistle stop, promising to fight for national health insurance, and that was a big reason he surprised Mr. Dewey like he did. But the doctors had their way with him in Congress too. Even Mr. Nixon had a plan, but it was different from Teddy Kennedy's and never went anywhere. So my question is, will we ever see a time when everyone in our great country has health care?" The Lord paused a moment, and said, "Yes, my daughter, we will ... but not in my lifetime."

After 1994 I no longer began speeches with this story — it was too depressing. I would have had to add one more sad chapter to my friend's narrative — the collapse of the Clinton plan. The punch line had become a poignant epitaph.

History has weighed heavily on American health care reformers. We remain the only developed nation that does not provide health care as a right to its citizens. President Obama has frequently remarked that presidents dating back to Teddy Roosevelt have tried to win universal health care and fallen short. Here is a very brief version of health reform history in the United States, to provide a frame of reference for the push in 2009-10.

Progressive reformers began to promote health care reform in the first decade of the twentieth century. Teddy Roosevelt took up the cause after he left the presidency, during his unsuccessful run as a third party candidate in 1912. But the effort petered out as the Progressive era waned and the United States entered World War I. One historian writes, "Compulsory health insurance stands out as the only major reform goal of the progressive era that did not win enactment."[4]

That same epitaph was written by Frances Perkins, the Secretary of Labor under President Franklin Delano Roosevelt. She came to the newly elected President with a long list of issues in 1933 including: a forty-hour work week, minimum wage, workers and unemployment compensation, Social Security, and health insurance. President Roosevelt contemplated including health reform in the Social Security legislation, but opposition by the American Medical Association (AMA) convinced the President that including health care could sink the whole bill. Perkins left office in 1945 with only health care not checked off her ambitious list. It was her chief regret.

President Harry Truman was a heartfelt champion of national health insurance, and when Congress resisted during his first term in office he made it a major theme of his underdog 1948 campaign for reelection. A huge opposition campaign mounted by the AMA succeeded in torpedoing Truman's drive to enact the legislation and led to Truman becoming the most prominent of the list of reformers who were bitterly let down. He said, "I have had some bitter disappointments …, but the one that has troubled me most, in a personal way, has been the failure to defeat the organized opposition to a national, compulsory health insurance program."[5]

The one happy chapter in this tale is the enactment of Medicare. President Lyndon Johnson made it his top priority when he was elected in 1964, picking up the mantle laid down by President John F. Kennedy, who had campaigned for national health insurance for seniors when he was elected in 1960.

Johnson told his top health aide, "The President begins to lose power fast once he has been elected.... We've got to get this legislation fast. You've got to get it during my honeymoon." Which, using his mastery of the legislative process, he did.[6] Johnson also twisted arms in Congress to enact Medicaid that same year, 1965, providing government health coverage for some of the poor.

Readers who remember President Richard Nixon only for the Watergate scandal will be surprised to learn that he was a major proponent of universal health care during both his terms. At the same time Massachusetts Senator Edward Kennedy was the leading Congressional champion. The modern politics of health reform, with conflicted agendas from the health care and business community, divisions among reformers, and big chasms between the White House and Congress, led to the collapse of both the Nixon and Kennedy proposals. A similar fate awaited a more faint-hearted attempt to enact universal health care by President Carter late in his presidency.

Readers are likely to be more familiar with the titanic struggle over health care reform under President Bill Clinton, a battle marked by the emergence of the private health insurance industry rather than the AMA as the leading opponent, and the Republican right under Newt Gingrich taking aim at Clinton's health care plan as the ticket to winning at the ballot box in 1994.

President Clinton was the first president since Kennedy and Johnson to make health care a top legislative priority. He made that commitment in his first address to both houses of Congress, handed responsibility to his wife, to whom he had pledged to give a major role in the administration, and declared to the nation that he would not sign a bill unless it covered everyone in the nation. So what went wrong?

Despite Clinton's passion and commitment, the administration made several crucial mistakes. In taking months to develop a detailed policy plan, he forgot Johnson's crucial advice about how short a president's honeymoon period is. That detailed policy proposal was very complex and hard to understand. It prided itself on being new, when what Americans generally want in health care reform is the comfort of familiarity. Drafting a highly detailed proposal insulted Congress, which takes pride in both its role and expertise in developing legislation.

The traditional opponents of reform were much the same as they had been ever since the growth of private insurance for most working people after World War II and the establishment of Medicare for seniors and Medicaid for some of the poor in 1965, had created the modern health coverage system. By 1993, health care was a huge industry, making up more than 11 percent of the economy and growing rapidly. The rising cost on individuals, employers, and taxpayers was pinching the budgets of all three groups. Still, higher costs to the system translate into greater revenues for the industry. Everyone in the industry — doctors, hospitals, other health care providers, drug companies, and even insurers — acknowledged that some systematic issues had to be addressed. But they opposed any reforms that would harm them financially.

As a result, when the Clinton plan was finally released in 1993, the AMA, AHA (American Hospital Association), and other provider groups organized their members to oppose specific provisions of the plan, while insisting that they wanted to see passage of some sort of comprehensive bill that aimed at universal coverage. Three groups in particular emerged to play powerful roles in defeating the Clinton plan: the insurance industry, the business lobby, and the Republican Party aligned with their growing right-wing base.

The leading symbols of opposition to the Clinton plan were Harry and Louise, an upper-middle-income couple featured in television ads run by the Health Insurance Association of America (HIAA), an association that represented mid- and small-sized health insurers. The ads attacked "mandatory government health alliances" and "bureaucrats." Hillary Rodham Clinton attacked the ads saying they distorted the proposal that she had developed. The notice given by the First Lady to the ads brought them to the center of national media attention, although the spots had only run in a few elite media markets.

The small business attack was led by the National Federation of Independent Business (NFIB) and had its biggest impact in Congress. The NFIB adamantly opposed the requirement in the Clinton plan that employers either provide health coverage or pay a portion of their payroll to the government to subsidize their employees' health care. Even when Michigan Congressman and chair of the House Energy and Commerce Committee John Dingell dropped the payroll tax to as little as 1 percent of payroll for very small businesses, which would have resulted in a huge bargain for small employers, the NFIB still objected. For the NFIB, this was an ideological fight as much as it was a fight about dollars. The NFIB's intransigence led to the bill's death in Dingell's committee.

The major big business associations also joined the opposition. Some CEOs whose firms had employees with good coverage supported reform. These included auto manufacturers and the president of American Airlines, who saw an opportunity to reduce their companies' costs. But the major business groups such as the Business Roundtable and Chamber of Commerce fought the Clinton plan. In doing so these business groups followed the lead of those of their members who would have the most to lose, including insurance companies, drug companies, and fast-food chains (who paid little if anything for employee coverage). The business lobbies also responded ideologically, opposing government becoming the major regulator of health coverage.

The Republican attack was led by the House minority leadership, Newt Gingrich and Dick Armey,* who regarded the defeat of the Clinton health care plan, or any plan at all that the President could take credit for, as their means to a majority in the 1994 elections. Gingrich and company followed a strategy developed by William Kristol to "defeat the Clinton plan root and branch ... as a model for routing contemporary liberalism and advancing an aggressive conservative activist agenda."

---

* In August 2009, I debated Armey on PBS's *The News Hour*, when as president of Freedom Works he was helping to organize the tea party demonstrations at Congressional town halls.

Gingrich employed the Kristol game plan of "sight unseen, Republicans should oppose it."[7] When Gingrich captured the House with fifty-two seats flipping from Democratic to Republican, the Kristol strategy was vindicated. Health care reform had become a political football once again. As a result, all of the problems that supposedly everyone wanted to resolve continued to fester, like an open sore on the body politic.

The Origins and Rise of the Public Option

The defeat of the Clinton health care plan sent me into a one-year funk. I finally found relief for my blues in American history, particularly in reading Eric Foner's classic *Reconstruction: America's Unfinished Revolution 1863-1877*. The book tells of the rise of a host of progressive initiatives during the Civil War and its aftermath — women's suffrage, public funding for higher education and others, and of course the end of slavery — and then the subsequent rollback of many of those measures in the following decade. The leading example was the transition of slavery to serf-like conditions on southern plantations. So why did Foner's account make me feel better? Because eventually progress triumphed: women got the vote in 1920 and the Civil Rights era gave blacks the right to vote. In words popularized by Dr. Martin Luther King, but first spoken by the abolitionist Theodore Parker: "The moral arc of the universe is long, but it bends toward justice."

By 2003 the arc in the United States was bending back to universal health care. It was remarkable really, given the utter rout of the Clinton plan. After Republicans took over the House of Representatives in 1994, any discussion of comprehensive health reform was considered political suicide. I assumed that the issue was dead politically for a generation. But in less than a decade, the enormous contradictions in the American health care system were reclaiming their place on the political stage, as they had done repeatedly for a century. Health care costs were gobbling up a growing share of the economy, putting pressure on families, businesses, and government while more and more Americans were uninsured or staggering under the burden of medical debt.

So I decided to write the story of our eight-year campaign for health reform that culminated in the defeat of the Clinton plan in 1994. I was addressing the new crop of organizers and activists who were entering the fray. I wanted them to think seriously about what had happened and not rush to do the same things over again.

I did not anticipate when I wrote "Will It Be Déjà Vu All Over Again? Renewing the Fight for Health Care for All — Tales, Hopes and Fears of a Battle-Scarred Organizer in 2003," that I would devise a new policy approach to comprehensive reform. But the process of recounting the history of the Clinton fight gave me a fresh perspective. I realized a fundamental paradox: People want reform up until the time that reform is about to happen, but when faced with specific solutions that may become law, the public easily becomes alarmed by the prospect of change. Once the public discussion switches from problem to solution, the solution becomes the problem.

The first time I encountered this phenomenon was in Albany, New York, in 1992, when we held a big march outside the State Capitol in support of a single-payer bill. Single-payer refers to proposals for universal, government financed health insurance. We'd been organizing for universal health care in New York for more than five years and had never received any negative press coverage until that day. The press had always sympathetically portrayed the story we were telling: soaring health care premiums, high out-of-pocket costs, shrinking coverage, stories of people losing their insurance, and others scared that they might. But with the prospects of actual legislative action, an enterprising reporter found a local business that would have to pay more for its employees' health coverage if our bill became law. Overnight, the press sympathy moved from the uninsured working mom to the small business owner oppressed by new costs.

The reason that health care reform keeps rising to the top of the political agenda, no matter how often it goes down in flames, is that people deeply care about health care. When we meet an old friend, we often ask, "How have you been? How is your family?" If things are going badly, we may repeat the old adage, "At least I have my health." We vow to stick with our betrothed "in sickness and in health." So when we have to pay more to hang on to shrinking health coverage, when we can't retire early or switch jobs or start a small business because we might lose our health insurance, when a serious illness threatens to drive us into bankruptcy, we demand that our political leaders do something!

But when we care about something so deeply, change can also be terrifying. Specific solutions prompt people to ask, how will that change affect me? Will I be worse off than I am now? What will I lose?

We cannot lose sight of the fact that our health care system does work for most people, most of the time. Five out of six people under the age of sixty-five — and virtually all seniors — have health coverage. Most people believe they get good care from their doctors. Almost everyone knows a family member or close friend whose life has been saved by treatments delivered in a hospital or by other medical miracle cures. Even people who aren't insured generally have access to some care, often in the emergency room.

The reason that President Clinton's message mavens called the administration's plan the Health Security Act is that people were most scared of losing coverage. This in turn reflects the fact that people place a high value on keeping what they have, and are willing to pay for something as valuable as access to health care.

In the two-trillion-dollar health care industry, every policy solution results in winners and losers. The underlying problem for most American families and businesses is high costs. But any solution that saves money — Medicare negotiating the price of prescription drugs or stopping overpayments to insurance companies, to take two examples — will create many health industry losers. Opponents of reform learned early on (back to the Progressive era) that the most effective way to block change is to scare people about how change will "ruin" their health care.

The infamous Harry and Louise ads effectively exploited people's fear of change and of losing what they now have. If the ads had challenged the premise that there was a health crisis, they would have been ineffective. Instead, the ads acknowledged the problem while attacking the Clinton proposal, saying that it would take away the choice of doctors and ration care. One of the ad's tag lines was, "There must be a better way."

Rather than proposing a policy solution that reassured people, Clinton made the mistake of doing the opposite. Clinton ran as a "new Democrat" and wanted to come up with a solution that would appear to break the mold. He proposed a policy known as "managed competition," which would have restructured much of the private insurance system.

In turning their back on the old, both Bill and Hillary Clinton rejected the familiar. But faced with the actuality of reform, the exotic quickly becomes suspect. The lure of being innovative clashed directly with the need to offer security.

The Clinton plan also failed to rally supporters, whose enthusiastic support was crucial to countering the organized opposition. Since managed competition is based on regulated private health insurance, Clinton alienated supporters of single-payer national health insurance, who had been leading the grassroots forces for change. In their attempt to fully remake the private insurance system, the Clintons confused and worried other potential supporters. As a result, most groups offered lukewarm general support for the proposal but emphasized their specific objections on details key to their organization. They nitpicked. What most members of Congress heard from these groups was a drone of mind-numbing, technical nit-picks.

After I had spent several weeks writing and reliving the bitter history of the Clinton fight, the proverbial light bulb went off. If the solution was the problem, we needed a policy solution that would reassure the public. We also needed a solution that would appeal to those who support a single-payer system. At the same time, a solution should not gore the ox of every player in the health industry.

My father loves to tell a story about his mom, who when asked by a waiter whether she'd like peas or carrots with her dinner, would answer "yes." In past debates on health reform, two distinct options had always been offered: building on the private insurance system or offering national public health insurance. But why did we have to choose? Why couldn't we just say "yes"?

From that insight, the blueprint of a new policy approach followed easily: Offer people the choice of either keeping their private health insurance or getting health insurance through Medicare. Private health insurance would need to be regulated, to stop companies from discriminatory practices like refusing to cover people with preexisting conditions or charging more for people who have health problems. And Medicare's benefit package would need to be brought up to the level of private insurance, including offering prescription drug coverage and limiting out-of-pocket costs. This simple framework would provide the public with two familiar options, and appeal to both sides of the reform camp. It was also better policy than simply regulating private insurance. Medicare has a better record of cost control than private insurance and, unlike private insurers, does not routinely deny care recommended by a doctor. As a new option in the private market, Medicare would force private insurers to compete on price and access.

I posted my "Déjà Vu" article on the Internet in March 2003. Much to my surprise, it garnered a lot of attention, particularly for a piece that was more than 11,000 words long and had not appeared in a journal. It created a buzz among the large community of single-payer organizers.

A month letter, I got a call from Jacob Hacker, a professor at Yale. Hacker told me that he had thought of the same idea a couple of years earlier, and it was published as part of the Robert Wood Johnson Foundation's "Covering America" project.[8] He had begun developing the new approach after writing a book called *The Road to Nowhere* about the failure of the Clinton plan. "My basic goal," he told me, was to capture the "advantages of public insurance as a powerful player in the context of a system that relies on private insurance for working-age people. Medicare would be better able to control costs and provide security. And it was familiar."

Hacker's detailed plan was very close to the ideas that I had sketched out. Employers would offer coverage at work from private insurance or pay into a coverage pool for their employees. Employees who didn't get coverage at work could choose from either Medicare or a number of private insurance plans. The only issue that I challenged Hacker on was the title of his proposal, "Medicare Plus." I thought framing it as a Medicare plan was a mistake. The proposal had to indicate a choice of either private insurance or Medicare. Hacker changed the name when he updated his proposal in 2007 to the Health Care for America Plan.

Hacker's paper caught the attention of other progressive activists, including Roger Hickey, co-director of the Campaign for America's Future (CAF), a progressive think-tank. Hickey liked it because, "It was simple and easy to explain to a grassrootsy audience, unlike the Clinton plan, which was impossible to explain. And I liked that it challenged the insurance industry." Hickey also understood that expanding Medicare to people under 65 could create a bridge to those on the left who were fighting for Medicare for All (as single-payer advocates were starting to call their approach), as well as to others on the left who were looking for a plan that had more chance of becoming law.

Hacker's idea also came to the attention of Diane Archer, who had founded the Medicare Rights Center, a leading consumer advocacy and policy organization based in New York City. Archer's organization ran a hotline that received more than 10,000 calls a year from seniors on Medicare. She noticed that after private insurance plans were allowed to offer Medicare in 2003, the number of consumer complaints soared. "As many issues as we saw on the traditional Medicare side, they paled by comparison to problems on the private side. This got me interested in being sure there was a public Medicare option in health care reform."**

** A Medicare public option had been included in a universal health care bill that passed out of Representative Pete Stark's House Ways and Means Committee in August 1994. Yet, by the time Stark's committee acted, the Clinton reform movement was all but dead and reformers weren't paying much attention.

Hickey and Archer began to promote the Hacker plan. Their strategy was to increase its academic credentials and make it attractive to pro-reform groups. They focused particularly on key unions that progressives would regard as leaders and that Democratic presidential candidates would court in the 2008 election campaign. Hickey got the Economic Policy Institute (EPI), a leading labor-backed think-tank, to publish an updated version of Hacker's paper as part of EPI's Agenda for Shared Prosperity project, which aimed to put out progressive economic approaches in advance of the 2008 election. He also convinced the American Federation of State, County & Municipal Employees (AFSCME) and the Service Employees International Union (SEIU), two unions with strong records of working on progressive political change, to release statements endorsing the plan on the day it was unveiled.

In early February 2007, less than a month later, John Edwards unveiled his health care reform proposal. Part of Edwards' strategy for attracting the support of progressives was to announce substantive policy proposals early, positioning him as a candidate with ideas and pressuring the other major candidates, Hillary Rodham Clinton and Barack Obama, to respond. As CAF blogger Bill Scher wrote the day after Edwards' plan became public, "*The New Republic* reports today that a core feature of the plan is 'the essential idea behind another health care reform plan that has been quietly generating a great deal of enthusiasm among reformers — a plan composed by Yale University political scientist ... Jacob Hacker." In fact, Hickey and Hacker had been talking with Edwards' issue and health policy advisors, one of whom was Peter Harbage. Edwards appeared on *Meet the Press* and noted, "One of the choices, by the way, available in these health markets is the government plan. So people who like the idea of a single-payer insurer health plan, that is actually one of the alternatives that people can choose."

The public option was a part of Edwards plan, but not the centerpiece. In many ways Edwards' plan was modeled after the health reform plan passed in Massachusetts in 2006. The Massachusetts legislation combined a requirement that state residents have health coverage with a variety of ways of expanding coverage. The major innovation was the creation of a new regulated marketplace, called a "connector," where individuals could purchase private health insurance. Low- and moderate-income people who earned too much for Medicaid and did not get health coverage at work received income-based subsidies to pay for the coverage. The regulations included bans on insurance companies denying coverage or charging people more for preexisting conditions.

The next major candidate to announce a health plan was Barack Obama. As he did with the Edwards camp, Hacker had briefed Obama on the public plan idea earlier that winter, just after Obama had announced his run for president. MIT economist Jonathan Gruber, a designer of the Massachusetts plan, also participated on that call with Obama. Hacker told Obama that the Massachusetts plan needed two crucial improvements: clear responsibility for employers to provide for or pay for health coverage, and the inclusion of a public insurance plan in order to control costs.

In the weeks before Obama released his proposal, Hickey and Archer sent Hacker's plan to Obama's health care advisors and arranged for Hacker to talk with some of the Obama team. While the advisors asked Hacker about various aspects of reform, he believes that they mainly wanted his ideas on structuring a public plan.

In late May 2007, Obama announced his proposal in a speech at the University of Iowa, but the policy details weren't clear. He said, "Everyone will be able buy into a new health insurance plan that's similar to the one that every federal employee ... currently has for themselves." At one point he referred to a "new national health care plan and other participating plans." Was he speaking about the Federal Employee Health Benefits Plan, which is a choice of private insurance plans, or was he proposing to introduce the choice of a new public insurance plan?

The confusion was noted by several bloggers, and threatened to ruin the reception of Obama's plan among progressives. An Obama campaign advisor rushed to reassure potential critics: "If you don't have health insurance through your employer, you will be enrolled into a new, comprehensive public health insurance plan that emphasizes prevention, chronic care management and quality care. The benefits will be similar to those available today to every federal employee.... This plan will enjoy the great efficiencies we see in public plans like Medicare but, if you still cannot afford it, you will receive a subsidy to pay for it. Of course, you can choose private insurance if you prefer but the private plans will have to compete on a level playing field with the public plan — without the extra payments that tip the scales in favor of private Medicare Advantage plans today."[9]

The Obama campaign erased any further ambiguity by prominently including the following in the official health care issue section on the campaign's website: "Specifically, the Obama plan will: (1) establish a new public insurance program, available to Americans who neither qualify for Medicaid or SCHIP (State Child Health Insurance Plan) nor have access to insurance through their employers, as well as to small businesses that want to offer insurance to their employees."

This growing progressive focus on the public option was not lost on Hillary Clinton's campaign, whose advisors called Hacker, Hickey, and Archer at 1:00 on the morning of the day that her plan was unveiled in mid-September. Her proposal included offering people the choice of private or public coverage. *The New York Times* columnist Paul Krugman, who had been following the primary debate around health coverage closely, summarized the results after the Clinton plan became public: "The Edwards and Clinton plans as well as the slightly weaker but similar Obama plan achieve universal-or-near-universal coverage through a well-thought-out combination of insurance regulation, subsidies and *public-private competition*. These plans may disappoint advocates of a cleaner, simpler single-payer system. But it's hard to see how Medicare for all could get through Congress any time in the near future, whereas Edwards-type plans offer a reasonable second best that you can actually envision being enacted by a Democratic Congress and signed by a Democratic president just two years from now."[10] (Emphasis added.)

Hickey and Archer's discussions with the presidential campaigns were backed by an important finding. Research showed that the choice of a public health insurance plan was popular with the public, when it was included within a larger framework for reform. That was the conclusion of a unique and intense public opinion research project that we had begun two years earlier.

A Frame for Selling Reform to the Public

Philippe Villers was five years old when his father rushed his family out of Paris a mere two hours before the Nazis entered the city. That helps explain Villers' ambition to make a significant contribution to social progress. After hearing a powerful sermon following the assassination of Dr. Martin Luther King, Villers decided to take action. "I was a mechanical engineer. And thinking like an engineer I realized that I had no experience or training in doing direct work on social progress. So I started a company with the specific intention of getting enough resources to make a difference. It was called Computer Vision, a firm that developed systems for computer-aided design. Over the next ten years it became a Fortune 500 company."

Phil Villers and his wife, Kate, decided to use their newly amassed wealth to tackle the health problems of senior citizens, particularly the lack of coverage for long-term care. He contributed $40 million to start the Villers Foundation, which after several years became the consumer health advocacy organization, Families USA. As president of Families USA, Phil became deeply immersed in the fight for health care reform in 1993-1994, coming away anxious for his next opportunity.

In early 2005 Phil invited me to a meeting that he was planning in Herndon, Virginia. He and another Families USA board member, Bob Crittendon, a Seattle primary care doctor and longtime reformer, decided to invite a broad array of health care advocates for the three-day meeting in Herndon, with the goal of building bridges so that people would cooperate in the next battle for reform.

One of the presenters was Michael Shellenberger, who, along with Ted Nordhaus, headed up a new firm, American Environics, which employed an unusual public opinion methodology developed in Canada, designed to provide a much richer view of public attitudes than conventional focus groups and polling methods. Using sophisticated statistical methods, American Environics drew maps of how people view politics and society on a number of issues. The methodology — which he told us was being used by large corporations to develop highly sophisticated marketing strategies — could be used by progressives to change the conventional way of approaching reform and perhaps find the key to keeping public support for health reform even when it was under attack.

Another Herndon presenter, pollster Celinda Lake, who had a long history of polling on health care, put the dilemma Shellenberger was addressing this way. "Why is it that year after year large majorities of Americans tell us in polls that they support a government guarantee of health care for all, including a major government role and higher taxes, but we keep losing?"

The meeting led to the formation of a new group called the Herndon Alliance, under the leadership of Bob Crittendon. I volunteered to chair a committee on public opinion research, and with funds raised from several foundations and organizations, we hired both American Environics and Lake Research to engage in an extensive public opinion research project to change the old paradigm.

The first step in the American Environics process was examining the issue of universal health care through their database. The database includes 170 diverse values, ranging from religiosity and patriotism to propensity to buy brand-name items. Two contrasting values illustrate the richness of the data. One value, "modern racism," expresses the view that we have moved beyond racism in this country. The contrasting value, "acknowledgment of racism," represents the belief that racism is still a problem in our society.

Shellenberger and Nordhaus returned with a fascinating portrait of the American electorate, divided into six segments.

One group, which they labeled "the anti-health justice base," would not support any government role in health care. Luckily, that made up only 4 percent of the population. Many more Americans fell in the "health justice base," which would support an expansive government role, but still they added up to only 15 percent. The other 81 percent of Americans were somewhere in the middle, with most of them divided into two groups. The biggest swing segment, a full 40 percent of the electorate, was labeled "proper patriots." More men than women, often professionals or executives, they live in small towns or the suburbs, have a great deal of national pride, believe in the traditional family, and are somewhat religious.

Lake and her staff held focus groups with people in each of the three largest swing segments. Bob Crittendon attended the sessions, and he was amazed to find that people who would never appear together in a typical focus group — an African American senior citizen and a young white office worker — would share the same values and worldview. The research team identified a number of crucial values and views of health care held by the swing-values groups.

- People take health care solutions very personally and pay attention to how the solutions have an impact on their lives. People put their families and themselves first, wanting to know what a proposal will do for them and how it will affect them as taxpayers and as people with coverage provided by an employer or government.

- People want to make their own choices of doctors, tests, specialists, drugs, and second opinions. They believe choices are being reduced by employers and insurance companies.

- If "personal responsibility" does not occupy a central place in proposals, voters are turned off. However, once others demonstrate personal responsibility, people become more generous.

- People want government to be a watchdog and rules enforcer, but do not want the government to provide health care. People understand that only the government is powerful enough to protect consumers against insurance companies, drug companies, and hospitals. At the same time, people are deeply suspicious of a government role in providing health care or the government's ability to run anything.

- Voters would eagerly embrace a uniquely American solution. They believe American ingenuity can produce the best solution to the health care problem.

With this information in hand, Shellenberger and Nordhaus asked the Herndon communications committee to come up with proposals for health care reform that would take into account public perceptions. We were specifically encouraged to look for innovative, breakthrough ideas that the research had suggested. Members of the group came up with three proposals, one focused on universal cancer screening, another on children's health, and a third on health insurance consumer protections. However, none of these was a comprehensive proposal to provide coverage to everyone.

I had been waiting to introduce the idea of a public option as part of comprehensive reform but was hesitant to do so. I felt I was so closely associated with it that my advocacy would seem self-promotional. Fortunately, Diane Archer had no such compunctions. To my surprise, Nordhaus and Shellenberger roundly applauded the public option as exactly the kind of breakthrough thinking their process was meant to generate.

This is the initiative we tested:

Guaranteed Affordable Plan: Health insurance companies should be required to offer a standard comprehensive health plan so that everyone knows what they are getting and that their health care needs will be met. Every American would have guaranteed access to a choice of standard, affordable health plans, either buying it from a private insurer or from a public plan. Employers and insurers could choose to offer more coverage beyond the standard plan, but all plans would have to cover at least the standard package of benefits. Everyone would have a choice of plans, private and public, that would be affordable to them based on a sliding scale.

The next step was another round of focus groups and polling to test the initiatives. Much to my delight, the Guaranteed Affordable Plan tested very highly, especially with swing- and base-value groups. Finally, we had a message frame that described an effective, comprehensive approach to health reform that would be popular with these key groups.

As we continued our research we learned more about how people view reform. People want new choices, starting with the very important assurance that they could keep their current plan. Once people hear that, they relax and are more open to change, including a willingness to help others who don't have coverage.

The public insurance plan was seen as an important fallback to private insurance. Most people thought it would not be as good as private coverage but valued it as an affordable option if they lost coverage at work. The choice was also perceived as putting health before profits. We found that basing the cost of coverage on income assured people that it would be affordable and also that everyone would have some responsibility to pay. Finally, the government was seen as having a positive role: controlling greedy health insurance companies, rather than providing health care.

We also tested the proposal against powerful attacks that the right would employ: it would hurt small business, ruin the quality of health coverage, and introduce too much government. Even after these criticisms were presented, the surveyed voters still supported the proposal, because by reassuring them that they could keep what they have, they believed the threat would not apply to them. Plus, by offering a choice of other quality, affordable options and protection from insurance company abuses, they were hopeful that the proposal might offer help if they ran into problems with or lost their current coverage.

The research also taught us language that we should avoid, including one term that health reform advocates had used for years, "universal health care." For many people its meaning is not clear. Did it mean covering everyone in the universe? For others, it sounded so far-reaching that America clearly couldn't afford it. Or a program to pay for people who some saw as undeserving. As an alternative, we found that the strongest language was "quality, affordable health care for all." This language felt inclusive in a positive way. The phrase resonated with the 85 percent of Americans who have insurance as well as the minority who don't. The fact that the vast majority of Americans are insured underlay the entire communications strategy. A focus on the "uninsured" did not speak to most Americans. The narrative had to include the high costs and insecurity of people who have coverage.

The Herndon research emphasized the need to avoid scaring people about change, because fear was clearly the biggest weapon that the opposition would use. We learned the importance of avoiding messages that health reform advocates had long relied on, the specter that people would lose their health coverage or be forced into bankruptcy if the system wasn't changed. Those messages simply reinforced fear. To get people past fear to "I'm mad as hell," we needed to incite anger and then offer hope.

Anger needs a target, and the obvious one was the health insurance industry. That became the focus of the last round of research, which Lake Research undertook in February 2008, as we were planning to launch the HCAN campaign. I attended the focus groups, watching panels of two of the American Environics segments, proper patriots and another called "marginalized middle-agers," in Denver, Philadelphia, and Richmond, Virginia. We started the focus groups with an open-ended question about what people thought of the health care system, and the first answer in every group was the same: people immediately started complaining about health insurance companies. I listened to middle-aged white male businessmen from Denver stating that insurance companies were jacking up premiums, cutting benefits, denying care and doing it all to increase their profits. When we probed further, high insurance company CEO salaries really made people mad. In our subsequent polling, we found that four out of five people thought that the best description of insurance companies was "putting profits before people" and 70 percent agreed they were "greedy." Only 39 percent regarded insurance companies as "reliable."

We didn't need to do formal research to discover what almost everyone already knew: Americans are ticked off at health insurance companies. But we did learn that we could use language that some might have seen as too left or ideological. Plus, we could use the research to demonstrate to candidates for Congress and president that the insurance companies made a ripe target.

With the 2008 election on the horizon, we also tested two of the candidates' health care proposals. One was based on the premise of guaranteed affordable choice, an accurate summary of the proposals supported by Hillary Clinton and Barack Obama. The other proposal was based on Senator John McCain's health care proposal, although at the time it did not include a provision he added later — taxing health care benefits — that would prove to be toxic to voters.

An earlier Herndon poll had asked surveyed voters to choose between a guaranteed choice proposal and two conservative health proposals and a single-payer plan. The results were startling. Guaranteed affordable choice was preferred by a ratio of about three to one to all three alternatives.

Now we were testing the two plans that we expected to be presented by the candidates for president, labeled proposals from candidates A and B. We found that voters preferred the Democratic plan by 55 to 28 percent. Even Republican women liked it much more; only Republican men were evenly split.

Finally, we leveled tough attacks against both plans and then asked voters to compare them again. We found that attacks on both plans raised significant doubts in voters' minds. The good news was that the Democratic plan weathered the assault better than the McCain proposal. The Democratic plan remained the choice of 55 percent of voters, while the Republican plan dropped in support to 23 percent, with the balance undecided.

We had completed research lasting more than two years to garner a rich understanding of how Americans view health care reform and develop language that would allow us to explain a progressive proposal to the American people that they could support, even when the plan was attacked. But so far this was all just an academic exercise. Now we needed to build a campaign and raise the resources to broadcast our message in a real political contest.

3

Building Health Care
for America Now

I clearly remember the actual moment when Health Care for America Now was conceived. In January 2007, I had come to the Washington, D.C., office of Jeff Blum, USAction's executive director. We were joined by Alan Charney, USAction's program director. They had both cut their teeth in the student anti-war movement. Jeff Blum had led sit-ins at the University of Chicago that resulted in his expulsion from the University. Alan Charney helped to organize the most famous of the college sit-ins, at Columbia. By now both were also veterans of the Clinton health care wars. The three of us had worked together for twenty-five years.

At the small round conference table in a K Street office building that housed a number of progressive organizations, I told them simply, "It's time for us to build a new health care campaign."

Neither was surprised. They'd been doing this work long enough to understand that prime moments of political opportunity had to be seized. But unlike me, they were experienced in coalition politics in Washington. The first step, they said, was to have two major unions, SEIU and AFSCME, help found the new effort. Both unions were represented on the USAction board, but during a major split in union ranks in 2005, SEIU had led a number of unions out of the American Federation of Labor and Congress of Industrial Organizations (AFL-CIO) while AFSCME remained deeply committed to the federation. We knew that getting the two unions to work together would be a big challenge.

SEIU, the Service Employees International Union, repre-sents more than 1.2 million health care workers and one million other workers, including janitors and others in blue-collar jobs. AFSCME — the American Federation of State, County, and Municipal Employees — represents some 1.6 million workers in state and local governments in forty-four states, including many health care workers.

Blum summarized the importance of inviting SEIU and AFSCME to the same table. "They both have institutional power, congressional relations, members, money and history. Both have been major forces on health care issues. They stood out as being the most active on big federal issue campaigns and working in coalitions. You could imagine they'd put money in and would attract other money.... Trying to bring them to-gether was an early test of whether we could create a broad co-alition."

For assistance, Blum turned to Brad Woodhouse, the execu-tive director of an organization originally called Americans United to Protect Social Security (AUPSS). It was formed in 2004, immediately after President Bush pledged to use his re-election political capital to privatize Social Security. With the backing of both AFSCME and SEIU, which served as co-chairs of the effort, money raised with the help of the Democratic leadership in Congress, and a field operation led by USAction affiliates around the country, AUPSS had run a devastatingly effective campaign. The campaign sank Bush's effort and sent his poll numbers sliding sharply downwards. By the summer of 2005, as the war in Iraq claimed more and more American lives, Bush's standing never recovered. AUPSS changed its name to Americans United for Change and continued to work promoting issues backed by Democrats in Congress and their outside allies.

In April, leaders from the two unions joined USAction and Americans United to talk about forming a new health care campaign. The union leaders agreed to work together, and so in June 2007 I flew from Albany to Washington International Airport for our first planning meeting. I had high hopes for our project, but could never have imagined that I was beginning what would become a weekly commute for the next 18 months.

Joining us were two AFSCME staffers. Steve Kreisberg, the director of collective bargaining and health care policy, brought a deep knowledge of health care issues both in Congress and at the bargaining table. Barbara Coufal, assistant director of their legislative department, contributed extensive health care expertise to the group. SEIU sent their government affairs director Ellen Golombek, who had once led an effort to collect "I am a health care voter" pledges from constituents in presidential battleground states, and Khalid Pitts, who had come to the SEIU after being a leader in the gun control movement and was now responsible for coordinating issue campaigns and coalition relationships.

As we began to discuss building the health care coalition, I made a simple proposal. We first needed to see if we agreed on a common vision for health care reform. A health care coalition that comes together around vague principles, such as making health care affordable or improving quality, will promptly fall apart once a real legislative battle is engaged. It's easy to agree to platitudes. The tough job is agreeing on core policies that will shape reform. The group concurred, and I was charged with drafting a statement of principles to bring to the next month's meeting.

I based my draft on the key elements of the guaranteed affordable choice plan, fleshing them out to include core essential reform policies. These ideas were also included in plans that had been released by John Edwards and Barack Obama — Hillary Clinton's plan was still in the works.

When we met again in July, the groups agreed to use the statement I had drafted, with some edits, as the basis for building a new health care campaign. The group then decided to invite other organizations to the table. AFSCME chose the AFL-CIO, bringing in the nation's biggest labor organization. AFSCME's president, Gerald McEntee, chaired the AFL-CIO's health care committee. SEIU chose MoveOn.org, adding a powerhouse netroots group with millions of members. USAction invited the Center for Community Change (CCC), a large network of local and state community-based organizations, including faith-based, communities of color, and rural groups. Finally, Americans United invited the Campaign for America's Future, the progressive think-tank and communications shop that had led the way on the Hacker plan and had been a leading voice in the campaign to save Social Security from the Bush proposals.

The leaders representing these organizations formed our Organizing Committee. Together, at biweekly meetings over the next few months, we wrestled with tough decisions. As an outside evaluation of HCAN compiled after the health care bill passed in 2010 found, much of our eventual success was because we made the right decisions early on.

A Field Plan

From the beginning we were convinced that we could not compete with the insurance industry and other corporate and health care opponents within the Beltway. They would have a battalion of lobbyists, with much better access to members of Congress and their staffs. The heart of our campaign had to lie outside the Beltway, where we could organize at the grassroots level. A major field program could organize people to speak out locally, attract the attention of the local media and directly engage their members of Congress. Here's how the HCAN evaluators, who had substantial experience in running issue campaigns, described the choices we faced:

> HCAN's decision to invest heavily in field operations should not be glossed over. Field campaigns are labor intensive, challenging to build and manage, and usually require patience before seeing a return on investment. It is far easier to raise money and put it directly into television or other paid media, or hire subcontractors to run state-by-state grasstops campaigns to generate letters and calls from influential constituents, than it is to design and implement a field program that mobilizes the grassroots. For these reasons and others, large-scale national advocacy campaigns do not often invest in building strong and broad field operations.

The question that occupied the Organizing Committee was how to structure the field campaign. The evaluators did a good job of framing that choice too: "Two models were contrasted for HCAN's field program — the first a more traditional electoral campaign model, which would hire national staff and organizers to 'parachute' into states, the second a network model where investments would be made to support existing networks of organizations in states to work on HCAN's agenda. The discussion about the two models was a major early debate and critical decision for the fledgling HCAN campaign."

I had very strong opinions about why we needed to build the campaign on the backs of existing organizations. I had been working for such state organizations for almost thirty years. The state groups had experience, active members, extensive relationships with other organizations, an understanding of state politics, and relationships with state legislators and, to a lesser extent, members of Congress. They were built to run issue campaigns, so why would anyone think you could hire people to come in and do a better job?

Among those who argued for hiring outside staff, modeled on election campaigns, the issue boiled down to accountability. National or statewide campaigns have long found that local political parties are too often inept, sucking up their money and delivering next to nothing. That is why electoral campaigns almost always hire their own field staff, holding them responsible for reaching specific voter contact goals. People running issue campaigns in Washington also become frustrated working with state and local organizations, which by definition aren't solely accountable to them. These organizations have many issues on their plates and have their own needs, which may come into conflict with that of the national campaign. What if the state organization has a lobby day planned at the state capitol or is holding its annual meeting at the same time that the national group is planning simultaneous events in twenty states? Organizations don't always deliver; sometimes they take the national money and run—doing as little as they can get away with.

I'd had extensive personal experience with this choice. In 2005, for example, USAction groups had been the foundation for the successful field campaign to oppose President Bush's push to privatize Social Security. That model contrasted with a campaign pushing for withdrawing troops from Iraq in the summer of 2006, in which large numbers of organizers were hired directly by the national campaign and given uniform, detailed tasks to accomplish. These organizers struggled to reach unrealistic goals and were usually successful only when they were bailed out by organizations that were already doing the work in their states. Of course, the state organizations really resented this, since these groups always struggle financially, and they could have hired staff with the money that the national office used.

USAction state groups were largely fed up with national campaigns. The leaders had vowed never again to participate in a campaign in which they were forced to do the work of outside staff or a campaign that gave them money but didn't listen to their opinions about what worked in their own communities.

We struggled through this disagreement for several weeks before we finally came to a resolution. We would run the field campaign as a two-way street, discussing strategy and planning tactics in conjunction with our state field "partners." We would give the state partners leeway to modify the campaign plan as long as they came up with a better approach for their state. If we could not find a local organization that could carry out the campaign, we would hire a staff person to work directly for the national campaign. Most important, we would base the campaign on contracts with state organizations that included achieving clear results, during regular review periods. In that way, if an organization didn't produce, its funding could be stopped. This resolution sounded straightforward on paper but I knew that unless we had a national staff who really understood the dynamics, it would fall apart.

Coalition Buy-In

We also talked about the membership and decision-making structure of the campaign itself. We'd already made one very important decision. The glue that held the coalition together would be the statement of principles. The HCAN evaluators summarized why this mattered: "Many coalitions attempt to articulate core principles; what makes HCAN's Statement of Common Purpose significant is that it was actively used in the formation and management of the entire coalition campaign. At the outset, these principles played a valuable role in attracting members and shaping the coalition. It allowed HCAN to bring together groups and organizations that did not trust each other and that may have had disagreements in the past, but could recognize mutual beliefs and goals embodied in the principles."

The campaign's members would be any group that endorsed the principles. The big question was, who would govern the campaign? In most campaigns, governance is obscure. Many organizations are encouraged to sign on to the campaign, while decision-making is left to a steering committee that includes relatively few groups. Behind the scenes, a very small number of organizations — those that are putting in the most money or have the most political clout — have the biggest voice. Usually, the staff make most of the decisions, ensuring that decisions are supported by those few big players.

If that had became the structure, it would have doomed the health care campaign. For a campaign this big to work, we needed the major organizations to invest their money, their staff, and their members in the effort. Moreover, since this would be a big, bruising battle, a number of issues could potentially divide the coalition. The only way to keep the groups together was to design a structure where the group would make the tough decisions together.

At this juncture Jeff Blum pulled me aside to make a startling proposal. Every steering committee member should have to make a large contribution, on the order of $100,000. Coming from USAction, this was a daring proposal, because groups like

USAction have to raise every single dollar they get from scratch, and coming up with so much money would be difficult. Progressive non-profits rely on foundation grants, support from labor unions, gifts from individual donors, and fund-raising events. Every dollar is precious and the process of raising the money is often frustrating and exhausting. But after participating in a number of D.C.–based issue coalitions, Jeff had become convinced that power belonged to groups that put in real money. No matter how big a role grassroots groups played in organizing the field, they would not be respected in Washington if all they did was receive money, not contribute themselves.

Blum also understood that even for well-funded organizations, writing a big check is significant. We needed the major unions to write big checks. So by volunteering that USAction was willing to pony up big time, Jeff challenged the unions to at least match him, if not ante up much more.

Blum's proposal had one downside. We needed the coalition's leadership to be representative of the major progressive forces. Still missing were women, communities of color, and faith-based groups, each an important pillar of the progressive base. We could reach out to them, but could any afford to pay substantial dues?

Another barrier was that at least two other members of the Organizing Committee would be hard pressed to contribute major dollars. Undeterred, Blum convinced Deepak Bhargava of the Campaign for Community Change and Roger Hickey of the Campaign for America's Future to support his proposal. But several members of the Organizing Committee remained concerned about the financial threshold for other constituency groups.

The final terms for membership in the Steering Committee were: make working on health reform a major priority; commit substantial internal resources toward engaging the organization's members; dedicate two senior staffers to work on the campaign; and contribute at least $500,000 in resources, $100,000 of which had to be in cash. However, we decided to consider making exceptions for faith-based groups and groups that represent communities of color, as long as they met all the conditions except the cash contribution.

Targeting Congress

A legislative campaign must have a strategic focus. What would ours be? For the previous few years, with Bush in power, issue campaigns had focused on "swing" members of Congress. These were either conservative Democrats or moderate Republicans. So when we started to discuss how we would target our efforts, it was natural to propose a similar swing-member strategy.

To me, however, the history of health care had taught us a different lesson. Focusing on swing members would not be enough. I feared that the attack by the opposition would be so strong that even moderate Democrats would wilt. Another consideration was that we needed to play to our strength. Progressive organizations do not have many members in more conservative districts. In campaigns that focused exclusively on swing members, we had to construct an organizing base with very little building material. Instead, we needed to energize the substantial progressive base around the country if we had any chance of building the kind of movement we would need.

The Organizing Committee agreed in principle that we needed to focus on virtually every Democrat, not just the conservatives, but where would we get the money to organize a grassroots campaign in hundreds of Congressional districts? In addition, we absolutely had to raise enough money to run a multi-faceted, national campaign with not only a strong grassroots presence but also enough paid media to appear credible to the national press, White House and Congress. How much was that? The total sum was mindboggling, but we estimated that we'd need $150 million—$50 million a year for three years.

Where we would ever find that much money? Fortunately, we already had a lead.

Spending Boldly and Quickly

I met Chuck Feeney only once, at a board meeting of The Atlantic Philanthropies held on a balmy late winter day in 2009 at the venerable Willard Hotel, a few blocks from the White House. It was hard to miss him. Everyone else in the elegant room was dressed as you'd expect for a business meeting of a multi-billion dollar foundation, held at a prestigious venue. Charles F. Feeney was wearing a faded white-and-black checked flannel shirt. Of medium height with a solid build and a full head of white hair, the seventy-seven-year-old's lively blue eyes engaged me as we talked briefly after my presentation to the Board. Feeney's biography is titled, *The Billionaire Who Wasn't: How Chuck Feeney Made and Gave Away a Fortune Without Anyone Knowing*. Feeney was as unassuming as the book's title implies.

Feeney had made his fortune in the duty-free business. In 1984 he transferred almost his entire wealth to The Atlantic Philanthropies, inspired by Andrew Carnegie to see the impact of his charitable giving in his lifetime. Feeney, a brilliant entrepreneur whose idea of planning is to follow opportunities, believed that "spending too quickly and boldly would be a lesser evil than spending too slowly or too timidly." In 2002 the Atlantic Board formalized that philosophy, deciding that it would spend down by 2016, distributing most of its four-billion-dollar endowment.

In January 2007, Gara LaMarche became the third president and CEO of The Atlantic Philanthropies. Before he was hired, LaMarche told the Atlantic board of directors, "Atlantic needed to make some bigger bets that might have bigger pay offs, and that he wanted to move more into a social justice sphere, becoming a sizeable backer of community organizing."

Gara LaMarche grew up in a working-class family in Rhode Island. After graduating from Columbia in 1978 — LaMarche paid his own way, working at a nursery school — he took a job with the American Civil Liberties Union. After several years he became the director of the ACLU's Texas chapter. His career took him to the Freedom-to-Write Program of the

PEN American Center, to Human Rights Watch and then to George Soros' Open Society Institute (OSI), where he established a focus on social justice and democracy. In his position at OSI, LaMarche met the heads of the major progressive organizations in the country, including Roger Hickey and Jeff Blum.

Hickey and Blum were eager to talk with LaMarche in his new position at Atlantic. They separately approached him in the summer of 2007 about the possibility of Atlantic funding our national health care effort. LaMarche wasn't inclined to take them up on the idea. Atlantic made its grants from four program areas, and health care wasn't one of them. But he was intrigued enough to agree to a meeting in October 2007, which would include several members of our Organizing Committee.

Stuart Schear joined LaMarche at the meeting, as a new Atlantic staffer hired to help the foundation with communications. Schear was an expert on health policy and politics. He had covered the Clinton health care fight as a reporter for PBS's *MacNeil-Lehrer NewsHour*, had worked for President Clinton in the White House, and then became the head of the Robert Wood Johnson Foundation's "Covering the Uninsured" project, an effort to keep expansion of health coverage in the public eye during the Bush Administration.

Jeff Blum began the meeting by declaring that if a Democrat were elected as president a year later, it would open the door for "a generational moment to win health care for all in America." He suggested that if Atlantic made a major commitment to historic health reform, it would create a lasting legacy for the foundation. We had begun laying the groundwork for the coalition, he said, and we thought we needed a total of $150 million, $50 million a year for three years. Finally, he asked LaMarche to consider contributing $45 million of that, a huge sum for one foundation.

The group continued to expand on Blum's opening points, focusing on how the coalition would have unified labor support and would organize at the grassroots. They talked about the impact of health reform on racial justice. The group reviewed the progress whereby all three major Democratic candidates for president were on the same policy page.

Gara LaMarche had a number of questions. What would happen if a Democrat did not win the presidency? How many other groups, who are not part of your coalition, are likely to approach me with the same request? Will your coalition include more mainstream and even some conservative supporters of reform, which other funders will want to see in order for them to help fund the effort? How far along are you in planning, because we would need a very detailed plan to consider making a grant of this magnitude? How would you spend $150 million?

Despite his many questions, LaMarche was clearly interested. He said, "I'm driven by a sense of opportunity that this is the biggest social justice issue in the U.S. If the opportunity arises and the stars are in alignment and significant resources would help, that's why I'm having this conversation. I'm also interested in building organizations."

After addressing LaMarche's questions, the conversation began to focus on the planning process. LaMarche said that while he did not usually make planning grants, this situation called for funds to undertake detailed planning. Doing so, he suggested, would allow the Organizing Committee to develop a much more detailed campaign plan, including a well-thought-out budget and fund-raising plan. He said he would consider a planning grant in "the low six-figures" and that "I could give that without prejudice. It wouldn't bind me to more and it wouldn't preclude more."

While cautious, LaMarche did not have sticker shock from the $45 million request. "The fact that I haven't screamed at the number still doesn't mean that I don't think it's highly unlikely. But we will try to do something significant. Don't feel discouraged."

Discouraged? We were anything but let down. Blum was buzzing and told me that I should work with Diane Archer right away to frame an outline for the planning grant.

Later, when I talked with LaMarche about his recollections of the meeting, he told me, "I remember thinking that it was an audacious request, but what are we here for? I was new to the foundation and thought that one way to make strategic change is by doing something. A lot of foundations are into strategic plans and they have their place. But it made sense to be defined by actions. If someone were to say that Atlantic took a major risk on health care reform, that's worth more than a ton of strategic plans. We could have a huge impact in people's lives."

Diane Archer and I quickly set up a meeting with Stuart Schear, and then kept in regular contact with him as we wrote a planning grant. However, our Organizing Committee was one of several groups that approached Atlantic about funding health care work, including the health consumer group, Families USA. In late December, Schear, working with a group of his colleagues at Atlantic, settled on giving planning grants to our Organizing Committee and to Families USA.

The Big Plan

When Phil Villers established the Villers Foundation, he hired Ron Pollack to be the executive director. He chose well. Pollack turned Families USA (as the Villers Foundation was renamed) into a respected and effective "Voice for Health Care Consumers," as the organization branded itself. It was the largest national public interest organization that focused exclusively on the full range of health policy issues from a consumer perspective.

Stuart Schear had worked with Pollack closely on the Covering the Uninsured project, including an effort to find common ground on a health reform proposal among a group of "strange bedfellows," which included organizations representing health insurers, hospitals, doctors, drug companies, and labor.

Like all of us, Pollack and the Families USA Board were anticipating a new opening for reform if a Democrat won the presidency in 2008. The strategy Pollack brought to Atlantic had three components. One, Families would give grants to a number of health care consumer groups (including some USAction affiliates) in fifteen battleground presidential states to fund the release of a number of reports that highlighted why health reform was needed in that state. Second, he wanted to find common ground and build relationships among potential adversaries. Third, he hoped to form a coalition of major stakeholder groups that supported reform, each of which would make a substantial contribution to a joint effort. The Families USA Board agreed to commit $5 million to the venture, to demonstrate the seriousness of its commitment and attract other groups.

With planning grants to both our health care Organizing Committee and Families USA before them, Atlantic decided to take the unusual step of having both groups come in together and present their ideas to the Atlantic staff.

As Gara LaMarche told me, "I've known Ronnie for a long time. We'd funded him for various things. And he had a relationship with Stuart, who was initially inclined toward funding Pollack. All I knew was that I didn't want to split the difference. Instead, I wanted to look at the options and make a choice."

So in late February, Families USA and the Organizing Committee made presentations together to LaMarche and ten Atlantic staffers.

LaMarche remembers, "I knew the players in the HCAN coalition whom I would want to be allied with: more bottom up, grassroots, organizing. A group with organizing networks and labor unions. Unlike Pollack, who was working with the industry, working inside, top down. I was in the process of moving Atlantic to being less tied to traditional work, to take on messier work like organizing."

Stuart Schear was impressed by another big difference. Our campaign was based on principles for reform, whereas Pollack said that the coalition he brought together would avoid discussing any common framework for reform. "We were very impressed with the HCAN principles. Families decided it would not have principles because having principles would divide their group. What we found more appealing in the HCAN strategy was that while not entirely an outsider plan, it was an advocacy plan based on continued pressure from those left of center, although not so left as to be out of the discussion."

What finally clinched the deal for Schear was the plan we submitted at the end of March 2008, which he said had an impressive level of detail, unlike the Families plan, which was "much more impressionistic." We had used the Atlantic planning money to turn the campaign plan that the Organizing Committee had developed during the fall into a detailed roadmap that included everything we'd need to launch the campaign. The first part of the 895-page plan was a 61-page funding proposal to Atlantic, followed by 140 pages of more detailed narrative and 635 pages of data tables. The data included everything we would need to start working on the campaign, including: profiles of potential state field partners in all fifty states; information on hundreds of potential organizational members from fifteen different constituencies; Congressional targeting analysis; and information on foundations and individual donors. It included detailed plans on communication, creating a new small business coalition, building support among academics and elite opinion makers, and policy research. The plan also included detailed budgets for 2008 and 2009, in three tiers, ranging from $63 million to $120 million for the two years.

By the time we submitted the proposal to Atlantic on April 1, 2008, we had another major funder interested as well. The California Endowment (TCE) had been established in 1996 when Blue Cross of California was acquired by the for-profit health insurance giant Anthem (which later became part of WellPoint). Starting in the mid-nineties, for-profit insurers started taking over non-profit insurance companies around the nation, most of them members of the Blue Cross Blue Shield Association. Laws in many states require that when a non-profit becomes a for-profit, stock in the for-profit company or other proceeds from the conversion be given to a non-profit foundation. TCE was one of the biggest "conversion foundations" in the nation, with an endowment of more than $3 billion.

During the past several years, TCE had invested heavily in preparing the ground for universal health care in California. In 2003 the State Legislature enacted a law that would have required most businesses to pay for their employees' health coverage, but in 2004 the law was rejected in a voter referendum by a small margin, after a huge opposition campaign led by retailers such as Macy's. In 2006, the city of San Francisco enacted a law that provided coverage for virtually all residents. In 2007, with the backing of Governor Arnold Schwarzenegger, California came tantalizingly close to passing a reform bill. But the state's growing financial crisis and the enormous difficulty of passing any reform measure, including opposition from single-payer supporters in the State Senate, ended up sinking the effort.

After the California legislation failed, The California Endowment realized that it should apply the lessons from its recent experience to national reform efforts. Robert Phillips, a program officer at TCE, had been in touch with Stuart Schear about Atlantic's conversations with our Organizing Committee. "We'd learned a number of lessons from the California fight," Phillips told me. "We saw that we got the biggest bang from our buck from advocacy. We realized that it was important to push for specific reforms, not just say 'get something done.' And that we needed to be prepared to fund the effort for more than one year."

In June 2008, Gara LaMarche at Atlantic's board meeting recommended a grant of $10 million to the coalition. The first $8.5 million would be made in July with another $1.5 million in November. Atlantic would also consider a $20 million grant to HCAN for 2009. In October, the TCE board made a $2 million grant to the Tides Foundation to support HCAN's work, with the expectation of another $2 million being available if needed.

In the meantime, we got a name. The Organizing Committee chose the name Health Care for America Now, which was the most popular choice among several that we had presented in our February opinion poll, and we formally voted to become a Steering Committee, which became HCAN's governing board. The Steering Committee chose three co-chairs: Barbara Coufal from AFSCME, Khalid Pitts from SEIU, and me, representing USAction. We were almost set to go. We had a plan of action, money to carry it out, and leadership to steer it. Yet a question remained open: Who would actually run the day-by-day, nuts-and-bolts operation?

Accepting the Job

I didn't plan to become HCAN's campaign manager. In fact, I resisted the notion for several months. During the planning process I had facilitated the meetings and coordinated the work. I had the time, unlike most of the other people who were on the Organizing Committee. In September I'd given up some of my responsibilities at Citizen Action of New York and started working half time as the coordinator of USAction's health care work. I also had significant experience organizing coalitions. In New Jersey, I had started a USAction organization that was structured as a coalition. For twenty years I'd headed the New York State Health Care Campaign, which also gave me extensive experience in health care. Also, for several years I'd been helping to prepare the intellectual ground for a new health reform fight.

The final reason was a matter of temperament. Directing a coalition effort takes a subtle blend of listening and leading. It's not enough just to be a good facilitator, someone who can listen carefully to diverse opinions, draw out people who are being quiet, understand which comments aren't resonating with the group even if nobody actually challenges a remark, and finally synthesize the group's discussion. You also have to know when to lead. Sometimes group dynamics can lead to weaker outcomes than the best the group is capable of. Other times the group can become sidetracked or fail to see a problem in a new light. Often all the information for making the best decision is on the table, but the group needs some sensitive shoving to reach it. That's where the leadership comes in.

As the Steering Committee met over the fall, I had taken on a leading role. Still, in January when we started to talk about hiring a campaign manager, I didn't think I would be interested in the job. The reasons were personal. Claudia and I lived in a rural community in upstate New York, outside Albany. Claudia had a job teaching literature and journalism at the state University at Albany and I don't like living in cities. I was intent on continuing to commute a couple days a week to D.C. rather than moving there full-time, which the job would require. So I joined a small committee that started looking for a campaign manager. As the committee continued its work from January to March, I coordinated the complicated planning process that led to writing the 895-page campaign plan.

By the time we were ready to make an offer to a candidate, I realized that I was feeling increasingly torn about my role. In many ways I was uniquely qualified for the challenge of running HCAN. I had an understanding of the complex interactions between health care policy and politics, and had experience balancing the conflicting agendas of our coalition partners. I understood the complex dance required to make our field model work and had years of experience running issue campaigns, although not at the national level. So by the time we made a job offer to a candidate, I told him that he should expect me to work closely with him. I am not sure whether that figured in his decision not to take the job. What I do know is that he asked for a very high salary, and we wouldn't quite meet it. And that he was very skeptical that the coalition would hold together as the legislative fight unfolded.

A week before the candidate declined, Claudia came down to Washington with me for a couple of days. She knew that I'd become very conflicted about the job but still would never take it without her approval. To our mutual surprise, she liked Washington a great deal, which is particularly pleasant in late March, when the cherry trees are in bloom, the air wonderfully mild. The city has an open feeling that is a far cry from New York City's intensity. "I could live here," she said.

So when our three-month search process ended without a campaign manager hired, I announced that I was available. The response all around was along the lines of, "What took you so long?" I told the Steering Committee that I had one condition: While I'd work full-time for HCAN, I'd continue to commute from Albany to Washington until we knew who would win the election for president in November 2008.

I broke the news to Karen Scharff, co-executive director with me of Citizen Action of New York for more than twenty years, and began to look for staff for a campaign that we planned to launch by early summer. We had a lot to do in three months. Yet we were ready to come out with all guns firing.

4

Ready, Set, Go!

O n July 8, barely three months after accepting the job as national campaign manager for HCAN, I took the podium in front of a jam-packed room at the National Press Club for HCAN's public unveiling. I had imagined a formal room at a fancy club, with well-dressed reporters in neat rows and a bank of cameras from elevated risers, but it wasn't like that at all. The nondescript room was packed with folding chairs, and most of the reporters in front were not wearing jackets or ties. They were surrounded by 200 HCAN supporters carrying our new red, white, and blue signs. The great thing about the name "Health Care for America Now" is that it's both an organizational name and a slogan. The other side of the sign carried our tag line, "Quality affordable health care we ALL can count on." These signs were to become a ubiquitous feature of hundreds of rallies and demonstrations over the coming months. A few TV cameras were pointed at me from thirty feet away, and next to me was a drop-down screen on which we were about to show our first TV ad.

This event was one of fifty-three taking place simultaneously around the country. I opened the press conference by saying, "We are announcing the campaign today in Washington. But what is really emblematic of our campaign is that we are also launching today in fifty-two cities, including thirty-eight state capitals, around our nation. The heart and soul of Health Care for America Now lies outside the Beltway, where we are mobilizing millions of Americans at work, at home, in their neighborhoods and online to make good, affordable health coverage a part of the American Dream. "

Those widespread events symbolized how HCAN would be different from anything that had come before. To be taken seriously inside the Beltway, a launch of a major issue campaign in Washington, accompanied by prestigious organizational leaders making short statements, a new website and a national TV buy, was expected. But pulling off fifty-three simultaneous events around the country, each with local leaders, was unprecedented. For me, it was early evidence of the wisdom of building a new health care campaign on the shoulders of organizations that had members and credibility around the country.

The NBC news affiliate in Trenton, New Jersey, was one of the many local TV stations that ran a story on that evening's news, capturing the New Jersey launch, held in a formal room of the State Capitol, with wood panel doors and the American and New Jersey flags at the front. The news anchor introduced the story saying, "A national grassroots effort kicks off for an American solution that will guarantee family health care based on need and not ability to pay. A new organization is calling on the next President and Congress to make health care legislation the first order of business in 2009."

The story then turned to a quick parade of local New Jersey activists. Ev Liebman, of USAction affiliate New Jersey Citizen Action said, "It's time we had an American solution that provides quality affordable health care for everyone." Rex Reid of AFSCME echoed the need for change, saying "working families are being choked by raising health care costs, yet still nothing gets done." Jeanne Oterson of Health Professionals and Allied Employees, an American Federation of Teachers (AFT) local that represents nurses, added, "Few of us anymore can count on quality, affordable, accessible care, when we need it in our own communities."

Reverend Bruce Davidson, director of the Lutheran Office of Government Ministries, argued, "Justice demands that health care be provided based on need, not simply on a person's ability to pay." A physician described his daily experience: "As a doctor, I come across patients every day who cannot access care because they can't afford it. No one should have to choose between paying for a medication and putting food on the table."

The reporter asked, "So this grassroots effort is calling on legislators and citizens to answer just one question: Which side are you on? The side where patients are at the mercy of private insurance companies, or on the side where every patient has an equal and affordable choice for insurance?" Bingo! The message that we had spent months developing was delivered on our opening day by a local news reporter.

Back in Washington, I was joined at the press conference by the leaders of some of HCAN's most powerful members. But the guy who stole the show was an auto mechanic. David White began, "I own a small auto shop in Bar Harbor, Maine. This is my busiest time of the year and I shouldn't be here now." David was the only speaker who was not all dressed up. His hair was a little disheveled and he was clearly flushed as he admitted to the crowd that he was a little nervous. But he captured the attention of the room in a way that none of the rest of us, polished and practiced, had managed.

David, who had become a volunteer after he was canvassed by Maine People's Alliance, told his story. "I'm proud to have paid the entire cost of platinum health coverage for my employees and their families. I considered it the right thing to do. However, when our insurance doubled in two years, something had to change. With over 12 percent increase in gross income in 2002, we had a stellar year. We all deserved a raise. Instead, a 50 percent increase in the price of our coverage in that same year ate up more than we made. No one got a raise. I had to do three things to make up what turned out in the large picture to be a small difference. All three of these: choose a lesser-priced and of course lesser benefit package, raise our rates, and lay one person off for six months — just to pay the difference. This is about more than the money. I was literally in tears laying this out to my men — and I'm not really fond of crying before my men. Then it hit me. No matter how hard we work, ultimately our entire community foots this unreasonable bill or we go out of business. Like noticing someone pouring poison in the water supply, I was compelled to act. I quickly learned that my circumstance is not at all unique."

We launched HCAN online too, with an initial email to more than 5.3 million addresses. That campaign was coordinated by our new online director, Levana Layendecker, who had come to HCAN from the American Friends Service Committee, better known as the Quakers. MoveOn led the online campaign, with a blast to its 3.3 million members, a number that was to grow to more than 5 million by 2009. Our major labor partners and groups like Planned Parenthood and True Majority, which had become the online affiliate of USAction, emailed to another 2 million homes. We asked people to send us their insurance company stories, and more than a thousand stories of woes caused by insurance company malfeasance poured in. The initial email blast also became the basis for HCAN to build its own email list, which grew to almost 40,000 by Election Day.

In addition, we unveiled our first national ad, which ran on CNN and MSNBC as well as on D.C. cable and broadcast TV, including the weekly and Sunday morning news shows that members of Congress and their staffs would be likely to view. The message of the ads was captured most simply by a print version, which we placed in *The Wall Street Journal, The New York Times, The Washington Post* and several of the newspapers read closely on Capitol Hill, like *CongressDaily,* the *Hill,* and *Roll Call.* The headline, "Trust insurance companies to fix the health care mess?" ran on top of a picture of a question-answering "Magic 8 Ball." The answer: "Not on your life."

The television version showed a number of people interrogating the Magic 8 Ball at home. A mother asked about her young son, "Will they pay for his inhaler?" The 8 Ball responded, "Not likely." A dad asked, "Is my surgery covered?" only to hear "Don't bet on it." A pregnant woman wondered if she could choose her doctor and the 8 Ball answered, "Better not tell you." A woman worried, "Will they cover the chemo?" and was told, "Doubtful." Finally, the ad returned to the mom who is seen angrily shaking the 8 Ball and asking, "Will health insurance companies ever put your health before their profits?" The verdict: "Not a chance." The announcer's voice intoned, "We can't trust the insurance companies to fix the health care mess. If you're ready to demand quality, affordable health care now ... Join Us," as the Magic 8 Ball said: "HealthCareforAmericaNow.org."

We focused on the question of trusting the insurance companies for several reasons. We knew from our research that the best way to reach the public was to generate anger at big insurance. Moreover, the insurance industry was starting a "charm offensive," a public relations campaign to convince the public that the industry had turned a new leaf and would support reform. But we also knew from our research that people were highly suspicious of any reforms backed by insurers.

We had another audience too: those in Congress who might be tempted to swallow the insurance company line that they backed reform. We wanted, early in the debate, to show the powers in Washington that cooperating with big insurance was a dead end.

An online version of the ad ran on the websites of the major national and Capitol Hill newspapers and on twenty-seven national blogs and eighteen state progressive blogs. All told, our ad firm estimated that the campaign delivered 34,126,174 impressions. That may sound impressive, but it's really not. We spent only $1.1 million on the total buy, a small sum for a national campaign. Our audience wasn't the broad public, who needs to see commercials over and over again to make any kind of impression. Instead we were aiming at a small sliver of movers and shakers, who expect any major effort to shape public policy to include paid advertising.

The fact that money is the main political currency in Washington was underscored by the headline of the Associated Press article, running in 175 papers around the country, "Money, ads give health care top political billing." The article went on to say, "A coalition of labor unions and Democratic-leaning organizations called Health Care for America Now on Tuesday was announcing a $40 million campaign to promote affordable health care coverage for all." The emphasis on the $40 million was echoed by local reporters around the country.

AP wasn't the only national outlet to lead with the money story. *The New York Times* ran an article a few days earlier under the banner, "New Health Reform Group to Spend $40 Million." The article began, "It could be a version of the 'Harry and Louise' television commercial that helped kill Hillary Rodham Clinton's health care plan in 1994, only this time, it will be in favor of reform. A national advertisement by the newly formed group Health Care for America Now, to be released on Tuesday, will take on insurance companies and argue for comprehensive, affordable health care in the United States, a spokeswoman for the group said Wednesday."[11]

The Associated Press and *The New York Times* articles were no accident. I had spent the two weeks prior to the launch introducing HCAN to the national press. We had hired the progressive Fenton public relations firm to arrange for introductions for HCAN's new communications director, Jacki Schechner, and me to the national press. Jacki had joined the HCAN staff from CNN after a career in journalism that included being the first TV reporter whose beat was the online world. Our whirlwind tour of the Washington press corps included visits with the major national print and TV news outlets and national bloggers.

The combination of extensive pre-launch coverage and fifty-three events around the country led to sixty-six local TV reports viewed by 2.3 million people as well as numerous articles in newspapers, on radio, and online. It was a good start.

After we showed the Magic 8 Ball ad at the press conference, I started taking questions from the press. Looking back at the video of the event, one question stands out. *The Washington Post*'s Perry Bacon asked if we would "accept a plan if it does not include a public option." This was a question that we would hear over and over again for the next seventeen months. The same question would cause the next president and many of his top health officials much public consternation. While I hadn't prepared an answer, without hesitating I answered, "We're fighting for our principles, all ten of our principles. And we will push hard to get the Congress and the next President committed to our principles.... A core of our principles is to get a public plan so we are not at the mercy of the private insurance companies."

Insurance Company Rules

Nine days after HCAN launched, we learned that another health care campaign was going to make its debut, announcing a strategy that sounded remarkably like HCAN's. It boasted a name that could have been taken right out of HCAN's message book. *Politico* reporter Chris Frates wrote:

> "Ahead of the approaching health care reform storm, the insurance industry is building an ark: a nationwide education campaign aimed at raising an activist army at least 100,000 strong. The unprecedented effort by America's Health Insurance Plans, called the Campaign for an American Solution, includes a nationwide listening tour, advertising and an intense recruitment effort aimed at signing up Americans who are satisfied with their private insurance coverage. AHIP President and CEO Karen Ignagni plans to launch the campaign Tuesday by hosting a discussion among a group of uninsured people in Columbus, Ohio....
>
> "On an issue as big and far-reaching as health care reform, you need to be working with real people and you need to have a reach outside the Beltway," AHIP spokesman Michael Tuffin told Politico in an interview outlining the industry's strategy. "The issue isn't going to be settled just by lobbyists in Washington. The American people are going to have their say."...
>
> Tuffin continued, "To spread the AHIP gospel and sign up true believers, the group has planned dozens of unscripted roundtables in cities from Albuquerque, N.M., and Denver to Boston and New York. The discussions will include union members, working families, faith and community leaders, and small-business owners and employees."[12]

If you've never heard of the Campaign for an American Solution, there's a good reason. Four days after the announcement in *Politico* we stopped the Campaign dead in its tracks, crippling its tour and sending it underground.

AHIP stands for America's Health Insurance Plans, the major trade association for the health insurance industry. Their president, Karen Ignagni, came to the insurance industry in 1993 after heading the AFL-CIO's health policy work, a head-turning switch even by Washington standards. Ignagni personified the consummate Washington insider, with pay of $1.9 million in 2008 and strong relations on the Hill and with the press.

AHIP had chosen to launch in a battleground state. As *The Columbus Dispatch* reported on July 20, "It's no accident that AHIP is launching the campaign with an event Tuesday in Columbus, a demographic test market for the country and a key state in the presidential race."

Luck had a little to do with our ability to ruin the AHIP campaign's launch. As it turns out, SEIU was holding a political action training for more than 100 of its members in Columbus on the same day that AHIP planned to hold its first roundtable, which it billed as a "listening session" at a YWCA a few blocks away. The AHIP event would be the first chance to test the ability of HCAN's local partners to engage in rapid response, an essential component of any campaign in this age of instant communication. We decided to hold a press call with Ohio reporters on the day before the AHIP rally, so that we could provide our spin on the story and alert the press to the protest we had planned for the next day. On Monday at 11:00 I was joined on the press call by an SEIU member and representatives of the three local HCAN partners that we had contracted with to organize in Ohio: Brian Rothenberg, the Director of Progress Ohio, an online group that worked with USAction; Katy Gall, an organizer with Ohio ACORN; and Stephanie Beck Borden, a member of a faith-based organizing project called AMOS that was part of the CCC network. Stephanie had a personal story to tell about a problem accessing health coverage. Unlike AHIP's outsiders coming to "listen," we were represented by actual people from the Buckeye State.

On the call, Michelle Grey told the press, "I'm a state nurse here in Ohio and a member of the SEIU District 1199 WKO. My grandson has autism and my daughter, a single mother who works hard yet barely gets by, has a very difficult time providing for his very sensitive medical and health needs and insurance does not provide the coverage she needs. It is a horrible feeling to watch my grandson and daughter suffer because health insurance companies care more about making money than actually helping people get the care that they need."

We gave the press research that contrasted the rapid rise in the cost of health insurance premiums to Ohio families and businesses with stagnant wages for Ohio families. The research demonstrated that the net earnings of Community Insurance Company, the Ohio subsidiary of WellPoint, had more than doubled from $204 million to $420 million, from 2003-07.

The press call was covered by Ohio newspapers and radio, progressive blogs, and *The Nation*. MSNBC played a copy of our Magic 8 Ball ad.

The press coverage also brought forth a new ally. We received a frenzied email from Randi Schmitt, the senior advocacy associate at the YWCA USA, who was alarmed that we would be holding a protest outside their building, since the YWCA represents many low-income families. Randi was worried that it would look like the YWCA was endorsing AHIP, which was the last thing the organization wanted. When the YWCA rented space to the Campaign for an American Solution, the organization had no idea that it was a front group for the insurance industry. I assured Randi that we would move the protest to the side of the YWCA's building and avoid any mention of her organization. A short time after the rally, the YWCA became a member of HCAN, making sure that no one doubted which side they were on.

On the morning of the AHIP event, 200 marchers paraded to a parking lot next to the YWCA, where a small red pickup truck served as a stage for the rally speakers. Walking in a long line, the marchers, most of them wearing SEIU's purple T-shirts with the logo "I am a health care voter," banged on makeshift drums made from large plastic containers and carried hand-made signs that read: "AHIP, which side are you REALLY on?" and "We can't count on AHIP to fix health care." Another sign said "Honk if you want to get rid of for-profit insurance. "And many people held the ever-present HCAN red, white, and blue signs.

Inside the forum, as the session was nearing its end, an SEIU member confronted Ignagni with ammunition provided by Angela Braly, the CEO of WellPoint. A key message of the AHIP charm offensive was that health insurers wanted to expand their "membership," i.e., the number of people who had insurance. But that was not the story Braly had told Wall Street investors in April 2008. On a call with Wall Street analysts to review WellPoint's first-quarter profits, Angela Braly told a group of analysts, "We will not sacrifice profitability for membership." In other words, the company would not sell health coverage to more people if it meant it would lose money.[13]

Kim Gooden, an SEIU activist from New York, stood up and told the audience what Braly had said. Gooden said, "How do you guys sit in this roundtable and have this discussion and this woman [Braly] is making these type of comments? ... When you talk about profitability, you guys have all these different rules and regulations on how not to pay out money! And you make profits off of that. And people are dying, people are sick, it's disgusting."

California Representative Pete Stark, the chair of the Health Subcommittee of the House Ways and Means Committee, piled on, too. Stark was a longtime critic of the health insurance industry and a fearless champion for consumers on health care. Any health reform legislation would have to go through Stark's committee. On the morning of AHIP's Columbus action, Stark released a statement that read, "America's Health Insurance Plans' new 'Campaign for an American Solution' rings as true as the tobacco industry's efforts to end smoking. There is nothing grassroots about it. It is designed, financed, and coordinated through their Washington trade association with the singular goal of protecting their profits. I hope it is true that these companies intend to be a positive force in health reform efforts, but I tend to be cautious when the fox starts drawing up plans for a new henhouse."

AHIP gave us another opening to poke fun at their "listening tour." The Campaign for an American Solution promoted a toll-free number for consumers to call. But when we dialed in, we got the following message, "Thanks for calling the Campaign for an American Solution. No one is available to answer your call right now." Our online team immediately created a thirty-second ad for YouTube, showing an unanswered phone and playing the voice mail recording. Our ad was covered by *Politico*, guaranteeing that it got a big audience inside the Beltway.

An enterprising reporter for the online magazine *Slate* identified the toll-free number used by AHIP. "The same phone number was previously used in a lobby campaign by the Poker Players Alliance, whose chairman is former Sen. Alfonse D'Amato of New York, aka 'Senator Pothole.'" AHIP was running the classic example of an Astroturf campaign — a campaign backed by corporate money but designed to look like a genuine grassroots effort.[14]

We were hoping for more opportunities to rain on the AHIP parade, but the "listening tour" decided to put in earplugs. Some of our staff signed up for Campaign for American Solution emails and regularly monitored the website in the hope of finding out where AHIP would pop up next. As HCAN blogger Jason Rosenbaum reported on the NOW! blog for August 13, "The insurance industry front group America's Health Insurance Plans is continuing its 'listening' tour on short notice. After a month of silence, they are announcing the 2nd stop in their tour in Detroit. The announcement was sent out an hour ago. The tour stop is *today*. There is no information on where or when the event will be held."

A few days later AHIP showed up in Utah, as Salt Lake City's *Deseret News* reported on August 27, "A group of small business executives and state lawmakers in Utah met this week with insurance industry leaders to discuss health care access, quality and affordability, as part of the Campaign for an American Solution."

On October 2, AHIP popped up at an Arkansas Governor's roundtable. As Rosenbaum wrote, "They gave no notice that they were attending. Zero. And yet they still say they're 'listening' to the public."

We did catch up with them in Rhode Island, though. As *The Providence Journal* reported on September 27:

> Yesterday, AHIP held a "roundtable discussion" in Providence as the seventh stop in its Campaign for an American Solution, meetings to discuss what citizens want from their health-care system. And the first thing the "listening tour" encountered was a protest. A group called Health Care for America Now!, comprising unions and other activists, gathered a dozen or so people under umbrellas outside the Foundry building.... Inside, at a discussion moderated by former Lt. Gov. Charles J. Fogarty, Ignagni spoke with eight people, most either public-employee union representatives or small-business owners.

Eight people. The Campaign for an American Solution would maintain a website and continue to facilitate some Astroturf activities, but it never tried for any of the lofty goals to reach "real people." Unfortunately, this didn't stop the health insurance industry from trying to bend health reform to its own purposes. It just found other front groups to hide behind.

Chasing the AHIP listening tour wasn't the only way that we went after the insurance industry in the summer and fall of 2008. On the weekend before the Columbus protest we released a hilarious video called Insurance Company Rules, produced for us by a Los Angeles-based political comedy troupe called Public Service Administration. The lead-in for the sketch is, "Americans are beginning to take notice. You can play the fair way. Or you can call 'insurance company rules.'" In a series of increasingly ridiculous vignettes, losers of chess, tennis, and golf make up for their losses by taking outlandish measures, as the announcer says, "Insurance companies rewrite the rules so that they win every time." The video went modestly viral, with 125,000 hits on YouTube in a short time, after being featured on MNBC and several progressive blogs. I know that at least one ten-year-old was impressed. A lobbyist who was active with HCAN heard her son declare, while playing with a friend, "I call insurance company rules."

In June, as we prepared for the HCAN launch, we had identified HCAN partner organizations in almost forty states. Margarida Jorge, our new field director, coordinated the difficult task of identifying organizations that could organize a field campaign and work well with other coalition partners. She was uniquely equipped to handle this tough job, having been an organizer for AFSCME for ten years, working for USAction's Missouri affiliate and then coming to SEIU to run their Americans for Affordable Health Care Campaign.

Throughout the campaign we asked HCAN's state field partners to undertake specific activities. In addition to holding the July 8 launch event, each field partner was responsible for organizing a public event aimed at the health insurance industry in July or August. We assisted our state partners by contracting with the Northwest Federation of Community Organizations (NWFCO) to write a report contrasting the profits of major insurers in each state with the shrinking number of people that the insurers covered.

Typical was a protest organized by Maine People's Alliance outside the office of Anthem Blue Cross and Blue Shield (a WellPoint subsidiary) in Augusta, Maine. As the local NBC affiliate reported on August 7, "A national health insurance reform group is slamming Maine's biggest health insurance company, saying Anthem Blue Cross Blue Shield is making exorbitant profits at the expense of Maine people. It's part of an effort to force politicians in Washington to dramatically change the country's health insurance system.... Ali Vander Zanden, a member, said, 'The report shows that in Maine between 2004 and 2007, Anthem's profits increased by almost 90 percent while its membership increased just 2.4 percent.'"

Some of our HCAN state partners were more creative. In Seattle, Washington, Community Action Network organized a life-sized board game outside the headquarters of Regence Blue Shield. Volunteers were the game pieces, demonstrating the various ways that the health insurance industry denied coverage and care. Outside the Regence building in Portland, Oregon, an activist put on a plastic bare butt, carrying the sign, "No more bare coverage."

On September 14, we organized 350 house parties in forty states and 180 cities, at which we showed a nine-minute video made for HCAN by Brave New Films. "Diagnosis Now" featured the stories of three families that had become victims of health insurance company abuses. At the parties we generated more than 5,000 letters to members of Congress. More than 400 people, including Representative Pete Stark, also joined a virtual house party online, hosted by the progressive blog FireDogLake.

Why Not Single-Payer?

One positive by-product of our early attacks on the insurance industry was an improvement in the tense relationship with organizers who were working to promote single-payer reform. Single-payer health insurance means replacing private health insurance with a government-financed plan.

It is impossible to overstate how important the idea of the public option was to creating the powerful unified coalition that became HCAN. The comments of Bill Raabe, who represented the National Education Association (NEA) on the HCAN Steering Committee, were typical. "The NEA had been committed to single-payer for a long time. Our leadership are social justice people. They saw the public health insurance option as another path to social justice. It was another way of providing access to everybody and having a fair impact on controlling costs. It went after the people making millions and billions and would hold them accountable."

As HCAN formed, many unions and other organizations engaged in internal debates about whether to put aside the long-held goal of working for a single-payer national health insurance plan in preference of advocating for a set of principles for health reform, including a public option. AFSCME's Barbara Coufal explained, "There was definitely a strong, very active single-payer contingent in the union. They wanted to see the union embrace single-payer and not compromise. We had a debate in our 2008 convention about competing resolutions, on single-payer vs. the public option. Ultimately, it was the real practical point of view of the 3,500 delegates to support what could be achieved, a public option. And it was also a way to help Obama succeed. Having the public option in a reform proposal allowed most of the single-payer people to stay engaged in the fight."

During the summer of 2007, we had held a similar discussion at Citizen Action of New York, which had long supported the single-payer cause. We brought together sixty of our key volunteer leaders to deliberate about whether we should campaign for single-payer or instead campaign for principles of reform, including a public option.

We structured the discussion around a "power map." Its purpose is to help organizations make fact-based decisions about strategies to employ in an issue campaign by doing a careful, detailed analysis of the ideological position and power of each of the forces that will engage in the political debate. After creating the power map, we had a mini-debate. I made the case for the principles with a public option, and others in our group argued for a single-payer campaign. After several hours in which the group delved more deeply into the implications of the two competing strategic approaches, we took a vote. At the beginning of the day, the Citizen Action leadership had been evenly divided between backers of each approach. But after engaging in a systematic discussion of what would create the best chances of a winning campaign, the group voted for the principles with a public option approach by four-to-one.

The AFL-CIO had a particular challenge in supporting HCAN instead of focusing on single-payer. The California Nurses Association, a member of the AFL-CIO's Executive Committee, firmly believes that single-payer is the only reform worth fighting for. Gerry Shea, who had succeeded Karen Ignagni as the director of the AFL-CIO's health policy work in 1993, observed, "We had lots of interest and resonance in working with HCAN in the fall of 2007. Then we quickly went into the single-payer fight. We always maintained that single-payer was our goal, but that we had to engage in national political debate as it was presented to us. There was no credible single-payer candidate for president. It was a constant issue but it was not a difficult issue, unlike 1993 where there really was a division among our unions. This time the presidents of our national unions were united that the road to comprehensive national health reform ran through the 2008 elections. This meant we had to push the candidates for as strong a health proposal as possible, but accept that our policy advocacy would have to pivot on the prevailing candidate's position."

While a growing number of groups decided to support HCAN's approach, many single-payer advocates remained highly skeptical. Rumors circulated on the web that we were an insurance industry front group. I was even asked by a prominent single-payer advocate if Atlantic Philanthropies was financed with insurance company money (it's not). Other single-payer advocates engaged in convoluted dissections of the Herndon research to show that it was biased and based on faulty assumptions.

While I respected the single-payer champions' concerns about the many potential shortcomings of reforms that kept much of the nation's health financing system in place, we were no longer debating theory. We were actually trying to get a president and Congress to pass a law that provided affordable health coverage to everyone in the United States.

The most resonant argument made by single-payer advocates was based on strategy, not policy. These activists recognized the impossibility of enacting single-payer reforms and understood that the public option was a reasonable compromise. But they argued strenuously that it made no sense to start at the compromise position. Why, they would ask, would you go into negotiations with your fallback position?

Yet that argument ignored a crucial fact that was the hardest for single-payer supporters to swallow. We knew that a political fight around single-payer would frighten Americans about government health reform, playing into the opposition's strongest hand. Everything we had learned from the history of reform underscored the enormous difficulty of keeping the public with us in a legislative fight.

The public option gave us the high ground with the public because it could withstand attack against the charge of a government takeover of health care. We could always argue that it was an individual's choice whether to keep their private insurance or enroll in a public health insurance plan. Time proved that we were correct. Even after the right spent tens of millions of dollars and mounted a big campaign against the public option, polling — even in conservative states — still found strong support for giving people the choice of a public health insurance plan.

One other observation on the single-payer debate lies at the heart of the gap between the many single-payer activists who worked with HCAN and those who continued to criticize our approach. John Meyerson, a longtime activist who directs the legislative and political work for Pennsylvania United Food and Commercial Workers (UFCW) Local 1776, asked me, "Have you noticed that the single-payer or bust people all have great insurance?" He's right. The activists on the left who insisted that only single-payer was worth enacting didn't really have any skin in the game.

Still, I knew we had to address the issue among the large base of activists whom we wanted to include in HCAN. Our communications staff asked me to write what would be my first contribution to *The Huffington Post*. It was also my first post anywhere, as I had been a Luddite when it came to "new media." I started the post, entitled "Why Not Single-payer?," by restating the official HCAN position, which was that a properly designed single-payer plan could meet our principles. I went on to recount my history as a champion of single-payer reform in New York and the thought process that led me to propose the public option as an alternative. I also clarified a common misunderstanding among many single-payer advocates, who often equated single-payer with universal health care. One of the myths about health care around the world is that "everyone but us has single-payer." In fact, that is the way Canada provides a government guarantee of good health coverage. Other countries — including the European countries usually held up as models — do it differently, with all sorts of variations of public, private, and non-profit insurance and socialized medicine. But what's true in all these countries is that health care is guaranteed and regulated as a public good.

I'm told that the post helped persuade some single-payer supporters. Toni Lewis, a physician who heads up an SEIU-affiliated union of 13,000 doctors called the Committee of Interns and Residents, told me that she gave out "Why Not Single-payer?" constantly when she talked to the many members of her union who were single-payer supporters.

I had always believed that what would really turn around many single-payer activists was our actions, not our words. The anti-AHIP action in Columbus, Ohio, was the first proof that I might be right. On the morning of the action, Eve Gittleson, a prominent single-payer advocate who was a regular contributor to the popular progressive blog *Daily Kos* wrote, "Though many of us respectfully disagree with the overarching philosophy of Healthcare for America Now (HCAN), to their credit, they will be out in force protesting the parasites. This is good." Later that morning, the Ohio group called SPAN, Single Payer Action Network, joined the march. It was the first of many times that single-payer activists were to join HCAN demonstrations and rallies around the nation.

We had hoped that all of our insurance company actions in the summer and fall would help make the repugnant behavior of health insurance companies a prominent public issue. But the media was focused on one issue: Who would be the next president of the United States. Any communications not directly related to the election made barely a ripple in the public discourse. Fortunately for us, health care had become a major issue in the presidential campaign, starting with the primaries and accelerating into the race between Barack Obama and John McCain.

5

Health Care in the 2008 Election

Clinton and Obama

Barack Obama did not have an auspicious start on the campaign trail in the health care debate. On March 24, 2007, SEIU and the Center for American Progress hosted a debate on health care among seven Democratic presidential candidates at the University of Nevada - Las Vegas. Obama's responses were vague; he stuck to broad generalities. He was completely eclipsed by John Edwards, who had released his plan a few weeks earlier, and Hillary Clinton, who had managed her husband's health plan in 1994. Afterward, Obama told his campaign manager that he had "whiffed" at the forum.[15]

Obama got his act together by the time the Center for Community Change brought together 3,000 people at the Heartland Presidential Forum in Des Moines, Iowa. The forum provided a rare opportunity for community activists to have an extended public discussion with the Democratic candidates, including Obama, Edwards, Clinton, Ohio Representative Dennis Kucinich, and Connecticut Senator Chris Dodd. Each candidate had a segment of the forum to him or herself. When it was Obama's turn, the first two questions he was asked were on health care. Obama famously remarked, "Now, if I were designing a system from scratch, I would probably move in the direction of a single-payer system," a comment that the right would later throw back at him whenever they could. Obama went on to argue that since we had to assure that everyone was covered as quickly as possible, we needed to build on what we had already in place. He said that is why he would expand existing government programs and give people with private insurance the new choice of a more affordable government plan.

At the Heartland Forum, Obama recounted the dilemma that his mother had faced when, from her hospital bed, she fought with her insurance company about whether they would cover treatment for her ovarian cancer because her illness was regarded as a preexisting condition. Obama included his mother's story in an ad that he ran before the Iowa caucuses, saying, "My mother died of cancer at fifty-three. In those last few months she was more worried about paying her health care bills than getting well." It was a story that Obama would retell often over the next two years.*

A short time later, the primary fight narrowed to the Democratic Party's two rock stars, Clinton and Obama, who faced off in their first one-on-one debate in Los Angeles, broadcast by CNN. Health care quickly took center stage. Obama mentioned it first in his introduction. When Clinton talked about it in her opening remarks, it earned her first round of applause. But the biggest reason that health care became such a prominent issue in the Democratic primary was that it represented one of the few policy differences between the two candidates.

When columnist Doyle McManus asked Clinton to identify differences between the two candidates, the first issue that she mentioned was health care. The next question from newspaper journalist Jeanne Cummings was directed at Obama, inquiring why his plan would leave out 15 million people. The ensuing back-and-forth between the two senators lasted twelve minutes, occupying fully one-fourth of the entire debate.

Whenever the question of differences between their health plans came up, Obama always leaped to point out that "95 percent of our health plan is similar." He was right that the two plans did have the same basic structure, which would become the framework for the Democratic plans introduced in Congress

---

* A 2011 book by former *New York Times* reporter Janny Scott (*A Singular Woman: The Untold Story of Barack Obama's Mother*) raised questions about the story, saying she had been denied disability coverage rather than medical treatment. But whether he remembered the details correctly or not, clearly Obama was deeply moved by the story and the preexisting conditions issue was one that was familiar and resonant with many voters.

in 2009. Both plans would have required all but small employers to provide health coverage for their employees or to pay into a government fund that would subsidize people who did not have employer coverage and who earned too much to qualify for Medicaid. Both plans would establish new insurance market-places, called "exchanges," through which those lacking coverage from their employer or a public program could choose between a number of private insurance plans or a new government plan. Small businesses could also access the exchange to find better deals for their employees. Insurance companies would be required to comply with a new set of consumer protections, such as not turning people down because of preexisting conditions or charging higher premiums because of a history of illness. The plans would also require states to provide Medicaid to many more low-income families.

The big difference was that Clinton would establish an individual mandate, requiring everyone to be covered or pay a fine, whereas Obama would only require children to be covered. As a result of this difference, one study estimated that 15 million people would remain without coverage under the Obama plan, allowing Clinton to declare that only her plan would achieve universal health care, which she repeatedly called "a core Democratic Party value."

Here's how Obama framed the dispute:

> It is true we've got a policy difference because my view is that the reason people don't have health care ... is they can't afford the health care.... My belief is that if we make it affordable, if we provide subsidies to those who can't afford it, they will buy it. Senator Clinton has a different approach. She believes that we have to force people who don't have health insurance to buy it, otherwise there will be a lot of people who don't get it. I don't see those folks. And I think that it is important for us to recognize that if, in fact, you're going to mandate the purchase of insurance and it's not affordable, then there's going to have to be some enforcement mechanism that the government uses.

Clinton responded that by providing subsidies and controlling costs, her plan would make coverage affordable. She went on to say that without a mandate, some people who could afford coverage would still not be covered. She also stressed that the government would need to ensure that insurance companies did not exclude people because of preexisting conditions. She was referring to the fact that if you both allow insurance to be voluntary and prohibit insurers from excluding those with preexisting conditions, then the price of coverage will soar, as would the cost of government subsidies. The reason is that the people who most need health care, those who have a health condition or who are older, would be the first to choose coverage. Since they use the most care, the cost of coverage would go up. As a result, those who are least likely to use coverage, people who are healthier or younger, would be less likely to purchase coverage until they got sick or had an accident, at which time they would decide that it is time to buy insurance. Over time, as this imbalance escalated, the insurance pool would become filled with older and sicker people, and the cost of coverage would go through the roof.

The solution was to require everyone to have coverage, so that the young and healthy were sharing risk with the old and sick. We should all remember that no matter how young or healthy we are now, anyone could have an accident at any minute or could be diagnosed with a serious health condition tomorrow. However, if everyone is in the insurance pool, the costs can be shared among the temporarily healthy and those who already need health services. That sharing of risk is the fundamental principle of insurance.

So was Clinton right and Obama wrong? Not quite. Both the Obama and Clinton plans would have provided subsidies, but what if they weren't sufficient? It is unfair to make people pay for something they can't afford. And fining people for not being able to afford something they want would lead to a public backlash against the program. When Massachusetts enacted its health reform law in 2006, the plan addressed this dilemma by giving certain people a hardship exemption if the cost of coverage was considered unaffordable.

Attempting to achieve universal coverage by jury-rigging the current health system is not easy. Still, as Obama said, we can't start from scratch, either by instituting a single-payer system or some other variant on a plan that would automatically cover everyone in the country. Politics are never academic. Health care politics start with the reality of 310 million Americans participating in a $2.5 trillion health system that consumes one-sixth of our economy. I always felt that our job was to do the best that we can, remembering that 50,000 people die every year because they do not have coverage, that hundreds of thousands more suffer from unnecessarily severe illness, and many of these people and others are forced near or into bankruptcy by medical debt.

For millions of people, the best we can achieve will be really good, as I can personally attest. A year after our younger daughter, Lindsay, graduated from college, she moved to Boston to live near her older sister. Lindsay took a low-wage job, with no health coverage, and couldn't afford the regular medications and visits to the doctor she needed. We paid $300 to fill her regular prescription when she first got to Boston. But a month later she had qualified for Massachusetts' Commonwealth Care, which is the model for the plan that both Obama and Clinton supported. Finally, Lindsay had a good insurance plan that she could afford. As a parent I felt enormous relief. As a health policy strategist I regard the fact that 98 percent of Massachusetts residents have health coverage as success.

If the small difference between Clinton and Obama on health care was exaggerated in the primary campaign, the chasm between their plans and the proposal put forth by the Republican candidate, John McCain, was immense.

McCain's Radical Health Care Plan

When John McCain launched his campaign in 2007, he prescribed the usual Republican policy platitudes for health reform, "remedies" that would expand coverage for next to nobody while increasing the number of people with lousy coverage. McCain's proposal included promoting high-deductible plans, which attract the healthy and wealthy while making coverage more costly for others; permitting insurance companies to sell policies across state lines, which would allow the companies to escape basic consumer protections; and promoting the use of high-risk pools that concentrate the very sick in one insurance pool and had already proven to be a costly failure in various states around the country.

However, by the time McCain had wrapped up the Republican nomination, he had added a radical centerpiece to his plan. Under current law, individuals do not pay income taxes on the value of health care benefits paid by their employer. McCain proposed to tax health benefits and at the same time to offer tax credits for a family that purchased their own coverage.

The problem with the McCain proposal was pretty easy for Americans to understand. His tax credit would be worth $2,500 to individuals and $5,000 to families. But in 2007 the average cost of an individual policy offered through an employer was $4,479 and the average family policy cost $12,106. As a result, if the plan succeeded in encouraging employers to drop newly taxable health coverage, workers would be forced into a private insurance market with not nearly enough money to buy a decent health insurance policy. Theoretically, employers would increase employees' wages to make up for the loss of coverage, but those new wages would be taxed and it was highly unlikely that employers would provide a big enough wage increase to pay for the cost of health insurance.

The philosophical argument behind the McCain plan was that it would promote a free market in health care and that in turn the market would control health care costs. Conservatives want to replace employer and government-purchased health coverage with a market approach in which individuals directly purchase health insurance. The right believes that our high spending on health care in the United States is because employers or government pay for our coverage, isolating consumers from the cost of care. Instead, conservatives promote "consumer-driven" health care, under which consumers pay for their own coverage, thereby becoming better "shoppers." According to the free-market view, health insurance should cover only catastrophic care while consumers pay for routine or preventive care out of pocket.

The theory that health care is a consumer good like any other commercial product and that health care markets work like other markets is pure fantasy, at odds with everything we know about how health care is actually consumed. Health care markets violate the fundamental tenets of market economics. The theory of consumer demand, which is the foundation of market economics, makes two assumptions. One is that consumers create demand for a good based on their preferences. The second is that consumers shop for a good based on having complete information about their choice of products. To give an example, a consumer decides it's time for a new car and then shops around for the best deal she can find on a car she likes.

But health care isn't like shopping for a car. First of all, we rarely choose to enter the health market, particularly when we suffer the serious illnesses that are responsible for most health care spending. Would you prefer cancer to heart disease? What's on your gift list for your seventieth birthday, rheumatoid arthritis or dementia? People end up in the health care system quite against their wishes.

Once you are forced into the health "market," consumers should not be making decisions on treatment based on cost or their preferences. If you have cancer, would you shop around between chemotherapy or radiation based on which is cheaper? Would you trust your opinion on the best treatment, or would you rely on doctors who have spent years in medical school and practice? You might do some research on your own to help you ask your doctor better questions and you might get a second opinion, but the medical professional will still set the course of treatment.

In health care, consumers do not have the most information and they don't drive demand. We spend hundreds of thousands of dollars to educate a doctor or other health care practitioner so that they can make informed decisions about what the proper supply of health care should be. We give the suppliers of health care the legal authority to determine demand. Doctors prescribe tests and medications and order medical procedures. While good practitioners listen to their patients, they use their training and experience to determine the best course of care — that's their job.

Consumers do play a limited role in generating demand. The explosion of drug company consumer advertising is aimed at urging consumers to ask their doctors to prescribe medications, based on the scanty information and slick spins of the ads. Still, drug companies spend much more money pushing drugs on the doctors who will decide whether to prescribe the medications than they do advertising to consumers.

Health care is a public good, not a commodity. The reason that other developed countries spend so much less on health care, and cover all their people and deliver higher health quality care, is that these countries recognize this fact. As a public good, health care must be made available on an equitable basis to all, and prices and supply must be regulated. In the rest of the developed world, almost everyone has their health coverage supplied by the government or by a regulated non-profit insurer, and the coverage comes with very low out-of-pocket costs. In other words, other developed countries follow a course exactly opposite the one recommended by conservatives, and achieve systems that are much more efficient economically.

We may have the most-market driven health care system in the world now, but not nearly free-market enough for conservatives. McCain's proposals would have pushed America toward a full free market in health care. However, Americans didn't need a policy lecture on consumer-driven health care to hate McCain's proposal. All they really needed to hear is that McCain would tax their health benefits.

Which Side Are You On?

The contrast between the Clinton/Obama plans and the McCain plan became the basis for the campaign that HCAN ran between the organization's launch in July 2008 and Obama's inauguration seven months later. In April 2008, HCAN's new Legislative Committee, comprising lobbyists from HCAN member groups, came up with a brilliantly simple strategy. We would ask sitting members of, and candidates for, Congress to choose between the two competing approaches to health care proposed by the Democratic and Republican candidates for president.

On one side, under the heading "On your own to get health insurance," we provided our description of conservative approaches to health reform, all of which applied to the McCain plan. These included: no guarantee of coverage; taxing health benefits; encouraging plans with $10,000 deductibles; allowing insurance companies to deny coverage for preexisting conditions and escape from state consumer protection laws; and not offering the choice of a public plan.

Opposite, under the heading "Quality, affordable health care for all," we listed a shortened version of the HCAN principles, all of which were part of the Obama and Clinton plans. Our list had: a guarantee of coverage; a choice of private or public plans; regulation of insurance; requirements that health coverage be comprehensive and that cost would be based on a family's ability to pay; measures to address inequities in health care in communities of color; and cost controls that encouraged quality and lowered administrative costs.

Above the two choices was the headline, "Which Side Are You On?" The introduction read, "It's time for an American solution that will guarantee our families' health and a healthy economy. The first order of business for the new President and Congress in 2009 should be health care legislation that guarantees quality, affordable health care for all."

We were careful not to make this a Congressional "pledge," which implied that candidates for Congress were bound to follow the statement if they signed it. Had we made it a formal pledge, many candidates who agreed with us would refuse to sign it, and with good reason. The legislative process is long and complicated and impossible to predict. A "pledge" implies a promise that shouldn't be broken, potentially putting members of Congress in the difficult position of not being true to their word if they voted for a bill that violated some part of the statement.

We did not want to play a game of "gotcha." Instead, our goal was to engage candidates for Congress in the health care debate and force them to focus on the specific measures that we wanted the legislation to include, in advance of Election Day. These were new issues to most members of Congress, who had not been in office during the last health care reform debate or who had, at best, vague memories of the issues raised in 1994. We also wanted to win their written endorsement of our principles, so that we could argue publicly that we had a big base in Congress behind our approach to reform now. If we were successful, the "Which Side Are You On?" campaign would be a great practice run for the Congressional debate on reform we hoped would take place in 2009.

The Congressional outreach effort was spearheaded by our HCAN state field partners, the organizations with which we had contracted to build local HCAN coalitions and to organize grassroots activities. During the summer of 2008, the local HCAN partners began requesting coalition meetings with members of Congress and candidates who appeared to have a chance to win. At the same time, many of our major labor partners asked their members involved in legislative and political action to request that candidates for Congress sign on to the HCAN statement. We focused on Democrats, as we had little reason to believe that Republicans would endorse a statement that rejected their Party's traditional nostrums.

We also carried out the campaign's first grassroots lobbying activities, starting in the fall. In addition to the 5,000 letters to Congress that we generated at September 2008 house parties, we scheduled national call-in days and canvasses. Our first call-in day, on October 8, was modest, producing some 2,300 calls. We did better two weeks later, with 3,056 calls. By Election Day, we had generated 9,445 calls to Congress in support of our sign-on statement. While this wasn't bad for an effort that had no real legislative focus, it was a far cry from what we would need in the midst of a real legislative fight. As much as anything, the call-in campaign was a way to help the coalition and our field partners to start evaluating the best ways to generate mass numbers of calls to Congress.

For example, the call-in days gave us the opportunity to introduce a high-tech tool that would make it easier for people to contact Congress. The "Click-to-Call" tool on our website eliminated the need for a volunteer to dial the phone. Instead, all he had to do was enter his ZIP code and telephone number on a computer by going to the HCAN website. In a minute his phone would ring and connect to his member of Congress, and then to each of his senators' offices. The click-to-call technology produced about 30 percent of our first round of calls, and the remaining were placed through our new toll-free number, 1-800-264-HCAN.

We staged our first national canvass day on October 18, when 5,064 volunteers went knocking on doors in thirty-two states, collecting postcards that carried a shortened version of the "Which Side Are You On?" message. Throughout the fall, Working America — an arm of the AFL-CIO that went door-to-door in battleground electoral states — collected signatures in support of health reform on cards that looked like colored band-aids. Their canvassers garnered the signatures of more than 300,000 people, all of whom were entered into a database of voters who cared about health reform.

On October 16, we held public events in twenty-three cities including a large rally in Philadelphia, where hundreds of activists gathered across the street from the Liberty Bell and Independence Hall. As HCAN's online director Levana Layendecker reported, "The hall blazed with brightly colored T-shirts from UFCW, ACORN, AFSCME, SEIU, Philadelphia Unemployment Project, and many other groups. Spontaneous chants rang out: What do we want? HEALTH CARE! When do we want it? NOW!!!" At the event, two members of Congress from Pennsylvania, Representative Bob Brady and Representative Allyson Schwartz, and one Congressional candidate signed our statement, as did a representative of Pennsylvania Governor Ed Rendell. Pennsylvania Senator Bob Casey and Philadelphia Representative Chaka Fattah also signed the statement that day.

The field outreach was backed by HCAN's legislative team on Capitol Hill. We had only one paid lobbyist, Doneg McDonough, who had joined the staff as our legislative and policy director in July. Doneg had been a legislative assistant for Representative Pete Stark during the Clinton debate and had then worked for the District of Columbia helping to establish programs to provide health coverage to low-income families. When I checked his references, a longtime Democratic Hill staffer told me that McDonough was the best of hundreds of legislative assistants he'd worked with through the years.

Using only one official lobbyist for such a big campaign seems absurd, but we could rely on our coalition structure. McDonough worked with the HCAN Legislative Committee, led by AFSCME staffer Barbara Coufal, and built a team of veteran lobbyists to help him. Starting in the summer of 2008, the legislative team arranged for a series of briefings of Democrats on Capitol Hill. We showed them the results of our polling, which demonstrated the popularity of the Candidate A, Democratic reform plan, as opposed to the Candidate B, Republican plan. The presentation also conveyed HCAN's advice about how best to talk about health reform.

We began another major strategic campaign component: organizing Congressional champions. On September 22, Illinois Representative Jan Schakowsky, who was also a member of the Democratic leadership, and Connecticut Representative Chris Murphy brought together a handful of their colleagues to meet with some of the HCAN legislative team. Also joining us were California Representative Hilda Solis, the leader of the Hispanic caucus's health committee, and newly elected Maryland Representative Donna Edwards, who had headed the progressive Arca Foundation before her election. While Edwards was still at Arca, its board had made a key grant to help launch HCAN. The gathering led to the formation of an informal HCAN caucus, weekly meetings among key staff of a number of House members and the HCAN legislative team to share information and plot common strategy. The meetings continued through March 2010.

Moving Health Care in Congressional Races

We decided to back up our lobbying campaign with an effort focused on making health care a prominent issue in a handful of swing Congressional races, six in the House and one in the Senate. The goal mirrored our "Which Side Are You On" effort — educating voters about the differences between the two major party candidates.

The campaign was built around a single television ad, written for us by Jonathan Cranin of Fenton Communications, a former Madison Avenue ad man who decided to bring his skills to progressive politics. Cranin had created the original MasterCard "priceless" advertising campaign and the E*TRADE "baby" campaign, two of the most effective ad campaigns in recent years.

Our target audience was undecided voters for whom health care was an important issue. Celinda Lake told us that the key demographic groups that would respond to a health care message were older white women and women of all ages who were not enrolled in a political party. The "Fighter" ad that Cranin and his team created shows a very determined middle-aged woman power walking through a neighborhood of modest, well-kept suburban homes, with American flags waving. The actress, who actually is a cancer survivor, says: "I've never faced an enemy like cancer. But it's okay. I'm a fighter. Now I find out that Republican Congressman Tim Walberg [or whoever was the Republican candidate] sponsored legislation that would let insurance companies make the rules. They could even deny coverage for preexisting conditions like cancer. He wants me to fight cancer and the insurance company? Fine, I'll take you both on."

We purchased time for the ads on television shows, both broadcast and cable, which are watched more heavily by the women we were working to influence. In addition, we created two campaign mailings, each sent to 45,000 women who met our demographic profile in five Congressional districts

I wanted to know if the $3.5 million we were spending on the ads was worth it, so we designed a study to measure the impact of the ads. We polled women in the district before and after we ran the ads to see if their opinions had changed. We also left out one group of women from the mailings to act as a control group so that we could separately measure the impact of the mail.

The results were gratifying. Our ads swayed an average of 13 percent of voters toward the Democratic candidate. Voters who had received the mail and phone calls moved more than those who had just been exposed to TV.

MoveOn decided to fund HCAN to run the "Fighter" ad in North Carolina, this time aimed at John McCain. We made a substantial ad buy in mid-October. In any close election, every little bit adds up. Obama carried North Carolina only by 14,000 votes. In addition, five of the seven Republicans whom we had criticized for their health care positions lost their elections.

As Election Day approached, we had succeeded in our goal. We had the signatures of 139 members of the House and seventeen Senators for the HCAN principles of Quality, Affordable Health Care for All. The House members represented a diverse array of Democratic philosophies, rather than a narrow group of progressives. We had the support of thirty-eight members of the progressive caucus, twenty-nine members of the centrist New Democratic coalition, and thirteen members — more than one-quarter — of the conservative Blue Dogs. We also had the support of many members of the three House committees that would consider health legislation.

We had also won the support of House Democratic Caucus Chair Rahm Emanuel, who would soon become the next White House chief of staff. And yes, much to my surprise, we'd gained the backing of the man who would soon become Emanuel's new boss too.

Obama Campaigns for a Health Reform Mandate

A campaign staffer for the Obama campaign told me in the summer of 2008 that Obama, disregarding the advice of key campaign aides, decided to make health care a major issue in his general election campaign for president. It was the first of several times over the next year and a half that Obama would reject the advice of top advisors and press ahead with the fight for a comprehensive health reform bill.

A week after Obama accepted the Democratic nomination in Denver, I flew to Chicago to meet with his campaign staff. Jan Schakowsky had arranged the meeting. As a fellow member of the Illinois Congressional delegation, Schakowsky had been an early Obama supporter and had strong relationships with the staff. We were joined by Shakowsky's chief of staff, Cathy Hurwit. Hurwit had been the legislative director for the national Citizen Action for a dozen years and was my closest colleague during the Clinton health care fight. Rounding out our team was William McNary, who is president of USAction and co-director of Citizen Action Illinois, where McNary had come to know Obama well when he was an Illinois state senator.

The Obama campaign headquarters, located in a glass skyscraper in downtown Chicago, buzzed with the activity of energetic young people, several of whom were ushered out of the conference room with their laptops in hand to make way for us to meet with Obama's campaign policy staff.

Jan Schakowsky began the meeting by emphasizing that health care was a key way to talk about the economy during the election campaign. The President also had to take the lead on the issue once he took office. She stressed that only the President could cut through all the turf battles in Congress and impose the discipline necessary to keep the issue on track in what would be a very tough fight. She was prepared to organize a group of supporters inside the House, but the campaign would also need a strong outside force, which is what we were building at HCAN.

I presented highlights from our polling data and then outlined the campaign we were building to win health care reform. We had persuaded over a hundred members of Congress to sign the HCAN principles. We were building an army to pass such a plan next year. However, I did not plan to ask for Obama's signature on our "Which Side Are You On?" statement. Given how nervous so many politicians are about putting their name on an issue pledge, I didn't imagine that a presidential candidate would agree.

So I was completely taken aback when one of the Obama campaign staffers said, "You know, Obama is a Senator. He could sign. He supports all these principles and this is totally consistent with our message."

I didn't let my surprise show. Still, I was skeptical that the offer would hold. Two weeks later, Cathy Hurwit sent me a one-line email that she had received. The email simply said, "Please sign Obama onto the HCAN pledge, tx!"

I wrote Hurwit back, "This is amazing! This is real, no joke, right?"

It wasn't a joke. Later that day I received an email telling me that Senator Obama would be signing on. On October 6, *Politico*'s Chris Frates reported:

Obama backs Health Care for America Now

> Sen. Barack Obama (D-Ill.) has signed on to the progressive Health Care for America Now campaign's principles — a move that bolsters the clout of the nascent organization and could provide him with artillery support as he starts to pound the health-care issue on the presidential campaign trail.... Obama said in a statement released by the group. "... I am proud to join HCAN's efforts to tackle the tough challenges we face in reforming our nation's healthcare system."

Obama endorsed the HCAN principles two days after delivering his major campaign health care address at Newport News, Virginia. Much of the speech was taken up with attacking McCain's health care plan, including McCain's proposal to tax health benefits. We were responsible for one line in his speech, "You may have heard about how, in the current issue of a magazine, Senator McCain wrote that we need to open up health care to — and I quote — 'more vigorous nationwide competition as we have done over the last decade in banking.' That's right, he wants to deregulate the insurance industry just like he fought to deregulate the banking industry. And we've all seen how well that worked out."

There's a great story behind how that McCain quote found its way into Obama's speech. On September 19, I had received an email from Jennifer Lindenauer, who had coordinated the production of the "Fighter" ad. She attached an article that McCain had written for the September/October issue of *Contingencies*, the magazine of the American Academy of Actuaries. One line was underlined in the article, "Opening up the health insurance market to more vigorous nationwide competition, as we have done over the last decade in banking, would provide more choices of innovative products less burdened by the worst excesses of state-based regulation."

This line was political dynamite. Lehman Brothers had declared bankruptcy just a few days before. Bank of America had just taken over Merrill Lynch so it would avoid the same fate. Treasury Secretary Henry Paulsen was scurrying to stop the entire banking system from collapsing.

I was advised that the best way to draw attention to the McCain quote was to send it to *The New York Times* columnist Paul Krugman. By that evening Krugman had added a new post on his blog: "You might want to be seated before reading this. Here's what McCain has to say about the wonders of market-based health reform." After reporting the McCain quote, Krugman went on, "So McCain, who now poses as the scourge of Wall Street, was praising financial deregulation like 10 seconds ago — and promising that if we marketize health care, it will perform as well as the financial industry!"

From Krugman it leapt to a screaming headline on the front page of *The Huffington Post*: "OUCH" above a pained picture of McCain. The next day Obama added an attack on McCain's pronouncement to his stump speech: "So let me get this straight — he wants to run health care like they've been running Wall Street."

The next day, September 21, the Obama campaign's new campaign ad stated, "We've seen what Bush-McCain policies have done to our economy. Now John McCain wants to do the same to our health care. McCain just published an article praising Wall Street deregulation. Said he'd reduce oversight of the health insurance industry too. Just as we have done over the last decade in banking. Increasing cost and threatening coverage. A prescription for disaster. John McCain. A risk we just can't afford to take."

The ad attacking McCain's quote in *Contingencies* was just one of many health care-related ads that the Obama campaign ran through Election Day. On October 23, *Politico* reported, "Democrat Barack Obama has spent $113 million in health care television advertising so far this year, eight times that of Republican rival John McCain — an investment that polls show are paying big dividends as the election enters its closing weeks…. Obama has devoted 68 percent of his total TV advertising this year to ads that include health care themes, and McCain has devoted 13 percent…. In October, McCain spent 1.5 percent of his TV ads on health care, while Obama upped the ante to 86 percent of his total budget."

Many of the ads included attacks on McCain for his support of taxation of benefits, including a spot that showed Democratic vice-presidential candidate, Delaware Senator Joe Biden, making fun of the Republican vice-presidential candidate, Alaska Governor Sarah Palin's claim that she had refused funding in Alaska for a spending project that was a "bridge to nowhere." The spot showed a clip from the vice-presidential debate in which Biden quipped, "Taxing your benefits. I call that the ultimate bridge to nowhere." Another Obama ad ended with the tag line, "John McCain, instead of fixing health care, he wants to tax it."

An admission by McCain's top policy adviser, Douglas Holtz-Eakin, provided another opening for Obama ads aimed at senior citizens. On October 6, the *Wall Street Journal* reported, "John McCain would pay for his health plan with major reductions to Medicare and Medicaid, a top aide said, in a move that independent analysts estimate could result in cuts of $1.3 trillion over ten years to the government programs." The Center for American Progress apportioned that $1.3 trillion between the two programs and came up with an estimate of $882 billion of cuts in Medicare. The Obama campaign soon put up two ads, each of which attacked McCain for taxing benefits and then paying for his plan with the Medicare cuts. Obama's campaign ran a third spot, targeted at seniors, which focused on the Medicare cuts alone.

Obama wasn't the only one making a big issue of taxation of health benefits. The issue had become the labor movement's biggest weapon against McCain. For the previous two decades, unions had often foregone wage increases at the bargaining table in order to preserve good health benefits. Health care had been at the center of virtually every major labor negotiation, and union members were acutely aware of the sacrifice in wages that they had made.

While many people may think that labor's biggest political clout derives from campaign donations, that is far from the truth. Where labor support really matters is in educating and mobilizing their members to support pro-labor candidates. Starting in the 1990s, unions had developed increasingly sophisticated ways of using issues to motivate members to vote for candidates supported by labor, almost always Democrats. One key result was that white male and Catholic union members had voted Democratic in presidential elections, unlike non-union members in these same demographic groups.

In more heavily unionized states in the Midwest, inspiring these labor members to vote for Obama was crucial to improving his prospects. A union organizer in Ohio told me that the most effective message to reach these union members was: Obama will not take away your gun. McCain will tax your health benefits.

Unions sent millions of mailings and made millions of phone calls to their members attacking McCain's proposal to tax benefits. The United Auto Workers even ran a $3 million TV ad campaign in four Midwest states featuring a young mother with an asthmatic son who said that the McCain plan would raise her taxes by $2,800 a year, "That's gas money, grocery money.... We can't afford a health care tax. We can't afford John McCain."

By September 2008, the Kaiser Health tracking poll reported that "health care has crept up in importance as an election issue in recent months among a key voting group: political independents, who ranked it as highly as Democrats did in this poll. Roughly one in four (26 percent) independents rank health care as one of the top issues they would "most like to hear the presidential candidates talk about." Health care's importance had risen among independents by eight percentage points since April 2008. At the same time, health care dropped even further down Republicans' priority list (now mentioned by 11 percent, a new low).

Nowhere was the gap between Republicans and the rest of the electorate reflected more visibly than in the presidential debates between Obama and McCain. In the three debates, besides their answers on specific questions about health care, Obama said "health care" twenty-five times while McCain voiced the words just nine times. Unfortunately for McCain, two of the debates included long segments addressing specific questions on health care, dominated by McCain trying to defend his plan to tax health benefits.

It is worth noting that McCain's major attack on the Obama plan would be the central Republican message throughout 2009 and 2010. During the first debate, held on September 26, 2008, in Oxford, Mississippi, McCain said, "I want to make sure we're not handing the health care system over to the federal government, which is basically what would ultimately happen with Senator Obama's health care plan. I want the families to make decisions between themselves and their doctors. Not the federal government."

The shining moment of the debates for me occurred at the second debate, in Nashville on October 7, when NBC's Tom Brokaw asked, "Is health care in America a privilege, a right, or a responsibility?" While I listened to McCain equivocate in his answer, I wondered what Obama would say. But Obama was crystal clear: "I think it should be a right for every American."

Even so, storm clouds loomed on the horizon, in particular Obama's commitment to the public option. In his October 4 campaign address on health care at Newport News, Virginia, Obama provided a fairly thorough description of his health care proposal, but he left out any mention of the public option. Instead, after saying that individuals could keep their insurance if they liked it, he said, "But if you don't have insurance, or don't like your insurance, you'll be able to choose from the same type of quality private plans as every federal employee — from a postal worker here in Virginia to a Congressman in Washington." He did not mention the other choice in his health plan — a public health insurance plan.

In the same month, the Obama campaign's website replaced the description of his health care plan, which had contained several prominent mentions of the public option, with a new description that buried one mention of the public plan deep in the text. Roger Hickey brought this to the attention of the Obama campaign staff, who assured him that the campaign's position had not changed. But the abrupt shift made us nervous.

A week later we celebrated Obama's election. According to Jonathan Alter, author of *The Promise*, Obama told himself on election night that enacting health reform was the single achievement that would most help the average American.[16]

We didn't know what the President-elect was thinking at the time. But for me one line of his acceptance speech at Chicago's Grant Park in Chicago, on that clear early November evening, held great meaning. "This victory alone is not the change we seek — it is only the chance for us to make that change."

Now we had our chance.

6

The Economy or Health Care?

I suffer no illusions that this will be an easy process. It will be hard. But I also know that nearly a century after Teddy Roosevelt first called for reform, the cost of our health care has weighed down our economy and the conscience of our nation long enough. So let there be no doubt: health care reform cannot wait, it must not wait, and it will not wait another year.

—*Barack Obama before a Joint Session of Congress,*
February 24, 2009

With those words, in his first address to Congress, the new president laid to rest the big question: Would he really try to pass health reform?

From the day after his election on November 4, 2008, until he addressed Congress on February 24, 2009, the question that reporters kept asking me was, "He is not really going to try to enact health reform, is he?"

Headlines after the election reflected this skepticism. A *Bloomberg News* headline filed after the votes were in on election night read, "Obama Health-Care Plan Collides with Financial-Crisis Spending." The next day, a Reuters headline read, "Even with mandate, Obama faces health care pain." Both articles emphasized that the financial, budget, and economic crises would all create huge obstacles to Obama trying to enact health reform.

In talking to reporters, my job was to insist that the President-elect was intent on moving rapidly on health reform. I used the report that he had spent 86 percent of his campaign advertising in October as strong evidence of the President's resolution. The inevitable follow-up question from reporters reflected their general cynicism, suggesting that they thought it would be nearly impossible to move any major legislation through Congress. They pointed to interest group opposition, partisan politics, and above all to the need for sixty votes to break a filibuster in the Senate — where the Democrats held only fifty-eight seats. I could appreciate their skepticism, since even modest legislation led to partisan gridlock; nothing as big as health care reform had happened in their entire careers.

My response was to place Obama's election within a historical context. I agreed that enacting health reform would take a historic shift in American politics, but Obama's mandate for change signaled a new era when the traditional roadblocks to progressive change would be overcome. I also said that the last people to see the potential for major change would be Beltway insiders who were blinded by the money-driven, interest-group politics that had been dominant for decades.

It turned out that the reporters had some cause for their skepticism. Obama's advisors would have preferred that the President put health care on the back burner early in his term, according to reports by Jonathan Alter in *The Promise* and *Getting It Done* by Tom Daschle. Both his political and economic advisors worried about the high political price tag for health reform and the need for the administration to focus sharply on economic recovery. But Obama insisted that money be included in his budget proposal to move ahead with health reform. He told Daschle, "Tom, health care is the most important thing we will ever do. And it is more important to me now than ever before. Don't ever doubt that."[17]

We did not need to know about the debate inside the White House to understand that the economic crisis threatened to wreck our strategy of moving ahead aggressively on health reform early in 2009. We decided to make a television ad that showed Obama making the case for us. Using video from his Newport News speech, the ad showed Obama saying, "The question isn't how we can afford to focus on health care—the question is how we can afford not to. Because in order to fix our economic crisis, and rebuild our middle class, we need to fix our health care system too.... It is clear that the time has come—right now—to solve this problem." The spot included piano music that built emotionally to the President-elect's final promise, followed by the words on screen "We Agree" and the HCAN logo.

A series of reports by reformers reinforced that message. On November 17 the New America Foundation released "The Cost of Doing Nothing," which detailed the adverse impact on family budgets and the nation's economy if the nation failed to provide good health coverage to everyone and also to control health care costs. In January, Families USA released a report on the number of newly unemployed Americans who could not afford to pay for health coverage on their own.

HCAN partners around the country released individual state reports a few days before the President was to deliver his late February address to Congress. The reports, entitled "Next Step: Health Care—To Fix [State's] Economy, We Need to Fix Health Care," included individual states' data on how health costs were hurting families, businesses, and state governments. Also in February, the Center for American Progress released a report showing that 14,000 people a day were losing health insurance during the recession. The report was released on a conference call with reporters that I joined, along with several people we recruited: a doctor, a representative from the United Food and Commercial Workers, and a small business owner recruited by the Main Street Alliance.

The Main Street Alliance (MSA) was the new small business organizing project funded by HCAN. We had seen the power of small business opposition to reform in the Clinton era and knew we needed a voice on our side. Created by the Northwest Federation of Community Organizations (NWFCO), MSA was based on a strategy piloted by two of our HCAN partners, Washington Community Action Network and Maine People's Alliance. The organizations took old-fashioned door-to-door canvassing and applied it to canvassing small businesses. Canvassers went storefront to storefront in a business district with a survey designed to ask small business owners about health reform. Through this process, an organizer identified individual small business people who were interested in becoming more engaged in the issue, oftentimes by sharing their story with the media or writing a letter to the editor. Over time, many MSA leaders became the most effective spokespeople and grassroots lobbyists in the entire reform campaign.

The Main Street Alliance also weighed into the economic debate by releasing a report in mid-January that showed small business support for progressive principles for reform. On February 3, *The New York Times* ran a front-page article entitled "Small Payroll, but Big Woes on Insurance," which included the stories of three business owners recruited by MSA.

Several of our HCAN Steering Committee members also helped raise a big business voice for reform during this crucial period. Better Health Care Together was the name of a loose coalition formed in 2007 that included three HCAN members — SEIU, the Communications Workers of America, and the Center for American Progress — and several major corporations including: Wal-Mart, AT&T, Intel, Embarq, and Kelly Services. Shortly after the election, the CEOs of the Better Health Care Together members sent Obama a letter that stated, "As leaders of Better Health Care Together ... we know that addressing the needs of our nation's health care system *is essential to the country's long-term economic growth and prosperity.*" (Emphasis in the original.)

Throughout this period, HCAN performed another inside-the-Beltway function, adding our perspective to media-hyped stories and trial balloons floated by the administration. For example, we pushed back when Obama was rumored to favor appointing Tennessee Governor Phil Bredesen to be Secretary of Health and Human Services. Bredesen was perversely proud of cutting back on a pioneering Tennessee program that had extended Medicaid to many low-income families. We also criticized South Carolina Representative Jim Clyburn, the third-ranking member of the House leadership, when he suggested Obama should seek "incremental" reform.

I learned another important lesson about working in the D.C. bubble when we met with two of Senator Kennedy's Health, Education, Labor and Pensions (HELP) Committee staff members the week after Obama was elected. Shortly after I returned from the meeting, I received an alarmed email from a staffer complaining that a story about our meeting had appeared in the closely watched political blog, Talking Points Memo (TPM). The story reported, incorrectly, that Kennedy's staffers had agreed with our suggestion that health reform be paid for through the economic stimulus package being debated in the lame duck session of Congress. Someone in our group had received that impression from the meeting and then called a reporter at TPM to leak the story. I learned firsthand how Washington insiders like to feed stories to the press to curry favor and generate spin. It was a lesson I would be forced to learn over and over again.

While I wasn't looking for press coverage about private meetings, we did want HCAN to be named regularly in major newspapers, especially *The New York Times*. In mid-December, I finally was quoted in an article by Robert Pear, the dean of national health care reporters. I had read Pear's work for years but had only met him in early July. Robert looked like a sixty-year-old version of the high school nerd, a small man with thick, owlish glasses. He spoke softly and always with great respect and deference. His reporting was revered so much that *Politico*'s daily health news summary designated articles he wrote under the heading, "Pearwatch." Getting HCAN staff quoted by Pear was one of our campaign goals. When it started to happen regularly, we regarded it as a milestone in HCAN being viewed as a key D.C. player in health reform.

Being quoted in the *Times* was also part of our strategy to raise my personal profile. That was another step toward HCAN becoming an inside Washington player. In early March, *Politico* ran a two-page profile of me. Around the same time I was added to the very long list of people profiled on *The Washington Post*'s website whorunsgov.com.

The HCAN staff team grew after the election as well, as we prepared for the legislative fight. Melinda Gibson was the first staff person I had hired. Melinda had been a member of the Organizing Committee representing the Campaign for America's Future. She virtually created the nuts and bolts of the organization single-handedly during the period before we launched, and continued to serve as our operations manager.

Esther Garcia was responsible for recruiting organizations to join HCAN and keeping them involved in the campaign's work. By Election Day we had more than 550 member groups, a number that eventually grew to more than 1,100.

Kerry Greeley joined the campaign in June as our development director. Kerry had been a key fund-raising staff person for John Kerry's presidential campaign and began to set up fund-raising meetings for me in New York and Los Angeles, with the help of several consultants. She also hired an experienced hand, Shadia Garrison, to coordinate foundation fund raising.

After the first of the year, Tara Straw joined the legislative team, leaving the American College of Obstetrics and Gynecologists, where she had been a lobbyist. We added one more lobbyist in the early spring, Darren Fenwick, who had worked for two of our Steering Committee members, ACORN and UFCW. In February, Avram Goldstein left Bloomberg News, where he had been covering the health insurance industry, to become our first research director.

With the prospect of a huge legislative fight and an expanding staff, we needed to hire a deputy campaign manager. I had first met Ethan Rome in the early 1990s, when he was a very young organizer for Connecticut Citizen Action Group, working on the Clinton health care fight. He had played a key role in Connecticut's successful campaign to institute a state income tax in 1991, and then he had become the chief political operative for Connecticut's speaker of the House, a position that gave him inside political experience to complement his work as an outside agitator. For the past nine years he had worked for AFSCME, most of the time directing its internal and external communications. Ethan joined the HCAN staff in mid-January, taking responsibility for supervising many of the senior staff and overseeing our paid advertising.

Just after the New Year, Claudia and I packed up her Subaru Forester and drove to D.C., where we had rented a furnished apartment in a neighborhood about a mile from my K Street office. The apartment was also an easy bus ride from the Georgetown University campus, where Claudia had accepted a job teaching literature and journalism. She was nervous about the change, while I was eager to stop commuting every week from Albany to Washington. As it turned out, Claudia fell in love with Washington, while I was ever eager to get out of the city and back to the rural serenity of our home in upstate New York.

During the fall and winter we continued to expand HCAN's Steering Committee, which eventually grew to include twenty-one organizations. We also continued to recruit members of Congress to sign on to the HCAN principles. On the day that Congress returned to Washington in early January, we ran print ads in *The Hill*, *Roll Call* and *Politico* thanking President Obama and Vice President Biden and the 170 members of the incoming Congress who had signed the HCAN principles, which the ad also enumerated.

Key members of Congress were also pushing to put health care on the top of the agenda. Shortly after the election, from his convalescence in Hyannis Port after surgery for brain cancer, Ted Kennedy appointed several members of his HELP Committee to lead three reform task forces. His staff also quietly kicked off a "workhorse" process, which brought together a big group of diverse stakeholders — hospitals, doctors, unions, insurance companies, business, consumer groups — to discuss reform proposals.

The most welcome surprise was delivered by the chair of the Senate Finance Committee, Montana Democrat Max Baucus. He had made his name running what was arguably the Senate's most powerful committee, responsible for approving any measures involving taxes and the financing of government programs. Most Democrats viewed him warily, as he was proud of making bipartisan deals through his friendship with the ranking Republican on the Committee, Iowa's Charles (Chuck) Grassley. Baucus had greased the way for Bush's 2001 tax cuts, heavily weighted to benefit the rich, and for the 2003 Medicare prescription drug bill, which prohibited Medicare from negotiating with drug companies for lower prices and handed over the entire new Medicare drug business to private insurance companies.

During the summer and fall, health advocates had been nervously awaiting Baucus's "white paper" on health reform. To our relief, the 98-page document released on November 12 largely followed the Democratic consensus on health reform. Notably, it included an individual mandate for adults as well as children, the position that Obama foreswore during his campaign.

The President and his team had been busy too. On December 11, Obama announced the appointment of former Senate Majority Leader Tom Daschle to be both the Secretary of the Department of Health and Human Services (HHS) and the White House health care "czar." Daschle quickly announced that the White House transition office would encourage Americans to hold house parties to discuss health reform, using a discussion guide provided by the incoming administration. In a short time, more than 4,200 meetings were scheduled. HCAN worked with its coalition partners to encourage our members around the country to hold house parties, and more than 1,500 agreed to do so, giving us a huge presence. On the opposite side, as Robert Pear reported in *The New York Times,* "The health insurance industry is encouraging its employees and satisfied customers to attend," as were the AMA and drug companies.[18]

Pear filed a report from a house party that he attended in Vienna, Virginia. The article began by saying that the dozen consumers who had assembled "quickly agreed on one point: they despise the *health insurance* companies." (Emphasis in the original).[19] Early in the article, Pear reported that most of the house party attendees supported the public option.

The public option was the major point of contention as well in Pear's earlier article on insurance companies recruiting their employees to attend the house parties.

Here it was, barely one month after Obama had been elected, and the public option was already the biggest controversy in the health care debate.

The Public Option Leaps to Center Stage

At times in the long months that followed, officials in the Obama administration would become frustrated with the progressive community for our focus on the public option. They would point out that the public option was only one provision in a huge piece of legislation with many essential proposals for making care affordable. It would affect only a small percentage of Americans. They would ask, why is it taking up so much of the public debate?

I have explained why the public option was essential to building a broad, largely unified movement for reform. Yet we did not choose to make the choice of a public health insurance plan the biggest issue. Our message included several key points — a guarantee of quality, affordable care; good benefits; regulating insurance practices; and the choice of a public plan. It was our opponents who seized upon the public option. As Chris Frates reported in *Politico* on November 25, "The one principle conservatives seem to agree on is a willingness to fight the Democrats' push to create a public plan, which they view as a back door to a single-payer system."[20]

Two weeks later the insurance lobby AHIP, joined by the Blue Cross and Blue Shield Association and the American Hospital Association, released a report that the groups had commissioned to indirectly attack the public plan. Two powerful interests were teaming up to stop the public option, even though these groups clashed on many issues. The insurance industry did not want to compete with a public health insurance plan, and the hospitals did not want another new payer who would refuse to pay inflated prices. And while doctors did not take part, we expected that they too would oppose a public option that was based on Medicare rates, which are usually lower than those paid by commercial insurers.

We had to respond swiftly to the widening campaign against the public plan. I was driving home from my office in Albany in a blinding snowstorm the week before Christmas when I phoned Celinda Lake and David Mermin from Lake Research. I remember squinting through the windshield at a flurry of giant snowflakes as I told them that I wanted to do a poll as quickly as possible to test the strength of support for the public option. I suggested that we test the strongest attacks on the public option against our best defenses and see where the public stood.

As Lake went into the field the week of January 8, calling 800 likely voters around the country, I held my breath. For example, we asked those surveyed to choose between the following arguments:

> A new government health insurance plan will cost taxpayers a huge amount of money we cannot afford right now during an economic slowdown, and because the government is involved, it will make the health system less efficient and increase costs.

OR

> Private insurance companies currently have little incentive to control premiums and deductibles, reaping huge profits while working families struggle to pay the bills. A public health insurance plan that competes directly with private insurers will help control health care costs for all Americans.

The poll presented voters with a series of arguments like these, for and against the public plan. It contained all of the arguments against the public plan: it would be a big government bureaucracy with higher costs to taxpayers; a public plan would result in rationing health care with long waiting times for treatment; government regulation was sufficient to protect consumers so there was no reason to establish a government plan; a government plan would force people to lose their private insurance; a public plan will raise the cost of health coverage; and a public plan would have an unfair advantage over private insurance companies.

In every instance our counter-arguments won, usually by margins of two to one. Before doing the poll, I thought that we would come out ahead, but I never suspected that the public would vote so heavily on our side. We immediately arranged for briefings on the results with the new administration, five days after the President was inaugurated, and with key Democratic staff in both houses of Congress.

The survey also led to the naming of the public health insurance plan. The poll results underscored that the best way to frame the public plan was as a choice. We decided to start calling it a "public health insurance option" rather than a "public plan." But that was a mouthful, which the White House also realized. They soon were referring to a "public option," the label that stuck.

On February 24, President Obama addressed the joint session of Congress, promising that "health care cannot wait, it must not wait, and it will not wait another year." Two days later he introduced his budget, which included a $634 billion reserve fund for health reform over ten years. The administration acknowledged that the budget did not contain enough money to provide coverage for everyone and that it would work with Congress to identify other needed funds. The bottom line was that Obama was going to push for reform in 2009. To start the ball rolling, he invited members of Congress and outside groups to come to the White House for a health care summit on March 5. There, a Republican Senator would place the public option on center stage.

Going to the White House

The last time I had visited the White House, I was ten years old. As I waited in line with my grandfather, a helicopter landed on the wide lawn. Through some trees I saw the suit pants of a man striding from the chopper and a little girl, younger than me, running up to the man and giving him a hug. It was five-year-old Caroline Kennedy. The year was 1963, a few months before her dad was killed.

Now I joined a line of suit-coated men and women as we passed through the security checks at the East Wing entrance, walking along a long hallway lined with pictures of presidents relaxed and at play. Formally uniformed guards, dressed in their starched navy blue jackets with white stripes, pointed the way up the stairs to a crowded East Room. Seats had been placed on three sides of a small podium facing a bank of television cameras. The White House is far grander than it looks from the outside, gazing through the black wrought iron gates where tourists typically stand on a visit to Washington. When you stand under the front portico, which we walked through later on our way to breakout sessions in the Old Executive Office Building, it soars overhead. The ceilings in the main floor rooms are twenty feet high. The building has a palpable energy even when you find a quiet spot, and that day in March it buzzed with excited conversations as we were seated, waiting for the President to enter.

Chief of Staff Rahm Emanuel entered and leaned against the large open entranceway to the room, thirty feet from where I sat. I thought of going up and reintroducing myself. He had been on the staff of Illinois Public Action Council with me in 1981, hired to raise money from political donors. I remembered that the twenty-three-year-old Emanuel, who had studied classical ballet, would sometimes take an athletic ballet turn in my office. But I kept my seat. The President was expected at any moment and the work with Emanuel happened a long time ago.

HCAN had generated our own press spin of the summit before it took place. Anticipating that the big theme of the day would be the broad variety of interest groups working together, we held a press call to emphasize that "health insurance companies, drug companies, and high-paid lobbyists should not be allowed to steer or derail health care reform." On the call, which included California Representative Xavier Becerra, the fourth-ranking member of the House leadership, we announced that we would deliver CDs with the signatures of 301,012 people on a MoveOn petition that read, "Don't let the insurance lobbyists delay health care any longer." The call helped shape the press coverage, including an article by Robert Pear in the *Times*.

His first report on the summit led with the President's vow not to allow lobbyists and special interests to block reform and included quotes from speakers on our press call.

HCAN was well represented among the summit attendees. Of the eighty-two representatives of stakeholder groups, twenty-four were HCAN members. In addition, twenty of the fifty-five members of Congress who attended had signed the HCAN statement of principles for reform.

After the President made his opening remarks, we were assigned to one of five breakout sessions. A few highlights in my discussion group stood out. Tom Donohue, the head of the U.S. Chamber of Commerce, said that unlike in the past, when employers were uniformly opposed to reform, business was now divided. He even said that some businesses were open to the idea of a public option. Donohue looks like the director of a funeral home, with a full head of white hair, a dour countenance, and a dark suit. As it turns out, Donohue was just blowing smoke. His organization would serve as a front group for the insurance industry, spending $86 million of secret insurance industry contributions to kill the legislation.

Senator Jay Rockefeller of West Virginia was the only one who expressed skepticism about the prospects for success, saying that any serious effort to control health care costs would be squashed by health care provider groups. At the time he seemed unaware of the new policy approach that had been developed over the past few years and was now embraced by the President. But Rockefeller would soon get up to speed and emerge as one of the strongest champions for aggressive reform, including a public option that controlled how much doctors and hospitals were paid.

Teamster President James Hoffa provided a hot spark of reality to the discussion, after Oregon Senator Ron Wyden spoke in favor of modifying the tax deduction for health care benefits. Hoffa hit the roof. He had spent months energizing his members to vote against McCain's push to tax health benefits.

After the breakout sessions, we returned to the East Room for the emotional high point of the summit. Once we were all seated, the President escorted Senator Ted Kennedy into the room. Kennedy was leaning on his cane, his ruddy face clearly pained, but he had a smile on his face. We all stood to deliver long, heartfelt applause. The President asked Kennedy, whom Obama called "a knight," to address the group. The Senator steeped his brief remarks in his sense of history, saying that what distinguished this debate from others, going back to Truman, was that all the interest groups were participating. As a result he said, "This time we will not fail."

Before asking Kennedy to speak, Obama quoted remarks that several people had made during the breakout sessions. I was half-listening when the President got my full attention, "With respect to the cost of care, Richard Kirsch with the Health Care for America Now said that we can't have a false dichotomy between coverage and costs, that by covering more people we can also lower costs at the same time...."

I'm told that there was cheering back at the HCAN office, particularly from the fund-raising staff who thought that Obama quoting me would give us a big lift with potential donors. Unfortunately, they were wrong.

After Kennedy spoke, Obama asked several key members of Congress to weigh in, including Chuck Grassley. He promptly attacked the public option, saying, "So the only thing that I would throw out for your consideration — and please don't respond to this now, because I'm asking you just to think about it — there's a lot of us that feel that the public option, that the government is an unfair competitor and that we're going to get an awful lot of crowd out, and we have to keep what we have now strong, and make it stronger."

Obama responded in what would become his familiar professorial manner: "The thinking on the public option has been that it gives consumers more choices, and it helps give — keep the private sector honest, because there's some competition out there.... I recognize, though, the fear that if a public option is run through Washington, and there are incentives to try to tamp down costs and ... that private insurance plans might end up feeling overwhelmed."

It was the first of what would be a maddening pattern of equivocation on the public option by Obama that would end up generating lasting outrage and disappointment among the substantial progressive base of Obama supporters. However, this interchange at the White House in March did not raise alarm bells widely; it was still too early in the debate.

I could see the long shadow of 1994 when the President asked the heads of the two most effective opponents of the Clinton plan to speak. He first called on Karen Ignagni, tripping over her name by pronouncing the silent second "g." Ignagni said that she knew that the insurance industry had to "earn a seat at the table" and that it was committed "to play to contribute and to help pass health care reform this year." By September, however, the industry would be playing another game, secretly funneling tens of millions of dollars to the Chamber of Commerce to try to kill reform.

Obama also asked Dan Danner of the National Federation of Independent Business (NFIB) to comment. Danner said that he was looking "forward to finding a solution together that works for America's job creators." That solution would not include any provision requiring employers to help pay for coverage, which the association vigorously opposed.

Still, we had good reason to hope. The President had made it clear that the nation's economic crisis was a reason rather than a deterrent for enacting health reform in 2009. He concluded his opening remarks at the summit saying, "It will not be easy. There will be false starts and setbacks and mistakes along the way. But I am confident that if we come together, and work together, we will finally achieve what generations of Americans have fought for and fulfill the promise of health care in our time."

In a short time we had put HCAN on the map in Washington. I had no illusions that our firepower inside the Beltway could stand up against the onslaught I knew was coming. Yet we had other weapons in the treacherous time that was sure to come. Unlike the fat cats, we were slowly building a grassroots movement of people who would raise their voices across the country.

7

From the Ground Up — Champions

A Mom in Tennis Shoes

The long line of marchers, stretching as far as the eye could see, streamed toward a downtown Seattle plaza on a sparkling day at the end of May 2009. Under a forest of banners and signs, dressed in a rainbow array of T-shirts, walking to the beat of bass drums, they sent up a chant that reverberated between the buildings that lined the avenue: "Health Care Now! Health Care Now!"

Later, from a podium on the plaza, Democratic U.S. Senator Patty Murray addressed the crowd of more than 5,000. She stood in tennis shoes, in front of a huge banner that read "Health Care for All — Health Care Can't Wait," wearing a powder-blue, zipper-front sweatshirt. Murray exclaimed, "Look at this crowd. If this turnout doesn't send a message to Washington, D.C., that there is a groundswell of support for real health care reform this year, I don't know what would."

Despite the welcome, Murray had only agreed to attend the rally a few days before. Only after long months of planning and weeks of steady pressure was the Senator persuaded to put aside her caution and address the rally. For the Senator, as well as for the HCAN coalition in Washington state, the Mothers March for Health Care was a turning point that led to her becoming a strong champion of reform. It also paved the way for her colleague in the Senate, Maria Cantwell, to become a reliable advocate for progressive change as well.

Convincing Senators Murray and Cantwell to become leaders in the fight for reform is a splendid example of how we reaped advantages from the key strategic decisions that we had made at the beginning. Among them was the plan to build a strong coalition, focused on grassroots activity around the nation, which would create Congressional champions and pressure swing members of Congress. The stories of some of the people who organized the Seattle march serve to illustrate the efforts of the many leaders who led the fight around the country.

One of them, Robbie Stern, grew up in Charlotte, North Carolina, and went north to college, to Syracuse University where he came under the influence of George Wiley, who founded the National Welfare Rights Organization. Stern's youthful experience in the civil rights and anti-war movements convinced him that a strong labor movement was the key to winning social justice. So even though he earned a law degree, he became a pipefitter, working in shipyards and for a utility company in Washington State. He then drew on his early political experience and education and went to work for the AFL-CIO, doing policy development and coalition building. Eventually he became the state labor federation's head lobbyist.

When HCAN started in 2008, Stern recalls, "One of the advantages that we had here is that we had a longstanding coalition that had been working on health care reform. Several years ago we had formed the Healthy Washington Coalition, which had a history of working together and working with state and federal policymakers. We had built long-term relationships between the hospital association, community health clinics, the medical association, all the unions, including both the AFL-CIO and SEIU. Until the election of President Obama, we had been focused on state-based legislation. So when we called for a big rally, all of the organizations stepped up."

Stern also explains, "It took a lot of work to get Murray to the rally. We had a lot of people from labor calling her, including the president of the State Labor Council. SEIU was totally committed. Planned Parenthood and a lot of women's groups helped. We were able to inundate her with: 'this is important, you need to be there.' People in D.C. have a Beltway mentality, they are risk adverse. But we had a person on Murray's staff in Seattle who understood that the constituency that Murray would need in 2010 cared deeply about this."

As the HCAN coalition leadership met in January 2009 they were looking for a way to accomplish two goals: energize their base and engage Senator Patty Murray, who was a member of the Senate Democratic leadership, in what they knew would be a hard-fought campaign. Murray had been a community activist before entering politics. As president of her local PTA, she, according to her official biography, "led a grassroots coalition of 13,000 parents to save a local preschool program from budget cuts." When a state legislator told her that she couldn't make a difference because she was just "a mom in tennis shoes," she proudly adopted that moniker in successful runs for school board, the State Senate, and in 1992 for the U.S. Senate. As a Senator, she continued to champion mothers and families.

While Murray's history meant that we did not have to worry about her voting for health care reform, that did not mean she would become a champion of the issue, someone who would speak out strongly in support of reform both publicly and among her Democratic Senate colleagues. Because health care reform would be the subject of such intense interest group pressure, including from groups like hospitals that often supported Democrats, the easier route would be for Murray — as it would for most members of Congress — to not become a visible advocate, because doing so would risk alienating some of her supporters. However, for our campaign to succeed, we needed to turn liberal leaders like Murray into full-throated champions who would fight hard when opposition forces threatened to kill or dramatically water down the legislation. To make Murray and others into a champion, we needed to demonstrate the intensity of support among Democratic activists and to personally drive home the moral issues underlying our campaign.

The HCAN leaders decided to plan a large rally for late May, after the weather in gray, drizzly Seattle improved. Looking for a theme for the event, a volunteer leader named Deana Knutsen recalled the signs that mothers in Argentina hold up to remember their children who had disappeared in the 1990s, as victims of military repression. Deana, whose son was born with a disability that required medical care, had been recruited years earlier by a canvasser for the Washington Community Action Network (WCAN), which was HCAN's field partner in the Evergreen State. She had risen to leadership in the state organization and was elected secretary-treasurer of USAction and to the board of a public hospital. Knudsen's suggestion connected with Murray's "mom in tennis shoes" persona. The organizers decided to frame the rally as a "Mothers March for Health Care." They would aim for a big turn out, at least 2,500, and try to invite a prominent mother, such as Michelle Obama, to induce Senator Murray to attend.

The rally organizers focused their outreach on organizations that had not been involved in the campaign, including groups representing the African American, Latino, and Asian-Pacific Islander communities. The effort also became a way for each HCAN coalition partner to awaken their own members to the fight for reform. As the organizing for the rally gathered steam, so did the campaign to get Murray to speak, which was proving to be a tall order.

Will Pittz says that the crucial moment in his life that led him to become an activist was when President Clinton signed a welfare reform bill in 1996, legislation that many saw as abandoning families like his who had relied on welfare to survive. Welfare had given his parents the opportunity to get ahead. His parents' rise from poverty paved the way for his admission to Northwestern University and graduate work at Harvard's Kennedy School, where he decided to work for social justice. In 2006, at the age of thirty-two, he became the director of WCAN.

Will Pittz looked through his calendar and told me what it took. The coalition met with Murray's staff on March 3 in D.C. and pushed for the May march, but could not get a commitment. On March 10, they met with her staff in the state. They held a conference call with her staff and the HCAN coalition on March 27. On April 2, Will met with her staff. On April 13, forty-three small business owners met with Murray's legislative director at Seattle's Pike Place Market. The HCAN coalition groups met with her state director on April 27 and with her staff again two days later. On May 12, they met with her staff and small business leaders to talk about how Murray could work with small business owners. Pittz relates:

> On May 13, I was in D.C. with one of those owners, a painting contractor named Michelle Molton. Murray has a regular breakfast meeting that is open to visiting constituents. There were about twenty people around a big table. Murray talked a little and then took questions. As soon as she opened the floor, Michelle thanked her for her vote to expand the Child Health Insurance Program and invited her to come to the May 30 rally. She said, "We're having a march with five thousand people in Seattle and we would love to have you be our keynote speaker." Murray said that it would depend on her schedule.

They continued to pressure Murray, but did not get a commitment to attend. By late May they were not expecting her to show. But a few days before the scheduled march, Murray's office confirmed that she would be at the rally.

The HCAN organizers were granted their wish for a beautiful spring day. More than 5,000 people marched, leaving from Pratt Park in Seattle's historically African American Central District, through the international district, turning a corner to stream down a steep hill to the West Lake Center, to a plaza in the center of downtown. Mothers pushed their children in strollers, while at the front, an older woman was pushed in her wheelchair.

Among the marchers were 800 members of SEIU, including Linda Arkava. She had worked at Swedish Hospital for twenty-three years, starting in the kitchen, then becoming a secretary, before coming a nurse in 2002. She became active in SEIU after her nurse manager notified Arkava and her co-workers that they would be working in two different campuses of the hospital, in violation of the rules governing how changes at the workplace were to be made. Arkava says that while her manager intimidated many of her fellow workers, she knew that her longshoreman husband had benefited from his union, and so she was not afraid to assert her rights. As a result, her nursing unit was kept together.

As front-line health care workers, nurses see the failures of the system every day. Arkava told me, "I had always been a supporter of health reform but never had been active. I had lived in Denmark in college and I'd seen that national health care really could work. I have a young adult daughter whose friends are uninsured. I've worked in an oncology clinic for a long time, where you have people who have reached the maximum on their insurance and are finding paying bills to be really stressful. As a nurse you hear so many stories."

Linda Arkava took her place on the rally podium, under a white awning. A thin woman, wearing a purple SEIU T-shirt that read "Health Care Can't Wait," she had a red-and-white bandana carrying the same message tied around her waist. She told me, "At the rally I picked out one of those stories to tell, about one of our patients. The guy comes in and he has acute heart failure because he can't afford his meds and we spend huge amounts to care for him. There are so many other stories: a man in his forties who never goes for screenings because he has no health care and ends up with coronary heart disease. Or the fifty-year-old stroke patient who can't get good rehab so he is not able to return to work. As nurses we see the negative cycle where lack of preventive care or inadequate care costs the system so much money. And we see that the hospital eats the bill, which impacts our livelihood."

In one picture, Linda stood with Patty Murray, who was grinning, clearly buoyed by the huge crowd. But an encounter with a ten-year old would leave the Senator with the most lasting impression of that day.

Three Generations

In 2001, a WCAN canvasser knocked on Gina Owens' door and began talking to her about legislation in Congress that would fund food stamps and soup kitchens. Gina told me, "I liked that the canvasser really wanted my opinion. I was working at the Indian Health Clinic as a medical assistant and I did a lot of work with the homeless. I hadn't been active, because you need to find something that you're passionate about so that you'll keep going."

A week later, Owens found herself marching to a meeting of the National Governors Association in Coeur d'Alene, Idaho, in a demonstration organized by WCAN and a sister group in Idaho to pressure the governors to support funding for food assistance. "The theme was no empty plate. We decorated bowls and plates with messages and then marched with a group of elementary school children who delivered the plates to the governors."

WCAN soon began to work on health care issues, including testifying at the legislature in Olympia about the plight of single moms who held down low-wage jobs and who did not have health coverage. Gina knew one of those moms well. Her daughter Tifanny had worked her way up to management at a Jack in the Box restaurant after three years of working without health insurance. Tifanny Owens told her story to the legislature and joined her mom as an active member of WCAN, attending weekly meetings of the Seattle chapter. Gina says, "WCAN puts a lot of trust in their leaders, unlike other organizations that are staff driven. Leaders really plan actions."

In 2006 Tifanny became seriously ill. "Her legs would swell and she couldn't walk. Her lungs would fill and she'd throw up. But her condition wasn't diagnosed. She missed a lot of work, and in October '06 she was told if she didn't come to work she'd be fired. But of course she was too sick to work. They even denied her unemployment." She lost her health insurance.

Tifanny Owens was eventually diagnosed with pulmonary hypertension, a rare, life-threatening lung disorder in which the arteries that carry blood from the heart to the lungs become narrowed. Treatment can include medication and surgery, which were by then both out of Tifanny's reach.

"Tiffany got sicker. When it got really bad she went to the ER, but mostly she delayed getting care because she couldn't afford the out-of-pocket costs. I still have unpaid bills from her care that I'm trying to get settled. Finally, she was so sick that they put her in the hospital. After an eight-day admission a doctor said she wasn't getting proper care and got her moved to the University of Washington hospital, but it was too late. The doctors called a family meeting to decide on end-of-life care. As they went around the room, Marcelas — who was only seven — insisted on speaking, saying, 'I'm my mother's son.'"

Tifanny died a few days later. When I sat down with them in September 2010, I asked Marcelas Owens what he remembered about his mother. "She liked to sing Beyonce songs."

The day after learning that his mom died, Marcelas Owens told his grandmother that he wanted to be an activist. Joshua Welter, the WCAN health care organizer, was skeptical — after all, Marcelas was just seven. But the boy insisted that he be given a chance, and Joshua arranged for him to speak to a breakfast gathering of homeless kids.

At the Seattle rally, three years after his mother died, Marcelas Owens waited backstage for his turn to speak. He asked his grandmother to point out Senator Murray. Gina pointed to the short woman wearing tennis shoes, but Marcelas didn't believe it was the Senator because he thought members of Congress always wore suits.

After Murray spoke, Marcelas introduced himself. The diminutive Senator bent down to look the ten-year-old boy in the eye, gently putting both her hands on Marcelas' outstretched arm and heard his simple plea.

"After I spoke," Murray later told reporters, "I turned around and there was this little boy looking right straight up at me with his big brown eyes. And he said to me, 'You can't let anybody die like my mom did.'"[21]

Marcelas Owens then told his story to the crowd. Wearing a cherry-red WCAN T-shirt, he stood on a riser so he could be seen over the top of the podium. "Were you nervous?" I asked him. "No," he said. "It's like speaking to someone individually.

People want the same thing. Like talking to the mirror — they want the same things you do."

This poised young man would have several more opportunities to tell his story, on national television and before the D.C. press corps, in the coming months.

The Public Option Fight in Two Washingtons

Senator Grassley's challenge to the public option at the White House summit further cemented the issue as a central point of contention. In response, HCAN pushed back against Grassley in Iowa, generating 698 calls to the Senator's office in a few days to support the public option. In mid-March HCAN ran an ad in Iowa that starred a nurse from Des Moines. Dressed in blue scrubs, she said that we need a public option so that we can control our health care instead of being at the mercy of private insurance companies.

On April 29, sixteen senators sent a letter to Senator Ted Kennedy and Senator Max Baucus, the chairs of the two committees that would consider reform, endorsing the public option. Sherrod Brown, a first-term senator from Ohio, organized his colleagues to put their names on the letter, a common way for members of Congress to show unified support for a position. Brown was rapidly becoming a leading HCAN champion in the Senate. As a seven-term congressman, Brown had been a close ally of progressives but had hesitated in taking on health care in the Senate, respecting both his own junior status and the leadership role of Ted Kennedy. But by March, with a tacit nod from the ailing lion, Brown began to step out. On April 17, he spoke before 500 people at an HCAN rally in a church in Cleveland Heights. The gathering was one of 123 public events that HCAN partners held around the country during the spring Congressional recess. The events included more than 15,000 people and forty members of Congress.

The letter from the sixteen senators was released the day after a dramatic change in the Senate's political composition. On April 28, Pennsylvanian Arlen Specter announced that after forty-four years as a Republican elected official, including twenty-eight years in the U.S. Senate, he would become a Democrat. Specter's switch, and the anticipated seating of Minnesota Democrat Al Franken, whose razor-thin Election Day victory was still being disputed, would give Democrats the sixty votes they needed to overcome a Republican filibuster. As *Forbes* magazine wrote that afternoon in its online edition, "Sen. Arlen Specter's historic decision to jump parties is a huge shot of adrenaline to the new administration's health care agenda."[22]

But four days later, Specter spoiled his surprise in an appearance on *Meet the Press*. As *The Huffington Post* reported, "Democrats eager to see what kind of Senator Arlen Specter would be now that he has left the Republican Party likely weren't counting their blessings after watching his appearance on 'Meet the Press' this Sunday. The Pennsylvanian, while insisting that his switch in party affiliation was driven as much by values as politics, nevertheless came out forcefully against two of progressives' most cherished policies."[23] One was the Employee Free Choice Act, legislation that aimed to restore effective collective bargaining rights to unions. The other was the public option, which Specter said he would vote against.

The HCAN coalition in Pennsylvania, with support from our team in Washington, immediately sprang into action. Within a few days we generated a flood of calls to his office from constituents. Marc Stier, HCAN's Pennsylvania director, also had a number of "grasstops" leaders, from labor unions, the Jewish community, and Democratic donors, call Specter. The Senator would need their support in his bid for the Democratic nomination for Senate in 2010. Stier arranged for critical op-eds in newspapers in Philadelphia, Scranton, and Erie. The HCAN coalition planned protests outside all five of Specter's offices, capped by a march to his Pittsburgh office. Stier kept Specter's staff informed about the upcoming op-eds and rallies.

The strategy worked. On the following Friday, I received a fax from the Senator. It contained Specter's sign-on to the HCAN principles, with a caveat on the public option. Specter wrote, "With respect to the third bullet — 'to join a public health insurance plan' — I look forward to discussing and considering this issue. A starting point could be the proposal made by Senator Schumer earlier this week which seeks to maintain a level playing field between the private and public sector and any public plan."

As I wrote Marc Stier, "Good job! We got one nervous Senator." Specter's letter, while a clear retreat from his unequivocal statement on national TV that he would vote against a public option, was still not an outright endorsement. Keeping the pressure on, HCAN's Pennsylvania coalition canceled the Pittsburgh march but still held the demonstrations outside the Senator's other offices. Pennsylvania newspapers and *The Wall Street Journal* reported the Senator's change of position.

HCAN was spurred to produce a new television commercial, in cooperation with the National Physicians Alliance (NPA). NPA was founded in 2005 by doctors who had been active in the American Medical Students Association (AMSA). AMSA captured the youthful idealism of students who went into medicine to care for people, a sharp contrast with the AMA, which is primarily concerned with boosting doctors' incomes.

The television spot we produced featured NPA's president, Valerie Arkoosh, a Philadelphia anesthesiologist who specialized in caring for pregnant women. Arkoosh says, "My passion comes from seeing every way that women can fall through the cracks in the current medical system. I worked for eight years at a health care system in Philadelphia, which went bankrupt in 1998. It was bought by the for-profit hospital chain, Tenet, and I became chair of the anesthesiology department. I quickly found that it was really challenging to have short-term goals around quarterly earnings, which were tied to CEO compensation, and still provide quality care."

We decided to run the ad in six states that were represented by Democrats who were wavering or opposed to the public option. Arkoosh later heard that the University of Pennsylvania, where she had since moved, received complaints from Specter's office about the ad, even though the commercial did not identify her as a UPenn doctor. To its credit, the university responded that this was a matter of academic freedom, and they never raised the issue with Dr. Arkoosh.

Inside Jockeying on the Public Option

The public option had become a key issue in the House too. On the day after the letter that Brown organized was sent to Kennedy and Baucus, 117 members of the Progressive Caucus, Black Caucus, Hispanic Caucus, and the Asian Pacific American Caucus in the House, signed a letter that read "…our support for enacting legislation this year to guarantee affordable health care for all firmly hinges on the inclusion of a robust public health insurance plan like Medicare."

That last phrase captured a key policy difference that was beginning to emerge. With a "robust public option" the new public insurance plan would pay health care providers the same or similar rates as Medicare paid, which would be key to delivering lower premiums. This was the feature of the public option that raised hackles among doctors and hospitals.

As the debate raged on the public option, Senate Finance Committee Chair Max Baucus was searching for a way to bridge the differences between members of his committee, including liberal Democrats, more conservative Democrats, and the handful of Republicans that Baucus hoped he could bring to the table. He asked New York Senator Charles Schumer to see if he could come up with a compromise that would meet the objections being raised by public option opponents, while maintaining liberal support.

Schumer had risen to become the third-ranking Democrat in the Senate and held a coveted seat on the Senate Finance Committee, primarily due to his success running the Senate Democratic Campaign Committee, which made huge Democratic electoral gains in the 2006 and 2008 elections. Schumer is brilliant and backs up his intelligence with bulldog tenacity and a willingness to fight. His politics reflect both New York liberalism and the Democratic Party's need to raise buckets of money. With his assignment in hand from Baucus, he quickly educated himself on the policy issues at hand and on May 5 proposed a "level-field" public option. Most of what Schumer proposed was designed to refute claims by opponents that the public option would be structured to have a competitive advantage against private health insurance plans. Schumer included a proposal that the public option pay more than what Medicare pays, but he did not foreclose the possibility of the public option being linked to Medicare rates.

The Schumer compromise wasn't enough to entice conservative Democrats like Nebraska's Ben Nelson or moderate Republicans like Olympia Snowe, another member of the Senate Finance Committee, to support the public option. On May 20, Snowe proposed her own public option "compromise," which was anything but. She would have established a trigger mechanism whereby a public health insurance plan would be established only if there was not enough competition in the private health insurance market. As HCAN quickly pointed out, that question had already been settled. According to data collected by the American Medical Association, 94 percent of all health insurance markets in the United States were already anticompetitive in 2008. To us, Snowe's trigger was modeled after a similar provision in the Medicare Part D prescription drug law, which had been used to stop Medicare from competing with private insurance plans to sell prescriptions.

Soon another public option "compromise" was generated by Senate Budget Committee Chairman Kent Conrad, a North Dakota Democrat who also sat on the Senate Finance Committee. Conrad proposed that the government help establish health insurance co-ops, run at the state or regional level, owned by the people who bought insurance. If the trigger was designed to kill the public option, the co-op was meant to render it totally ineffective. As HCAN explained in a meeting with Senator Conrad, no member-owned health insurance plan could possibly compete with insurance industry behemoths like WellPoint or United Health Care. Conrad hoped his proposal would entice Republicans to soften their objections, but even though he had no Republican takers, he continued to push his co-op plan.

Buying Off the Health Care Industry

During the spring, the White House continued to focus on bringing traditional opponents of reform to the table. One of the biggest lessons that the White House had taken from the history of health reform, including the defeat of the Clinton plan, was the need to placate as many industry opponents of reform as possible. Dennis Rivera, who headed SEIU's health care council, was working with the administration to win support from the insurance industry, doctors, hospitals, drug companies, and medical device manufacturers. On Mother's Day, I was attending a Yankees-Orioles game at Baltimore's Camden Yards with my wife and our three children when I got an email saying that the White House would hold a "conference call on a major initiative to reform health care and reduce costs" at 3:00, which would be about the sixth inning. I could imagine the groans of the entire press corps and every health lobbyist in D.C. at having to interrupt their Mother's Day. Couldn't it wait a day?

The White House released a statement that acknowledged the history behind the agreement it was announcing. "It is a recognition that the fictional television couple, Harry and Louise, who became the iconic faces of those who opposed health care reform in the '90s, desperately need health care reform in 2009. And so does America. That is why these groups are voluntarily coming together to make an unprecedented commitment. Over the next ten years — from 2010 to 2019 — they are pledging to cut the growth rate of national health care spending by 1.5 percentage points each year — an amount that's equal to over $2 trillion." The next day President Obama appeared with leaders of the health industry trade associations at the White House to formally announce the deal.

Since the announcement included no details on how these savings were to be accomplished, the "news" was largely met with skepticism. Few believed that the cost savings would be real. But the lack of specificity still didn't reassure those who were worried that the deal might actually do what it promised. As Robert Pear wrote in the *Times* a few days later, "Hospitals and insurance companies said Thursday that President Obama had substantially overstated their promise earlier this week to reduce the growth of health spending."[24]

The announcement paved the way for a series of secret backroom deals with Senator Baucus and the White House, under which the industry groups — including hospitals, insurance companies and drug companies — agreed to specific amounts of revenue reductions in return for a promise that they would not be asked to give up more. The most important of these deals was cut with the powerful prescription drug industry, which had put aside a $100 million plus war chest for the health reform fight. The drug industry had already started running ads to support reform, but they let it be known that their war chest could also be spent attacking the legislation if its interests were threatened. During his campaign for president, Obama had supported giving Medicare the authorization to negotiate prescription drug prices. But blocking the authorization for the government to use its huge purchasing power to get lower drug prices — as every other nation in the developed world does — was number one on the drug industry's agenda.

The deal struck by PhRMA, the prescription drug trade association, conceded some loss of projected revenues in Medicare (although the industry would still reap huge profits from the expanded market as uninsured Americans entered the ranks of those with coverage) in return for a promise by the White House and Baucus to oppose other proposals that would lower drug prices. Among the proposals that were taken off the table were both Medicare negotiations and another popular proposal: allowing Americans to re-import drugs from Canada — where they sold for much less — into the United States. In return, PhRMA would use its huge war chest to support reform.

As a result of the agreement, over the next ten months the drug industry spent $80 million on television ads promoting reform. The ads constituted by far the biggest paid advertising for reform, although the ads' content was much less effective than the money behind it. That is because PhRMA insisted that the message in the ads focus on the benefits of reform rather than portray what we knew would be much more powerful, drawing a sharp contrast with insurance company abuses. PhRMA would not tolerate a hard-hitting message that demonized their biggest customer. Still, having that $80 million on ads that lifted reform was much better than the alternative. If PhRMA had spent that money attacking the legislation — changing the balance in paid media by $160 million — reform might well have failed.

The White House may have struck one more deal with Baucus and the major industry players, to kill the robust form of the public option. In August 2009, *The New York Times* reported, "Several hospital lobbyists involved in the White House deals said it was understood as a condition of their support that the final legislation would not include a government-run health plan paying rates — generally 80 percent of private sector rates — or controlled by the secretary of health and human services."[25] In an interview given in October 2010, former Senate Majority Leader Daschle, who kept in close contact with the White House and Senate leadership throughout the debate, gave credence to the story. Daschle told Igor Volsky, a blogger at the Center for American Progress's Wonk Room, "I don't think [the public option] was taken off the table completely. It was taken off the table as a result of the understanding that people had with the hospital association, with the insurance (AHIP), and others."[26]

However, Volsky's reporting and Daschle's response missed an important nuance that was included in the *Times* article. It's not clear whether there was tacit understanding to oppose any form of a public option or, as the *Times* reported, one that gave the government a role in setting rates tied to Medicare. Either way, it seemed that privately the White House was willing to give up a public option, even as the President had finally started making the case publicly.

Obama Supports the Public Option — For Now

Claudia and I were returning from a hike to the Grand Gorge of the Potomac, on a glorious Sunday in early June 2009, when she started to feel chest pains. By late Monday night the pain had sharpened and moved lower into her abdomen. Early Tuesday morning I drove her to the hospital. The next two days Claudia spent in a fog of pain before and after emergency gall bladder surgery. Meanwhile, I shuttled back and forth on the phone and by email with the White House and HCAN allies about what President Obama was about to announce on the public option.

Just after I got to the hospital I received an alarmed email from a friend on Capitol Hill. Later that day at a meeting with Congressional Democrats, Obama would lay out an ambitious agenda to pass reform by October 1. As part of that, he would announce that he must have "a public option, with or without a trigger."

This would be a disaster, as I quickly informed Patrick Gaspard, the White House political director, in an email. "This will cause a huge problem — a firestorm. A trigger is a way to kill the public option. It is and will be viewed that way by the whole progressive base. It will undercut what Kennedy, Schumer and the House are doing. And it's my worst nightmare because our campaign is based on lifting the President's plan."

As I reached out to others in the coalition who could contact the White House, I felt badly that I was paying so little attention to my wife, moaning in the hospital bed. I would check in on her, ask the nurses to deal with her needs, then turn back to my Blackberry. Later, Claudia told me that I had no reason to feel guilty; she was totally out of it, and had no recollection of my being at her bedside.

Finally I heard back from Patrick, "Sorry, Richard, in mtg and can't call. But your info is completely wrong. Pres will be strong in his public statements on his desire for a public option. … it will be in the letter we are putting out tomorrow."

Sure enough, the next day — June 3 — the President released a letter that he sent to Baucus and Kennedy. For the first time he put in writing the specific provisions that he wanted to see in the health reform legislation. What the President asked for included most of HCAN's key principles: regulating health insurance plans in an exchange; a mandated benefit plan (although not as comprehensive as we supported); responsibility by employers to pay for coverage, with special consideration for small businesses; and cost-control measures that promoted quality as opposed to cutting benefits. For the first time the

President endorsed an individual mandate, while calling for a "hardship" exemption, the obvious compromise to the dispute he had had with Hillary Clinton during the primaries. Last, to the relief of the entire progressive community, he wholeheartedly supported the public option. "I strongly believe that Americans should have the choice of a public health insurance option operating alongside private plans. This will give them a better range of choices, make the health care market more competitive, and keep insurance companies honest." Yahoo!

Three days later, the President's grassroots arm, Organizing for America (OFA) kicked off its health care organizing drive with thousands of house party meetings around the country, followed a few days later by a national petition drive, which included calling for a public option. OFA was the successor organization to Obama for America, the huge grassroots mobilization of volunteers and small donors that was key to the election. Now housed at the Democratic National Committee, Organizing for America had the challenge of transforming electoral energy into grassroots action on issues. While the press had disparaged OFA's initial steps because it could not match the breadth of the campaign's grassroots activism, I thought that if even a small proportion carried over, it would be a huge boost for progressive organizing. But to harness that enthusiasm, the President would need to stick to his progressive principles. His earlier silence on the public option had made enlisting OFA in the health reform fight next to impossible. Now OFA was able to swing into action without worrying about a deluge of negative feedback from its members.

For the next few weeks Obama would continue to strongly endorse the public option, whether in a speech to the AMA or in a series of three large town hall rallies, part of an aggressive push to pressure both houses of Congress to enact reform before it recessed in August.

From the Inside Back Out

Former Speaker of the House Tip O'Neill famously said, "All politics is local," but in today's world of instant national communication, that truth is receding. The HCAN coalition in

Washington state was well aware of the national debate on the public option when it turned its sights from Patty Murray to her junior colleague in the Senate, Maria Cantwell.

Like Murray, Cantwell is a liberal Democrat, but that's where the similarities ended. Cantwell would never appear in front of a crowd in tennis shoes. Unlike Murray, who entered politics from the grassroots, Cantwell is a more typical member of the U.S. Senate. She moved to Washington in 1983 to volunteer on a presidential campaign and was elected to the Washington state house three years later, at the age of 28. In 1992 she was elected to Congress but served just one term, a victim of the Gingrich–led rout of Democrats in 1994. After her defeat, Cantwell turned to Seattle's booming high-tech sector, becoming a multimillionaire as an executive at RealNetworks. In 2000, she used her newfound fortune to finance a return to politics, successfully joining the millionaire's club that is the U.S. Senate. More than two-thirds of its members had a net worth topping a million dollars in 2009.[27]

While Cantwell championed the environment and reproductive rights, she was not always a reliable progressive. She voted for the Central American Free Trade Act and sponsored Democratic Senator Ron Wyden's health reform bill, which included taxing health benefits. Cantwell served on the Senate Finance Committee, so hers would be one of the first votes needed to move health reform forward.

Seattle is home to the one sizeable health cooperative in the country, Group Cooperative of Puget Sound, which provides health coverage to more than 600,000 people. Cantwell had been meeting with Puget Sound executives but had not been accessible to the HCAN coalition. On June 22, she told Seattle's National Public Radio (NPR) affiliate that she preferred the co-op idea to the public option. The word in Washington was that Cantwell did not respond to grassroots pressure. But HCAN decided to see if that was true, with a boost from a well-respected Seattle blogger.

As Rachel Berkson, then an organizer for SEIU recalls, "The HCAN coalition blanketed her with phone calls, emails, letters. Every time she appeared in public we were there with questions on the importance of the public option. We held protests outside her office in downtown Seattle."

One of those who raised her voice was Jody Hall, a small business owner of Verite Coffee and Cupcake Royale in Seattle. Hall had been one of Starbucks' original employees, starting as a barista when the fledgling chain had thirty stores and leaving as a marketing executive eleven years later when Starbucks had more than 3,000 locations. She loved the tradition of coffee houses as community hubs. "Someone once called coffee shops a Penny University — pay a penny and get exposed to poets, artists, bankers, politicians." She also had seen how independent coffee houses that were in tune with the community and offered a better cup of coffee could outcompete Starbucks.

Hall heard about the Main Street Alliance (MSA) from a friend. "I was far enough along in my business that I felt like I had the time to help. I realized that only small businesses would stand up for small businesses. So I went to Olympia and testified about the high cost of health coverage, in a room with all these suits," — a big contrast with Jody, who dressed casually even when she brought cupcakes to the White House. "I testified that small business insurance coverage is not as good as coverage available to big businesses like Starbucks. I also said that insurance companies have no accountability for rate hikes. While I was testifying, I noticed that most of the senators were busy texting. I wondered if they were interested, although a few of them seemed interested and asked good questions. I thought, so this is how laws are made?"

When the national health reform debate heated up, Hall became a leader of MSA's local group, attending meetings with Senator Murray, who like Hall's Congressman, Jim McDermott, visited with her at her Seattle coffee house. So she was a perfect spokesperson for the HCAN coalition when she talked with Eli Sanders, who wrote for a popular Seattle blog called *The Stranger*. Talking about Cantwell, Hall told Sanders, "I'm really frustrated by her inability to listen to her constituents. I don't know if Big Insurance has her in its pocket or what, but it seems like she's watering down what could be a really good transformation in health care."

Sanders followed Jody's quote by writing, "A person active in the local health-policy-reform community added that compared to Murray, Cantwell doesn't seem to care. 'Senator Murray has been very responsive,' he said. 'She's done multiple public events and expressed her support of a public health-insurance plan. Consumers and small businesses have tried to meet with Senator Cantwell on this issue without as much success.'"

Hall added to the grassroots lobbying campaign by stamping "Health Care Now!" on her coffee cups, along with HCAN's toll-free number for calling members of Congress. She also recruited other Seattle small business owners to join the "small business stamping revolution" by stamping their products.

Through the grassroots pressure and press attention, Cantwell got the message. As the AFL-CIO's Robbie Stern told me, "I was gardening, putting in a new rhododendron, when I got a call from Maria's chief of staff saying, "STOP, STOP, we're there!"

Cantwell would become a vocal advocate on the Senate Finance Committee for both the public option and aggressive insurance regulation.

The common lesson that Murray, Cantwell, and Specter learned from their interactions with the HCAN coalitions was that they could ignore an impassioned grassroots base of support for reform only at their peril. While the specific demand that activists emphasized was the public option, the underlying message was that a big, organized constituency expected them to fight for health reform. The stories that they heard from their constituents about their problems with the health care system and the encounters they had with voters helped them understand that they could not walk away from the issue when the going got rough in Congress, as it was certain to do.

8

From the Ground Up — Swings

A Northern Blue Dog

"If I had not gone to the doctor for a checkup, you and I would never have met," Dan Sherry said as he shared his story on his fifty-third birthday in August 2010. The doctor found nothing more than elevated cholesterol. Yet his insurance company's reaction would turn Dan from an armchair activist into a national leader in the fight for health care, taking him to the White House, where he met the President, and to the steps of the Capitol, where Speaker Pelosi invited him to tell his story to the national press corps. Most important, he would sway his own member of Congress, conservative Illinois Democrat Melissa Bean. The complement to HCAN's strategy of creating strong Congressional champions was winning the support of "swing" members of Congress like Bean.

Sherry grew up south of Boston, and you can still hear a trace of a Boston accent in his voice. His wife Marcia's family had a small business in the Chicago suburb of Evanston, making pet tags. Dan and Marcia both wearied of working for big corporations that left them with little control over their lives and decided to go into the family business. With 120 million dogs and cats in the U.S., they recognized the huge potential for growing the business. Within a few years, their revenues had grown by twenty fold. When the advent of big chain stores like Petco and Petsmart threatened their business, Dan opened up a trophy and award business. He even invented a board game to play with a dog that became the rage in the dog obedience world, called, "My Dog Can Do That!"

Ironically, the explosive growth of their pet-tag business caused Dan Sherry to lose his health insurance. In the summer of 2003 he received an order for 100,000 pet tags. In the rush of trying to deliver such a huge order, Sherry missed one payment on the high-deductible health insurance plan that he had been purchasing for fifteen years. "With such a high deductible, we'd never used the insurance, even when our children were born. When I tried to make the missed payment, they said they first wanted to see our medical records. I hadn't been to a doctor in years. And I'd even run the Chicago Marathon two years earlier. But in spring of 2003, I had decided to get a checkup and sure enough, they found high cholesterol. Since then I've had an MRI and my pipes are clean as a whistle. But the insurance company refused to cover me. It agreed to take my wife and children but jacked up our rates. I was left uninsured. I looked for other coverage, but once you get rejected, the insurance companies share their data. I went years without insurance and was really angry. Until you've walked in the shoes of someone without insurance, you don't know what it means."

In 2008 Jamie Meerdink, the Main Street Alliance organizer in Illinois, walked into Dan's store and asked him to sign a petition to support health care reform. Sherry remembered, "Jamie asked if I had a story. His timing was perfect. I had just seen a lawyer who told me that the only way to protect my wife and kids from the medical costs that would result if I got seriously ill was to get divorced and give my wife the house, the car and all the savings." Jamie invited Sherry to MSA's first meeting in Illinois. "I had no idea of what I was getting involved in. I couldn't tell if they were well organized or not. But I was intrigued about getting involved in a grassroots organization. You literally took someone who was feeling angry, alone, impotent, frustrated and took me to the steps of the Capitol and I'm really appreciative of the entire journey."

Sherry's congresswoman, Melissa Bean, represented a traditionally Republican district northwest of the city. She had squeezed into Congress by winning 52 percent of the vote in 2004. She cast herself as a fiscal conservative, joined the Blue Dog Democratic caucus in the House, and described herself as pro-business and fiscally conservative. Her voting record reflected that: She had a higher rating from the U.S. Chamber of Commerce than from AFSCME, the big public employee union. Bean had operated a small business from her home before she ran for Congress, and she regarded herself as a champion of small business. She would be as tough a vote to get on health care reform as any Democrat north of the Mason-Dixon line.

Citizen Action/Illinois and the Main Street Alliance set out to build a base of supporters in Bean's district. The organizing strategy was designed by John Gaudette, who in the fall of 2008 started working on the HCAN campaign. John's father, Tom Gaudette, was a top lieutenant to Saul Alinsky, the godfather of twentieth-century community organizing in the United States. Gaudette came to work for Citizen Action/Illinois because he respected their method, which he said was old-fashioned organizing but updated. "The group understood you still had to talk to people directly and build relationships, rather than thinking it all could be done through technology."

Gaudette was assisted by Citizen Action/Illinois organizer Jessica Palys, and together they reached out to churches, suburban Democratic groups, and other progressive organizations, including activists. One of the first people they turned to was David Borris. He was a small business owner, the proprietor of an off-premise catering company called Hel's Kitchen. He was active in the anti-war movement, where he connected with Citizen Action/Illinois, which was organizing a campaign for withdrawal from Iraq. As he told the press at HCAN's July 2008 launch event at the Illinois State Capitol in Springfield, health insurance premiums for Borris' business had doubled from 2002 to 2008. "When the press was asking questions at the launch event, I was so aggravated at one question that I walked to the podium. It was so empowering. That's how I would sum up the feeling that people had who got involved. That moment realizing that what I have to say matters. It felt good."

Jessica Palys also reached out to Hal Snyder, a local Democratic activist. Snyder was fifty-eight years old but had only been involved in politics for a few years. He had earned a degree in medicine but realized that he didn't want to be a doctor and instead spent twenty-five years developing software for sophisticated computer networks. "I had been apolitical; apathetic. I was too smart. Political parties were for those who lacked imagination, who could not see more than one point of view at a time. But then around 2003, I became politically involved overnight. It was like being hit by a cattle prod, or Paul on the road to Tarsus [*sic*]. It looked to me that the Republicans had vacuumed the treasury to line the pockets of their friends. I wanted to end all the evils of the Bush administration: war, lies, depression. I wanted to share my new insights with my friends at work — who weren't exactly receptive. I became dysfunctional at work. It didn't seem important anymore. I'd look out the window and see people whose lives were being destroyed."

Snyder became active in opposing the Iraq war, where he met David Borris and William McNary, a dynamic organizer and speaker who was the co-executive director of Citizen Action/Illinois and the president of USAction. "In December '08 Jessica invited me to a health care meeting in Arlington Heights," Snyder told me. "I was suspicious of HCAN. I'd read about them having $50 million, so I thought it must be the insurance companies trying to water single-payer down. There were about twelve people on a snowy morning. John [Gaudette] was there. He endeared me to him. He said we invite single-payer people to speak their minds and he emphasized our points of agreement. I realized that these were my people. They know how to put together an event. I saw that there was skill and a strategy and tactics to organizing for social change."

Citizen Action was using meetings like this to build a base of activists. John Gaudette told me, "People told stories and then shared their frustration. We did a training on building power and had a strategic discussion on how to move members of Congress. We asked people what they thought we should do. Organize call-ins? A rally? A press event? Over time we did trainings on how to get media, or other things people needed. In three months we went from twenty people to 100 and eventually to 150 active volunteers."

Snyder left his job and became a full-time volunteer for the HCAN campaign, one of many super-volunteers around the country. "We began holding health care summits, at local churches and public libraries. We would start with panelists: Gaudette; Sherry; Borris. Then we broke people up into small discussion groups, which built connections between people. I was hooked when I saw people learning about the health care crisis and seeing that we could do something about it."

Citizen Action and MSA started to turn their sights on the main prize. Snyder says, "We started bird-dogging Bean as early as February 2009. On very short notice she would send robo-calls to people within five miles of where she'd be meeting with constituents. The message would be, 'I'll be at the Jewel Food store in Palatine at 11:00 in the morning.' We would rush to send people to talk with her, but they never got a satisfactory answer. We went to a parade in Grey's Lake and ran into her before the parade started. She said, 'I know what you are going to say. I've been hearing from your people.'"

Starting in April, HCAN activists visited Bean's local office at least once a month, bringing with them people who could tell stories. Dan Sherry's daughter attended high school with Bean's daughter, and he remarked, "She's here in a swing district where it's very tough for her to keep her seat. She's very coy, on the fence. Sometimes she sounded like she was talking from the Republican playbook. She spouted right-wing talking points. We'd push back on her. We'd counter them. It became a little contentious."

In my experience, contentious can be good when you are trying to move someone in politics. One of my favorite quotes comes from Frederick Douglass's eloquent treatise on power: "Power never concedes anything without a demand; it never did and it never will."

Bean's office became particularly tense at on June 25, the day that HCAN held a 10,000-person rally in Washington. Hal

Snyder didn't want to make the trip to Washington. Instead he proposed to John Gaudette that he organize a rally outside Melissa Bean's office in Schaumburg, Illinois. The rally would be aimed at pushing Bean, who had continued to avoid taking a position, to become a vocal supporter of reform. At 11:30, forty people gathered outside Bean's office, an impressive count for a weekday morning. Snyder and a few others went up to Bean's office and requested that one of the Congresswoman's staff address the crowd and the TV cameras. Bean's staff asked them to wait outside.

At the same time, John Gaudette, David Borris and others from HCAN Illinois were meeting with Bean's chief of staff in Washington. Her chief got a call from Bean's staff in Illinois, asking for advice about how to respond to the HCAN demonstration in front of their offices. The angry chief of staff demanded to know why HCAN was protesting against Bean. They told her that it wasn't a protest, rather a show of support for health reform.

Bean's office refused to speak to the press covering the demonstration and the next day cancelled a scheduled meeting in Illinois with HCAN. But the HCAN organizers all agree that the demonstration marked a turning point in their relationship with Bean. David Borris told me, "She needed to understand we had access to a power base that could be vocal and visual. Soon they needed our help to turn people out against the tea partiers." John Gaudette said, "After that we started hearing from her chief of staff, who started asking us to react to proposals, like the co-op or small business pools. They wanted to know how we believed the proposal would impact small business."

A Southerner on Obama's Coattails

The prime organizing focus for the HCAN coalition in North Carolina was its newly elected Democratic senator, Kay Hagan. Since every one of the sixty Democrats in the Senate would have to vote to break a Republican filibuster, winning the votes of Democrats like Hagan who represented more conservative states was essential.

The director of the HCAN partner organization in North Carolina was Lynice Williams. Williams was raised in public housing in Queens, a community where social action was a part of attending church. She married a minister and in 1980 they moved to Raleigh, North Carolina. Williams was a stay-at-home mom, but as her kids got older, she started to volunteer with her local YWCA, which had much fewer resources than the YWCA frequented by whites. She then started volunteering for a local women's center, working on issues of particular concern to African American women. When she heard that the local hunger coalition was looking to hire an assistant director, the news left her shocked. "In all the years I volunteered, I never knew you could get paid. So I worked for a year as a full-time organizer for the hunger coalition until the organization went broke. I then took a job as a community organizer for North Carolina Fair Share and in 1996 became the executive director."

The membership of North Carolina Fair Share comprises churches that provide regular funding to the organization, other community groups, and 3,000 people who are dues-paying members and who are invited to participate in one of nine chapters around the state. NC Fair Share coordinated the state's HCAN coalition, which included most of the progressive infrastructure in the State, including local affiliates of five national HCAN Steering Committee groups: ACORN, the NAACP; SEIU; the National Education Association; and the AFL-CIO.

Obama carried North Carolina in 2008, the first Democratic candidate to do so since Jimmy Carter in 1976. Obama's victory was due to two factors. The first was a changing electorate in the state, as more northerners moved there for jobs or to retire. The second was a big push by the Obama campaign to register and turn out African Americans and young people. His election helped carry Kay Hagan to a surprise victory over the incumbent senator, Elizabeth Dole.

Williams later recalled, "I had worked with Kay Hagan when she was in the North Carolina Senate, where she was a moderate. But when she became U.S. Senator, we didn't know where she'd be. She ran for the Senate saying that she would support Obama's platform, and we were going to hold her accountable to that — she won on his coattails. She knew that — but we had to continually remind her. And remind her that North Carolina has one million uninsured people."

In the U.S. Senate, Hagan was appointed to the HELP Committee, chaired by Ted Kennedy, making her one of its few moderate Democrats. Kennedy, whose cancer was advancing rapidly, had asked his close friend, Connecticut Senator Chris Dodd, to serve as acting chair of the Committee. In early June, Dodd unveiled a first draft of the health care legislation. The draft had blank, place-holder sections for two crucial issues that were facing unexpected controversy among the committee's usually reliably liberal membership: how employers should be made responsible for paying for their employee's coverage, known in shorthand as "employer responsibility," and how the public option should be structured.

Hagan had an important role to play in answering that question. She was getting a lot of pressure from North Carolina's dominant health insurer, North Carolina Blue Cross Blue Shield. The company had 53 percent of the commercial health insurance market in the state and 97 percent of the individual health insurance market.

In mid-May, HCAN received an email leaking a plan by the company to launch a TV advertising campaign against the public option. We realized that this would be news, so we forwarded the Blue Shield plan to Ceci Connolly at *The Washington Post*. Connolly broke the story on May 18, under the headline, "North Carolina's Blue Cross Blue Shield Trying to Kill Key Plank of Obama Plan." Connolly wrote, "In three 30-second videos, the insurer paints a picture of a future system in which patients wait months for appointments and can't choose their own doctors." One of the ads concludes, "We can do a lot better than a government-run health care system."

The company never ran the ads, I assume because the rest of the health insurance industry jumped all over them for being off message from their "charm offensive" with the President and Congress.

HCAN had received the leaked information indirectly from Dana Cope, the executive director of the State Employees Association of North Carolina, a local of SEIU, which represents everyone who works for the state: 55,000 employees from "the janitor that cleans the Capitol to the Governor," as Cope told me. But that representation comes without effective bargaining rights. "What's frustrated me and our members is that we have public employees on food stamps. At the same time we're lining the pockets of corporate CEOs."

One of those CEOs was the president of Blue Cross Blue Shield of North Carolina. SEIU staffers discovered that the CEO made $4.5 million a year, some of that from a secret cost-plus contract between North Carolina and the health insurance company. Cope said, "The contract gave the company higher profits every time health costs went up. And they could charge everything to the taxpayer and make more money, from Frisbees given out by the marketing department, to the corporate jet, to ads run against health care reform."

Clearly, the state's insurance giant was working hard to lobby the junior U.S. Senator from North Carolina. So did the HCAN coalition, which decided to include her in the big rally that HCAN was planning in Washington on June 25. The coalition invited Hagan to attend a town hall meeting to be held after the rally at the Stewart Mott house, across the street from the Capitol.

To prepare, the HCAN organizations in North Carolina started calling their own members and asked them to do two things. The first was to call Senator Hagan and tell her to support health care, including the public option. The second request was to attend the HCAN rally in Washington. Some of the HCAN coalition leaders called Hagan to ask her to meet with the North Carolina activists when they arrived in D.C. The president of the North Carolina NAACP made sure the Senator understood how important it was that she meet with her constituents. Still, Dana Cope recalled, "She wouldn't promise to meet us. We didn't know until she came in to the rally that day whether she would make it."

HCAN also contacted both the mainstream press and progressive bloggers in North Carolina. On June 18, a blogger at *Progressive Pulse* wrote, "Why Hagan would not want to give her constituents another option for health insurance when the only place most of them can go is one NC company — North Carolina Blue Cross Blue Shield — is beyond me."

Three days later, HCAN launched a new TV ad in ten states, including North Carolina, that attacked high insurance company profits, CEO salaries, soaring co-payments and constant denials of care. The ad then pivoted to deliver the same message as Obama had been preaching: The solution to our health care problems was to enact reforms that allowed individuals to keep their own plan or have a choice of a new plan, including a public health insurance plan that would, as Obama had argued, "lower costs and keep insurance companies honest."

In response, Hagan's office told the Greensboro *News & Record*, on June 21, "Sen. Hagan is looking at all the public option proposals. She's going to be working with her colleagues to ensure private health insurance isn't going to be destabilized."

The howl from progressive blogs was immediate. "We didn't dump Liddy Dole to deserve this," wrote Pam Spaulding in *Pam's House Blend*, which calls itself "An Online Magazine in the Reality-Based Community."

And because Hagan was another Senate multimillionaire, the coalition also let Hagan's office know that her image could be further tarred if it became public that her family fortune had been increased through investments in Aetna, United Health, and a long list of drug companies.

On the morning of the big rally and lobby day in Washington, Bob Geary, a reporter for the North Carolina blog INDYWEEK.COM, boarded one of the buses with the HCAN coalition and later gave a detailed account of what happened when the activists got to D.C., arriving still without any confirmation that Hagan would see them. At 9:00 A.M, the bus riders took out their cell phones and called Hagan's office, urging her to meet with them later in the day. On one bus an organizer for the Campaign for Community Change told her fellow riders,

"I've got her picture on this milk carton! She is MIA, and we are going to find her!"

The Big Day Arrives

I walked to the podium to greet a sea of upturned faces over a rainbow of T-shirts, stretching all the way to the foot of Upper Senate Park, a wide, tree-lined lawn that runs the length of the Russell Senate Office Building almost all the way down the hill to Union Station. Behind me, the Capitol Dome soared against a luminous blue sky. It was going to be a hot day.

"You are a sight for sore eyes!" I began. I really meant it. After six months of being isolated in Washington, where the national press corps and internecine Congressional politics define America, it was wonderful to see the HCAN army we had been building around the country stretched out in front of me. I started the chant: "Health Care for America ..." The crowd roared back, "Now!" I then turned the microphone over to the Emmy award–winning TV star Edie Falco, the first of a parade of speakers that would follow for the next ninety minutes.

For almost a year, we had been organizing separate HCAN coalitions around the country. In April, we decided that it would give our effort a big boost if we could bring our activists together. We also anticipated that the health care battle would be heating up in Congress over the coming months. The unions on the HCAN Steering Committee thought that a national gathering would be a good way to mobilize their members for the fight.

We also knew that if we brought all those people to Washington, their representatives in Congress had better know they were there. We decided that we would aim for 5,000 people but not just for a rally. We'd create a huge lobby day, bringing the whole group up to Capitol Hill.

The twin effort worked much better than expected. We turned out 10,000 people on that early summer day, who arrived in 207 buses and by car, train, and plane, from almost every state in the union. The huge crowd, sunshine, soaring Capitol Dome, and exuberant rally lifted the crowd's spirits.

The only sour note was that the footage taken by the banks of TV cameras filming the rally never made the news. One story dominated that day: Michael Jackson had died.

After the rally, we scheduled three issue-based town halls to which members of Congress were invited: one focused on racial equity in health care; a second for doctors and nurses; and a third for small businesses. We also held ten town halls for people who came from individual states, so that our activists could meet with the members of their state's Congressional delegation as a group. Other rally goers fanned out to lobby their members of Congress across Capitol Hill.

Confronting Hagan

After the rally, the North Carolina HCAN delegation held their town hall in a backyard patio of the Mott House, a gathering place for progressives located across from the Hart Senate Office Building and the Capitol. The North Carolinians still didn't know if Hagan would appear. While they waited, they heard from people with health care stories. One of them was Rhonda Robinson, a forty-four-year-old mother whose health care nightmare had led to her becoming a spokesperson for the HCAN coalition. Robinson had lost her job with the North Carolina State Department of Health and Human Services, which in the recession reduced its work force. As a result, she also lost her health coverage. Robinson suffered from epilepsy and while she worked had been under regular care from a neurologist. She had been taking two medications. When she lost her coverage, she could not afford the $800 a month for the drugs and had stopped going to her doctor, whom she had not seen for more than a year.

At the Mott House, Robinson stood up to address her fellow North Carolinians. As the *INDYWEEK.COM's* Geary reported, "In tears, her voice shaking with frustration, Robinson couldn't read the speech she'd written. 'This is not a game to me,' she struggled to say. 'I have two kids, and I don't want them to find me dead in my bed.' When Robinson sat down, several of her Durham allies — fed up by Hagan's absence — swept in to take her with them to Hagan's office. They met the

Senator in the lobby of the Dirksen Building as she headed for the elevator en route to the meeting they had just left. 'Tell her your story,' her friends urged Robinson. And she did, calmly this time. 'I'm a single mom, I have a preexisting condition, Senator, and I'm one of the 47 million people who don't have health insurance,' Robinson remembers saying to Hagan. Hagan listened intently, Robinson says, gripping Robinson's arm. 'That's exactly the people we want to help,' Hagan said finally. 'People like you. C'mon, let's go.'"[28]

Geary continued, "Moments later, Hagan was speaking at the town hall meeting. 'She kept looking at me whenever she said preexisting condition,' Robinson says. 'She kept talking about it like Obama when he was talking about his mom and her preexisting condition.'"

Hagan walked to the podium wearing a white skirt suit and a string of white pearls. She thanked the group for making the long trip to D.C. and then described in general terms the health reform legislation that she was working on as a member of the Senate HELP Committee. After Hagan delivered her remarks, an HCAN organizer asked her a series of questions, including whether she would support equal access to health coverage to all. Hagan responded that she wanted to address the fact that insurance companies charged women of childbearing age more for health coverage than men of the same age. "It takes two to make a baby," she told the crowd in a slightly lilting southern accent.

The last question that Hagan was asked was whether she would support a plan that allowed people to keep their own coverage or choose either a new private plan or a public plan. Here she punted, earning groans from the crowd. She said that she wanted to be sure that the "200 million people" with private health coverage could keep their plan and that states had to have a key role in the new system. She never referred to the public option, but several times said "whatever you name it." The crowd started chanting "support the public option" while she left the stage.

SEIU's Dana Cope recalls, "She didn't make a commitment to the public option at the rally. At that point she said no more questions and she walked out. We had had this huge campaign for her election; she'd beaten Elizabeth Dole. We were stunned. We came back to North Carolina and met with her in her office in Raleigh and let her know that if she didn't commit to this we'd put huge public pressure on her. She told us that she was getting pressured from Blue Cross Blue Shield and the North Carolina Chamber of Commerce. We told her, we got your back, and this is what you and Obama were elected to do."

A Brew With Specter

We also used the massive rally on June 25 to finally cement Arlen Specter's commitment to the public option. We invited Specter to join more than 2,000 HCAN activists from Pennsylvania who crowded into the Capital City Brewing Company, housed in the massive Beaux Arts style Postal Square Building, built in 1911. Desperate for large enough spaces to hold town halls with our bigger delegations, Melinda Gibson, the HCAN staffer who was coordinating logistics for the rally, had rented the huge hall, lined with dark wood around a long, massive bar. HCAN demonstrators hung over the banister that lined the second floor balcony, peering down on the long room filled shoulder to shoulder, with the crowd pressed around the huge, shining metal brewery tanks. Some of the rally goers ordered glasses of brew from the bars.

For an hour they chanted and listened to speeches from members of the House of Representatives from Pennsylvania and leaders of HCAN member organizations. They were wait-ing for Pennsylvania Senator Arlen Specter, who was at the White House at a meeting on immigration reform. It was hot and the crowd was trickling out, but a thousand activists still remained when Specter finally joined them.

Specter stood in front of a bright metal cooking hood under which three chefs were preparing for the restaurant's dinner crowd. "I agree with you that health care is a right... I know that you are very interested in the public component. And I think that Senator Schumer has a public component that has a level playing field with the private sector but the public compo-nent can be included." As he left to cheers, Specter said, "Your passion and your presence here and your rally and your enthusiasm has a big effect on what goes at the Capitol three blocks away. We will get health care this year."

Double-Teaming Feinstein

The HCAN coalition in California held rallies in their home state on June 25. But these events were meant as protests aimed at Senator Diane Feinstein. As Anthony Wright, the executive director of Health Access, HCAN's lead partner in California explained, "To our dismay, early in the health reform debate, Senator Feinstein became a regular voice of caution, warning against moving too fast, and instead arguing for a more incremental approach. Consequently, even with fifty-five members of Congress from California, the Senator became our primary statewide focus, starting with a series of call-in days in May 2009." The California HCAN coalition sent two hundred activists to join the June 25 D.C. rally and planned local rallies outside her offices around the state.

The rallies turned into demonstrations when Senator Feinstein appeared on CNN's Sunday news program on June 21 and told host John King, "To be candid with you, I don't know that [President Obama] has the votes right now [for health reform]. I think there's a lot of concern in the Democratic caucus."

HCAN partners promptly changed the message of the rallies. Wright told me, ""We wanted to respond forcefully that these comments were a problem, while not declaring war, because we still wanted her vote in the end. Our message was that California could not afford to go slow on health care reform, and that we needed Senator Feinstein to be a champion, not a skeptic. So June 25 became an opportunity to make a statement — to hit all five of her offices, in D.C. and in the state, protesting outside, visiting staff inside, and getting media. In Los Angeles and San Francisco we had more than 100 people at the events and dozens of folks in Fresno and San Diego. We got television press coverage in every location, and a delegation of several leaders met with her staff in each office. I was part of a delegation of about ten leaders who met with her health staff in D.C.

On the same day, the head of the California Labor Federation, Art Pulaski, already had a meeting with Feinstein's chief of staff in D.C., and he brought the comments up in his meeting as well."

MoveOn also made sure that Feinstein got the message. The organization sent an email to its huge California membership asking them to contact Feinstein and to donate to ads that would press her to support reform.

Over time, Feinstein would become a stalwart supporter of reform, in particular of regulating health insurance company premiums and profits. On August 28, she started publicly indicating her change of heart. She sent out a press release detailing the health crisis in California and credited HCAN for data on the increase in insurance company profits. Her release said, "I have received over 293,324 phone calls, letters and emails about health care reform — and climbing. Additionally, several thousand Californians have visited our offices and met with staff, revealing their fears and concerns about cancelled policies, denied treatments, increasing premiums, and other problems with our health care system."

Feinstein heard our message.

An Organizer Sums It Up

A final look at the multiple impacts of that day of rallying demonstrates clearly the impact that grassroots organizing can have on our elected officials. All across Capitol Hill on June 25, HCAN members were meeting with members of Congress. One was Congressman Brian Higgins, a Democrat who served on the House Ways and Means Committee. Diana Cihak, an organizer for Citizen Action of New York, described how Higgins was moved from being cautious to becoming a champion.

"Higgins represents a fairly conservative district. As an Irish Catholic who has been bashed publically for his pro-choice stance, he has to walk a fine line with his constituents. He signed the HCAN pledge, but he wasn't ready to make any solid commitments.

"It wasn't until our meeting with him on Capitol Hill at his office during our June 2009 rally that I saw his full commitment to reform. He was with us — finally! About fifteen of us crowded into his office and he let everyone speak.... There was a doctor with us who ran a clinic that is the main source of health care for the refugees in Buffalo. There were members of labor from SEIU and CWA talking from a labor perspective and also as health care workers on the front lines of this fight everyday. And I had brought along my ten-year-old daughter and fourteen-year-old niece who spoke from their hearts about the future of their nation. We went way over our allotted time, as his staff was shooting me annoying glances every couple of minutes. But Higgins stayed with us. And in the end he vowed to fight to the end and to use his position on Ways and Means to assure a good, strong bill."

Returning to Buffalo, Cihak invited Higgins to a rally the following Saturday. "Higgins came and spoke passionately about his commitment to health care reform — about how this single issue was the most important piece of the puzzle to put our economy back on track. I was relieved and amazed — this was much stronger than any speech he had made before.... I knew that he had become one of our most passionate supporters."

Higgins was not the only House member who had been swayed. The House was about to start making history, finally moving reform legislation further through Congress than ever before. But neither the House nor the Senate was moving as fast as reformers, starting with the President, had hoped.

9

The Happy Warrior

In looking through the archive of blog posts and news clips on the HCAN website for June and July of 2009, to refresh my memory in preparation for writing this next chapter, I noticed an unmistakable difference between these and earlier months. There was a newly intense swirl of activity, from Congress, from supporters and opponents of reform, and from the White House. The press was covering a growing number of health care issues, recounting numerous engagements on a rapidly expanding battlefield. According to a study by the Pew Research Center's Project for Excellence in Journalism for the ten months that began in June 2009, when the text of the first health reform bills was released, through March 2010, when the legislation became law, health care reform was the top issue in the national press.[29]

In writing this book, I'm trying to give the reader a feeling for what it was like to live through the campaign to win health care reform. "Campaign" is a military term, and it is appropriate for the health care battles. The advances and reversals centered on a cause that is a matter of life and death, literally as tens of thousands of people die every year in this country because they do not have health insurance.

Living through the battles required calm and perseverance. In June the press reported that Senate Finance Committee Chair Max Baucus was about to release a reform proposal that dropped the public option. There were many very long faces among the HCAN staff in our D.C. office. This was the first concrete bad news that we had received. Our online director, Levana Layendecker, suggested that I might want to address the staff's funk. So I quickly walked around the ring of outer offices and inner cubicles that housed our staff and asked everyone to come into the conference room.

I didn't know what I was going to say, but I was speaking from the heart, not from the head, so no preparation was needed. This was my message, which I delivered with quiet, intense passion: "We are going to go through a long series of ups and downs, good news and bad, twists and turns, over the next few months. We are lucky to have gotten this far without any real crises. There are three ways that I think you can deal with the emotions. One is to ride the roller coaster, up each hill and down, going from high to low, at the edge of your seats. But for me at least, that would just tear me up inside. Another way is to not react emotionally to anything; don't get excited when the news is good or let yourself get down, when the news is bad. Remember that things can and will change quickly, so just watch it all happening and get your job done. I'd recommend that before staying on the roller coaster. But not if it means that you turn ice-cold emotionally — that would be like never even taking the ride. Missing the whole adventure.

"Here's what I'm going to do," I continued. "I'm going to remember how incredibly lucky we are, how privileged we are, to be helping to lead this fight. We have a shot, a real shot, at doing something historic, something that people have dreamed about and fought for a century, making health care a right in our country. I'm incredibly grateful to have this opportunity. So when the news is good I'm going to feel excited and use that to keep me going forward. But I'm not going to think it really means anything definitive: just another step forward. And when the news is bad, I'm going to take the punch, exhale and smile, and figure out what we do next to solve the problem or face the next challenge. They called Hubert Humphrey the Happy Warrior, and that's what I'm going to be, a happy warrior, loving that I get to be in this fight, the fight of our lives."

The House Marches Forward — But Not Fast Enough

President Obama had set an ambitious goal for both houses of Congress: pass legislation before the August recess. With that accomplished, the President aimed to then work with Congress to reconcile the legislation passed by each house and push for enactment of a final bill by October.

On June 19, the chairmen of the three House committees responsible for passing health care reform bills announced a common draft for what became known as the tri-committee bill. The fact that all three committee chairmen — Charles Rangel (NY) of the Ways and Means Committee, George Miller (CA) of the Education and Labor Committee, and Henry Waxman (CA) of the Energy and Commerce Committee — would present the same bill to their committees was a powerful indication of both the consensus that had emerged among Democrats on the shape of reform and of the determination among House Democrats not to allow traditional ways of doing business, such as Congressional committee fiefdoms, to interfere with moving health reform legislation forward.

Typically, each committee chair would develop his or her own legislation, and then the Speaker's office would need to go through a difficult process of reconciling the several different bills passed by each committee. But the House had taken a very different course. The staff of all three committees had been working together for months to write a unified bill. While each committee would certainly make some amendments when the committee considered the bill, reconciling changes to a piece of common legislation would be relatively easy.

It helped that all three chairmen were liberals who had lived through the 1994 Clinton health care fight. Their common beliefs meant that they would not have to negotiate major ideological differences. Their common experience of failure was a sharp reminder of the necessity of working together. Their cooperation was also a tribute to the leadership of House Speaker Nancy Pelosi, who wanted to move expeditiously toward reform.

The legislation that the House produced was the best version of reform we were sure to see, since the Senate was certain to weaken the bill on a host of fronts. It largely met the HCAN principles, containing a number of key provisions that would become bones of contention as the legislation moved forward.

I always believed that the most important test of reform was whether it provided people with good, affordable coverage. The House bill largely met that test. Most people would continue to get health coverage at work. To assure that coverage at work was affordable, the tri-committee bill would establish new regulations on employer-provided coverage. The rules would require that coverage at work be comprehensive, from preventive through chronic care, and would have limits on out-of-pocket costs. The bill would also require employers to pay a significant portion of the premiums for their employees and for family coverage.

Under the proposed legislation, people who did not get coverage at work, and some small businesses, would access insurance through the new health insurance exchanges. The exchanges would be regulated nationally and include stringent consumer protections and comprehensive benefits. The exchange would include a public option, a new, national insurance company, run out of the Department of Health and Human Services. Initially, the public option would pay hospitals and doctors at the same or slightly higher than Medicare rates, making it a "robust" public option that would result in considerable cost savings to the government and lower premiums for consumers. After two years the public option could negotiate rates with providers.

People who earned less than four times the poverty level — which was $88,000 a year in 2009 — would receive financial help from the government to pay for their premiums. The legislation extended Medicaid eligibility to 133 percent of the federal poverty level; currently states set their own Medicaid eligibility levels, which are as low as 25 percent of the poverty level in some states. Providing Medicaid eligibility to low-income people across the nation was the third leg of the framework that made good health coverage affordable to all.

The cost of expanded coverage in the bill, roughly $1 trillion over ten years, would be paid for principally through savings in the Medicare program and a new surcharge on incomes of upper-income taxpayers. The savings in Medicare did not come from cutting Medicare benefits, but from ending excess payments made to "Medicare Advantage" plans, private insurance plans that were receiving payments from Medicare that were 13 percent higher than the cost to the government of providing coverage directly to people through the Medicare program. The bill would have provided new benefits to seniors, including coverage for preventive care and gradually closing the Medicare prescription drug "donut" hole under which seniors have to keep paying Part D drug coverage premium, while at the same time paying the full cost of the prescriptions. Other Medicare and Medicaid savings came through cutting hospital and drug payments, reflecting the agreements that these industries had reached with the Obama administration.

The legislation dealt gingerly with two potential "wedge" issues in health reform: abortion and immigration. The abortion issue turned on whether government funding would fund abortion coverage by subsidized plans in the exchanges. The legislation was silent on this issue, meaning that plans that offered abortion coverage could do so even if a portion of the coverage was subsidized. However the legislation did not change the Hyde Amendment, which prohibited government funding for abortion except in the case of rape or incest, resulting in virtually no federal funding for abortions in Medicaid.

However, the House tri-committee bill failed to correct a major inequity in Medicaid coverage of immigrants. Under current law legal immigrants had to wait five years before they were eligible for Medicaid coverage. The bill did allow most legal immigrants to be eligible for subsidies in the exchange, and it did not prohibit immigrants who were not in the country legally from using their own money to purchase coverage in the exchange.

HCAN's Legislative and Policy Committee prepared a detailed analysis of the legislation, including proposals for improvements. We were ready to do this thanks to an exhaustive policy process that we had undertaken earlier. Beginning in the fall of 2008, the HCAN Committee spent eight months drafting detailed policy recommendations that fleshed out each of our ten guiding principles. By hammering out these issues early, we avoided internal disagreements when faced with real bills.

We knew where coalition members stood. The long process of carefully writing the policy documents, which were adopted by the HCAN Steering Committees, created a great amount of good will and shared purpose among the sizeable number of HCAN coalition members that participated.

While HCAN had some reservations about the tri-committee bill, overall it was a monumental achievement. The Congressional Budget Office — the official referee on the cost and impact of proposed legislation — estimated that it would result in 97 percent of Americans receiving coverage. We believed that the structures and consumer protections would mean that, for most people, coverage would be affordable and meet their health care needs.

The House was working aggressively to meet the President's target of passage by the first week of August. On July 16, the Ways and Means Committee passed the tri-committee legislation with a manageable number of amendments (including changes proposed by Republicans) by a vote of 23-18; three of the twenty-six Democrats on the committee voted no, along with all the Republicans. The Education and Labor Committee followed the next morning, by a margin of 26-22, again losing three Democrats.

We celebrated those milestones, but typically the press buried the good news in a cloud of doubts. Robert Pear's reporting in *The New York Times* usually avoided most of the skepticism that pervaded the Washington press corps. Pear's long history gave him the ability to see the big picture rather than being distracted by the barrage of attacks focused on every minute spurt of progress. But the *Times* editors had assigned David Herszenhorn to write with Pear, and their joint coverage began to contain the same negative spin and inside the Beltway tunnel vision common to the national press corps. An example was the *Times* article the day after two House committees passed almost identical health reform bills on the same day. Under the headline, "Dems Grow Wary as Health Bill Advances," the co-authors led off, "Three of the five Congressional committees working on legislation to reinvent the nation's health care system delivered bills this week along the lines proposed by President Obama. But instead of celebrating their success, many Democrats were apprehensive, nervous and defensive."

The same negative slant distorted the press coverage of a historic event. The American Medical Association endorsed the House bill, even though it included a public option that was tied to Medicare rates. The AMA opposed that provision, but they decided that it was time to be on the right side of history. The association was also hoping that by endorsing the House bill, Congress would be more likely to raise physician rates under Medicare. As the longest-serving member of Congress, Representative John Dingell of Michigan, told *The New York Times*, "The historical significance of the A.M.A.'s support should not be underestimated. Quite honestly, it has been difficult to win the support of this organization going all the way back to the 1930s."[30]

But as a progressive media watchdog group noted on July 22: "A Media Matters for America analysis of transcripts available in the Nexis database has found that broadcast and cable news featured almost twice as many segments mentioning the American Medical Association's (AMA's) reported opposition to a public insurance plan as segments mentioning the AMA's recent announcement that it supported the House Democrats' health care reform bill, which includes a public plan."

We still faced real obstacles. The next hurdle was the highest yet, the House Energy and Commerce Committee, where the Clinton bill had died in March 1994. The committee had more conservative Democrats than the others, including seven members of the Blue Dog Caucus.

One of them was Mike Ross of Arkansas, who chaired the health committee of the Blue Dog Caucus. Ross had been one of the first members of the House to endorse HCAN's "Which Side Are You On?" statement, but on July 17, *Politico Pulse* reported that Ross was unhappy with the House tri-committee bill. A few days later, Ross and several other Blue Dogs on the committee met with President Obama and Committee Chairman Henry Waxman to discuss a number of concerns that they wanted addressed. Over the next ten days, negotiations that included White House Chief of Staff Rahm Emanuel continued at a furious pace.

While the Blue Dogs pride themselves on being fiscal conservatives, the list of changes they wanted revealed interest-group pressure more than fiscal prudence. They demanded two items that would increase costs to the federal government but please interest groups. One measure was to decrease the number of small businesses that would be required to help pay for their employees' coverage, which meant that the employees and taxpayers would have to pick up more of the tab. Another measure — the one that caused the most uproar — was to require the public option to negotiate rates with providers rather than initially pay providers rates tied to Medicare. This concession to hospitals and doctors would increase the cost to the federal taxpayer by some $75 billion over ten years.

To reduce the cost of reform to the federal government, the Blue Dogs wanted to eliminate subsidies to people who earned above three times the poverty level, forcing middle-class families to pay the full cost of health coverage. As HCAN pointed out, that would require families who earned more than $55,000 to pay three times as much as a member of Congress pays for coverage. The Blue Dogs also wanted states to pay for a higher share of Medicaid costs, shifting costs from federal taxpayers to state taxpayers.

To pass the bill out of his committee, Waxman agreed to several concessions. However, progressives on the committee — led by two close HCAN allies, Tammy Baldwin of Wisconsin and Jan Schakowsky of Illinois — limited what Waxman had to give up. I saw this as an important shift in dynamics; Waxman and the White House had to negotiate with progressives to secure enough votes for passage rather than acquiesce to all the Blue Dog demands.

Still, we shared the feelings of progressives in Congress who were tired of the small group of conservative Democrats using their power to impose their will on the majority. After all, in the first two House committee votes, more than 88 percent of Democrats had voted for the bill. The Blue Dogs represented only seven of the thirty-six Democrats on the Energy and Commerce Committee. On July 30, the Progressive Caucus held a rally on Capitol Hill to protest the weakening of the public option and affordability provisions in the bill. In support, we sent an email to our D.C. area activists, asking them to attend the rally. We also issued a two-paragraph press release that said that the demands by "some Blue Dog Democrats will result in higher costs to families."

Our very mild two-paragraph release sparked outrage from both the White House and some of Speaker Pelosi's staff. We issued it on the same day that I met with Speaker Pelosi to describe what we were doing to promote reform. After the meeting, one of the Speaker's press officers confronted me angrily, swearing that the release could be used as ammunition against the Blue Dogs in an election. It was D.C. paranoid insanity to the max. I laughed it off, but the press staff made a big deal of it with others in the Speaker's office, and shared their unhappiness with our White House liaison.

When I returned to the office, Jim Messina, the deputy chief of staff in the White House, wanted to know why we were "participating in rallies blowing up Blue Dog members who made a deal that white house was a part of (if reluctantly)?" I responded that we had simply sent an email to our D.C. activists to support progressives but that we were "telling every one of our allies on E&C to vote for the bill." I also pointed out that we had spent $2 million in July on TV ads promoting reform. Messina wrote back: "Just play it straight, this is exactly what people don't like about you there is always some other agenda. Just play it straight."

Taken aback, I asked Ethan Rome, HCAN's deputy director, to look at the email. I couldn't figure it out. I was always very careful to be clear with people about what we are doing, just to avoid accusations of double-dealing. And I had only talked to Messina once, months before, and briefly, so where was this coming from? When I tried to talk to Messina about it, he wouldn't return my calls or emails. As I later realized, the "other agenda" was promoting our views of the best reform possible, even when the White House had taken another tack. I came to find out that being berated like this was an old habit of

Messina's, learned while he was chief of staff to Max Baucus. As it turned out, this was only the White House's opening salvo.

When the dust had cleared, despite the concessions made to the Blue Dogs, the bill maintained the same strong framework as the tri-committee bill passed by the other committees, including a national public option run by the Secretary of Health and Human Services who could use that power to negotiate lower rates and expanded coverage to tens of million of uninsured people. The committee approved the bill on July 31 by 31-28, with five Democrats joining all the Republicans in opposition.

Yet that was the last Congressional vote before the August recess. Time had run out for both houses of Congress to pass bills before they left Washington.

A week earlier, Senate Majority Leader Harry Reid conceded that the Senate would not make the deadline. The Senate was tied up by the crawling pace of negotiations in the Senate Finance Committee, where Chairman Max Baucus was insisting on reaching a bipartisan agreement with Republican Senator Chuck Grassley and four other Senators, who had become known as the "Gang of Six." Baucus' attempt to reach an agreement with his Republican counterparts would prove to be one of the biggest blunders of the entire effort to win reform.

10

No HELP for the Gang of Six

Kennedy Takes the First Step

The two Senate committees that had jurisdiction over the health reform bill — HELP and Senate Finance — were drawing up separate bills. Even though the staffs of the two committees met regularly to align the two pieces of legislation as they were drafted, the bills produced by each committee reflected the real ideological differences between the more liberal members of the HELP Committee, who were planning to pass a bill regardless of Republican support, and the Finance Committee, where Chairman Max Baucus was intent on producing legislation that would win several Republican votes.

When Acting HELP Committee Chair Senator Christopher Dodd released the first draft of the legislation on June 9, two crucial sections were missing: the requirement that employers provide or pay for coverage and the structure of the public option. At HCAN, we were not happy that a committee known for its liberal makeup was having trouble reaching consensus among its Democratic members on two such important provisions. The public option was the issue that received the most public attention. But while the "employer responsibility" provisions had not been the focus of much public debate, they would actually have an impact on many more people than the public option. At most, ten million people were expected to enroll in a public option in the first few years, while 160 million people would continue to receive health insurance at work.

In 1994, business groups had run a major public campaign against the provision in the Clinton bill that would have required employers to help pay for coverage. But in 2010, the business groups ran a stealth campaign against a similar provision. Since they knew that it had strong support in the House, their goal was to kill the "employer responsibility" proposal in the Senate. The employer groups lobbied the Democrats on the HELP Committee and found a few sympathetic ears, but they planned to make their stand in Baucus' Committee. So after negotiations with the two most conservative Democratic members of the HELP Committee, Kay Hagan of North Carolina and Jeff Bingaman of New Mexico, a watered-down version of the House employer responsibility provisions was included in the HELP bill, meeting HCAN's principles, and allowing us to support it. We'd ducked another bullet, at least for now.

To ensure that the HELP bill included a strong public option, HCAN asked our state coalitions to lobby the Democrats on the committee. Chief among them was the committee's acting chair, Senator Dodd. The lead HCAN partner in Connecticut was the USAction affiliate, Connecticut Citizen Action Group (CCAG), which had a long history of helping to elect progressives to office.

CCAG's political prowess meant something to Senator Dodd, who was facing the prospect of a tough reelection fight in 2010. He faced allegations that he had improperly received low-rate financing from Countrywide Financial; as chairman of the Senate Banking Committee, he had regulated the company. Now CCAG's Director Tom Swan and politically powerful allies in the labor movement informed Dodd's office that the HELP Committee's failure to pass legislation with a public option would wreak havoc among Democratic voters, the base Dodd had to hold on to if he had any chance of winning reelection.

Another, surprising source of trouble on the HELP Committee came from Rhode Island Senator Jack Reed, who we had assumed would be a reliable vote. However, on June 12, Reed wrote a letter to Obama in which he said, "Like a significant number of my colleagues, I favor a public option. But this public option may be accomplished by building on existing not-for-profit arrangements involving Federally qualified community health centers." Ugh! The last thing we needed was one more watered-down proposal, like Conrad's co-op idea, that would have no chance of competing with huge insurance companies.

Our coalition in Rhode Island, led by Ocean State Action, immediately sprang into action. It generated "grasstops" calls by organizational leaders to Reed's office from prominent unions, the state nurses association, and members of the State Legislature and grassroots calls from activists in the state who were alerted by email. Within a few days, Reed's staff had called Tara Straw, HCAN's deputy legislative director, to find out how to make the calls stop.

Reed's colleague from Rhode Island, Sheldon Whitehouse, also served on the HELP Committee. Ocean State Action had opposed Whitehouse on consumer issues when he had served as the director of the Rhode Island Office of Business Regulation, even picketing his office. Many years later, after Whitehouse had served as Rhode Island attorney general, he asked Marti Rosenberg, who was at the time the executive director of Ocean State Action, to serve on the board of a health quality initiative that Whitehouse founded. Marti remembers, "When he began to consider a run for the Senate, he asked to meet with me. We talked about the issues that had been problematic, and resolved our differences. Various organizational members of Ocean State Action began to endorse him in early 2006, and then we ran an independent get out the vote program that helped get him elected. Whitehouse publicly credits Ocean State Action and the progressive political community for helping him win."

Rosenberg, who was now the development director of USAction, called Whitehouse to ask for his help with Reed, which led to Whitehouse and his staff helping to sort out the growing problem in the HELP Committee on the public option.

Rosenberg arranged for a call with Whitehouse's health staff person, who — much to our horror — described the HELP public option under consideration. We could see North Carolina Senator Kay Hagan's hands all over this. It would be called the Community Health Option and allow each state to set up and govern its own public plan. Whitehouse's staff stressed that some on the Committee wanted to be certain that the new public plan was responsive to the particular conditions in the health care market in each state. We declared that such a proposal was lousy policy and would be met with an angry response by the progressive Democratic base. Fifty separate public plans would not have the size or bargaining clout to compete with the big insurers. Plus, the lobbying clout of the insurance and health care industry at the state level, combined with conservative state legislative bodies, would doom the public option to failure in most of the country. But remembering the concerns that Hagan had voiced at the town meeting, we raised no objections to the name change. We suggested that HELP establish state advisory committees that would advise HHS on the best way to operate the national public option in each state's exchange. A few days later we learned that our suggestions had been accepted and would be included in the HELP Committee's next draft, which was released on July 2. The HELP bill included a version of the public option that resembled the Energy and Commerce Committee's in the House. Not all that we hoped for but, still, within the HCAN principles. Another bullet ducked.

I was reminded of a few lessons in politics from this near defeat. First, even legislators who share our values can easily lose sight of what's at stake as they face the pressures of negotiating with their colleagues. Second, state organizations that had relationships with those in power could give us access and credibility when we needed them the most. We could never have achieved the same access if we had simply parachuted in campaign operatives to carry out our field activities.

On July 15, all thirteen Democrats on the HELP Committee voted for the reform legislation, with all ten of the Republicans voting no. The vote followed thirteen days of debate and included the adoption of 160 Republican amendments. Republicans were so intent on slowing down the pace of deliberations that when Dodd proposed accepting a combined package of their amendments on one vote, they refused, forcing the committee to spend hours in debate.

On the day that the HELP Committee passed the bill, HCAN started running a TV ad in Connecticut that thanked Senator Dodd for his leadership. The commercial featured Jenny Bass, a Connecticut woman who had received notice that Anthem Blue Cross was going to hike her insurance premiums by 22 percent. This was the first thank-you ad that HCAN ran. Over the course of the campaign, as more bills reached various Congressional milestones, thank-you ads would become an HCAN specialty and, not surprisingly, a favorite of the members of Congress whom we showered with gratitude.

Grandpa Twitter

On the Senate Finance Committee, Chairman Max Baucus launched efforts to seek bipartisan agreement on legislation between a small number of Democratic and Republican members. Baucus rested his hopes on his long history of collaborating with Iowa Senator Chuck Grassley, the ranking Republican member (the ranking member is the senior member of the minority party on a committee). Baucus and Grassley were friends, both avid runners from rural states. The two had partnered on a number of bipartisan efforts on contentious legislation, including the Bush tax cuts in 2001 and the Medicare prescription drug legislation in 2003.

Baucus was frequently quoted as saying that for the legislation to endure, it needed bipartisan support. But Grassley's most recent health care vote might have given Baucus some pause. In January, Grassley had voted against a major expansion of the State Child Health Insurance Program (SCHIP), because the legislation ended the requirement that immigrant children who were in the United States legally wait five years before being eligible for health care. Up until that point, Grassley had been a supporter of the SCHIP program.

In mid-June, Baucus brought together two other Democrats and four Republicans to begin a series of intense deliberations. Soon one of the Republicans, Utah's Orrin Hatch, dropped out, which left six senators: Baucus, Democrat Kent Conrad, Democrat Jeff Bingaman of New Mexico, Grassley, Republican Mike Enzi of Wyoming, and Republican Olympia Snowe of Maine.

For the next three months they would be called the "Gang of Six."

The HCAN coalition in Iowa had been working for months to influence Grassley, regularly attending town hall meetings that he held around the state. Amy Logsdon, the lead HCAN organizer, had moved to Iowa to attend Grinnell College and then joined the Iowa Citizen Action Network (ICAN) as a door-to-door canvasser. ICAN, a USAction affiliate, was the lead HCAN partner in Iowa. Logsdon traces her activism to her parents, who taught her that it was important to serve others, and to a disability in the family. "I had an early awareness from my brother's disability that the world isn't always fair and that no matter how hard you struggle you won't always get ahead."

Of Grassley, Logsdon says, "At first we thought he would be open to reform. He had advocated for an individual mandate in the past. He had a special relationship with Baucus. When Grassley started to make negative comments about reform, the HCAN partners did not immediately attack him. Instead, the coalition partners kept encouraging their members to attend the numerous town hall meetings that Grassley held around the State, encouraging the Senator to support reform. We arranged for a conference call with the Senator. I was surprised by how testy he seemed on the phone." Amy was also taken aback by the unfriendly attitude of Grassley's D.C. staff, with whom they met after the big HCAN rally on June 25.

Logsdon thinks that the major factor was pressure from right-wing Republicans in Iowa. In 2008, the Iowa Republican Party had slighted Grassley when it did not select him as a delegate to the national convention. "There were stirrings that he might be in a tough race for reelection in 2010, with a primary challenge from the right. There were murmurings among conservative blogs that a red-meat Republican needed to primary him. He was hearing that Republicans didn't want a negotiator; they wanted someone to vilify the Democrats. And conservatives at town halls yelled at him not to work with the enemy."

In June, only two weeks into the Gang of Six negotiations, Grassley said that a mere three or four Republican votes would not be enough for him to support the bill. That alone should have been a warning sign, since Republicans had not to that point provided more than three votes for any major Obama initiative. On July 6, Grassley told *Politico*, "I take pride with being an obstructionist," in referring to his scuttling a deal with a public option. By July 14, *The Wall Street Journal's* Greg Hitt reported that the only role that Grassley had played in shaping the health care legislation "has been to delay."

A verbal scuffle with a constituent at a Grassley town hall held in late June provided an opening for the HCAN coalition in Iowa to focus public attention on the Senator's opposition to reform. At the town hall, a constituent told Grassley, "I think that I should have the same insurance that you have." In response, Grassley first told the man that to get good insurance he should get a job with John Deere, the big farm-equipment manufacturer, which is based in Iowa. A few moments later, Grassley made another suggestion: "Go work for the federal government."

In response, we created a job application that people in Iowa could fill out online. HCAN pointed out that "Senator Grassley pays $356.59 per month for health care, and the most he pays when visiting a doctor or hospital is $300. Senator Grassley's health care bills are paid by you and me." As most Iowans knew, these benefits were far more generous than theirs: The average Iowan paid $600 a month in premiums for a plan with a $500 deductible.

On July 20th, ICAN held events at public libraries in three cities in Iowa, at which people filled out job applications and then walked to Grassley's office to deliver them. More than 7,000 applications for federal jobs with good health benefits were left at the Senator's offices.

The HCAN coalition kept after him at town halls, but he gave no indication that anything would change his mind. Instead, the seventy-five-year-old Senator used a new social medium to make sure that right-wing Iowans appreciated his increasing contempt for health reform. Using twitter.com, on July 24 the Senator cogently tweeted, "Misinformatio accuses me of supportin ObamaCare. NOT TRUE. I M at table making sure Govt takeovr doesn't happen, protect patience and tax-payers."

Grassley made his point on Capitol Hill as well. On July 31, *The Hill* reported that Grassley "has assured his GOP colleagues that he will not sell them out and strike a private deal with Democrats on healthcare reform, according to Republican senators." It was a public admission that Grassley was negotiating in bad faith.

In early July, Senate Majority Leader Harry Reid had tried to push Baucus to meet the looming deadline, telling him to stop negotiating with Grassley and move a bill. Still, Baucus persisted in trying to make a deal with his longtime partner. By the end of July, all hope of legislation being passed by the Senate Finance Committee, let alone the whole Senate, by President Obama's pre-August recess, was gone. Baucus just ignored Reid, who threw in the towel two weeks later by admitting that there was no way the full Senate could consider a bill before the August recess.

So why did Obama and Reid allow Baucus to persist in a clearly failed effort, which was increasingly making the entire Democratic leadership look foolish? Daschle says that Reid's style was to give his committee chairmen autonomy and that Obama thought it was important to allow the Senate leadership to do their jobs without being pressured publicly by the White House. Another problem was that Obama had assigned Jim Messina, who was Baucus's former chief of staff, to be the White House's chief liaison with Baucus. Messina's very close relationship with Baucus may have led him to give the Senator extra leeway.

At HCAN, we too shared some responsibility. Throughout this period HCAN and other progressive groups held fire. We didn't do any of the myriad things we could have done to pressure Baucus, Reid, and Obama. We could have mounted a grassroots campaign in Montana against Baucus, for instance. Still, we gave the young Obama administration the benefit of the doubt. At every one of the weekly meetings that progressive groups held with Messina, we were told to hold our fire, because a Gang of Six agreement was just around the corner.

Yet the main reason that Baucus stubbornly pursued his negotiations with Grassley and the rest of the Gang of Six may be simply because he knew no one would dare to stop him. Baucus was masterful at stifling any pressure from the left. He'd been using his power to suppress dissent in Montana for years.

The Boss of Montana

"Max Baucus has been in the Senate as long as I've been alive," Molly Moody told me. Molly, the HCAN organizer in Montana, hired by the Northwest Federation of Community Organizations (NWFCO), was only slightly exaggerating. Baucus was elected to the House of Representatives from Montana in 1974, two years before Molly was born, but didn't enter the Senate until January 1979.

Max Baucus is not an eloquent speaker, but he's still a very successful politician who had to conquer a youthful speech impediment. He has thrived as a Democrat for thirty-five years in a state that has been red for most of that time. While he often made alliances with conservatives in the Senate on economic issues, he also championed progressive causes. He was a key sponsor of the Clean Air Act and protected a key part of the Rocky Mountains from mineral exploration. He had a strong pro-choice voting record and had fought for Indian issues in Congress.

The President of the Montana Education Association, Eric Feaver, told me that the best speech he ever heard Baucus give was when he helped lead the opposition to the Bush plan to privatize Social Security. Feaver remembered that Baucus passionately recounted how Social Security began in Montana. Feaver said, "It was his shining moment."

That was one side of Baucus' record. The other was his history of working with Republicans to pave the way for important legislation that violated Democratic principles, most notably the Bush tax cuts for the rich.

Baucus' political success in Montana relied on more than being a moderate on the issues. He sought to squelch any dissent from Democrats in Montana about his positions and to use old-fashioned machine politics to control others in his party.

Jim Messina was one of the people who had run Baucus' political machine. Messina was often referred to as Baucus' second son. He had managed Baucus' campaign for reelection to the Senate in 2002, then became chief of staff for North Carolina Senator Byron Dorgan and, starting in 2005, had assumed the same role for Baucus. In 2008, Messina became the chief of staff of Obama's presidential campaign. After the election, he was appointed as a deputy chief of staff to President Obama.

As Molly Moody told me, "Montana is like a small town, everybody knows everybody, and tries to stay loyal to your friends, so it's hard to push them. When I started working in politics in Montana, Jim Messina was a friend and confidant. He was good about making politics fun. He comes from field organizing."

Eric Feaver told me, "Messina is a campaigner. He's outstanding at the strategy for winning elections. He learned at the hands of people who had a hard-core don't take any prisoners mentality. Messina plays real hard ball — you're either with me or against me."

Moody hadn't seen that side of Messina before she assumed the job of organizing the HCAN coalition. At the beginning of the health care campaign, she and others had met with the staff of Baucus' Senate Finance Committee and been encouraged by what she had heard. "There was a lot of optimism and hope that his proposal would be progressive and he would be a champion of health care reform. Even though everybody knew he would play both sides of the aisle, we were optimistic."

SEIU had made Montana a priority state, and established a Change That Works organization there, run by Jim Fleishman, who had run Baucus' reelection campaign in 2008. Jim grew up in a liberal family — *The Nation* was on the coffee table — and attended Harvard before starting a career that included running Montana People's Action, a grassroots community organizing group, for ten years.

After the election in 2008, SEIU established Change That Works (CTW) organizations in twelve states. Anna Burger, SEIU's Secretary-Treasurer at the time, told me, "We came into the election in 2008 with high hopes of both winning the election and changing public policy in a new administration. We wanted to be prepared for moving our issues after the election, when people are usually exhausted. Our goal was to organize for an economy that works for all of us, pushing for health care reform and the Employee Free Choice Act. We were even hoping to move legislation in the first hundred days. We wanted to build a grassroots organization, based on engaging voters in what was really going on, by holding conversations in kitchen tables, living rooms and church halls. We were tired of politicians telling people one thing at home and then doing something else in Washington."

To accomplish that goal, SEIU made a huge investment in building a field operation through CTW, spending $30 million from 2009 through early 2010, when the union closed the organization after health reform passed. Jim Fleishman describes the CTW organization that he ran in Montana. "We had four offices with from nine to thirteen field staff. Calling through a list of potential health care activists that SEIU had created through a door-to-door canvass in 2006, our organizers set up meetings with people in their homes to build a trust relationship and to draw out stories of people who had been harmed by the health care system. People would tell stories of not being able to see a doctor, concerns about losing their health coverage. We had a really capable press person and we'd get press on everything, which created the impression that we were powerful. We would put the people we found front and center with the many community papers in Montana. When Baucus and Tester [Jon Tester was the other Democratic senator from Montana] read clips from the Flathead Lake rural weekly, it helped them keep in the center, instead of moving to the right on health care. We did a lot of outreach — we held nine pancake breakfasts in small towns. As part of an ambulance drive around the state, we held an ice cream social in Big Sandy and a buffalo feed on an Indian reservation."

Starting in the fall of 2008, Molly and HCAN were also organizing their network of organizations and activists. Jim Fleischman says, "Molly got off to a bad start with the Baucus people, which is easy because they are very sensitive." Moody told me that the first sign of tension with Baucus' office was in October 2008 when Montana HCAN did what every HCAN organization in the country was doing, generated calls into their Congressional offices asking their senators and representatives to support the HCAN principles. But Moody was the only organizer in the country who got a call from a Congressional chief of staff. Jon Selib, who had replaced Messina, told Moody that the calls were not needed and asked her to stop them.

In January 2009, the HCAN coalition in Montana joined many HCAN groups around the country in generating calls to Congress asking for support for providing the children of legal immigrants with health coverage. Concerned that Baucus' office might take offense if they received constituent calls, Moody had informed the Senate Finance Committee staff about the grassroots effort. One of the people who was on their list and received a call from HCAN asking people to call Baucus was Selib. He was furious. He told Moody, "You're dead to me."

"Dead to me?" Another prominent Montana organizer, who has worked for Baucus, told me off the record, "They run the organization like the fucking mafia. If in any way you are perceived as standing in their way, they will shut you out. People in Montana with substantial bases have to go around them. Part of what makes them difficult to work with is that the Senator can control everything in the State. The Baucus organization was shaped largely by Messina and was still in place when he went to the Obama campaign."

Messina may have left Baucus' employment but he still was in constant communication with his former boss, and the person responsible for being the liaison between the White House and Baucus all through the Gang of Six negotiations. Molly Moody recalled, "Messina said I can't believe that you're on the wrong side of Max because we were pushing for the public option. That's when I realized that every communication that I sent out to the coalition members and grassroots would go directly to Messina."

It was no secret that another way that Baucus attempted to control dissent was by using his power to deliver public funding to organizations in Montana. At one point a prominent progressive activist in Billings, at odds with HCAN because we weren't fighting for single-payer, accused an HCAN organizer of being a "Baucus fundee." In fact, in a low-wage state like Montana, in which federal jobs were better paying than most employment opportunities, many of the people who worked for non-profits or Democratic-elected officials had worked for Baucus at one time or another. Baucus also used his own state political action committee, called the Glacier PAC, to fund Democratic candidates for state and local office, giving him other leverage to squelch dissenting voices from Democratic elected officials in Montana. The press was also intimidated by the state's senior Senator; one Helena *Tribune* reporter had seen editors refuse to run stories critical of Baucus.

The bottom line, as one longtime Montana activist told me, "If they want to, the Baucus people can crush you."

While the Baucus operation worked to squelch any pressure from the left, that didn't mean that the Senate Finance Chair intended to hurt the prospects for health reform. As Eric Feaver told me, Baucus badly wanted to get health care done. "He spoke about his historical legacy, this as the defining moment of his career. That's exactly how he looked at it," Feaver told me.

So did his "adopted son," Jim Messina. After meeting with labor leaders on health care at the White House, Messina commented, "I want this as bad as a cold beer on a hot, desert day."

The Senator From Maine

While Baucus continued to attempt to woo Grassley, another Republican Senator — and member of the Gang of Six — was the focus of one of HCAN's most intense campaigns of grassroots pressure and paid advertising. Maine Senator

Olympia Snowe was widely considered the most likely Republican to buck her party and vote for reform.

After the big HCAN rally on June 25, the HCAN delegation from Maine was incredibly frustrated. They had asked to meet with Snowe, one of the Gang of Six, weeks before the rally. Instead they had only been given a meeting with two members of her staff. One staffer sat through the meeting signing letters that Snowe's office was sending to constituents. The other spent the meeting trying to defend Snowe's trigger proposal for the public option. Snowe was continuing to try to find a middle ground on the public option issue, conspicuously refusing to sign a letter sent to President Obama on June 8 by all the other Republican members of the Senate Finance Committee. The letter called the public option a "federal government takeover" of the health system.

Late that afternoon, about fifteen of the Mainers headed to Washington's Reagan National Airport for the flight back to Portland. They had gone through security and were waiting at the gate when a member of their group who had been delayed at the ticket counter ran up to them, very excited. "Guess who's on our flight?" he said. "Olympia!"

The group decided that Tamsin Kemos should talk to the Senator when the flight touched down in Portland. Kemos lives in Brunswick, "where Maine starts," and her family "goes way back" in the state. "I'm English, French, Cherokee and a little Irish for good luck."

After telling Snowe that the group was returning from the health care rally in D.C, Kemos recalled, "In a discouraged voice, Senator Snowe asked, 'As part of single-payer?' When I answered cheerfully that actually we preferred the public option, she smiled and said that she was working really hard on that issue. I told her that the cost of health care was a personal issue for me because my husband and I are self-employed and spend $16,000 per year just on premiums. She jumped in and said that that was 'outrageous, that 'the whole system is so dysfunctional.' I said that I could find a lot of ways to use even some of that money. She said, 'Absolutely.' I joked that I could do my own personal stimulus to the Maine economy and she said that that was exactly why we needed to do something, that there isn't enough competition to make the price of insurance affordable."

"I think the decision we made to speak in a conversational way made a difference. She was very relaxed, took a lot of time to explain her committee's process and what the concerns were," Kemos said. "She assured us that she would do whatever she could to make sure it happens now and that she really understood how bad the problem is in Maine."

Elected to the Senate in 1994, after sixteen years in the House, Snowe had been the upper chamber's most liberal Republican. She was a strong supporter of women's health issues, including reproductive rights, and had pushed for more funding for women's health research and gender analysis in FDA clinical trials. In 2003, when Republicans were the majority party in the Senate, she became chairwoman of the Senate Small Business Committee.

The HCAN coalition in Maine believed that Snowe did genuinely care about providing affordable access to health care. The challenge would be persuading her to once again buck the Republican leadership. The coalition agreed that the best way to bolster her best intentions was to present her with an endless parade of stories from Mainers, particularly small business owners and women who were struggling with the high cost of health coverage and care. The strategy was to demonstrate to Snowe, and to her colleague in the Senate, Susan Collins, that there was a groundswell of support in Maine for reform.

The HCAN coalition's grassroots work in Maine was led by Maine People's Alliance (MPA) and Change That Works. MPA had a strong group of active volunteer-leaders on health care and an individual membership of 32,000, built up over years of door-to-door canvassing on health care and other issues. CTW had made a huge investment in the state, with a staff of twenty-two, most of who were organizing in the field. The coalition came up with ideas for two grassroots activities built around Maine icons. In the early spring, MPA volunteers delivered carved-out lighthouses to each of Snowe's offices in Maine, thanking the Senator for being a guiding light of bipartisanship. Shortly afterward, CTW and MPA organized the delivery of 225 Maine blueberry pies to all of Snowe's and Collins' offices in the State, as well as to all seventeen district offices of Maine's two Democratic members of the House of Representatives. Some of the pies were baked in a church kitchen by a group of grandmothers and young girls, who cut moons and stars out of pie dough to decorate the top of the pies. Each pie carried a personal message from a Mainer about health care. The lighthouse and pie deliveries garnered local press throughout the state.

In June, CTW ran another campaign that captured an iconic symbol of the high cost of health coverage in small towns around the country, not just in Maine. CTW asked Mainers to send pictures of hometown appeals and fund raisers held in communities as a way to raise money to pay for health care treatments for a neighbor. CTW made a video called "Begging for Change" that shows a stream of such appeals. One was a homemade sign, taped to a window, with the words, "Brother Peter, 4 year old son Benjamin was seriously insured in a car accident!!! Please Donate!!!"

On July 18, the HCAN coalition held a lively demonstration in Portland, in which 600 Mainers from all corners of the state marched through the streets, with signs that said, "No more begging for change." The march culminated at a rally in Portland's Monument Square, where they heard from the speaker of the House in Maine and a Republican state senator. In addition, the remarks delivered by Olympia Snowe's representative at the rally, Cheryl Leeman, caused a brief national stir.

Leeman, who was a member of the Portland City Council, read the Snowe statement to the crowd. "Our collective mission is clear: to provide every individual with access to high quality, affordable health care. We can no longer be a nation that spends more than any other, but leaves one citizen out of four without comprehensive care.... Make no mistake, our mission represents a once-in-a-generation opportunity.... That is why it is so critical that now ... we truly transform the health care system.... Let me be clear I too share the goal of meaningful reform this year. It can be done and it will be done!"

Speaking for Snowe, Leeman went on to endorse key parts of HCAN's reform plank: insurance regulations, comprehensive benefits, and financial assistance to make coverage affordable. Then she said the words almost everyone was waiting for: "I believe that the reforms we are creating will result in more competitive, affordable and innovative options for Mainers, yet we can all agree that we must not leave universal access to chance. That is why I also support a public plan which must be available from day one." The crowd erupted in the loudest and longest cheers of the day.

Those cheers were echoed in Washington the next day, when we learned of Snowe's support for a public option. When *The New Republic's* Jonathan Cohn reported it in his blog, the word spread quickly through Washington. In response, Snowe's office sent out a statement with what they said was the full transcript of the Senator's remarks. The statement said that Snowe supported a public plan from day one "in any state where private plans fail to ensure guaranteed affordable coverage." It turns out that Leeman had left out the second part of the sentence, I suspect that because like most politicians, she was loath to deliver bad news to a big crowd.

The bottom line was that Snowe was still supporting a trigger mechanism for a public option. How would the trigger work? We had no idea, because Snowe had never produced any language describing her proposal. And other than a few sentences in a barely comprehensible paragraph, she never would.

So what did Olympia Snowe believe? And what would she do as she participated in the Gang of Six deliberations? I shared the confusion that the HCAN coalition had about Snowe. She seemed like she was sincerely committed to the goals of health reform and was looking for some way to reach a bipartisan agreement. Of course, that was the problem. The rest of her Republican Party was moving further away. Some Republicans believed that the key to defeating Obama in 2012 was killing health care. Others, like Grassley, were worried about the growing anger on their right. Both aspects of the mounting Republican resistance were on display the day before the Portland rally, when a Republican Senator who was helping to lead the right-wing forces didn't pull any punches. As Ben Smith reported in *Politico*:

> "I can almost guarantee you this thing won't pass before August, and if we can hold it back until we go home for a month's break in August," members of Congress will hear from "outraged" constituents, South Carolina Senator Jim DeMint said on the call, which was organized by the group Conservatives for Patients Rights.
>
> "Senators and Congressmen will come back in September afraid to vote against the American people," DeMint predicted, adding "this health care issue is D-Day for freedom in America.
>
> "If we're able to stop Obama on this it will be his Waterloo. It will break him."[31]

Yes, the story of the so-called tea party protestors would take over the airwaves. So why didn't the tea-party rebellion of August defeat health care and break Obama, when they staged the angry demonstrations promised by DeMint? The answer, lost to the national media narrative but appreciated by Democratic members of Congress across the nation, is that HCAN and its allies out-organized the tea partiers where it counted, in the districts of vulnerable Democrats. We had been preparing for a showdown for more than a year. It would be our finest hour.

11

The Guns of August

Representative Lloyd Doggett thought that the Saturday morning neighborhood office hours he had scheduled at a grocery store in Austin, Texas, would be like so many he'd held before during his fourteen years in Congress. He'd meet with constituents like the father and son in a Boy Scout uniform who came to talk with him on August 1 about applying to a military academy. But he was in for a surprise, courtesy of an activist with the local Republican Party and Americans for Prosperity, a right-wing group funded by the billionaire Koch brothers, Charles and David, who had made their fortune in the energy business. As Doggett told 4,500 HCAN activists on a national conference call ten days later,

> If you're not from Texas, you'll know me best as the guy with the red devil horns in that YouTube mob scene video. I had what I call neighborhood office hours gathering at a local grocery store. This Saturday, the first Saturday that we were back for the recess, it's usually very productive with neighbors gathering from the area. Well, the local Republican Party organized a huge protest, about two hundred people. This was all done for camera for the local Republican Party. And after talking with them for about an hour, amidst their jeers and the like, but discussing some of their concerns about the program, they began yelling "just no" so loudly that they scared off some people and prevented anyone from hearing. Their YouTube video picks up with my departure and tries to give the impression that I've been run out of Dodge.

The YouTube video succeeded in what its instigators hoped to do — create a national narrative about an angry, bordering on violent, grassroots revolt against health care, just as Senator DeMint had promised. But the tea partiers — as the protestors soon became known, borrowing their name from the Boston Tea Party protest that preceded the American Revolution — didn't deter Doggett, nor would it deter Democrats around the country. Doggett went on to tell the HCAN activists:

> Since that first meeting I've held five town hall meetings. I feel very confident about the [health care] bill. It represents a major step forward to dealing with the number one cause of bankruptcy and the number one cause of credit card debt. When I hear people talk about rationing, I think of a ... woman with breast cancer who doesn't have health insurance and is 60 percent more likely to die than a woman who has insurance. That's just not right.
>
> If anyone thought they could sit back and leave the job of enacting health care reform to President Obama and what is barely a Democratic Congress, well, that's not the case. Unless we get the active involvement of those who believe our health care system is not serving Americans, health care reform will stall. Let me make it clear that the protestors are committed to the goal that Medicare and Social Security have no place in our society. The underlying philosophy that these people have is as radical as the tactics that they've been using to disrupt public forums across America. The media, particularly at the local level, only wants to report the fight, not the substance of what it does to help people. If your representatives in Congress have not held town hall meetings, be on the phone with them tomorrow and encourage them to be out there, face to face.

For the rest of the four weeks in the August recess, stretching through Labor Day, we took Doggett's advice. But the first week of August was especially tough slogging. On Sunday, August 2, Dr. Valerie Arkoosh, the Philadelphia physician and president of the National Physicians Alliance, was attending a large town hall meeting held in the flag-draped auditorium of the National Constitution Center. This was a modern museum dedicated to the Constitution, located two blocks from Philadelphia's Independence Hall, the home of the Liberty Bell. The

Pennsylvania HCAN coalition had recruited more than half of the 350 people who filled the hall for a meeting with Pennsylvania Senator Arlen Specter and Health and Human Services Secretary Kathleen Sebelius. Arkoosh remembers being terrified by the protestors, "I was scared. We'd had a very cursory bag check — no metal detectors. The vitriol was frightening. There were people in the room who were against the bill who had perfectly legitimate questions but they didn't get to talk either. The tea party people would not let any factual answers to be given — if anything remotely positive was said they would start shouting. I was in awe that the two of them [Specter and Sebelius] stuck it out."

Marc Stier, HCAN's Pennsylvania director, was sitting next to Philadelphia Congressman Chaka Fattah, who told Stier, "You've got to do something." Stier told me, "I tried to lead chants but we were outshouted. We were back on our heels. The vehemence and rudeness. Specter's chief of staff told me that in twenty years of politics, no one had ever treated Specter like that. People kept interrupting, kept shouting about socialism, liars, high taxes, death panels. We were just not prepared for anything like this. Press reports said that the crowd was evenly divided even though three-quarters of the people were our folks."

Video of the event shows Specter and Sebelius patiently trying to respond to questions from the protestors, valiantly attempting to make their points among a chorus of boos and derision. But the Fox News coverage, broadcast over and over again on the cable network, was edited to make the Senator look foolish, by first showing a woman asking a question of Specter, and then cutting to him answering a different question.

A week later Specter held another town hall meeting, on a Tuesday morning in Lebanon, Pennsylvania. A sizeable crowd of tea party protestors, organized by groups like the Constitutional Organization for Liberty and the Berks County Tea Party, got there early, filling the 250 seats long before the meeting started, leaving supporters of reform along with many opponents, outside in the summer heat. Specter had tried to bring order to the meeting by giving out index cards to the first thirty people who wanted to ask questions. But that only provoked a man to stand up and shout at Specter, demanding that he be given the chance to speak. "I called your office, and I was told I could have the mic to speak. And then I was lied to, because I came prepared to speak, and instead, you wouldn't let anybody speak. You handed out — what? — thirty cards? Well, I got news for you. That you and your cronies in the government do this kind of stuff all the time. I'm not a lobbyist with all kinds of money to stuff in your pocket, so that you can cheat the citizens of this country." The man repeated one line several times, "You are trampling on my constitutional rights."

Tea party protestors invoked the Constitution at town hall meetings around the country. They included a woman named Katy Abram, featured in the Fox News coverage of the Lebanon town hall, who said, "I don't believe this is just about health care ... this is about the systematic dismantling of this country.... I don't want this country turning into ... Russia ... turning into a socialized country. My question for you is," she said, stopping because everyone is clapping so loudly, "what are you going to do to restore this country back to what our founders created according to the Constitution?" People cheered, whistled, and clapped even louder. It was difficult to hear everything she said on the YouTube video, but the last sentence was "George Washington is rolling over in his grave right now."

A sample of press headlines gives a flavor of the way that the town meetings were being covered in early August: "Tempers Flare Over Health Care Plan," "Health Care Town Halls Turn Violent in Tampa and St. Louis," "Swastika Painted Outside Office of Black Congressman." But my favorite headline was this from a column in *The Washington Post* on August 16: "Crazy Is a Preexisting Condition."[32]

In the column, Rick Pearlstein asked whether the protests are "genuine grass roots or evil conspirators staging scenes for YouTube?" He answered, "They are both. If you don't understand that any moment of genuine political change always produces both, you can't understand America, where the crazy tree blooms in every moment of liberal ascendancy, and where

elites exploit the crazy for their own narrow interests."
Pearlstein and others have pointed out that American history is
replete with examples of major progressive change generating
fear, loathing and insanity from the right. *The New York Times*
economics columnist David Leonhardt recounted some of that
history: "The federal income tax, a senator from New York said
a century ago, might mean the end of 'our distinctively American experiment of individual freedom.' Social Security was actually a plan 'to Sovietize America,' a previous head of the
Chamber of Commerce said in 1935. The minimum wage and
mandated overtime pay were steps 'in the direction of Com-
munism, Bolshevism, fascism and Nazism,' the National
Asociation of Manufacturers charged in 1938.... *The Wall Street
Journal* editorial board described civil rights marchers as "asking for trouble" and civil rights laws as being on "the outer
edge of constitutionality, if not more."[33]

Another part of the history of right-wing reaction has been
the role of instigators in fomenting populist zeal. During the
New Deal, Father Charles Edward Coughlin, a Roman Catholic
priest, used the radio to foster widespread hostility to FDR's
initiatives. Fox News, and in particular its popular host Glenn
Beck, have played the same role toward the Obama administration. In an October 18, 2010, piece in *The New Yorker*, historian Sean Wilentz explained how Beck taught the tea baggers
their fascination with a distorted view of the Constitution. Beck
put a book called *The 5000 Year Leap* on the top of his required
reading list. The book was published in 1981 by a man named
Willard Cleon Skousen, who was so far right that he even became a pariah among most conservative activists. Wilentz describes the book as "a treatise that assembles selective
quotations and groundless assertions to claim that the U.S.
Constitution is rooted not in the Enlightenment but in the Bible,
and that the framers believed in minimal central government."
As Wilentz went on to write, "Either proposition would have
astounded James Madison, often described as the guiding
spirit behind the Constitution, who rejected state-established
religions and, like Alexander Hamilton, proposed a central
government so strong that it could veto state laws." With
boosting by Beck, *The 5000 Year Leap* shot to the top of the Ama-

zon best-seller list, selling more than 250,000 copies in the first half of 2009 alone — the period right before the August tea party actions.[34]

The Bible joined the Constitution that it allegedly inspired as a frequently quoted source for tea party members at town halls. At the town hall in Constitution Center a middle-aged woman held up the New American Bible, while she told the camera, "This is the only truth. The only truth."

Fox News, the Republican Party, and right-wing groups financed by corporate money weren't the only ones helping to organize popular opposition to health reform. The insurance industry was adding fuel to the fire. In one example, uncovered by the blog *Talking Points Memo,* the health insurance giant United Health wrote its employees to encourage them join in tea party demonstrations.[35]

They Needed Our Help

Marc Stier walked out of the disastrous town hall in the Constitution Center and quickly realized what every great organizer recognizes: The opposition always presents the greatest opportunities to build power. "I realized that we needed to call Carney and Dahlkemper's offices right away." Christopher Carney and Kathy Dahlkemper were two Democratic members of Congress from central Pennsylvania who represented conservative districts. "Up until then they would never tell us when they were holding a town hall. But that event in Philadelphia pushed them into our arms; they needed our help."

Stier continued, "If we hadn't been doing all this work for months, sending regular delegations to their offices, meeting with them, generating press in their districts, they would have never come to us. From that point on, we got people out to all their town halls. We pretty much outnumbered the tea partiers consistently, even in rural areas. Now we had a partnership with these members of Congress."

Stier went on to tell me, "Specter did four big meetings and we coordinated closely with them. At one of Specter's meeting, we got twenty-five of the thirty-five questions asked by show-ing up at eight-thirty in the morning for an event scheduled for three in the afternoon. At most of the town halls held by Car-ney, we turned out about 60 percent of the people. It wasn't just that we had decent numbers but that we showed up in force at all. The tea partiers expected they had America on their side, but they came and found out they didn't represent everyone in those districts. It really popped their balloons. Also, Carney knows these folks and he always talked about how reform would help his district. We'd have people there with stories that would reinforce what Carney was saying."

Roxanne Pauline, a full-time volunteer for Pennsylvania HCAN, was organizing in Representative Carney's district, which bordered her hometown of Scranton. She traced her par-ticular passion for health care to the long struggle that her brother had with a debilitating chronic disease that he'd had since he was a young boy, and that eventually claimed his life at age forty-six. Pauline's family had owned a carnival, and she had worked for years putting on shows for rock bands and NASCAR. She also worked as the promotions director for a ra-dio station and did advance work for Geraldine Ferraro's vice-presidential bid in 1984. Pauline brought her combination of showmanship and political acumen to her volunteer job organizing HCAN.

> Once the craziness started with the town halls, we equaled or overran the tea partiers. There was a town hall planned for Honesdale, a rural town, on a midweek morn-ing, when you'd normally expect a crowd of fifty. The meet-ing was held in a courtroom and three hundred people showed up, with another hundred stuck outside. The crowd was split, about fifty-fifty. We took a blow-up giant purple gorilla, twenty feet high, which represented our strength. Really, it was the only prop we had. We put the gorilla in the back of a truck and put HCAN signs in his hands. We put up a big white tent and signed everybody up, collected two hundred signatures.

> It was very hot in the room and very tense. People would boo and cheer and scream and yell. As Carney had been in the military he has a cool, calm demeanor, but his

staff was on edge. The good part was we had talked to his staff earlier so they knew they had friends and would be covered. Carney did several town meetings after that, and the gorilla came to every one, generating tons of press. At every event we got bigger and bigger. And the tea partiers seemed to get smaller and smaller.

In a rare example of reporting on a town hall that wasn't confrontational, the *Philadelphia Inquirer* described a meeting held at a city church by Representative Joe Sestak on August 13, just two days after Specter was angrily met in Lebanon by tea partiers. This time the HCAN coalition was ready. Under the headline, "Sestak health-care meeting a spoonful of sugar," the *Inquirer* reporters wrote:

> About 650 people — diverse in age, race, and occupation, but nearly all supporters of a health-care overhaul — last night crowded into a Center City church for a town meeting with U.S. Representative Joe Sestak (D. Pa.) that, in sharp contrast to recent gatherings across the country, was overwhelmingly civil. Many said they went to Broad Street Ministry because they felt their point of view wasn't being heard. "We just haven't been getting our story told," said Antoinette Kraus, an organizer with Health Care for America Now. "The supporters of health reform have been missing from the debate. We support Obama's health-care plan, and we can't wait any longer for reform."[36]

Health reform supporters were responding to the tea party protests across the nation. By early in the second week of August, the field organizers for a number of national organizations began daily calls to coordinate rapid-response activities. The calls were coordinated by Organizing for America (OFA), which prepared a Google spreadsheet on which people could add information about any town halls, demonstrations, or rallies that groups learned about. While many groups participated, the organizations that most actively turned out their members around the nation were OFA and several members of the HCAN coalition: SEIU, the AFL-CIO, AFSCME, UFCW, MoveOn, and HCAN's local partners.

The groups would report on: how many people turned out for an event, both for and against reform; the tone of the event;

whether and how it was covered by the press; and how the member of Congress had reacted. Organizers would share lessons on what worked and what to avoid. Then upcoming events were discussed, flagging key ones for the biggest turnout. One group would take the lead responsibility for organizing each event and other groups would chime in on where they could help. Every few days, groups would share press clips and pictures from events. HCAN's field director, Margarida Jorge, particularly liked the fact that the calls included real numbers and were results-oriented.

AFL-CIO's Kate Gjertson told me that after each call, "I turned around and did a call with our national unions. We had great participation. It was incredible to get rapid-response intelligence. This is where we got competitive: we wanted to do better in terms of turnout than other groups." That's the kind of friendly competition we welcomed.

Up until August, many people who make up the progressive base in the country — individual members of unions, community and faith-based groups, online organizations, constituency groups that represent women, communities of color, seniors, Democratic Party activists — were standing on the sidelines. The legislation appeared to be on the way to passage, and they were not convinced that it was as progressive as they liked. But when they saw a virulent attack from right-wing crazies capture national attention, progressives knew in their gut they had to fight back.

A Lesson From the Grandfather of Health Care Reform

The tea party protestors would attack anywhere. In 1933, the year he took office as a member of Congress from Detroit, Michigan, John Dingell, Sr. introduced legislation to create a national health insurance system. That bill has been introduced into Congress every year since, as John Dingell, Jr. picked up the mantle when he was elected to his father's seat in 1955, after the elder man's death. Dingell, Jr., who is the longest serving member of Congress, chaired the House Energy and Commerce Committee during the Clinton health care fight. In 2009, California Representative Henry Waxman succeeded

Dingell as chairman but Dingell continued to be a revered figure among his colleagues in the House.

That reverence for Representative Dingell did not extend to tea partiers who lived in his suburban Detroit district, many of who were hard-pressed by Michigan's high unemployment rate. Valerie Przywara was an organizer for MichUHCAN — the Michigan Universal Health Care Access Network, an active member of HCAN's Michigan coalition. In August, she got a call from Dingell's office asking her if she could find an uninsured person to testify at a town meeting that the Congressman was planning the next day at a community center in the town of Romulus. Przywara told me, "I knew that there was some tension around town halls, so I asked Marcia Boehm if she would be willing to tell her story. Marcia has a visible disability; she is very short and on crutches. And she is uninsured. We were taken off guard by the number of people from the tea party. There was a huge crowd, with cars parked as far as you could see."

When the forum began, a man pushed his son Scott's wheelchair to the front of the room and asked Dingell, who uses crutches himself, "Why do you want to kill my son?" In an email that Przywara sent MichUHCAN members the day after the town hall meeting, she described the scene:

> I've been around, I'm not young anymore, I've seen a lot — but last night was like nothing I've ever experienced. Congressman Dingell's forum was stormed by hundreds of "teabaggers" intent on bringing down the forum. There was a huge picture of President Obama distorted to look like Hitler, shouting, vulgar language and physical intimidation. People screaming lies about the bill — like "they're going to euthanize you." Perhaps the saddest thing I saw was a father and his six-or-seven-year-old son — the father was trying to provoke a fight with reform supporters by calling them "stupid f**kers" and poking his finger in people's chests, all while his son stood by with his fingers in his ears to shut out as much as he could of the aggressive shouting....
>
> MichUHCAN member Marcia Boehm was the uninsured spokesperson for the forum. Marcia is a very short

person in stature and her disabilities require her to use crutches to get around. Marcia teaches at Madonna part-time and owns a small business. She has been uninsured since last December and can't afford insurance due to her "preexisting conditions." She was booed, heckled and physically intimidated. Marcia stood her ground with grace, dignity, authority and self-respect.

Przywara told me that a very large man got down on his knees so he could be face to face with Marcia Boehm and said, "They are using you. You're stupid. They're going to euthanize you."

Ken Brock saw what happened at the Dingell event and took action. Brock was the chief of staff to Michigan Congressman Mark Schauer, one of the freshman members of Congress whom HCAN helped elect. Schauer had worked in community organizing and social services before being elected to the Michigan State House and Senate and finally to Congress — he'd even been a door-to-door canvasser for a Citizen Action group in Pennsylvania.

Brock told me, "It was the second week of recess and we learned that the tea-baggers had planned a demonstration on Wednesday at four o'clock. We'd seen the abuse that Chairman Dingell, the grandfather of health care had undergone, just one district over; it was very motivating. We decided to put out the 911 to our entire network: our campaign volunteers, HCAN, labor, OFA. We asked our supporters to come early. We had 600 people on all four corners of the intersection across from our office, and for the first half hour it was all supporters. When it became clear to me that we would have a good turnout I made the snap decision to have Mark come down and talk to the crowd. We probably had a two-to-one advantage in terms of the number of bodies on the street. Doing this completely demoralized the protestors on the other side. They had scheduled a weekly protest, but after that their turnout was low."

Are You Guys Going to Do Anything About This?

We also made sure to support those who remained on the fence about health reform. The right-wing protestors who lived in

Melissa Bean's conservative Chicago suburban district weren't waiting for her to hold town hall meetings to raise their angry voices. After the tension caused by the HCAN demonstration outside of Bean's Schaumberg office on June 25, Bean had become more supportive of health reform and the public option. On Saturday, August 22, the HCAN coalition got word that the tea partiers were planning a protest outside of Bean's office. John Gaudette, HCAN's lead Illinois organizer, got a call from Bean's office asking, "Are you guys going to do anything about this?" Volunteer Hal Snyder remembered, "We got there forty-five minutes before them and outnumbered them most of the time."

A week later a local Democratic party activist alerted Snyder and other Obama supporters that a TV station was expected to cover "right-wing anti-health care protestors" picketing outside of a breakfast appearance by Bean at a meeting of the Lake Zurich Chamber of Commerce that was to be held at a local banquet hall. Snyder helped organize a support group, which arrived at 7:00 A.M. and stood across from the tea party protestors, holding competing signs at the entrance of Concorde Banquets.

Grown People Acting Like Three-Year-Olds

Late in 2007, Joe Szakos was surprised to see Tom Perriello show up at the Charlottesville office of the Virginia Organizing Project (VOP), the statewide community organization that Joe had founded in 1994. Perriello was exploring a run for Congress in Virginia's fifth Congressional District, which includes a big swath of south and central Virginia. Perriello told Szakos a little about himself: He grew up in a small town near Charlottesville and had received his undergraduate and law degree from Yale. He had worked in international human rights and helped found non-profit groups that link faith to public life, both in the United States and abroad. Perriello said that he wanted to talk with Szakos about issues in the community and about whom he should talk to. He said he wanted to anchor his campaign for Congress in spiritual beliefs. That made sense to Szakos, who had spent the past 25 years organizing in the South, where people naturally bring their spiritual selves to their community work.

Tom Perriello won by 727 votes, the smallest margin of victory for any member of the House of Representatives in the 2008 election. He benefited from a big turnout of African Americans, energized by Obama's candidacy, and by a concerted push by the local Obama campaign to pull votes for Perriello. Shortly after his election, Perriello signed the HCAN principles at a meeting with a delegation of twenty VOP members, including many who had volunteered to help on his election campaign. Szakos told me, "From that point on we tried to make it a regular relationship.... Tom told me that if he only served two years and we got health care and made other big changes, that will be a great two years. He asked VOP to keep organizing support in the community."

Even though Southern Virginia is a conservative place, Szakos was still surprised by the vehemence of the tea partiers that started showing at the twenty-one town halls that Perriello had scheduled for the August recess. "We misread the town halls; we didn't know they would be so messy."

Lydia Martin, a college student at Virginia Tech who grew up in the district, was working as a door-to-door canvasser for VOP in summer of 2009. Martin told me that people that she canvassed were receptive to talking about health care early in the summer. But by August, the mood had soured. "At the doors, people would say, 'I heard they were going to kill old people." Martin was aghast at the way people behaved at the town halls, "People kept interrupting people, shouting out. They didn't let anyone else speak. It was like grown people acting like three-year-olds."

Perriello's office asked VOP to help with turning out people who supported reform, although VOP and the local HCAN coalition — which included Change That Works, the Virginia Interfaith Center for Public Policy, AFSCME, the AFL-CIO, NAACP and the Communications Workers of America (CWA) — had already started to organize. The HCAN coalition was assisted by OFA, which had built a strong base of volunteers during the presidential election.

Brian Johns, who coordinated the HCAN campaign for VOP, said, "Each group would take the lead on coordinating and doing turnout for different town hall meetings. In the end we turned out just as many supporters of reform around the district as the other side turned out opposition."

Joe Szakos described the organizing strategy for the town halls. "We called people and asked them to come to the town hall meeting to support Perriello and bring homemade signs. We recruited well-respected people, like a local teacher, or doctor to tell their stories. We asked people to get to the town hall early and to line up to ask questions. We'd arrange for a local minister to speak early on, asking the audience to be respectful. At the meetings people would hush rude tea partiers and ask them to be polite. We would also talk to the press and ask them to not report just on the craziness. We would point reporters to people with health care stories so that the coverage would be more balanced."

In Charlottesville and some of the other of Perriello's town halls, supporters came out in force, outnumbering the tea partiers. But in some of the more southern communities in the district, like Danville and Bedford, the opposition clearly had the upper hand. In this Bible belt region, it was clear that many people were listening to Glenn Beck. At a town hall meeting held in the cafeteria of a local school in Bedford, the speaker who got the most applause talked about God and abortion, "Abortion is killing this country.... It's about family, and it's about God. In the Constitution, it's our bedrock."

Everyone — at least everyone on our side — who saw Perriello in action at the town halls, came away impressed. Richard Hatch, an Army veteran who was a lineman for Verizon and was now the head of CWA's State Council, remembered watching how Perriello dealt with a hostile crowd, "You had people who stood up and lambasted him. The questions were on health care, but not really. They went after him on cap and trade, on climate change." In June, Perriello had voted for the House bill to reduce climate change. "I remember someone asked how many don't believe in global warming. About 70 percent of people raised their hands. One guy told

Perriello that he respected him for standing up and going to these meetings and then proceeded to tell him why he was the most horrible Congressman ever. Perriello told the audience that he wanted to get each person's questions first and then he'd answer them. He stood there for an hour and a half. He stayed till he'd answered every question."

After the tougher meetings, the HCAN coalition worked to reassure Perriello. Joe Szakos told me, "We learned to have someone talk to Perriello right after a tough meeting, to talk about what good happened, like we got sixteen letters to the editor today. The tea partiers were really nasty to him. Tom's grandfather was a union organizer and Tom was a wrestler in high school. He may not be big but he's tough. He stayed focused and we stayed focused."

AMERICA! Only the Insured Survive

The rudeness of the tea party proved to be a turnoff to one key swing House member from Iowa, who responded much more favorably to the Main Street Alliance, the small business coalition that HCAN backed to give small business a voice capable of countering the conservative, Republican-aligned National Federation of Independent Business and Chamber of Commerce. A good example of MSA's success is the story of one small businessman and one Blue Dog Democrat.

Mike Draper was twenty-seven and looked it, fresh faced with a ready, twinkling smile that reflected the business that he had started while a student at the University of Pennsylvania: making funny, snarky T-shirts. After graduation, Draper moved back to his home state of Iowa, and opened a Des Moines clothing store called Smash, aimed at "twenty-somethings" to accompany his business creating and printing custom T-shirts. The business grew quickly: by 2009 it had expanded from two to seventeen people and had seen a ten-fold increase in revenues. He also went through different levels of health insurance. "I'd seen all phases starting the store. From being uninsured, to buying a policy for myself, to being on my wife's policy, to buying a family policy, to buying policies for my employees. I think that sometimes as a business owner you say that you did it on your own without help from your family or the government. But there's always the compassion factor. Still, the cost of health insurance isn't related to what you sell, and it can spike if an employee gets sick."

The New York Times' Robb Mandelbaum focused on Draper in his blog, "You're the Boss — The Art of Running a Small Business," on September 1, 2009. "Until this spring, Mr. Draper's sole public statement about health care was a T-shirt for sale in his store window that read, 'AMERICA! only the insured survive.'" Mike Draper became an HCAN activist after he received an e-mail message urging business owners to write a letter to the editor of the local paper and complain about Senator Charles E. Grassley's hostility to the public option. "His main point was that the public option would be an unfair competitor to the private industry," Mike said. "Which I thought was strange, because all I had heard before was that private industry was so much superior to something like Britain's National Health Service."[37]

The email message had been sent by Sue Dinsdale, an MSA organizer. MSA and the rest of the HCAN coalition in Iowa had been working for months to persuade Des Moines Congressman Leonard Boswell to become a health care champion. Boswell, who represented a swing district, was a decorated Vietnam veteran who still ran his family's farm. He was a member of the conservative Democratic Blue Dog caucus, although he had a mostly liberal voting record.

Mike attended a town hall meeting that Boswell held on August 23: "One of the reasons that I support Boswell now is that he was in the middle, as a Blue Dog, and when we first met with him, he said he didn't know enough to form an opinion. But he was one of the people who was turned off by the shouting at the town halls. He thinks: I used to be in the military, I had government health care; that worked."

The event that turned Boswell into a strong supporter of reform happened two days later. Dinsdale took the Congressman on what MSA called a "health care reality tour," during which Boswell visited a number of MSA member businesses located within blocks of his Des Moines Congressional office.

That evening, the Congressman sat down with Mike and a group of nine local business owners, whom Draper had brought together at the request of Boswell's chief of staff. Draper recalled, "The meeting hammered home these people weren't freeloaders — they were people that the whole economy was counting on. People who own small businesses aren't necessarily activists; they approached the issue with an open mind — they didn't know if the public option or reform would help. People shared their situations with Boswell. I remember one example of a woman who worked for Maytag, which stopped paying for her coverage without telling her. Now her child could only get insurance for conditions below his neck, because he had a preexisting problem with his neck. It was powerful for him to see people that were pretty level-headed."

A few days later, Boswell told the *Times*, "The Main Street Alliance is a positive voice for small business in my district, and I listen to what they say. They have been an important perspective in the health care debate."

When Boswell headed back to Washington after the August recess, MSA and the rest of the HCAN coalition organized a hundred people who lined the street across from the airport at six o'clock in the morning to give him a warm send-off. The coalition carried "Finish the Job" signs, the theme that HCAN had adopted for rallies we were holding all over the country to send members of Congress back to D.C. to pass reform.

Don't Pull the Plug on Grandma

Although progressive forces swayed hearts and minds by pushing back on the grassroots level, an important voice in the Senate drew a different conclusion. Mike Draper also met Senator Chuck Grassley several times. Draper told me, "What I really didn't appreciate was his pull the plug on grandma remark. It was disappointing to see him perpetuate what he knew wasn't true."

Draper was referring to a comment that Grassley made at a town meeting in Iowa on August 12. Grassley told the crowd of 300, "There is some fear because in the House bill, there is counseling for end-of-life, and from that standpoint, you have every right to fear. You shouldn't have counseling at the end of life. You ought to have counseling twenty years before you're going to die. You ought to plan these things out. And I don't have any problem with things like living wills. But they ought to be done within the family. We should not have a government program that determines if you're going to pull the plug on grandma."[38]

The "pull the plug on grandma" line was Grassley's own embellishment of a virulent lie about the health reform bill that had been started by one longtime right-wing critic of health reform. Former New York lieutenant governor Betsy McCaughey had started the lie on July 16, while appearing as a guest on a conservative radio show. "Congress would make it mandatory — absolutely require — that every five years people in Medicare have a required counseling session that will tell them how to end their life sooner."

McCaughey was referring to a provision in the House health reform bill that allowed Medicare to reimburse doctors every five years for providing counseling to seniors on preparing for end-of-life decisions. The proposal had enjoyed bipartisan support as a stand-alone bill sponsored by Oregon Democratic Congressman Earl Blumenauer. McCaughey lied about the provision in two ways. First, doctors were not required to provide the counseling; Medicare would pay for the counseling if a doctor gave it. Second, the counseling is to provide information to seniors on the choices they might make when facing a potentially terminal illness, not on how to end their lives sooner.

Sarah Palin's gift for right-wing populist propaganda gave McCaughey's cruel fabrication — designed particularly to frighten seniors — a national audience. On August 7, Palin posted the following on her Facebook page, "The America I know and love is not one in which my parents or my baby with Down Syndrome will have to stand in front of Obama's 'death panel' so his bureaucrats can decide, based on a subjective judgment of their 'level of productivity in society,' whether they are worthy of health care. Such a system is downright evil."

And so the "death panels" were born. Fox News and the rest of the right-wing press spread the "death panel" claim, and soon a sizeable proportion of seniors believed it was true. The rest of the press covered the issue as if it were a debatable policy point, not a bogus twisting of the truth. *Politico* health reporter Chris Frates later told Jacki Schechner, HCAN's communication director, that giving credence to the "death panel" charge was the low point of the media's behavior during the health reform debate. In 2009, PolitiFact.com, the Pulitzer Prize winning fact-checking service run by the Florida newspaper *St. Petersburg Times*, awarded McCaughey's distortion with the "lie of the year" award.

Chuck Grassley had a reputation for avoiding the scurrilous and taking policy seriously. That he would jump on the "death panel" bandwagon was a sign of how much he had moved away from any serious intent to support reform. Grassley's final turn to the right demonstrates the main lesson that Republicans around the country took from the tea party protests in August 2009: Entertaining any notion of bipartisanship on health reform would mean facing an angry attack from their right-wing base. If Max Baucus had been grasping for straws before August, he was now left holding thin air.

The President's Town Halls

In early August, as the national press narrative played up the tea party anger, the President decided to respond by holding three of his own town hall meetings, in New Hampshire, Colorado, and Montana.

The Montana town hall was held on August 14, in an airport hanger a few miles north of Bozeman. The Secret Service designated a hay field located a quarter mile from the airport as the site for any demonstrations. Change That Work's Jim Fleischman learned from monitoring the right wing and tea party blogs and email alerts that the President's opponents hoped to stage a big protest. The HCAN coalition was ready, bringing people to the hay field as early as 7:30 in the morning, more than five hours before the town hall was scheduled to begin. The coalition turned out 1,000 people, filling a bus from the AFL-CIO hall in Billings, vans from the Indian reservation at Fort Pack, and hundreds of individuals who made their own way. While health care supporters outnumbered opponents by some two-to-one, the day was filled with verbal and sometimes physical confrontation.

HCAN organizer Molly Moody remembers, "It was challenging because the tea partiers were loud. They had a water truck and some people thought they might try to run us over. They were playing Limbaugh on the radio very loud, trying to intimidate people. We had lots of people chanting and waving signs. We were more organized, but they were loud and crazy."

Jim Fleishman told me, "They'd chant and we'd chant. People got pushed around and knocked down, but no one got hurt. A tea partier got arrested for pushing a health care supporter. It went on all day." Moody said they didn't leave until six that evening, long after the President had flown on.

Jim Fleischman believes that the HCAN coalition's success in standing up to the tea party protestors that day was a turning point. "In some ways it broke the tea party movement in the state. Up to then they were so novel. After that point they did a few more things, but the novelty was worn off. It was the peak of their public presence."

* * * *

Obama's town hall meeting in Grand Junction, Colorado, the next day was a positive turning point for the HCAN coalition's relationship with U.S. Senator Michael Bennett. Hillary Jorgensen, who worked for the Colorado Progressive Coalition, was the lead HCAN organizer in Colorado. Jorgensen grew up in a small Colorado mountain town. Her own disabilities — she has a form of dwarfism and a cleft palate that required eighteen surgeries by her twentieth birthday — gave her "a very strong sense of fairness" and firsthand experience with the high cost of health care. Up until Obama's visit, Senator Bennett had been keeping the HCAN coalition at arm's length, despite numerous visits to his offices from people with health care stories. Jorgensen told me:

> After the speech we were loading everyone back on the bus and Senator Bennett happened to pass the bus. We asked the Senator's staff person for a few minutes to talk with the Senator. He got on the bus. He heard from almost every person on the bus why health care was important. There were some really moving stories. He stayed for about thirty minutes. That was a turning point with him.

> About ten days later we called his office and asked how we could help to get the Senator's vote for health reform. From then we were working as a team. Every time Bennett's office needed a story for a Senate floor speech about a Coloradan with a health care problem, his office would call us. He was on *Meet the Press*, and said that he was willing to lose his seat over his health care vote. I think for our members who had been calling him and writing him, it was a really important moment in galvanizing their support for him: we have a leader in D.C. who was willing to lose his seat to be sure that everyone in Colorado has health care.

The Groundswell Continues

While they didn't get the national press coverage given to the angry tea partiers, health reform supporters carried out numerous events, involving tens of thousands of people, throughout August and continuing through Labor Day, when Congress was to return to Washington.

AFSCME ran a rock and roll–themed Highway to Healthcare tour, stopping in twenty cities in ten states, where supporters and local elected officials greeted a large green RV. Ralliers received health care literature designed to parody an iconic rock album, like Bruce Springsteen's *Born in the USA*, and temporary tattoos with the tour's logo. The tour encountered opposition from the tea partiers only in Shreveport, Louisiana, where a Shreveport City Council member who spoke at the rally engaged in a verbal altercation with a tea party protestor.

On August 25 — the day Senator Kennedy lost his battle with cancer — *The Kansas City Star* reported, "After an August dominated by their opponents, health care reform advocates pushed back on Monday. Supporters clearly outnumbered skeptics among the 1,300 people who attended a health care town hall meeting in Kansas City — a first for session organizer Sen. Claire McCaskill. 'It's certainly the most vociferous support I've seen for attempts to reform health care so far,' the Missouri Democrat said. 'No question about it.'"[39]

Can you imagine what the national press would have reported if the tea partiers had organized a call with 140,000 people in August? That's what the faith-based organizing network PICO did on August 19, when it held a national tele-town hall with President Obama. All around the country people held listening parties for the event, many at local churches. The call-in with the President generated a good deal of local press coverage, but was virtually ignored by the national press, which insisted on portraying the mood of the country as souring on reform.

Naomi Rothwell emailed me about the 3,000-person rally that she and her friends organized in New York City's Times Square on August 30. "The August rally was conceived on the second floor of an Irish pub in midtown. The people who worked on it were mainly in their twenties and thirties and former Obama volunteers. It was one of the most moving and exciting rallies I've ever organized or attended ... and it was the very first rally any of us had worked on."

On September 1, HCAN Ohio held a campaign-style rally in Columbus, where more than 2,500 supporters also honored Kennedy's memory. *The Columbus Dispatch* reported, "An enthusiastic crowd rallied in Columbus last evening in support of President Barack Obama's drive to overhaul health care, hoping to take back the momentum lost during weeks of sometimes angry public debate.... Sen. Sherrod Brown fired up the crowd, telling how the late Sen. Ted Kennedy asked him to draft the bill's 'public option,' a federal insurance choice to compete with private insurance companies in an effort to make coverage more affordable."[40]

Pennsylvania volunteer organizer Roxanne Pauline was so fed up with the tea partiers shouting that nobody in Congress had read the 2,000-page bill that she decided to organize a reading of the House's legislation outside the courthouse in Scranton, Pennsylvania. She put up a tent and a stage, served coffee and iced tea, and from five in the morning until ten o'clock at night some forty readers read the bill out loud. Pauline told me, "Willie, who is nine years old, read the public option part. He said he wanted to read it so that he could get his uninsured Mom health coverage. He understood every word of it."

MoveOn members organized 264 candlelight vigils for health reform around the country on September 2, dedicated to the memory of Senator Kennedy. At the events, MoveOn members read the names and told the stories of people struggling with the health care system.

Unions in Massachusetts celebrated Labor Day by joining with OFA and Massachusetts Health Care for All to organize a march and rally at the Boston Common, which attracted 3,000 people, three times what the organizers expected. All of the Democratic members of Congress who were considering a run for Kennedy's Senate seat spoke, including Boston Representative Stephen Lynch, the sole Democrat in Massachusetts who had been raising doubts about health reform. Lynch was booed off the stage.

For the first time I felt that we had the momentum we needed to carry us over the finish line. We'd taken the oppositions' biggest punch, and while we teetered in the early rounds, by the end of the bout we were well ahead on points where it mattered, with the Democratic members of Congress who would be asked to vote for reform.

The Washington Post columnist E.J. Dionne reached the same conclusion on September 3, when he wrote a column entitled "The Real Town Hall Story." Dionne wrote:

> Health-care reform is said to be in trouble partly because of those raucous August town-hall meetings in which Democratic members of Congress were besieged by shouters opposed to change. But what if our media-created im-

pression of the meetings is wrong?.... There is an overwhelming case that the electronic media went out of their way to cover the noise and ignored the calmer (and from television's point of view "boring") encounters between elected representatives and their constituents....

Over the past week, I've spoken with Democratic House members, most from highly contested districts, about what happened in their town halls. None would deny polls showing that the health-reform cause lost ground last month, but little of the probing civility that characterized so many of their forums was ever seen on television....

The most disturbing account came from Representative David Price of North Carolina, who spoke with a stringer for one of the television networks at a large town-hall meeting he held in Durham. The stringer said he was one of 10 people around the country assigned to watch such encounters. Price said he was told flatly: "Your meeting doesn't get covered unless it blows up." As it happens, the Durham audience was broadly sympathetic to reform efforts. No "news" there.[41]

SEIU's North Carolina Director Dana Cope reported that most of the 800 people in attendance at the Durham town hall supported reform. "Congressman Price wouldn't stop thanking us. It got lots of positive publicity for him. It emboldened him; he had a meeting, and lo and behold, people supported reform! He found out that it's OK to vote for this — people want it."

While Democratic members of Congress came back to D.C. prepared to move forward, the national press would be stuck on the negative narrative for a little longer, until President Obama delivered a message at a venue that the Beltway understands, a joint address to both chambers of Congress.

12

The White House Waffles

Claudia and I were lucky that the summer of 2009 was much cooler than the typical sweltering-hot and humid D.C. summer. Almost every weekend, we took advantage of the fine weather to take a day hike. On August 16, a beautiful Sunday morning, we were about to head for the Grand Gorge of the Potomac when I received an email from *Politico* reporter Carrie Budoff Brown. She wanted my reaction to a statement made that morning on CNN's Sunday news show by HHS Secretary Kathleen Sebelius that the public option was "not essential" to reform.

My reaction was that I didn't need my Sunday ruined with more examples of the White House waffling on the public option, waffling that got me angry and sick to my stomach.

Brown had also sent the email to Jacki Schechner, HCAN's communications director, who had taught me never to react to a comment until I had reviewed the entire context and exact quote. When Brown sent us the transcript of the show, we saw that she had not given us the exact quote from Sebelius, let alone the several paragraphs that preceded it. In fact, Sebelius had defended the idea of having an entity to compete with private insurance companies, while leaving open the possibility that such an entity could be a co-op rather than a government-run insurance plan. The Secretary's final sentences were, "I think what's important is choice and competition. And I'm convinced at the end of the day, the plan will have both of those. But that is not the essential element."

We put the best spin on Sebelius' comments we could, emphasizing that the Secretary had defended the need for a competitor with private insurers and that when she said it wasn't "the essential element," that did not mean it wasn't very important.

The bigger problem was that Sebelius' comments were made in reaction to a comment from President Obama, delivered the day before at his Grand Junction, Colorado, town hall: "The public option, whether we have it or we don't have it, is not the entirety of health care reform. This is just one sliver of it. One aspect of it. And by the way, it's both the right and the left that have become so fixated on this that they forget everything else."

The President was clearly exasperated by the focus on the public option. Yet the "sliver" comment was made in response to the second of two questions that he had been asked about the public option. In his characteristically long and thoughtful answers, Obama had raised and answered potential objections to the public option, explained the rationale behind it and said that he supported the kind of level-playing field public option developed by New York Senator Chuck Schumer. But of course the press focused on the "sliver" comment. The White House tried to squelch the story after Sebelius' Sunday remarks, emailing reporters, "Nothing has changed. The president has always said that what is essential is that health insurance reform must lower costs, ensure that there are affordable options for all Americans and it must increase choice and competition in the health insurance market. He believes the public option is the best way to achieve those goals."

If anyone ever needed an example of the Washington press corps' group-think and eagerness to inflame controversy, the next day's headlines could be exhibit number one: *The New York Times* lead story, "'Public Option' in Health Plan May Be Dropped," *The Washington Post* lead story: "Key Feature of Obama Health Plan May Be Out," *The Wall Street Journal* lead story: "Chances Dim for a Public Plan," and *The Los Angeles Times*: "White House backs off public health option."

Prominent Democrats pushed back swiftly, in what *Politico* called a "revolt." The next day Senator Jay Rockefeller called the public option "a must." Wisconsin Senator Russell Feingold said that a public option was needed to "bring real change," and House Speaker Nancy Pelosi, backed by a cadre of House Democrats, reiterated that the House would pass a bill with a public option.

Republicans reacted too. Arizona's John Kyl, the second-ranking Republican leader in the Senate, rejected the co-op proposal, calling it "a Trojan horse." Representative Tom Price of Georgia said, "A co-op that is simply another name for a public option, or government-run plan, will be rejected by the American people."

All of this attention infuriated the White House, which never really understood what the issue meant to the left or to the right. Characteristically, the bulk of the frustration was focused on the left. An unnamed senior advisor told *The Washington Post*, "I don't understand why the left of the left has decided that this is their Waterloo. We've gotten to this point where health care on the left is determined by the breadth of the public option. I don't understand how that has become the measure of whether what we achieve in health-care reform." [42]

What was wrong with these people? Didn't they understand that Obama's base — who were not "the left of the left" — believed him when he said before the election, "The real solution is to take on drug and insurance companies" and "band-aids and half measures won't do." [43] That's why Obama got the loudest cheers at his summer town halls when he talked about the public option. His own grassroots organization, OFA, had found it nearly impossible to mobilize the President's most enthusiastic supporters until he embraced the public option in June.

The left always regarded the public option as the one issue that meant changing the status quo, taking on big insurance. The rest of the reform plan was based on attempting to regulate an industry that had utterly failed to control health care costs. Progressives had told the President's team early on during his campaign for president, and reminded him and his advisors every time they backed away, that the public option was key to maintaining our support. So why did they — and the President too, it seemed — refuse to believe what they were being told?

The answer has to do with deep contradictions in both Obama and in the Democratic Party, contradictions that underlay the White House's strategy on reform.

It was a cliché during his campaign for presidency that people tended to see what they wanted to see in Obama. Moderates and independents saw someone who was intent on transcending partisan politics. Obama ran as a post-partisan, appealing to people's strong urge for its elected officials to move away from rancor to unity of purpose. The left saw him as a transformative figure, the miracle that an African American who could actually be elected president also represented a sharp refutation of the Bush administration's domestic and foreign policy values. Obama promised to usher in a politics founded in the progressive values of community and common dignity.

Obama biographer David Remnick points to Obama as a great conciliator, a bridge between black and white America. To be that bridge, Obama learned to be successful in both worlds. Obama's cool demeanor is essential to his being accepted in a white America that could never tolerate an angry black man. Obama's spiritual grounding, his belief that "I am my brother's keeper, I am my sister's keeper," as he said in accepting the Democratic nomination in Denver, reflects the spiritual core that has allowed black America to endure centuries of oppression. Obama has a deep commitment to justice and a belief that getting there involves a continual process of reaching across divides and taking half steps.

The President's predilection to look for common ground, and his great intellect, were assets as a law professor, as he grasped and analyzed a multitude of views on an issue. That ability led him to believe that he could build consensus around rational policies in order to resolve difficult issues. Obama has said that a mistake he made in the first two years of his presidency was to pursue what he viewed as good policy, regardless of politics. But that's really a conceit; the two often cannot be separated. As a politician, the President should know better. The public option is a case in point, but far from the only example during his first two years in office or in the health care debate.

It is true that, as Obama and his advisors argued, the public option was not essential to the framework of reform proposed by the President and Democratic leaders of Congress. Under the legislation, the public option would have initially covered only a small percentage of people. That narrow policy view created the rationale for Obama and other policy advisors to throw their hands up at all the fuss. In doing so, they ignored the important *policy* reasons that the public option was so *politically* important to the left. The public option really did offer the potential to change the status quo, even if it began modestly. Having a government-run competitor to the private insurance industry would have created the foundation for a national health insurance plan that could do what the insurance industry was incapable of doing: putting the delivery of quality care ahead of maximizing profits. In doing so it would make a lot of powerful interests angry — which brings up other contradictions in the President and Democratic Party.

The best evidence that the public option had the potential to reform the American health care system is the vigorous campaign by the insurance industry and health care providers against it. If the public option was really just a sliver of reform, they would not have worked so hard to defeat it. Every time the political prospects for the public option dimmed, the price of health insurance industry stocks rose.

A fundamental element of the White House strategy to pass reform was to placate major interest groups. From the beginning of the debate, President Obama had sent out conflicting messages about the insurance industry: The industry that was responsible for tormenting his mother on her deathbed was now going to be part of the solution to the nation's health care problems. The White House message mavens wanted to have it both ways. While their research found that ending denials of preexisting conditions was the single most powerful message with the public, they told me that they did not want to link that issue to anti-insurance industry rhetoric. Doing so would contradict the President's image as being a bridge builder.

The White House had negotiated a number of deals with the health industry, designed to win their support for reform, including agreeing to oppose a robust public option, which would have the greatest clout to control how much providers got paid.

At the same time, many Congressional Democrats were swayed by industry campaign contributions and lobbying. I want to be clear: Many Democrats led with their values, and supported strong reforms including a robust public option and other measures opposed by well-financed interests. One example was the support in the House for requiring all but small employers to help pay for covering their employees. These Democrats stuck to their principles despite aggressive lobbying by well-financed interests in their districts and states. But with universal Republican opposition to reform — motivated by a lethal combination of ideology, politics, and corporate pressure — we needed the support of 85 percent of Democrats in the House and 100 percent of Democrats in the Senate. On some issues, like a public option tied to Medicare rates, lobbying by hospitals and doctors meant we lost the support of many Democrats in both houses of Congress.

It is also worth noting that some of the health policy staffers at the White House were close to the health care industry. For example, Nancy-Ann DeParle, the White House health care czar, had worked in and served on the boards of several health industry corporations after she left the Clinton administration, where she administered the Medicare and Medicaid programs.

Moreover, the President and White House's frustration with the left revealed an arrogance that was demonstrated in another remark made by that anonymous senior advisor to *The Washington Post*. In speaking about the left, the advisor said, "They're forgetting why we are in this." In another words, the left doesn't understand that the reason we are trying to pass health reform is to provide affordable coverage to people, not to achieve some sort of ideological goal through a public option. The people that I worked with understood this very well — we represented people who were dying and going bankrupt because of our lousy health care system. But unlike the White

House, we didn't think that because the public option was being attacked by powerful interests, the right wing and Republicans, we were supposed to stop fighting for the best possible reform that would actually fix the problem.

The White House also made a miscalculation about the right and Republicans. The administration seemed to think that if the public option were dropped, it would take the sting out of the Republican attack on "a government takeover of health care." I wrote a column for *The Huffington Post* in August entitled "The 'Government Take-Over' Isn't about the Public Option." I pointed out: "No matter what the president proposes on health care, the right will loudly label it a 'government take-over.'... Every component of Democratic health reform plans is characterized as a government take-over: establish standard benefit packages for insurance plans, require individuals and businesses to contribute to coverage, set up an insurance marketplace, etc.... If the public option weren't part of the Obama/Democratic reform plan, the right would still be screaming about a 'government take-over' as loudly as it is now.[44]

As we were to see, for nine months after the health care law was passed — without a public option — the Republicans continued to relentlessly demonize the law as a "government take-over." *PoliticoFact.com's* 2010 "lie of the year" was "the government takeover of health care."

The White House also knew that giving up the public option, or for that matter "compromising it" with a proposal like a co-op, would not soften Republican opposition. The President had directly asked Grassley if he could support the legislation without a public option; the Iowa Senator had said no.

Yet for all the waffling on the public option, the committed side of the President was evident too. Even before the August recess, White House chief of staff Rahm Emanuel had been pushing to drastically scale back reform, arguing that it posed too big a political risk. Instead, Emanuel advocated that the President propose legislation that would cover only ten million of the uninsured by expanding coverage for children and single mothers. But Obama refused to retreat from his fundamental goal of striving toward universal coverage. Comparing Emanuel's proposal to the estimates that thirty-two-million uninsured people would receive coverage under the plans making their way through Congress, he said, "Remember, if we do [retreat], twenty-two million go uninsured."[45]

The President's Speech

During the week before Labor Day, the White House announced that the President would give an address to a joint session on Congress on health care. The goal of the speech was to move the national narrative on health care from the angry tea-party opposition to the urgent need to realize the promise of quality, affordable health care for all.

In the run-up to the speech, the waffling from the White House continued. Assurances of support were mixed with trial balloons about abandoning the public option. The anxiety on our side soared. On September 3, MoveOn sent an email petition to their list of five million members that read: "President Obama, we're counting on you to fight for bold change on health care — including a strong public health insurance option. It's the key to breaking the stranglehold that private insurers have over our health care system."

We did a similar online petition at HCAN, which produced the highest online traffic we have ever had in a single day. A number of online petition efforts by several progressive groups gathered more than 400,000 signatures supporting the public health insurance option in the week before the speech.

Frustration on the left boiled over to the gates of the White House. On September 8, the Progressive Change Campaign Committee (PCCC), an Internet-based organization that had been pushing conservative Democratic senators to support the public option, organized a demonstration led by former Obama campaign staffers outside the White House. They delivered a petition signed by more than 600 Obama campaign staffers, 40,000 Obama volunteers, and 60,000 Obama donors, which read, "Any health care bill without a public option is not change we can believe in."

Two days before his speech to Congress, Obama went to Cincinnati and delivered what *The Washington Post* described as a "stirring, campaign-style speech to thousands of union members celebrating Labor Day." The *Post* reported, "Obama drew wild applause when he reiterated his support for a government-run insurance plan, one of the most contentious of the unresolved health-care issues and a key change that labor officials strongly support." I was glad to see the President out on the hustings, giving a fiery call to arms for health care. But I knew that didn't mean that he would be so strong two nights later when he addressed Congress.[46]

The night of the big speech Claudia and I were together at our apartment. The President delivered what was, in very many ways, a wonderful address. He began with a clarion call for health reform, saying, "I am not the first President to take up this cause, but I am determined to be the last.... We are the only democracy — the only advanced democracy on Earth — the only wealthy nation — that allows such hardship for millions of its people." He then called for bipartisan support and outlined the basic structure of reform before turning to "address some of the key controversies that are out there." He concluded by reading parts of a letter written by Ted Kennedy, which the Senator asked be given to Obama after he died. "Kennedy expressed confidence that this would be the year that health care reform — 'that great unfinished business of our society,' he called it — would finally pass.... 'What we face,' [Kennedy] wrote, is above all a moral issue; at stake are not just the details of policy, but fundamental principles of social justice and the character of our country.'"

In the section of the speech in which he addressed "controversies," however, the other Obama, the compromiser, came out. The President spent seven paragraphs — more than ten percent of the speech — discussing the public option. Most of those paragraphs were awesome. He quoted statistics from the HCAN report on the monopoly-like concentration of the health insurance industry. He quoted, without naming him, insurance company whistle-blower Wendell Potter's testimony to Congress that insurance companies are rewarded by "Wall Street's relentless profit expectations" for dropping coverage of the seriously ill. He clearly defended the public option proposed in Congress, and he reminded Congress "that a strong majority of Americans still favor a public insurance option of the sort I've proposed tonight."

But then he spoiled the party:

> The public option — the public option is only a means to that end — and we should remain open to other ideas that accomplish our ultimate goal.... For example — for example, some have suggested that the public option go into effect only in those markets where insurance companies are not providing affordable policies. Others have proposed a co-op or another non-profit entity to administer the plan. These are all constructive ideas worth exploring.

Within thirty seconds of the end of the speech — I'm not exaggerating — my phone rang. Robert Pear from *The New York Times* wanted to know what I thought of the President's possible compromise. I gave him an answer that I knew would not make news and that, while true, covered up my anger. I told him that the President's remarks were nothing new. The President did tonight what he had always done. Pear pushed me a number of times to express disappointment, but I wouldn't bite.

Why not? For two reasons. The first is that if HCAN, by far the biggest, most powerful progressive health care campaign in the nation, admitted that the President was willing to give up the public option, the game would be lost. Once we admitted defeat, many of our allies in Congress would follow and the media would write a final obituary. Instead, we had to focus on the President's strong preference for the public option and confidently state our commitment to help him pass what he most wanted. The second reason is that the HCAN Steering Committee did not want the campaign to be critical of the President, and I could only break with that if the Steering Committee agreed.

Dominating the news coverage of the speech the next day were two words shouted out during Obama's address by South Carolina Republican Congressman Joe Wilson. When Obama said that his plan would not insure illegal immigrants, Wilson shouted out, "You lie!" It was a remarkable breach of decorum, a bag of tea party anger delivered on national television to the President. And it would soon lead to one more weak-kneed policy concession by the White House.

While the President's advisors told progressives that Obama had taken on the health insurance industry, that wasn't the view from Wall Street. *The New York Times'* Reed Abelson reported:

> Even Mr. Obama, who had recently stepped up his crit- icism of the industry, seemed to soften his stance on Wednesday.... Additionally, he emphasized that he did not want a drastic move away from the current system, under which private companies provide coverage to the bulk of working Americans who are insured. "I have no interest in putting insurance companies out of business," he said.[47]

While the White House may have continued to pull its punches on the insurance industry, HCAN didn't. From the very beginning of our campaign, we knew that the only effec- tive antidote to the fear mongering that had reached fever pitch during the August tea party protests was to focus anger at the health insurance industry. After August, it was our moment to do that big-time.

13

If the Insurance Companies
Win — You Lose

I wish that I could start this chapter by having you watch a TV ad that HCAN began to run on September 15. If you want, you can view the ad on the Fighting for Our Health website, at www.fightingforourhealth.com. Below is the text and description of the ad, but if you don't actually watch it, you'll miss the wonderful baritone of the announcer, the ominous piano underscore and the energy at which the pages flip through the book that is shown on the screen, entitled "How to Get Rich," authored by "America's Health Insurance Companies." The book flips open to Chapter One, titled "Charge A Lot," which has a picture of a pile of money. The announcer intones: "Raise health insurance premiums four times faster than wages."

The pages of the book turn to Chapter Two, "Make A Lot," with an image of a mansion, and the announcer reading: "Pay your CEO $24,000,000 a year." Next the pages flip rapidly to Chapter Three, "Deny A Lot," pictured by a "DENIED" stamp on a pile of forms, and the announcer saying: "Deny one out of five treatments prescribed by doctors."

The screen goes black and the announcer reads the message displayed on the screen in white capital letters: IF THE INSURANCE COMPANIES WIN, YOU LOSE.

Then the mood and image change. As the piano becomes upbeat, the book flips back to the front cover, but now it has a different title, "REAL HEALTH CARE REFORM," along with a picture of a smiling family sitting in front of their home. The announcer reads the message on the white screen: "We want good health care we can afford, with the choice of a public health insurance option."

On the same day that we launched the television campaign, which ran on CNN and MSNBC cable news shows around the nation and on the big Sunday morning news shows, we ran print ads in all the Capitol Hill publications. At the bottom of the ad was our new tag line: "We want good health care we can afford, with the choice of a public health insurance option." The online version of the ad, which ran on Google, Facebook, and several political blogs, showed a slot-machine like row of "$ $ $" signs above our message, and then the web ad messages shifts to: "Let's not give them what they paid for."

A week after the first ads launched, HCAN partners held a "Big Insurance: Sick of It!" day of action around the nation. *The Wall Street Journal's* Avery Johnson led off her story on September 22, under the headline, "Protestors Rally with Gripes Against Big Health Insurers":

> Health-overhaul advocates turned out across the country today at rallies targeted against insurance companies and promoting a public insurance alternative as part of health legislation. MoveOn.org, Health Care for America Now and labor unions said they organized about 150 gatherings, which followed last month's raucous town-hall meetings focused on the health overhaul…. The Health Blog caught up with the rally in New York, where about 500 people holding signs and chanting "corporate greed has got to go" clustered outside UnitedHealth Group's Manhattan offices to deliver a list of demands to the insurer. One group, dressed to portray wealthy health-insurance executives, held signs that said, "Because nothing says freedom like denying claims."

New York City's "Big Insurance: Sick of It!" action outside UnitedHealth was one of six flagship demonstrations targeting the nation's biggest insurers. Rallies were held outside the Minneapolis headquarters of UnitedHealth, the Indianapolis offices of WellPoint, and the Cigna headquarters in Philadelphia. Two other large-scale actions took place in Hartford, Connecticut, where Aetna is headquartered and in Milwaukee, where WellPoint CEO Angela Braly was delivering the keynote speech at Marquette University's annual Business Leaders Forum luncheon.

The decision to launch the insurance campaign marked a new stage in HCAN's work. The basic message wasn't new — the Magic 8-ball ad we ran a year earlier was that you couldn't trust the health insurance companies to fix the health care mess. Yet now we were making a concerted bid to shape the legislative debate at a crucial time.

In the aftermath of the tea party protests, it was imperative that we bear down hard on the insurance industry. Even Republican message guru Frank Luntz had told Republican members of Congress, "The American people blame the insurance companies more than almost anybody else for why health care is such a mess in this country right now."[48]

One of the tensions that we faced in the HCAN campaign was whether to spend more resources pressuring members of Congress or protesting against the health insurance industry. While we had engaged in a few insurance protests in the summer of 2008, they had little impact on the national dialogue in the middle of the election campaign. With the support of the HCAN Steering Committee, I had decided to focus our energy on directly moving members of Congress. We had spent relatively little on television advertising during the first eight months of 2009, and what we had spent was almost all aimed at individual members of Congress.

As August ended, most people believed that the health care bill would be enacted before Thanksgiving, with an outside chance that it might be pushed until the Christmas break. It was time for us to change our strategy to meet the new challenges. HCAN's Deputy Director Ethan Rome urged a change in focus, which he summarized in a memo on September 1, "We need to weave together everything we do into a coherent story that redefines the national debate and takes back the momentum. Our job is to clearly define the two sides of the fight by driving the anti-insurance frame through aggressive media and field activities. We have to force members of Congress to choose which side they are on, in part by narrowing our public focus so we have a bigger voice and a more impactful message."

The message "If the insurance companies win, you lose" was the inspiration of Saul Shorr, the lead partner in the small political advertising firm Shorr, Magnus, Johnson. He had come up with the slogan when Rome and I interviewed him earlier in the summer, as we were looking for a new firm to do our advertising. Rome and I liked Shorr immediately; he had a sharp sense of humor, an instinct for the jugular, and even though his firm represented many prominent Democratic members of Congress, he was willing to take on the powers that be.

One of the questions that we asked potential ad firms was how they would spend the approximately $10 million we had available for paid advertising, which was very little for a national campaign. Shorr's advice was to focus the advertising relentlessly on the insurance message. Our audience for the advertising wasn't the broad American public — it would have taken $50 million to even begin making a dent in public opinion. Instead, our goal was to reach two groups. The first was the people most likely to respond to our message and act by sending an email, calling their member of Congress or simply talking to people they knew about the issue. The second audience was members of Congress and their staffs, along with the national press corps that Congress followed so closely. In addition, we would still target some ads at particular members of Congress, but only in specific circumstances.

Between September and December, Shorr and his partners created three additional TV ads and ran seven more print ads. The print ads, aimed at Congress and the press corps, were daring by D.C. standards. Each had the same format: white headlines against a black background. The second ad said: "The insurance industry employs 1,796 lobbyists in Washington. Do you think they are lobbying for you?" Another ad trumpeted: "Since January insurance companies have given more than $10 million to current members of Congress. Let's not give them what they paid for."

The second TV ad was launched on October 1. "Mansion" juxtaposed the home of UnitedHealth's excessively wealthy CEO Stephen Hemsley — who made $57,000 *an hour*, counting his stock options — with an average middle-class family home in foreclosure, which represented the 62 percent of bankruptcies caused by medical debt.

We actually delivered the "Mansion" ad to Hemsley's house in Minneapolis. Take Back Minnesota, the HCAN partner group, drove a moving van equipped with a video screen to Hemsley's home and showed the ad outside his residence. The moving van was a symbol for the people who were losing their homes due to medical debt, looking for a place to live.

An HCAN moving van also visited the home of the CEO of Cigna, Ed Hanway. Stacie Ritter rang the doorbell to Hanway's stately brick mansion, replete with a carriage house. HCAN's Pennsylvania director, Marc Stier, had met Ritter at an HCAN meeting when she told a moving story about how Cigna had refused to pay for the costly human growth hormone treatment needed by her young twin daughters. Her daughters, now eleven, were diagnosed with leukemia when they were four. They both needed stem cell transplants and other cancer treatments. The twins survived, but the glands controlling their growth were damaged. To continue growing, their doctor-recommended that they receive growth-hormone injections regularly, which CIGNA refused to pay for. Stacie and her family had already filed for bankruptcy due to the high out-of-pocket medical costs incurred from their daughters' treatment.

Ritter decided to ask Cigna CEO Ed Hanway if she could stay in his carriage house "just until we can get back on our feet." In 2009, Hanway made $12.2 million; Hanway's mansion in the Philadelphia suburbs was one of several homes he owned, including a beach house in New Jersey valued at $13.6 million.

After the moving van arrived at Hanway's house, Ritter walked up the winding front path, past beautifully manicured shrubs to the front porch of the brick mansion, ringed by four white columns and rang the doorbell. In front of the home, HCAN supporters held signs, including neighbors of Hanway who had earlier sponsored an HCAN house party. They had been unaware that their neighbor was the CEO of one of the nation's largest health insurers. Ritter stood there for a while before ringing the doorbell again, saying, "I'm going to give him one more chance." Finally, she got out a pen and loose-leaf paper and wrote him a short note asking him if he could stay at the carriage house and encouraging him to call her. She stuck the letter inside the entrance frame of Hanway's towering front door and left.

Although Hanway remained cold to the pleas of Stacie Ritter and others whose care he denied, one former Cigna employee had not been deaf to those cries. The unnamed "former insurance executive" whom President Obama quoted in his speech on September 9 was Wendell Potter, who had risen to the position of vice-president of communications at Cigna and was now working closely with HCAN to expose the industry's practices to the nation.

* * * *

I first met Wendell Potter at Philadelphia's 30th Street train station in April 2009. Potter looks like someone's kind uncle. He has short, thinning gray hair, wears old-fashioned black eyeglasses, and has a calm, gentle voice with a slight hint of his native Tennessee accent. He dresses in the conventional corporate garb of a boring big insurance company like Cigna — blue suits, blue shirts, and dark blue ties — where he worked for eighteen years, rising to the position of vice president of communications. But underneath Potter's quiet demeanor was a man wanting to scream out to the world: Don't trust the health insurance companies when they say they want to fix health care. It's all an elaborate game meant to distort the political process to increase their profits! I know. I did it for them for years.

Potter shared with me the story that had led him to want to make public amends. Potter had started out as a journalist, but when he moved back home to Tennessee, he took a number of public relations jobs, including working for a hospital system run by the Baptist Church and then moving to the Tennessee-based health insurance company Humana. As Potter wrote in his book, *Deadly Spin*, "One of the executives at Baptist begged me not to go 'to the dark side,' meaning cross over to for-profit health care. But I didn't fully understand yet how different it would be, and I saw it as a great career opportunity. Taking a well-paying job with great benefits at a Fortune 500 company seemed like a no-brainer." After a few years at Humana, he moved over to Cigna, climbing further up the corporate ladder.

Potter grew up in a struggling family in the Appalachian hills of eastern Tennessee. His father had been a tobacco farmer and then spent two decades working in a glass factory. On July 20, 2007, Potter traveled to the Wise County, Virginia, fairgrounds to hear presidential candidate John Edwards. What drew Edwards to the fairgrounds was a free health clinic that had been organized by the Remote Medical Group, an organization originally formed to provide health care to poor people in the third world but had found an urgent need for their services right at home. Potter wanted to hear what Edwards had to say, as part of his job at Cigna was preparing the health insurance industry's position paper on health reform.

What Potter saw, in a muddy field filled with stalls usually used for livestock shows, shocked him. Here were hundreds of people waiting patiently to get health care. They looked just like the neighbors he had grown up with, and whose conditions he had escaped. For many of them, it was their one opportunity a year to be treated. Here's how Potter described the scene in his book:

> Nothing prepared me for what I saw when I walked through the gates. The contrast to the calm on the outer side of the wall was stunning. The scene inside was surreal. I felt as if I'd stepped into a movie set or a war zone. Hundreds of people, many of them soaking wet from the rain that had been falling all morning, were waiting in lines that stretched out of view. As I walked around, I noticed that some of those lines led to barns and cinder block buildings with row after row of animal stalls, where doctors and nurses were treating patients. Other people were being treated by dentists under open-sided tents. Many were lying on gurneys on rain-soaked pavement. Except for cur-

tains serving as makeshift doors on the animal stalls, there was little privacy. And unlike health fairs I had seen in shopping centers and malls, this was a real clinic. Dentists were pulling teeth and filling cavities, optometrists were examining eyes for glaucoma and cataracts, doctors and nurses were doing Pap smears and mammograms, surgeons were cutting out skin cancers, and gastroenterologists were conducting sigmoidoscopies. Huge amounts of medications were being dispensed.[49]

Two weeks later, Potter boarded one of Cigna's corporate jets, where he was served a meal on gold-plated china. The contrast between what he had just witnessed in rural Virginia and the luxurious service on the Gulfstream Jet was too much for him. He could no longer hide from himself that his own good fortune and Cigna's obscene wealth derived from a health system that left millions of people destitute. After a few months of letting this truth sink in, he realized he had to come clean at a crucial time for health reform.

Quitting his job at Cigna was the first step. The second was figuring out the most effective way get his story out. Eventually he connected with Mike Morrill, a progressive activist in Pennsylvania who had worked with USAction. Morrill brought him to a Herndon Alliance meeting in D.C. where he met HCAN communications director Jacki Schechner, who encouraged me to talk with him. Potter also trusted HCAN's Research Director Avram Goldstein, whom he had gotten to know when Goldstein was covering the health insurance industry for Bloomberg News.

Potter needed help to become a whistleblower in two ways. The first was guidance on the best way to get his story out. The second was financial support. After leaving Cigna, he had been offered other corporate jobs — not in health insurance — and if he turned those down, he needed to have some income. I had to decide whether his story would resonate enough with the media to be worth raising money to broadcast it publicly.

In person, Wendell Potter is a very low-key guy. That would be one of his great strengths on television and as a public speaker, what *Time* magazine's Kate Pickert called "the soft-spoken Dad." Yet I didn't sense this power while sitting at a coffee table in the cavernous Philadelphia train station. And Potter didn't bring a smoking gun to the debate either, unlike Dr. Linda Peeno, the former medical director of Humana who confessed to being responsible for a man's death because she had denied him care. I liked Potter, but I wasn't sure that his story of how the insurance industry's business practices — dumping individuals and small businesses and promoting high-deductible plans — would attract more than fleeting media attention.

I asked Potter to put his story in writing, as he would if he were introducing himself in an op-ed for a major newspaper. Only after I read his article did I feel the power of what he had to say. He had managed to convey his passion and unique insight in a deeply compelling way on paper. The same story we had been trying to disseminate was being told by an inside source with rich detail and credibility. I was sold. Next, he needed an organizational home that made sense for him as a whistleblower, which he found in the Center for Media and Democracy. The Center's mission is "investigating and countering P.R. campaigns and spin by corporations." Perfect. I arranged for the Tides Foundation to make a grant to the Center to support getting Potter's voice out in the public.

To launch Potter, HCAN's legislative staff connected him with the investigative staff of Senator Jay Rockefeller's Senate Commerce Committee, which had extensive experience in grilling corporate witnesses. After a two-hour session and a background check by the Senate, Potter was asked to testify before the Commerce Committee on June 24, a day Potter said was, next to his wedding day, "the scariest day of my life." As he wrote: "Over the coming months, I would testify before two other congressional committees; appear at two press conferences with House leaders, including Speaker Nancy Pelosi of California; meet separately with dozens of members of both the House and the Senate and with scores of Hill staffers; and travel to more than half the states for speaking engagements and interviews."[50]

Potter's calm, avuncular demeanor, his obvious sincerity, and his old-fashioned looks and Southern accent all made him the perfect spokesman for revealing the health insurance industry's hypocrisy. After Labor Day, he became an instant celebrity, with appearances in the first half of the month alone on ABC's *Good Morning America*, CNN's *American Morning* and *House Calls with Dr. Sanjay Gupta*, and MSNBC. Over the next few months he became a regular guest on MSNBC's evening news shows, with invitations from Ed Schultz, Keith Olbermann, and Rachel Maddow.

He also became a celebrity at HCAN rallies around the nation. For example, during one month in the fall of 2010, Potter traveled to address audiences in Chicago, Washington, Little Rock, Los Angeles, New York, Boston, Nashville, Nebraska, and Iowa.

On September 22, Potter joined Stacie Ritter as a speaker outside his old employer's headquarters at an HCAN "Big Insurance: Sick of It!" demonstration with more than 400 people. Two weeks later, on October 6, Stacie and HCAN were back at Cigna's modern blue-glass-and-stone building in downtown Philadelphia as part of the next national wave of anti-insurance organizing. The theme of the demonstrations was "It's a crime to deny our care." HCAN activists draped the insurance company building with long rolls of bright-yellow crime scene tape, on which we had printed the slogan. In some places demonstrators even blocked the doors of insurance company headquarters as acts of civil disobedience.

Outside Cigna's Philadelphia skyscraper, a crowd of a hundred HCAN activists held signs and shouted out call and response chants, "Health care — Now" and "Cigna — Shame." Five demonstrators who had blocked the doors to the Cigna building were arrested, including: Joan Kosloff, whose son died in 2006 after he was denied health care; seventeen-year-old Michael Ladson, whose brother has a disability and has had problems getting the care he needed; SEIU member Dennis Short; Ray Torres, a member of the First United Methodist Church; and HCAN's Marc Stier, who was smiling and undaunted as he was led away in handcuffs.

Connecticut Citizen Action Group Director Tom Swan, who had joined the HCAN staff part-time to drive our anti-insurance activities, suggested that we take advantage of an AHIP conference to bring the action to D.C. The AHIP conference was scheduled on October 22 at the Capital Hilton, only a few blocks from the White. We decided we would crash their conference, both inside and outside the hotel. On the day of the AHIP conference, several Capitol Hill newspapers carried another of the now familiar HCAN print ads. However, unlike our other ads, which were basically a headline, this ad was an open letter to AHIP's president Karen Ignagni from seven individuals whose families had been harmed by the insurance industry, which read:

> We have lost siblings who could not get health insurance coverage due to preexisting conditions. We have been overcharged, only to have our policies cancelled when our health care needs became less profitable for your members. We have been given the runaround in the midst of hospitalization and been forced to declare bankruptcy due to medical bills that your companies refused to cover. We have had to move back in with parents as medical expenses swallowed up our salaries and our savings.

The families invited Ignagni to meet with them at the Hilton that afternoon. "We are siblings and parents and survivors who believe you should look us in the eye, hear our stories, and understand what you are lobbying against. We plan to be at the Capital Hilton Hotel at 3pm on Thursday and hope to see you there."

At 2:30 we held a press conference at the Hilton — the first in-person press conference we'd held in D.C. since our launch fifteen months earlier. Members of the seven families briefly told their stories to a large bank of news cameras and print reporters. Pittsburgh Congressman Mike Doyle came to the press conference to support one of his constituents, Georgeanne Koehler, whose brother Billy died because he lost his job and health coverage. Billy Kohl had received a cardiac defibrillator after he had a heart attack when he was thirty-nine years old. Several years later, he lost his insurance when the company he worked for went out of business. In 2007, he collapsed and was hospitalized. He was told that he needed to get a new defibrillator, which cost $10,000, money that he didn't have. He was working as a delivery driver at a pizza place, and his employer didn't offer insurance. The doctor told him to come back for the new defibrillator when he had the money. As Georgeanne told the press, "On March 7 he was coming home from work, drove two blocks, came to a stop sign, put his car in park and slumped against the steering wheel. The battery in his defibrillator was dead, so it was unable to stop his heart attack. He was 57 years old."

When the press conference was over, and Ignagni did not accept our invitation to come to the room we'd rented in the hotel, I led the seven families outside, where a crowd of more than 600 HCAN demonstrators waited to welcome them to cheers and chants.

We had another surprise for the AHIP conference attendees, one that could not be so easily ignored. As Republican pollster Bill McInturff was about to address a room full of health insurance representatives, a woman stood up and started to sing to the tune of "Tomorrow" from the musical *Annie*, a song called, "A Public Option Tomorrow." We had provided some support for a group of progressive pranksters called Agit-Pop to stage guerilla theater inside the AHIP meeting. One after the other, several of the "AHIP singers" stood and in fine, operatic voices, sang the song that concluded with "The option, the option, the public wants an option, without it reform is a corporate giveaway." As the song ended, the Hilton security guards escorted the half-dozen singers out of the room.

The guerilla theater action was captured on video by an Agit-Pop member in the audience. The video hit YouTube later that day, and it quickly had more than 130,000 views. The musical prank was reported on CNN and MSNBC and later by Jon Stewart on Comedy Central's *The Daily Show*.

More widely noticed on Capitol Hill was a comment by an AHIP lobbyist at the conference. While AHIP was still pretending to be supporting reform, Steve Champlin told the AHIP assembly: "There is absolutely no interest, no reason Republicans should ever vote for this thing. They have gone from a party that got killed eleven months ago to a party that is rising today. And they are rising up on the turmoil of health care. So when they vote for a health care reform bill, whatever it is, they are giving comfort to the enemy who is down."

Champlin's leaked admission to the closed AHIP group was further confirmation of what we had been saying since our first ad: "Trust the health insurance industry? Not on your life."

Wendell Potter said the industry would hide behind front groups, but not until a year later would the lengths that the industry had gone to cover up the spending of tens of millions of dollars to kill reform became known. In November 2010, Bloomberg News reported that the health insurance industry had funneled $86.2 million to the United States Chamber of Commerce. The Chamber wasn't just any ordinary front group, created by the health insurance industry to hide its involvement. It was the biggest business lobbying group in the country. Bloomberg reported that 40 percent of the $215 million in lobbying the Chamber spent in 2009 was provided surreptitiously by the health insurance industry. That money fueled an accelerating stream of television advertising in the fall, almost all of it aimed at vulnerable Democratic members of the House of Representatives or in states of swing Democratic senators. In October alone, the Chamber and other opponents of reform outspent proponents by two to one.

The good news was the reason the opposition was spending so heavily. Despite the tea party protests and virtually unanimous Republican opposition to reform, Democrats in Congress were inching their way toward passing the legislation.

The Colbert Report: Who Would You Save From Drowning — Health Care or a Little Old Lady?

At the end of July I went to a windowless room in the Cannon House Office Building for my interview with Comedy

Central's Stephen Colbert. I was really looking forward to it, and so were my three children (all of them in their early-20s) for whom — like a lot of their generation — Jon Stewart and Stephen Colbert were among the best windows on the news. I was a fan too, particularly of Colbert whose over-the-top act as a right-wing TV news host — a la Fox's Bill O'Reilly — I found to be very funny and incredibly incisive.

As we were taping the segment, Colbert advised me, "No matter how stupid and ridiculous I am, I want you to give me serious answers. Through your answers, people will actually learn something and one of the purposes of this segment is to actually educate people about an issue."

After introducing HCAN as "The fighting death panelers" and summarizing reform as "My doctor's office will now be in the DMV, " Colbert asked me to sell the bill to him with the admonition, "Keep in mind that I'm rich and I already have health insurance and I don't care about other people." When I argued — clearly forgetting the last part of his instructions — that 45,000 fewer people will die a year, he led me to admit that some Americans will still die. Colbert ended the argument with, "Not the best sell job. People will die: not everyone but a lot of people."

As the segment went on, he asked me to choose whom would I save from drowning, universal health care or a little old lady? I said I'd save both. He concluded the segment, with "Sadly after we taped that interview, Mr. Kirsch was put down by a death panel. He will not be forgotten? (Pause and smirk) *Who* will not be?"

14

The Baucus Bill Is a Failure

On September 16, Senator Baucus finally unveiled his bill. Even though he had never won agreement from Republicans in the Gang of Six, Baucus still introduced a bill with major provisions pushed by the Republicans, significantly weakening the bill's potential to deliver affordable health coverage.

There are several reasons that Baucus introduced a conservative bill, even without the support of the Republicans in the Gang of Six had. One is, Baucus still held up hope of a bi-partisan deal, which he desperately wanted. Two is that Baucus thought it was necessary to water down the bill to get conservative Democrats to support the legislation, since every Democrat would be needed to overcome a Republican filibuster. The third reason is that Baucus and his staff — many of whom had worked for the health care industry — were actually very responsive to the industry's lobbying.

The HCAN press release didn't mince words. Under the headline, "Health Care for America Now Calls Baucus Bill a Failure," the release summarized our intense disappointment with his compromises:

> The Baucus bill is a gift to the insurance industry that fails to meet the most basic promise of health care reform: a guarantee that Americans will have good health care that they can afford. The Baucus bill would give a government-subsidized monopoly to the private insurance industry to sell their most profitable plans — high-deductible insurance — without having to face competition from a public health insurer.

Under the Baucus bill, employers would have no responsibility to help pay for their workers' coverage and would be given incentives to have workers pay more for barebones insurance. Americans who don't get health benefits through work would still not be able to get good, affordable coverage.

Wendell Potter called the bill, "The Insurance Industry Profit Protection and Enhancement Act."

The decision by the HCAN Steering Committee to vigorously condemn the Baucus bill was not made lightly, since we had acquiesced to the White House strategy of withholding public criticism during the Gang of Six deliberations. But once the bill had been presented, we thought the Democrats on the Senate Finance Committee, and all the Democrats in the Senate, should know that the bill needed to be vastly improved. That's why our press release ended with the plea, "We urge Senators on the Finance Committee to replace the Baucus plan with legislation that will do what the Senate HELP Committee and three House committees have done: guarantee that Americans have good health insurance that they can afford with the choice of a strong national public health insurance option."

But we were too late. On the day that Baucus released the bill, I joined a group of lobbyists representing the HCAN Steering Committee to meet with New Jersey Senator Robert Menendez. He was a member of the Senate Finance Committee and the chair of the Senate Democratic Campaign Committee. By reputation, Menendez was a conventional "pol," with moderate politics who had risen to power through the Democratic Party in New Jersey. Yet he was thoughtful and well-informed about the issues that we were raising. Still, one comment he made stuck with me. After listening to our complaints about the Baucus legislation, he said, "I understand why you didn't raise these issues earlier, but I think it was a mistake. I wish you had let us know of the depth of your concerns before this."

Menendez was really saying that once the chairman had introduced his legislation, it would be very difficult to make many changes. In short, while we could lobby to make it better over the next several weeks, we had lost and we shared part of the blame.

So what was so wrong with the Baucus bill? I'll start with an issue that was dear to Menendez's heart, immigration. As a son of immigrant parents who left Cuba in 1953 to escape the Batista dictatorship, and the only Latino Democrat in the U.S. Senate, Menendez was a champion of immigrant rights and tuned in to the concerns of the Latino community. The Baucus bill contained two provisions on immigration that were the same as in the House legislation, one bad and one good. On the negative side, the bill did not end the requirement that legal immigrants had to live in the United States for five years before being eligible for Medicaid. On the plus side, the legislation did allow legal immigrants to qualify for subsidies to purchase health coverage through the new health insurance exchanges.

But the Baucus bill contained one other egregious provision, which had been elevated when Representative Joe Wilson shouted, "You lie!" at the President. Could people who were not here legally, using their own money, buy health insurance through the exchanges? The House allowed anyone who paid the full cost to buy health coverage through the exchanges. We knew from our polling that "free health care for immigrants" was strongly opposed by the public. We had also found that the best counter argument was to require them to pay for coverage like anyone else.

In this case, though, Baucus was not the only obstacle; the White House had caved in as well. Rather than support the Latino voters who had helped elect Obama, White House health czar Nancy-Ann DeParle told health care advocates that if illegal immigrants were allowed to purchase coverage through the exchanges, it would prove that Wilson was correct. Her logic was that since the government established the exchanges, it would amount to government health care for illegal immigrants. Of course, under this same line of reasoning, illegal immigrants should be prohibited from driving on the highway or buying government-inspected milk.

The Latino community was watching keenly. The day before the Baucus bill was released, Illinois Representative Luis

Gutierrez told the Congressional Hispanic Caucus, "Those who should be our friends, our allies, are more and more giving Representative (Joe) Wilson, R-S.C., exactly what he wants to continue with this prejudice against our community."[51]

Jennifer Ng'andu, who represented the National Council of La Raza (NCLR), the nation's largest national Hispanic civil rights organization, on the HCAN Steering Committee, told me:

> From a policy point of view, it means that everyone who wants to purchase coverage through the exchanges will have to go through a citizenship verification process, which will ultimately reduce the number of eligible people who get covered. This policy also ignores the fact that many families are of mixed immigration status. There are some 8.2 million Latino children who have immigrant parents; a sizeable proportion of those parents are not documented. Families in this situation may be scared to risk vulnerability to apply for coverage for their children, and some eligible children will end up without any coverage. And the concession didn't accomplish anything politically. The opposition still attacked the bill on the grounds that it would cover illegal immigrants — the facts never stopped a good sound bite. But it turned off the Latino community, who was paying a lot of attention to the public conversation and drawing conclusions about what the bill meant for them.

The Baucus bill had other huge problems that rankled reform advocates. The lack of a public option was not the only reason that we called the bill "a gift to the insurance industry." The Baucus bill contained very weak consumer protections against insurance company practices, with almost no help for the 160 million people who would continue to get health coverage at work and weak regulation for the thirty million people who would get insurance through the new exchanges. The Baucus bill compounded this failure by turning over responsibility for establishing the exchanges to each state. Since the insurance industry has much more political power at the state level than consumer advocates, this would almost certainly put the interest of the insurance industry ahead of consumers.

Letting Employers Off the Hook

Another major problem with the Baucus bill, which was only slightly improved in the final legislation, was the way it treated employer-based coverage. The Baucus bill created financial incentives for large low-wage employers to charge their employees a sizeable portion of their wages for lousy health coverage — insurance that had high out-of-pocket costs and skimpy benefits. As a result, many Americans, and particularly those who work for large low-wage firms, would continue to have health coverage that doesn't provide needed treatment and could leave them with substantial medical debts. In addition, the Baucus bill provided incentives for firms to hire part-time workers.

The lack of employer responsibility in the Baucus bill represented a defeat for HCAN, and reform advocates more broadly. The HCAN strategy had anticipated that the business community would resist being required to pay for employee health coverage. We had tried in two ways to build allies in the business community. The first was establishing the Main Street Alliance. But most of its membership were small businesses that would have been exempt from the requirement and as a result paid little attention to the issue.

Second, HCAN and several of its union members had tried various ways of lining up the support of big business for reform, but none had gotten very far. The Communications Workers of America (CWA) spent several years in conversation with AT&T and Verizon about the issue. The union had worked with AT&T to demonstrate how much health reform would save the company. But neither big telecom company was willing to endorse specific reforms.

Larry Cohen, the president of CWA, concluded that the resistance stemmed from a combination of ideology — opposition to government regulation generally — and class solidarity: resisting an economic cost imposed by government. Cohen observed that it was not just Republicans who believed that the only way to create jobs was to give corporate America a free hand; many Democrats shared that view as well.

CWA's research director, Louise Novotny, believes that the union's work with Verizon did bear some fruit. In June 2009, Verizon CEO Ivan Seidenberg was elected to be chair of the Business Roundtable (BRT), an association of the CEOs of many of the nation's largest companies. While the Chamber of Commerce and National Federation of Independent Business were lobbying hard against any form of employer responsibility, the White House pressed the BRT to remain neutral in the health care debate, and the BRT was willing to go along with the Baucus framework.

I had hoped that HCAN could mount a major effort to push real employer responsibility in the Senate bill. The House provisions were strong and the public was on our side. Such an effort required a big push by labor unions, which had a strong interest in non-union employers having to contribute to health coverage. However, organized labor was forced into a battle on another part of the Baucus plan, a provision that threatened to sharply cut their members' health coverage and erase years of difficult trade-offs that they had made at the bargaining table.

The Cadillac Tax

Valeria Castle-Stanley grew up near Wendell Potter, in Castlewood, Virginia, "right in the corner where Kentucky, Tennessee and Virginia come together." Her father worked in the coalmines, and when he and other United Mine Workers of America

(UMWA) workers went out on strike, she organized a demonstration at Castlewood High School to support the job action. She went on to get a B.A. in organizational management. At age thirty-seven she earned a master's degree in business. She worked at AT&T, helping people who have hearing and speech disabilities make calls through the use of a TTY machine. She also became active with CWA, becoming one of more than a hundred CWA Legislation and Political Action coordinators. Castle-Stanley told me:

> Everyone in this area was very anti health care. I organized a team that placed calls to Congressman Rick

Boucher and our two senators. I would go to work sites and we would have a large number of CWA members call one of the senators. We went to one of Boucher's town hall meetings in Abbington, VA. We brought twenty people with our CWA shirts. We were outnumbered. They booed us, when one of us stood up to speak they were told, "go home you're not welcome here."

Castle-Stanley had strong personal reasons for volunteering to help lead CWA's work on health care reform. As she told National Public Radio (NPR), "I have asthma and I've had it since I was probably ten, twelve years old. And it seems to be progressively getting worse. I pay over $1,500 a year for my medication. And I need those medications to live." With her preexisting condition, she was worried about whether she could get health coverage if she looked for another job now that she had her master's degree. In addition, she shared with me that her daughter "has some depression issues. It's been hard; we need to drive two and a half hours to see a child psychiatrist."

In 2009, Castle-Stanley made $42,000, a decent wage in rural Virginia, but less than it would have been if the union hadn't given up wage increases to keep good health coverage. As she told NPR, "I heard some senators wanted to tax our health care benefits. I just couldn't believe it."

Castle-Stanley wasn't alone. The entire labor movement was shocked that Baucus, with the tacit support of the White House, was proposing a steep "excise tax" — 40 percent — on health insurance policies that covered millions of workers, most of them not in unions. The supporters of the proposal called it a "Cadillac Tax," but President Obama knew better. He had argued vociferously before his election that taxes like this would fall on workers like Valeria Castle-Stanley. In his October 2008 health care address, Obama said:

> John McCain calls these plans "Cadillac plans." In some cases, it may be that a corporate CEO is getting too good a deal. But what if you're a line worker making a good American car like Cadillac who's given up wage increases in exchange for better health care? Well, Senator McCain

believes you should pay higher taxes too. The bottom line: the better your health care plan — the harder you've fought for good benefits — the higher the taxes you'll pay under John McCain's plan.

That same conclusion applied to the Baucus plan, even if the tax was levied in a different manner than McCain had proposed. It is hard to overstate the feeling of betrayal that the excise tax proposal created among unions and their members. This was the issue that unions had most relied on to convince their members to vote for Obama over McCain. Unions throughout the country had given up wage increases year after year after year in order to hold on to good health coverage. The AFL-CIO's Gerry Shea told me: "People were furious. Lots of our people still thought we should be supporting nothing short of single-payer and now they were hearing that their benefits would be taxed! Insurers were adding fuel to the fire by telling union locals that the tax will go to pay for the uninsured and trying to pit one group against the other. It generated enormous anger among the ranks and it endangered our support for health care reform."

It also put unions in the impossible position of having to choose between their obligation to their members and their commitment to social justice.

Peter Orszag, the Director of the White House Office of Management and Budget and a principal adviser to the President on health care, had first voiced the idea that the White House might be open to taxing health benefits in the spring of 2009. I had heard that White House Chief of Staff Rahm Emanuel reacted furiously to the prospect of the administration supporting an issue on which the campaign had spent $80 million attacking McCain.

In July, a number of union presidents met with Obama at the White House. Obama told them he would not push for passage of one of their two top issues, the Employee Free Choice Act, until he won passage of their other priority issue, health care. The President also promised the labor leaders that he would not support taxing health benefits.

Yet the very next week, Massachusetts Senator John Kerry, a member of the Senate Finance Committee, proposed a "Cadillac tax" on high cost health plans. The Kerry proposal differed from the McCain proposal in its structure, but not in its impact on existing health benefits. Kerry advertised his proposal as applying to firms like Goldman Sachs, which offered an array of health benefits that went well beyond corporate health insurance. But I was skeptical. For one thing, the only way such a proposal could raise enough money to finance a major chunk of reform was if it applied to a large number of workers, many more than enjoyed Wall Street–level perks.

After Kerry came out with his proposal, a group of union lobbyists, led by the AFL-CIO, met with the Senator's staff. The labor lobbyists were told that Kerry's excise tax was needed to get the bill out of the Senate Finance Committee and that it would not have an impact on many union members. Since the unions had a reservoir of good will toward Kerry, whom they had supported in his 2004 campaign against President Bush, they were inclined to trust him. As one lobbyist told me, "We couldn't believe that he would do this to us."

CWA had taken data to the meeting with Kerry's staff that demonstrated the proposal would tax many of its members. In September, CWA released a more complete analysis of the excise tax proposal in the Baucus bill, which showed that the excise tax would apply to all but one of CWA's twenty-six health plans. Nor would just phone company workers be taxed under the Baucus proposal. Using data from the Joint Committee on Taxation, CWA found that 40 percent of health care plans would be taxed, with the biggest impact on middle-class workers, older workers, and those in hazardous jobs.

While few would argue that teachers are paid Wall Street wages, they too would face higher taxes under the Baucus-Kerry proposal. The National Education Association (NEA) analyzed the impact of the Baucus excise tax in a dozen states and found that it would result in huge tax increases. In the state of Wisconsin, the tax would amount to more than $400 million over a decade on health insurance policies that covered 30,000 teachers. As the NEA reported, in order to avoid the tax, health plans would have to charge very high deductibles and co-payments, end coverage for dental and vision coverage, and scale back other health benefits.

The excise tax's popularity with Peter Orszag and other Obama administration health advisors derived from this financial mechanism. Forcing health plans to raise out-of-pocket costs and cut benefits was viewed as a way to control health care costs. This was an example of how some Democratic policy makers believed in the same conservative economics as Republicans. Their own personal privilege insulated them from the impact of health costs felt by ordinary Americans.

As I've discussed before, if high out-of-pocket costs and skimpy benefits were the keys to controlling health care costs, the United States would have the lowest health care cost in the developed world, not the highest. Raising out-of-pocket costs will decrease the amount of care people get, including discouraging them from getting the care they need. By contrast, the health systems in the world that provide the best care control costs by limiting payments to health providers and provide incentives for health providers to deliver quality care, rather than cutting back on benefits.

A spontaneous debate on the excise tax, broadcast on NPR's *Planet Money* in January 2010, captured the class differences in the attitudes toward the health care tax. Jonathan Gruber, an adviser to the Obama administration, appeared on the show to defend the Cadillac tax. As an example of how our health care system led to overuse, Gruber told a personal story. He said, "I hurt my knee playing tennis and went to the emergency room and it cost $75, which is not a lot of money. They told me that I should have waited [to get treatment] and I should have."

Neil Rausch, an NPR sound engineer, was listening to the story, and the host, Chanah Joffe-Walt, could see that Gruber's argument was getting Rausch "all worked up." So Joffe-Walt invited Rausch to join the on-air debate. Rausch had his own personal story to tell. His son was playing soccer when a ball hit him in the eye. Concerned, Rausch called his doctor, who told him to take the boy to the ER to be examined. That turned out to be the right decision, as the boy's eyesight could have been impaired if he had not been seen in the hospital. Rausch said that having to pay the $100 co-payment and wait around for hours in the ER were reason enough for him not to want to go to the hospital.

After hearing Rausch's story, Gruber admitted that his doctor had told him to go to the emergency room, a fact that he had conveniently left out of the story, because it proved that his basic thesis — that consumers were the main drivers of unneeded care — was wrong. In both cases the doctor's advice to go to the emergency room demonstrated that health care providers — not patients — are the main drivers of health care costs.

The class difference was revealed by the opposite reactions to the out-of-pocket costs. A well-off economist like Gruber may think that $75 is not a lot of money, but for most people, it's enough to give them pause. What might have happened if a family facing a $100 co-payment decided not to take their son to the hospital? How much more might it have cost if the boy needed more expensive care later, or lost his sight?

Unions were forced to walk a thin line, organizing their members to oppose the excise tax without driving them to reject the entire bill. NEA President Dennis Von Roekel captured the dilemma: "We had to keep in mind what's good for the whole middle class. There was a lot that was good in the bill for millions and millions of people who were not our members."

In the end, labor agreed to a compromise version of the excise tax in order to ensure that those millions of non-labor members benefited. I have extraordinary respect for the labor leaders who put the historic quest of economic justice ahead of the narrower interest of their members. But the fight over the excise tax had real consequences for other parts of the legislation, particularly requiring that employers help pay for good coverage for their workers.

As the AFL-CIO's Gerry Shea told me, "The tragedy of the excise tax was we had to devote so much energy to fighting it that we didn't have the capacity to focus on other important issues as much as we could have. Plus, it sapped people's morale and undermined their support for the whole issue."

The Individual Mandate and Affordability

In the President's September address to Congress, the President not only made a concession on the public option. He also said, "the plan I'm proposing will cost around $900 billion over ten years." Yet $900 billion was not enough money to make health care truly affordable to the uninsured. Why did the President make another, preemptive concession to the bill's opponents, one that would significantly damage his core goal? An article co-authored by Robert Pear and *The New York Times* White House correspondent Jackie Calmes summarized the impact nicely: "The number suggests a political and fiscal calculation to avoid the sticker shock of the trillion-dollar threshold. But it probably means that Mr. Obama could fall short of his goal of providing universal coverage for all Americans because the lower cost may force lawmakers to reduce the subsidies needed to help more uninsured individuals and small businesses seeking coverage for employees."[52]

If the President's goal was to get Republicans and the press to stop calling health care a "trillion-dollar plan," it didn't work. Four days later Republican Minority Leader Mitch McConnell's office issued a press release in which he castigated the "nearly trillion dollar plan." Likewise, when Senate Majority Leader Harry Reid introduced his legislation in mid-November, McConnell called it "another trillion-dollar experiment."[53]

If the goal was to appeal to the public, the White House's emphasis on a low price tag rather than affordability totally missed the mark. HCAN commissioned several polls, of the public at large, of voters in House districts represented by Blue Dog Democrats, and of voters in states that tended to vote Republican but were represented by Democratic senators, including Nebraska and Arkansas. Every poll found that large majorities of the public, including Republicans, preferred to "make sure that health care is really affordable to middle-class families and small businesses" rather than to "put a spending cap on health care reform at one trillion dollars so the cost doesn't spiral out of control."

I suspect that the White House set the ceiling to appeal to Democratic deficit hawks like Senate Budget Committee Chair Kent Conrad of North Carolina and Blue Dogs in the House, but that too was not necessary. The President had already promised that the bill would not increase the deficit.

When Baucus introduced his legislation, he proposed spending only $806 billion on covering the uninsured. As a result, the cost of health coverage that would be offered to families in the new health care exchanges was much more than some families could afford.

The inadequate provisions in the Baucus bill created a real dilemma for HCAN and other health care advocates. The single most important thing that people wanted out of reform was affordable health coverage. By September, the pollster.com average of support for the Obama health care plan had reached 50 percent opposed and 44 percent in favor. If we had run a big public campaign aimed at increasing the affordability provisions, our efforts would have further dampened public support for reform. HCAN did put out state-by-state reports that compared how much more a family would have to pay for coverage in the Baucus bill, but we held back from a major public push. Other advocates expressed their reservations to Congress even more quietly.

To add insult to injury, the Baucus plan levied high fines on people who did not purchase health insurance. Plus, it would have required a family to spend more than 10 percent of their income on insurance premiums in order to qualify for the hardship exemption that allowed a family to escape the fine. Fortunately, the high cost of coverage and stiff penalties were a real concern of Republican Senator Olympia Snowe. Unlike the other Republicans on the committee, Snowe had not ruled out voting for the legislation and both Baucus and the White House were courting her vote heavily. When the committee began to consider amendments to Baucus' bill, Snowe joined with New York Democratic Senator Chuck Schumer in introducing an amendment that lowered the hardship figure to 8 percent of income and significantly reduced the penalties to families who were not insured. When the amendment passed by a vote of

22-1, the health insurance industry panicked. In doing so, they began to turn the White House and friendly Senate Democrats like Baucus into industry opponents.

One of the biggest reasons that the health insurance industry loved the Baucus bill was the provision that required people to pay a lot for high-deductible coverage — the kind that insurers find most profitable — or face a steep fine. The Snowe-Schumer amendment weakened some of the industry's favored provisions. Estimates are that the amendment would have reduced the number of new insurance customers by two million people a year. Because of that, the industry broke the widely understood rules of the game: They attacked the Senate bill on the issue that people most cared about, affordability.

On October 13, the *Christian Science Monitor* summarized the widespread reaction to the release by AHIP of a study that it had commissioned by the accounting firm Price-Waterhouse. The study used heavily biased assumptions (by the firm's own admission when questioned later) to conclude that health premiums would soar under the Baucus legislation:

> Has the health-insurance industry shot itself in the foot? On Sunday, America's Health Insurance Plans (AHIP), the insurer trade group, released a study warning that the Senate Finance Committee's health bill would result in sizable hikes in insurance premiums. The timing of the release seemed intended to influence Tuesday's planned vote on the bill by the full Finance panel. But the study's methodology has been criticized as flawed by outside experts. And the salvo seems to have done something President Obama had been unable to accomplish: unite fractious Democrats in support of the legislation. "The insurance industry ought to be ashamed of this report," said Sen. John Kerry (D) of Massachusetts in debate prior to the committee vote.[54]

A few days later, the President used his weekly Saturday radio address to attack the insurance industry in what Jonathan Alter called "the strongest terms a president has used about the private sector since FDR." Obama called the AHIP-funded report "bogus," and said that the insurance industry was making "a last-ditch effort to stop reform" by "filling the airwaves with deceptive and dishonest ads." He accused the industry of using their revenues to figure out "how to avoid covering people" and spend their health dollars on "profits, bonuses, and administrative costs that do nothing to make us healthy."[55]

The President was not the only Democrat who was increasingly using anti-insurance company rhetoric. Before the summer recess, Speaker Pelosi's communications team instructed House members to focus on two themes in their public communications. One was the specific benefits of the bill. The staff of the Energy and Commerce Committee calculated the number of people who would benefit in each Congressional district from such provisions as covering the uninsured, protecting families from bankruptcy, and providing small businesses with tax credits. The other theme was protection from insurance company abuses.

In anticipation of the upcoming floor debate in the Senate, Majority Leader Reid's office also decided to focus on relief from insurance company abuses as the main message that Senate Democrats should push. While they were slow to come around — and the President still would not make it a regular theme of his communications — Democrats had come to realize that the only way they could rally the public around reform was to go after the insurance industry. But by then a lot of ground had been lost.

All the Way Down to the Wire

Any hope of getting a public health insurance option passed by the Senate Finance Committee rested on Maine Senator Olympia Snowe. She continued to talk about her "trigger" idea, without ever releasing any details on how the trigger would work. We continued to assert that the trigger would be written so as never to be pulled. That is, it would be designed to whitewash the killing of the public option.

We kept up our grassroots pressure in Maine. All summer the HCAN coalition in Maine had continued an array of grassroots activities. Change That Works drove a rented ambulance to events in small towns, which earned extensive local media coverage. The Maine People's Alliance's summer canvass generated thousands of personal letters to the Senator. On September 2, the HCAN coalition and Organizing for America held a big event at Snowe's office in Bangor, which the *Bangor Daily News* reported under the headline, "Health reform fans blitz Snowe with 35,000 messages."

On September 8, the coalition released two television ads, featuring local Mainers. The first showed a cancer survivor named Lee Roberts and her young towheaded son, picking apples to feed a horse at their Maine country home. In the ad, Roberts said:

> I'm happy to have health insurance — I don't like dealing with the health insurance company. As a twenty-five-year cancer survivor I worry about when I change jobs I'll lose my health insurance. We have to have reform that allows people to keep their health insurance if they like it but that forces the insurance companies to behave themselves. And gives us the public health insurance option so that all of us have coverage no matter what. We need Senator Snowe to continue her independence and show us that she cares more about the people of Maine than the insurance lobby.

The second ad, run on TV, on radio, and in print, was sponsored by the Main Street Alliance. The TV spot showed John Costin and several of his employees at work at his woodworking and furniture business. John explained, "We're not able to provide health insurance for our employees — we can't afford to do it. I get my health insurance through my wife's job, but she just got laid off this spring…. There's a bill in Congress that would lower health care costs for businesses and families — we need to tell Senators Snowe and Collins that they can make a difference."

But Snowe continued to put her political party first. Appearing on CBS's *Face the Nation* on September 14, she said that the public option is "universally opposed by all Republicans in the Senate" and "there's no way to pass a plan that includes the public option."

We were also working very closely with two prominent Democratic members of the Senate Finance Committee to build support for a public option amendment to the Baucus bill. One of our champions was Jay Rockefeller, whom Baucus had angered by totally ignoring him during the process of writing his bill, even though Rockefeller chaired the Health Subcommittee of the Senate Finance Committee. After Baucus had announced his legislation, Rockefeller immediately said that he would oppose the bill in committee unless it was changed. His statement earned him a private meeting at the White House with President Obama.

The second senator was New York's Chuck Schumer, who was the third-ranking Democrat in the Senate leadership and whose two terms as chair of the Senate Democratic Campaign Committee had earned him the loyalty of many Democratic senators.

On September 24, the two senators held a press conference call at which Schumer confidently predicted, "The health care bill that is signed into law by the President will have a good, strong, robust public option." Both senators said that passage by the Senate Finance Committee was possible. Schumer made a point of saying a large majority of Democratic senators supported the public option and that even if it was not passed by the Senate Finance Committee, it would have a "real good chance on the Senate floor." As I was listening to the press conference I was thrilled to hear the senators reject compromises like the trigger and co-op.

On September 29, the Senate Finance Committee defeated two public option amendments, one offered first by Rockefeller and a second by Schumer. The Schumer amendment earned the vote of ten Democrats. The three Democratic nay votes were from Baucus, North Dakota Senator Kent Conrad, and Arkansas Senator Blanche Lincoln. The vote demonstrated an important fact: Only a small number of conservative Democrats would vote against a public option, which meant that it had the support of at least 50 senators, a majority of the U.S. Senate. That was the good news. The problem remained that every Democratic senator would be needed to break a Republican filibuster of legislation that had a public option, even if some of those Democrats voted against the public option provision itself.

Two weeks after the public option amendments were defeated, the Senate Finance Committee voted to approve the health care legislation by a vote of 14-9. At the last minute, Olympia Snowe decided to vote for the bill, becoming the lone Republican alongside all the Democrats. However, Snowe asserted that her vote for the legislation did not in any way indicate that she would vote for the bill on the Senate floor.

The committee had taken fifty-eight hours debating the bill, the longest Senate Finance Committee bill "mark-up" in twenty-two years. It had accepted forty-one amendments, including nine offered by Republican Committee members. Several of the amendments improved the bill from our point of view, but the major problems with the legislation remained.

Still, we reached another major milestone. Now every Senate and House committee that had jurisdiction had approved health reform legislation that shared the same basic structure. The race was on to get the full House and Senate to each pass legislation in time for the two bills to be merged in one final bill no later than the Christmas holidays.

* * * *

The August tea party demonstrations, followed by the Senate Finance Committee deliberations, had fundamentally shifted the terrain of the health care debate. The insurance industry's charm offensive had collapsed. The Chamber of Commerce was spending tens of millions of dollars to kill reform. With the exception of Olympia Snowe, there was no longer any pretense of bipartisanship. Opposition among the public had risen to almost 50 percent from 25 percent the previous March. A growing part of that opposition, around one-third, included Americans who did not think that the bill was far-reaching enough. Between the "Cadillac" tax and the President's wavering on the public option, the base of support for reform was increasingly unhappy.

The tension with the White House spilled out at the national convention of the AFL-CIO in Pittsburgh, where Richard L. Trumka was elected as the Federation's new president on September 16. Referring to Obama, Trumka told the packed convention hall, "So long as you stand for a public option, we are going to stand with you." Addressing wavering Democrats, Trumka said, "a plan without a public option may be a lot of things, but it sure as hell isn't reform."

AFSCME President Gerry McEntee was more blunt. He led the union members in a new call and response chant, "The Baucus plan is — Bullshit!"

Just before Baucus had introduced his bill, the HCAN Executive Committee met to plan the campaign's public reaction. As we reviewed our decision to be highly critical of the Baucus bill I found myself saying over and over again, "I want to be certain that everyone is OK with this." The committee members said yes, but they were confused that I kept asking them to reaffirm their support. I wasn't really sure why I was doing it either, until Steve Kreisberg, an AFSCME representative, supplied the answer. "What I think Richard is asking us," he said, "is whether we will have his back if the White House goes after him."

That is exactly what I was getting at. The committee assured me that they would protect me. I needed the support, because the barrage was about to begin.

15

Did the White House Try to Get Me Fired?

Early on a September morning I got a call from a member of the HCAN Steering Committee. The message was brief: Someone at the White House had called SEIU and asked that I be fired.

Whoa. I felt for a moment that I was in a movie. This couldn't be happening to me. My mind started racing, considering how awful the White House would look if it became public that they were going after the head of a big progressive campaign for not toeing the White House line at every step. I might become a symbol for progressives of their growing alienation from the White House. But that was not what I wanted. I wanted to handle the crisis quietly and keep pushing for health reform.

Still, I was upset. When we began this journey, I had expected to take on the insurance industry, big business, the right wing, and conservative Democrats. I never expected to be blindsided by a Democratic president, particularly when I was spending every waking moment fighting for his top priority. And I had never expected politics to be so personal.

* * * *

Unlike what you might have seen on the television series, the West Wing of the White House is a pretty quiet place. I remembered a sunny afternoon the previous April, when the Marine guard on duty in the lobby of the West Wing checked my identity and let Patrick Gaspard's assistant know I had arrived. I waited for Gaspard in the stately reception area, decorated tastefully, as you would expect to find in an elegant colonial home.

I had worked with Gaspard for years when he was vice president for politics at 1199SEIU, the powerful health care union in New York. In the fall of 2007, Gaspard and I had discussed the upcoming Democratic primary. Gaspard was clearly excited about the prospect of Obama's run for President. Most of SEIU's members were African American or Latino. The union felt compelled to endorse New York Senator Hillary Rodham Clinton in the state's presidential primary, but after the New York primary was over, and Obama was favored to win the nomination, 1199SEIU joined SEIU nationally in endorsing Obama. Gaspard became a top staffer at the Obama campaign and after the election was appointed to the position of White House political director.

In the West Wing, we talked about how HCAN could work with the White House. We each had one question for the other. Gaspard asked, "Where might HCAN differ from the President on the policy issues?" I explained that Obama had endorsed the HCAN principles so that at this point we were aligned on policy with the President.

My question for Gaspard was, "How could we start coordinating closely with the White House?" Gaspard replied that soon the White House would assign a designated liaison with whom we could coordinate our work.

Looking back on that conversation, I'm quite certain that if Gaspard had been working with us, we would not have later found ourselves so at odds with the White House. Instead, it was the responsibility of Jim Messina, the deputy White House chief of staff. And as you'll remember from his track record as Baucus' chief of staff in Montana, Messina had used all of Baucus' power to stifle any pressure from the left.

I had talked to Messina only once, during the weekly meetings at the Capital Hilton between White House staff and the progressive community, run by the Common Purpose Project. The White House helped establish the Project early in 2009 so that White House staff could communicate regularly with organizations that were likely to support the President's agenda on his top priorities. At the weekly meetings, Messina delivered a report on the President's upcoming schedule and discussed the White House's top legislative priorities. Eric Smith, the Project's director, emphasized that a key purpose of the meetings was to air differences among friends. However, with rare exceptions, the meetings were a one-way street, in which the White House reported and groups asked questions but did not challenge the White House staff. Early on, in response to most questions, Messina took a tone that clearly discouraged dissent. He responded to being challenged with a mixture of defensiveness and aggressiveness that turned off, rather than invited, debate.

Although people in Washington tend to defer to the White House, this didn't have to be the tone. For example, White House Senior Advisor David Axelrod represented the White House at a meeting that Messina did not attend. As Axelrod answered each question that raised areas of potential disagreement with the White House position, he calmly explained the White House position. At the same time, he acknowledged that an organization might need to take a different stance. It was the polar opposite of the tone set by Messina. Axelrod recognized that the organizations at the table could be both strong allies of the White House and independent actors.

In one oft-quoted story, President Franklin Roosevelt met with the leading progressive groups of his day and after hearing their agenda said, "I agree with you. Now make me do it." But that was not the stance taken by the Obama White House. A White House insider told me that when he asked Messina what the "inside/outside strategy" was for passing health care reform, he replied, "There is no outside strategy."

Early in 2009 a number of leading progressive groups with strong White House ties, including SEIU and the Center for American Progress (CAP), started another coalition, named Unity '09. Its goal was to raise money to bolster campaign efforts to support the President's top agenda items including: health care, clean energy, financial reform, and immigration. Unity '09 hired a coordinator for each of the issue areas.

They hired Andrew Grossman to act as liaison between health care advocates and the White House. Grossman was an independent political consultant who had been executive director of the Senate Democratic Campaign Committee.

Once Grossman took the job, he moved quickly to establish a regular working relationship with HCAN. Each morning, at 8:30, Grossman conferred with us, wanting to know everything that we were doing. He was particularly concerned about any activities that might go beyond where Congress or the White House stood. On the other hand, he was able to offer little about the White House's strategy to pass reform, which he was not involved in setting. He was a messenger between us and the White House, with no decision-making ability.

* * * *

It was hard to keep my mind on work, while I waited to find out if the White House had really asked SEIU to have me fired. After a few hours, I learned that SEIU President Andy Stern said the White House had not called him. I breathed a small sigh of relief, even though I knew the story was far from over.

A few days later, HCAN Deputy Campaign Manager Ethan Rome and I met with staff from The Atlantic Philanthropies. We learned that Messina had complained to them about me. The Atlantic staff treated the issue gingerly. I did find out that the White House had complained about me to SEIU. But SEIU's response had been, "They are too sensitive."

I soon heard that Messina had also complained about me to Chuck Loveless, who was AFSCME's legislative director. Loveless promised Messina that he would talk with me, and a couple of weeks later he set up a meeting with several HCAN union leaders. Again, everyone was supportive. To improve the situation, they asked me to keep giving Andy Grossman a heads-up every time we did anything that might upset the White House.

I also checked with Bill Raabe, the National Education Association representative on the HCAN Executive Committee, to see if the White House had registered a complaint with them.

Raabe said that Grossman had asked someone at NEA whether it was true that I checked with the HCAN Executive Committee before making any important decisions. Raabe delivered the message: yes, absolutely.

I was relieved to be receiving unified support from the HCAN Executive Committee members. It was true the HCAN Executive Committee approved every key decision. As a result, they had my back when it mattered. Still, I found the machinations nerve wracking.

Even Andy Grossman became unhappy with how far out of hand the situation had become. He suggested that I write a personal note to Messina asking that we meet to try to reconcile. With Grossman's help, I gave the note to someone who could deliver it personally to Messina. I never heard back.

* * * *

A friend of mine in Congress told me that I had earned the White House's animosity because they thought I had lied about HCAN's role when I said that we were building an army to help the President pass his plan. The White House believed that I was promising that HCAN would be like Organizing for America, doing whatever the White House wanted. But OFA was part of the Democratic National Committee, controlled by the White House. HCAN was an independent coalition.

I guess I should have used a different metaphor than an army, because that implied that Obama was the general and we would follow every command. We were building an army only to pass the plan that Obama had run on. That didn't mean we would follow the President whenever he changed course.

HCAN's written mission was to pass health reform that was as close to our principles as possible. Our mission required us to simultaneously balance two goals: promote health reform broadly and fight for specific provisions in the bill. The White House only wanted us to be a campaign, not a lobbying group.

Here is one telling example. I was driving to the airport in Baltimore on a Friday afternoon in the summer, heading to my upstate New York home for the weekend, when Grossman called. He was angry because members of the HCAN Steering

Committee had agreed to each send a letter to Baucus and Reid expressing concerns about the Senate Finance Committee bill. The White House wanted the letters to stop, worried that if a letter were leaked to the press, it would look like some of their allies were unhappy. (Which we were!) I told Grossman that he could not stop us from lobbying for the bill we wanted; that was core to our mission.

The White House claimed that if our concerns became public, they could be used by opponents of reform. But by that logic, we could never say anything remotely critical — it would totally silence our voices. Plus, the restrictions seemed ridiculous to me. The opponents of reform had a huge arsenal they were firing every day. They didn't require our help to demonize the effort.

A White House insider also told us that they were particularly concerned about criticism from HCAN because we had a lot of credibility with Democrats in Congress. The assembled power of HCAN's Steering Committee members, backed by HCAN's considerable resources, elevated the impact of our positions.

Right after Obama was elected, the HCAN Steering Committee had strategized what would happen if the President took positions or made compromises that retreated from HCAN's principles. My contribution to the discussion was an analogy. We had come to the dance with Obama, and we had to hold him very tight when he tried to leave the dance floor. We had done that throughout the campaign. If I had a dollar for every time I had refused an invitation from the press to criticize Obama, I could have taken Messina out to dinner at the finest restaurant in D.C.

Throughout the fall, when the White House was compromising away the public option, many of HCAN's state partners — reflecting what they were hearing from HCAN volunteers — wanted us to start directing our grassroots lobbying against the White House instead of just focusing on Congress. But the HCAN Steering Committee decided to keep the grassroots pressure focused solely on Congress.

Fortunately, from my perspective, one of HCAN's most powerful members did not feel so constrained. MoveOn had built a list of more than five million Americans by listening closely to their concerns, conducting frequent surveys of their members. Most of them were growing frustrated with the president they had worked so hard to elect. MoveOn sent an alert to its list on October 23, under the subject heading, "TODAY: Call the White House." The email applauded a decision by Senate Majority Leader Harry Reid to support the public option. It also quoted a CNN report that the President was pushing Reid to kill the public option by supporting Olympia Snowe's trigger proposal. "The President has said many, many times that a public option is the best way to keep insurance companies honest and lower skyrocketing costs." The email urged MoveOn members to "tell President Obama to stand with Senate Democrats and the American public."

To improve HCAN's relationship with the White House, I started to keep them more apprised of our activities. On October 19, I sent a short email summarizing our past month's campaign activity, which included holding more than 200 insurance actions in forty-four states, generating a 246-page press summary; 204,000 constituent phone calls in support of reform to swing members of Congress; spending $3.7 million on ads that promoted reform; and spending $700,000 on an ad that said that there was a better way to pay for reform than through the excise tax on high-cost health plans.

All I heard back was an email from Grossman: "Geez — you are spending 700K on the financing ads? That's a huge amount of money."

In other words, rather than acknowledging the huge effort we had made doing exactly what the White House wanted us to do — promote reform — Grossman's only response was to attack us for the one activity that the White House didn't like: pushing for progressive financing of reform instead of taxing health benefits. And this was the position that Obama campaigned on when he ran for president!

So did the White House try to get me fired? I'm certain that Messina tried hard to undermine my position with both the

HCAN leadership and our primary funder. And I believe that in doing so, he hoped that I would be fired or that the HCAN leadership would reign in my actions to make them more acceptable to the White House. The problem with their strategy was that it was based on a false premise that I was personally deciding to challenge the White House. The failure of the White House staff to weaken my position or change HCAN's behavior was because the key decisions HCAN made, including any actions that might be seen as challenging the White House or Democratic Congressional leadership, were made by HCAN's leadership, not me or the HCAN staff.

Flare-ups with the White House would continue until Scott Brown was elected to the Senate in January. After his election, HCAN no longer pushed to improve the bill. We had one goal: Get the bill passed!

16

The House Makes History

On a cold, gray day in late October, Speaker Nancy Pelosi led a phalanx of her Democratic colleagues down the massive steps on the west side of the Capitol, facing the mall, where several hundred supporters, House staff members, and reporters waited. I was glad I'd worn a coat, as it felt more like my home in upstate New York than a fall day in the South. Pelosi announced that within a few days, the House would vote on the Affordable Health Care for America Act. The Speaker began, "It is with great pride and great humility that we come before you to follow in the footsteps of those who gave you Social Security, and then Medicare and now universal, quality, affordable health care for all Americans."

A few minutes later, Dan Sherry took the podium to tell his story. You'll remember him as the Illinois small businessman who became a leader in the Main Street Alliance, and a key voice in lobbying his member of Congress, Melissa Bean. Looking distinguished in a brown suit and gold tie, with reading glasses perched on his nose under a head of white hair, Sherry told how his insurance company had canceled his coverage when he missed one payment after fifteen years of being a reliable customer. After the ceremony Sherry headed over to the Old Executive Office Building to attend a press conference held by President Obama. As the press conference ended, Sherry caught the President's attention by shouting out that he was from Barrington, Illinois. Sherry told me, "When he heard me say that, he got a big smile on his face and his eyes popped. You could tell he was glad to see a hometown boy."

We'd reached this milestone by keeping the pressure on. On October 20, nine days before Pelosi unveiled her bill, the HCAN coalition and other health care advocates, including Organizing for America, Planned Parenthood, and Families USA, had held hundreds of local events around the country and produced a huge number of calls to Congress. OFA alone generated 315,000 calls on that one day. Throughout the reform movement, the volume of grassroots advocacy had soared since Labor Day. HCAN's list of email members had increased by 50 percent in September and October, to 194,000, and the number of unique visitors to the HCAN website had jumped by 75 percent since mid-August, an increase of a half million. While the HCAN list was not as large as those of many groups, it was incredibly responsive, as we had been cultivating people who were disposed to take action. An email sent in early November boasted astronomical rates of response for web-based advocacy: 40 percent of the recipients opened the email.

Our web team tried to make the online campaign fun as well as urgent. Before Halloween, we sent people a link to the "Health Care Mash," a horror video spoofing the insurance industry. It was recorded by Jon "Bowzer" Bauman, who had achieved celebrity as a member of the band Sha Na Na. A few days before the House vote we linked people online to a video recorded by Martin Sheen and Stockard Channing, who played the President and First Lady on *The West Wing*, urging people to call Congress.

After Labor Day, in response to a steady stream of calls generated by the right wing, HCAN partnered with AFSCME to begin a program of daily "patch-through" calls. We reached out to voters in districts represented by Democratic members of Congress who represented moderate to conservative districts or states. Under this program, a voter who responded to a recorded message on the telephone would be automatically connected to the office of their member of Congress or Senator to leave a message supporting reform. From September to December the program generated 396,082 completed calls to 86 House members and 20 senators, assuring that virtually every day Congressional offices would hear from between 50 and 200 supporters of reform. SEIU coordinated with HCAN on a similar program. HCAN volunteers also used web-based technology to call voters and connect them to members of Congress.

Each of the members of the HCAN coalition also organized their own members to communicate with Congress. HCAN members were hardly alone in generating extensive grassroots communications to push members of Congress on reform. Organizing for America, the grassroots organization built during the Obama campaign for president, reported that during the course of the campaign their volunteers made 1.5 million calls to members of Congress, and wrote and delivered 360,222 personal letters to Congress. The American Cancer Society ran an extensive program of bringing to members of Congress the stories of cancer patients who would be helped by reform. The faith-based network PICO ran a grassroots campaign to raise the voices of faith leaders in support of reform. Families USA organized the traditional national and state advocates of access to health care, particularly for low-income and vulnerable populations, to raise their voices. Community Catalyst organized state advocates to focus on issues like the affordability of coverage for moderate-income families. USPIRG organized students and small business people. And many other groups pitched in.

AARP mounted a huge effort. Like HCAN, AARP had identified specific health reform goals that it wanted to accomplish. While many organizations decided to focus almost exclusively on the Senate, AARP ran a two-chamber strategy, understanding that the House would create its own dynamic for reform. Most important, the foundation for AARP's entire effort was involving its members, which it did by organizing local forums and in-district lobbying meetings with members of Congress and their staffs and by holding huge tele-town halls, through which AARP members could ask questions of members of Congress and AARP staff on the phone. AARP calculated that 1,960,000 of its members participated in the tele-town halls.

Nationally, during the health care campaign, AARP collected 1,619,000 signatures on petitions in support of health reform and generated 1,278,000 emails and faxes to Congressional offices. The organization also ran TV ads and sent 39.4 million pieces of mail to its members, aimed at educating them about the bill and pushing back against the right-wing distortions of the proposed changes to Medicare in the legislation.

In early October, the HCAN legislative staff began working to identify members of the House whose vote for reform was not yet committed. We identified seventy-one House members who were leaning either against or for reform, and then focused on them with calls, emails, and door knocking. In the two weeks before the scheduled November 7 vote, members of the HCAN legislative committee spoke with staff at supportive Congressional offices each morning to share information and coordinate activities.

I also lobbied my own member of Congress, Scott Murphy. He had squeaked into office in a special election held on March 31, 2009, to replace Kirsten Gillibrand, who filled Senator Hillary Rodham Clinton's Senate seat after Clinton became Secretary of State. I'd never met Murphy, who owed his election to a big get-out-the-vote effort done by unions and the Working Families Party, a third party organized by unions and community groups including Citizen Action of New York. But I called Murphy's chief of staff and asked to meet with the Congressman. I was joined by two of my longtime colleagues at Citizen Action, Executive Director Karen Scharff and Shanna Goldman, the organizing director.

Murphy garnered the Democratic nomination to run for Congress because he was wealthy enough to finance his own election. I immediately noticed his distinctive pink Hermes silk tie, a pricey piece of attire. We talked for an hour, during which he said that the bill did not do enough to control costs but then admitted that he was worried about the opposition to reform by senior citizens in his district. He also complained that the bill raised money by ending a tax loophole for a biofuels firm in his district and also taxed a medical device manufacturer. Since his concerns were political, the message that Karen and Shanna delivered was straightforward: If you vote against the bill, the people who volunteered to get you elected will sit at home next time you run.

The more Murphy talked, the more uncomfortable I became. He seemed very cold and unconnected. I tried to bring in the personal side of what was at stake. I told him that my daughter, Lindsay, who has a chronic medical condition, had received affordable health care in Massachusetts because of their law. I said how much that meant to me as a parent. Murphy didn't look me in the eye or acknowledge my concern about my daughter. Instead he asked, "How have they controlled health care costs in Massachusetts?"

I wasn't surprised when he voted no. He would clearly need to be pushed hard to get him to change his vote when the bill came back to the House for final passage.

Being a Woman Is Not a Preexisting Condition

One of the speakers at the Pelosi rally was Jody Miller, a young mother from Maryland. Jody and her husband had spent $22,000 on infertility treatments and were finally blessed with triplets. Struggling to pay the huge cost of their current insurance policy, they applied for coverage from their local Blue Cross/Blue Shield plan. Their children were accepted for coverage, but Jody was turned down because her infertility was considered a preexisting condition. Her husband was turned down due to "spousal infertility!" As Jody told the audience on the Capitol steps, "Being a woman is not a preexisting condition."

That phrase was popularized in a campaign run by one of HCAN's Steering Committee members, the National Women's Law Center (NWLC), to address gender discrimination in health insurance coverage. NWLC had issued a report in 2008 that revealed the practice of charging women more for health coverage and another report in 2009 that exposed the use of gender-related preexisting condition exclusions. The later report found that in several states, pregnancy was considered a preexisting condition. In some states an insurer was allowed to reject a woman because she was a victim of domestic abuse. A Florida woman who had been raped was on a prophylactic treatment to prevent her from being infected with HIV; she was rejected because the rape was called a preexisting condition. In addition, women of childbearing age were routinely charged more than men for health coverage because a woman could get pregnant. That practice had prompted North Carolina Senator Kay Hagan to quip at the HCAN town hall on June 25, "It takes two to make a baby."

Hagan's raising of the issue showed the NWLC's widespread success in spurring women members of Congress to fight hard to end gender discrimination in health insurance. Both NWLC reports had received widespread attention in the press and support from editorial board writers. Maryland Senator Barbara Mikulski held hearings on the issue, which amplified the outrage. As a result, both the Senate and House bills prohibited insurers in the health exchanges from charging higher rates based on gender, and health reform had come to be seen as a women's issue.

Despite their success, women's health advocates and legislators would be sorely tested by the last obstacle that stood in the way of passing reform in the House: abortion. The abortion issue had first emerged when the Energy and Commerce Committee voted on the reform bill in late July. As Laurie Rubiner, who was the chief lobbyist for Planned Parenthood Federation of America (PPFA), explained to me, the organization had anticipated pressure in the committee to restrict access to abortions in the health exchanges. PPFA had focused extensive grassroots activity on a small number of Democrats on the committee who might support restrictions. On the opposing side, the U.S. Conference of Catholic Bishops had made totally banning access to abortions through the exchanges its top priority.

For years the bishops had elevated opposition to abortion above any other legislative issue. The Church said that it strongly supported universal health coverage, but the bishops were willing to kill the entire health reform bill if the exchanges gave women access to abortions, even if they paid with their own money for private insurance plans.

Under existing law, federal funds could not be used for abortion (except in cases of rape and incest), but abortion opponents went further, aiming to deny all access to abortions by insurance plans offered through the health exchanges. In July, Michigan Democrat Bart Stupak had almost succeeded in having an amendment passed in the Energy and Commerce Committee that totally blocked abortion coverage in the exchanges. Instead, a compromise was passed, which stated that abortion would not be paid for with federal funds; would not be considered a required primary care service; and that a choice of insurance plans were offered, some of which would not cover abortions.

Stupak's stand against abortions alarmed the HCAN coalition in Michigan. The United Food and Commercial Workers had 45,000 members in the state, and they asked Chris Michalakis, their chief political staff person, to organize pressure on Stupak. Stupak's Upper Peninsula district bordered Canada, where Michalakis was born, severely underweight. "The doctor wanted to be sure that I got proper health care," Chris told me. "Now I'm six-one. I have a lot of family over there. They joke about our health care system in the U.S."

Michalakis knew that Stupak would participate in a Lake Superior cruise planned for the first week of September, leaving from Marquette, Michigan. While UFCW had only a few members in the Upper Peninsula, he connected with AFSCME, students at Northern Michigan State University, and child-care advocates who had been working with HCAN. Together they assembled a crowd of fifty people who went to the dock to meet Stupak. When the boat could not leave the dock because of bad weather, Stupak went out to talk to the demonstrators. Michalakis said, "Stupak said that he supported health care reform but that he had issues that needed to be resolved. He promised us that he would not let abortion be the reason that he would not support it."

Just before the vote, another group of HCAN activists from the Upper Peninsula arranged for a phone call with Stupak. Paul Olson, who grew up in rural, iron-mining communities on the shores of Lake Superior, organized the call. Olson had recruited ministers and a doctor to be on the phone with Stupak; they told him that he needed to protect a person after they are born too. Stupak gave them the same message that he had relayed to the crowd at the Marquette dock. "Don't worry," Olson remembered Stupak saying. "There will be changes in the bill, and ultimately I'm going to vote for it."

Interestingly, that was also the perspective of Nick Ciaramitaro, who represented an AFSCME Council with 75,000 members in Michigan. Ciaramitaro had served in the Michigan state legislature. He told me, "I was a right-to-life Democrat in the legislature for years. It was clear to me that Bart was going to fight for as much as he could on the abortion issue, but ultimately it would not stop him from voting for the legislation."

If Stupak was just being a tough negotiator, it was working. As Pelosi was seeking to round up the 218 votes needed to pass the bill on the House floor, Stupak organized thirty-nine House members to join him in signing a letter saying that they would not vote for the bill if it included any access to abortions. Most observers believe that only a dozen members who otherwise supported reform would have stuck with Stupak on a final vote that resulted in killing health reform. However a dozen was enough to kill the bill, when added to the group of around thirty House Democrats who were opposed to the legislation regardless of how it dealt with abortion. As a result, Pelosi was forced to allow a vote on the Stupak amendment on the floor of the House. The amendment passed, with sixty-four Democratic votes, including many Democrats who had no intention of opposing the legislation because of the abortion issue, but still used the opportunity to register their opposition to abortion.

The Stupak amendment created a moral dilemma for many members on both sides of the abortion issue. It was an especially difficult decision for pro-choice women in the House, as well as women's health advocacy groups like Planned Parenthood and the National Women's Law Center. Passage of health reform would mean extending access to primary care, including the full range of reproductive health services, to tens of millions of uninsured women. At the same time, the legislation would have cut off access to abortion services to many women. But unlike the Catholic Bishops, most of the women in the

House — with the support of most advocates — chose to put the overall health of women and their families first, and voted for the bill. The issue did not end there, though. After the vote, Colorado Representative Diana DeGette, the co-chairwoman of the Congressional Pro-Choice Caucus, sent a letter to Pelosi signed by forty-one members, who pledged to vote against health reform when it came to final passage if the Stupak amendment were not removed.

With the abortion issue settled for now, the House moved forward to vote for reform on November 7. We were confident that Pelosi would be able to secure the votes of enough wavering members and deliver the 218 votes needed for passage. She was renowned for her skills at persuasion and vote counting. Still, I grew nervous watching C-Span as the vote tally slowly inched toward the magic number. My head told me that I shouldn't worry, but my heart wasn't so sure. Finally, the tally board reached 218 and then jumped to 220-215. Of the 258 Democrats in the House, 219 had voted yes: 85 percent of the Democratic caucus. The final vote also included support from one Republican, Joseph Cao, who had won election to a heavily Democratic seat in New Orleans.

It was a historical milestone, the first time that either body of Congress had passed legislation that promised to make health care a right in the country. But we had no time to catch our breath. To be sure that the victory wasn't spoiled, we had to start saying thank you, thank you, thank you! Right away.

It Was the Cherry on the Sundae

HCAN was taking advantage of a lesson learned the hard way by the environmental community. At the end of June, the House had passed legislation to address climate change, by a vote of 219-212. After the bill passed, the opposition — led by big oil and coal companies with the assistance of right-wing organizations and talk-show hosts — mounted a vigorous attack on Democrats from swing districts who had voted for the bill. Environmental advocates took a week to mount a campaign, including TV ads, to defend their beleaguered supporters. That experience had left a sour taste in the mouths of many electorally vulnerable Democrats, who were reluctant to cast another big vote that would be attacked by the right in the upcoming election.

HCAN had promised swing House members and the Speaker's office that we would not delay. As we neared the Saturday night vote, we prepared lists of members to thank, and we started recording the TV ads before the House had voted. Each House member would need a personalized ad, with their name and picture in the first frame and in the last, which ended with the tag, "Thank Congressman/woman XXX for standing up to the insurance companies and fighting for us." Our professional ad team, along with HCAN staffers Ethan Rome and Melinda Gibson, went to extraordinary lengths to have the ads ready to air Tuesday morning. The ads, which were sponsored by HCAN and AFSCME, ran in twenty House districts. We gave an advance copy of one ad to the Sunday morning talk shows, so that we immediately contributed to the national narrative in the aftermath of the vote.

While it was impossible to run the ads before Tuesday, that didn't stop us from launching thank-you activities on the ground even sooner, for both swing votes and reform champions. Working with the HCAN coalition and OFA, we had a delegation deliver a thank-you card and cookies or cupcakes at the office of almost every Democrat who voted for the bill on Monday morning and then planned bigger events on Thursday. Our biggest inspiration was to greet members of Congress at the local airports when they returned home on Sunday or Monday for the weeklong Veterans Day recess.

Willie Smith was the district director for Congressman Earl Blumenauer of Portland, Oregon. While Blumenauer represented the most liberal Congressional district in Oregon, it hadn't stopped him from, as Smith told me, "getting screamed at, at every event." Blumenauer had worked closely with the HCAN coalition for months. When HCAN organizer Betsy Dillner called Smith, saying that she wanted to organize a group to greet the Congressman at the airport, to be filmed by two of Portland's local TV news stations, he almost said no. "My first thought was that the poor Congressman was tired and anxious to get home," Smith told me. "But Earl agreed. When he got off the plane there were about forty people. He was so energized after it. It was one of those things. It had been a year and a half of trench warfare. Of getting screamed at every event, even if we had more people. He was incredibly happy to get off the plane to hear applause and see the thank-you signs. He stayed at the airport and said thank you to everyone who wanted to talk. It was the cherry on the sundae to know that people had recognized him for doing the right thing. I remember him telling me that it really validated the volunteers' work; we knew how hard they had worked on reform."

An issue in the thank-you activities was what to do about the members of Congress who had voted for reform but also had voted for the Stupak amendment. HCAN's principles included support for reproductive rights, including access to abortion. Before the House vote, while most groups that supported reform stayed out of the abortion fight, HCAN had weighed in. Our legislative team, backed by grassroots calls organized from the field and online, lobbied swing members to commit to vote for the health legislation even if the Stupak language was not included.

We did not run thank-you ads for members who voted for the Stupak amendment. However, other HCAN coalition members did run ads thanking the members of Congress in districts in which HCAN would not.

On the ground, we let each HCAN field partner decide what it would do. In Pennsylvania, the coalition decided to thank members like Kathy Dahlkemper, Christopher Carney, and Paul Kanjorsky. Each of them represented heavily Catholic, blue-collar districts with many senior citizens. The HCAN coalition had spent months telling these members of Congress that they would be strongly supported if they voted for reform. Pennsylvania HCAN director Marc Stier had learned how tough it would be for these members of Congress to vote reform without the Stupak amendment, when he asked some of the HCAN labor leaders to speak out against what Stupak was doing. Several HCAN leaders told Stier that if they did so, they would not be able to receive communion at church.

The bishops took retribution against HCAN for our admonishment of House members who voted to deny women access to abortion. The Catholic Church's Campaign for Human Development (CHD) is one of the largest sources of funding for community organizing to fight poverty in the country. Within three days of the House vote, CHD told HCAN members that it funded to disaffiliate from HCAN or lose CHD funding. As a result, eighteen groups — out of HCAN's 1,100 members — asked that their names be removed from HCAN's membership list.

She'd Better Start Packing Her Washington Office Now

Thanking was the easy part. We also had to address the issue of the Democrats who voted against reform. Among the thirty-nine Democrats who voted against the legislation, fifteen had been elected with significant support from labor and other progressive forces in their districts. The organizations and volunteers that had worked to elect these representatives were really angry when they were rewarded with a vote against an issue that represented what Hillary Clinton had often called during the primary, "a core Democratic party value."

A few days after the vote, MoveOn asked their members to contribute to a campaign of TV ads targeting "conservative Democrats" who "sided with Big Insurance." MoveOn told its members, "So we've got to act quickly and forcefully to demonstrate that any politician who sides with corporate special interests will suffer for it back home."

One Democrat who angered her constituents was freshman Susan Kosmas. Kosmas had owned an upscale real estate brokerage in New Smyrna Beach, Florida, east of Orlando. After serving in the Florida state legislature, she won the Congressional seat handily in 2008, defeating an incumbent Republican who had been implicated in the Jack Abramoff scandal. But it was a swing district; McCain had carried it by 51 percent.

The district Kosmas represented stretched from the Atlantic Ocean to suburbs east of Orlando, where the lead HCAN field organization was ACORN. Stephanie Porta grew up in Orlando and had started ACORN's Orlando chapter, which in 2004 had joined in ACORN Florida's successful effort to collect one million signatures for a minimum wage ballot measure that passed overwhelmingly. It also led the state's biggest voter registration drive, as part of the work ACORN did nationally to register more than one million voters in the 2004 election. The organization's huge success registering low-wage voters led to an attack by the Bush Justice Department, which pushed federal prosecutors to find evidence that ACORN had participated in voter fraud. It went so far as to remove prosecutors who did not go along with the politically motivated investigation — which never produced any evidence of wrongdoing. Right-wing interests also made a campaign of demonizing ACORN. Still, throughout this period of turmoil, ACORN chapters in several states had been under contract with HCAN as field partners and did an outstanding job of organizing grassroots pressure on members of Congress.

Like the other HCAN field partners, ACORN had been barraging Kosmas' office for months, with regular visits from constituents and a flood of phone calls. Earlier in the year, Porta had run into Kosmas on a flight back to Orlando. Porta told me, "She was sitting just behind me. She wears these huge sunglasses, like she was trying to hide. When we got off the plane, I introduced myself and told her that we were working on health care reform. She said, 'You know that's a very controversial issue.' Then we passed [Florida Representative] Alan Grayson, who I knew well, and the three of us started walking. I turned around and Kosmas was gone."

Doug Martin, who directed the legislative and political program for AFSCME in Florida, was also working hard to get Kosmas to vote for reform. The HCAN coalition chose Orlando as the site of a statewide rally with 1,100 people that it staged on August 29. While Representative Grayson spoke at the rally, Kosmas declined to attend.

As the vote neared, with Kosmas still waffling, Martin brought in AFSCME's biggest gun, President Gerald McEntee, who spoke at a press conference outside Kosmas' office in Daytona Beach. McEntee was joined by a wide array of other unions, and every speaker delivered the same message: "Vote for reform or face a backlash from the grassroots base that worked to get you elected."

But Kosmas had already made up her mind. That same afternoon she told a reporter at the *Orlando Sentinel* that she would be voting against the bill, because she preferred the proposal in the Senate bill that would tax high-cost health plans to the House provision of raising taxes on the wealthy. Clearly, Kosmas had been listening to her wealthy friends, not the public, which polling consistently found supported raising taxes on the rich.

The reaction was swift and sharp, starting with a quote from Doug Martin in the *Sentinel* article, "If she votes against health-care reform, it will end her political career. Her base will desert her. She better start packing her Washington office now."

After she had cast her vote against the bill, she started hearing from the labor volunteers who had worked to get her elected. As Doug Martin told me, "I'm a lobbyist and I tend to be diplomatic. But labor people will tell you what they think. I don't think Kosmas was ready for the blowback. But she should have been. She'd been hearing from us, but she refused to engage with us or take a position — which is her job. "

ACORN's Stephanie Porta told me that, "People were so pissed that they started sending out her personal cell phone number and Facebooking her, texting her. People were really angry and let her know it. These were people who had worked for her election, who had known her forever; they were furious, pissed as hell."

A few days later, Porta organized a big action outside Kosmas' office, where 150 people protested her vote. Every union told her that she would not get any more campaign contributions. If Kosmas had been unwilling to take a firm stand, her former supporters had no such qualms.

Betrayal in Colorado

The HCAN organizer in Congresswoman Betsy Markey's Northeast Colorado Congressional district had her own health care story. After graduation from Oberlin College in Ohio, Nicolle Hurt was working for a community organization that could not afford to pay for health coverage for its employees. She was in a serious car accident, and her pelvis was smashed. Unconscious, she was airlifted to Cleveland, but more than one hospital refused to treat her because she was uninsured. Fortunately, the hospital that finally admitted her had a good charity care program, or Hurt would still be saddled with debt. She told me, with a westerner's understated acceptance, "I didn't take the prescribed physical therapy because I couldn't afford it. I can feel storms coming, but I'm doing pretty well."

Hurt returned to her hometown of Greeley, where she started working for the Colorado Progressive Coalition — HCAN's state field partner — in the fall of 2008, shortly before Markey won election to the Congressional seat previously held by Marilyn Musgrave. Musgrave's hard right views on social issues had won her the enmity of the Colorado progressive community and even undercut her support in her conservative Congressional district. During her campaign, Markey often talked about the need to address the health care crisis.

Yet Markey was not eager to become a champion of reform. She was the only Democrat in the Colorado Congressional delegation who did not sign the HCAN "Which side are you on" statement of principles in 2008. She was being very cautious in her swing district, which McCain had carried with just 50 percent of the vote.

After Markey won, the Colorado Progressive Coalition (CPC) started recruiting activists to join in the health reform effort, most of them former volunteers on Markey's election campaign. Throughout the winter of 2009, Markey continued to avoid taking any position. During the next few months, CPC organized a steady stream of constituent pressure on Markey. Hurt told me, "We made formal delegation visits — a lot from small business since she was always talking about them — but also other delegations. We met her during every recess and during her meet and greet sessions; she likes to do individual meet and greets at a local coffee shop. I was seeing her monthly. It got tougher the closer we got to the vote. She kept assuring us that she was on our side, that she was for health care reform, but she also had concerns about how it was paid for. And that it was moving too quickly."

The tumultuous town halls in August didn't help. CPC staffer Hillary Jorgensen told me, "Markey gets flustered easily. In her district, where the tea party has a strong home, she had a lot of people yelling at her. It was a circus, and unlike Senator Bennett and his staff who were really good at keeping crowds under control, Markey was not as skilled. We turned people out too, sometimes as many as the tea partiers, so it became people on separate sides of the room yelling at each other. She ended up canceling a lot of town halls at the end of the recess."

Two days before the vote, CPC learned that Markey would vote no, so they were prepared. On the Monday following, CPC took a giant poster signed by Markey supporters to one of her offices, saying they were unhappy with her vote. CPC members wrote personal notes on campaign literature that had been sent out attacking Musgrave for her positions on health reform, and delivered the notes to Markey's office. Alarmed, Markey started to reach out to supporters and some of her donors to assess the damage. At one event, a donor walked up to her in a crowded room and ripped up a $5,000 check that he had made out to her.

Markey scheduled meetings with supporters to try to make amends. One of those who attended a meeting at a restaurant in Greeley was Tricia Smith. Smith had become permanently disabled in 1992 from the botched treatment that she had been given after a ski injury years earlier. Unable to work for eight years before qualifying for Medicare disability, she had no insurance. During that time she told me, "I had to crawl. I was bedridden. On top of that, qualifying for disability is a horrible and cruel process."

Smith had the opportunity to tell Markey directly how disappointed she was with her vote against reform. "We asked her, why did you do this when you know we've been working so hard on it? Markey said she was worried about cost issues and how it was paid for, that she had to go with her conscience. We told her you're there to vote *our* conscience. Her hands were shaking. She was very nervous. I felt bad for her."

The anger directed against Markey and Kosmas and others was more than a chance for people to express outrage. It served a vital purpose. The House vote in November wasn't the last one on health reform. We would need some of those members of Congress to vote yes when the final vote came around. But first we had to climb the tallest mountain of all: getting the votes of every Democrat in the U.S. Senate.

17

Harry's Dilemma

N ow it was Harry Reid's turn to announce the introduction of a health care bill. Like Speaker Pelosi, the Senate Majority Leader invoked history as he began his remarks in a packed meeting room in the Capitol Visitors Center:

> This bill is not just a milestone along a journey of a few months or even a few years. We have been working to reform health care since the first half of the last century. As the Senate heads down this home stretch, I am going to read just a short piece of a long letter by a former senator about the urgency of action on health care. This man wrote to Congress and I quote: "Millions of our citizens do not now have a full measure of opportunity to achieve and enjoy good health. Millions do not now have protection or security against the economic effects of sickness. The time has arrived for action to help them attain the opportunity and that protection.... We should resolve now that the health of this nation is a national concern, that financial barriers in the way of attaining health shall be removed, that is the health of all its citizens deserve the help of all the nation."

> That former senator was Harry Truman. And he wrote that letter to Congress on November 19, 1945, just months into his presidency and exactly 64 years ago today.

Harry Reid had a tougher job than Nancy Pelosi and the responsibility for doing what Harry Truman never did: delivering the votes in Congress. In the House, Pelosi only needed a simple majority. If Reid could have passed a bill with only a majority, he could have pushed through legislation that included a public option and other more progressive policies. But the Republicans were using the threat of filibusters to block the health care bill, and Reid needed the votes of all sixty Democrats to move legislation to the Senate floor for a final vote.

Beyond these votes remained the possibility of the one Republican who had voted for reform in committee, Maine Senator Olympia Snowe. Despite the lobbying effort being expended on her, Snowe showed no indication of bucking the rest of her party. The White House continued to plead with her. New York Senator Chuck Schumer kept trying to negotiate with her. But she never settled on any specific issues; she just kept raising an endless string of concerns that never could be resolved to her satisfaction. While our Maine coalition kept plugging away, national HCAN leaders decided to stop advertising in the state, focusing instead on getting every Democrat on board. That had become Harry Reid's assumption too.

Harry Reid reminded me of Harry Truman. Besides their physical resemblance — both short men with closely cut gray hair and a faint western twang — each had a deep commitment to the "little man" and a belief that government can lift people from poverty and provide opportunity. And both were fighters. Truman was a fiery verbal pugilist. Reid was not much of a public speaker, but he was an accomplished boxer and he brought that same toughness and persistence to the nightmarish maze that is the U.S. Senate.

Reid shared one other similarity with Harry Truman in 1948: His prospects for reelection in 2010 looked very slim. By October, only 32 percent of the state's Democrats viewed him favorably. Reid's popularity had suffered from the total collapse of the Nevada economy in the recession. The state had been leading the nation in growth for years, but it suffered a devastating turn downward, with a huge jump in unemployment and a flood of home foreclosures. Apparently, he was as good a target as anyone to blame.

As Majority Leader, Reid had to balance the interest of two constituencies: his voters at home in Nevada, a swing state that regularly elected politicians of both parties, and the other fifty-nine Democratic senators. He also had to balance concerns on the national level. He had to contend with Republicans and the right wing attacking him for backing the Obama agenda, while liberal Democrats were unhappy with him for not forcing through progressive policies.

Once the Senate Finance Committee completed its work, the next step was for Reid to propose his own bill — combining what the Senate Finance and HELP committees had enacted — and bring the legislation to the Senate floor for a vote. The biggest decision he had to make was whether to include the public option. Including it would make getting the sixty votes much harder, since several conservative Democrats did not want to support the provision. If he left it out, or included a provision like a trigger, he would anger the base of Democratic activists in Nevada, hurting his own election chances.

Reid was being pressured by the Progressive Change Campaign Committee, which ran an ad on TV and online in Nevada, featuring a Nevada nurse whose health insurance company had denied her treatment. The nurse, who identified herself as an independent voter, said, "I'm waiting to see if Harry Reid is a strong, effective enough leader to pass a public health insurance option into law."

The executive director of the Progressive Leadership Alliance of Nevada (PLAN), Bob Fulkerson, was furious at PCCC for harming Reid's chances of getting reelected, by running an ad that challenged him. As Fulkerson told CBS News, "Would these lefty blogger types be happy with a right-wing senator to replace Reid?... Because that's where their strategy could lead."[56]

Reid continued to be buffeted from the left and right. In early May, thirty Democratic Senators sent him a letter urging him to include a robust public option in the Senate bill. At the same time, the White House was pushing from the right. Even though Snowe had publicly stated that she was no longer promoting the trigger, the White House kept urging Reid to include the trigger in his legislation.

At home, Republican candidates were attacking Reid for his support of the public option. He responded by strongly defending his position, as he told his supporters in a September email, "As I've traveled the Silver State over the August recess, I've heard countless Nevadans proclaim their support for a public option meant to keep insurance companies honest, control costs, and promote competition — and that's exactly what I'm going back to Washington to fight for. Frankly, many Republicans are simply on the wrong side of what Nevadans are demanding — real health insurance reform."

HCAN's strategy was to campaign hard for the public option while applauding Reid for his support. After the Senate Finance Committee vote, we ran a television ad castigating Nevada's Republican Senator John Ensign for voting against the public option. The ad provided cover to Reid from the Republican attacks.

How would Reid escape being boxed between the left in Nevada and conservative senators? An interview with SEIU's president, Andy Stern, suggested a compromise that made political and policy sense. Stern suggested establishing a national public option with the stipulation that states be allowed to opt out. Under this proposal, a state legislature could vote not to offer the national public insurance plan in its state's exchange. From a policy point of view, such a compromise would still establish a national public plan, which would certainly include enough well-populated states to be viable. From a political point of view, it gave conservative Democrats the ability to argue that their state could decide not to have a public option.

While HCAN didn't endorse the opt-out publicly, which would represent another retreat from our policy ideal, with the permission of the HCAN Steering Committee I urged Reid's office and the staff of New York Senator Chuck Schumer to include the opt-out in the legislation. I argued that it was the only way that Reid could avoid being castigated from the left and avoid an internal war among Senate Democrats.

After two weeks Reid's office informed us that he would include the opt-out public option in his legislation. Here is how *The Washington Post* reported the news on October 27:

> Senate Majority Leader Harry M. Reid announced Monday that he will include a government-backed insurance plan in the chamber's health-care reform legislation, a

key concession to liberals who have threatened to oppose a bill without such a public option.

Reid's decision was a reversal from two weeks ago, when the Nevada Democrat appeared inclined to set aside the idea — among the most divisive in the reform debate — in an attempt to avoid alienating party moderates. Doubts remain about whether he has the votes to guarantee passage, but he said he concluded that in the interest of bringing the strongest possible bill to the Senate floor next month, adding a public option was a risk worth taking.

The public option had survived one more time, looking more and more like a cat with nine lives. I really thought we were going to defy all the skeptics who said it would never pass. But this cat wasn't immortal. It had only one, weakened life left.

* * * *

While the fight over the public option overhung the debate, the legislation that Senate Majority Leader Harry Reid introduced on November 19, 2009, contained a handful of other compromises that addressed some of the unhappiness among liberal Democrats in the Senate. Compared with the Baucus bill, it made health coverage more affordable for middle-income people, scaled back the excise tax slightly, and limited the amount that health insurance companies could spend on administration and profit. It raised additional revenue by increasing Medicare taxes on the wealthy. Unlike the House bill, it allowed insurance plans in the exchanges to provide abortion coverage, as long as the funding was provided by individuals or businesses, and not the government.

The next step for Senator Reid's bill would normally be straightforward: a motion to allow the bill to be debated. I was surprised to learn that this motion would be the first opportunity for Republicans to threaten a filibuster. Reid needed to get the votes of all sixty Democrats to even allow a debate on the health care reform bill. Two senators stood out as potential holdouts: Blanche Lincoln of Arkansas and Ben Nelson of Nebraska.

Solid as Nebraska

Nebraska presented one of the greatest challenges to HCAN's strategy of organizing from the ground up. The Cornhusker State did not boast a large, well-developed progressive infrastructure upon which we could readily build. It contained few labor union members and none of our national community partners had affiliates in the state. But there was one big reason that we couldn't ignore Nebraska: its senior senator, Ben Nelson, a Democrat who had been elected in 2000 after serving two terms as governor.

It's tough for Democrats to get elected in Nebraska. Ben Nelson had succeeded by being a conservative Democrat who championed his state above all. His campaign slogans were, "Nebraska First ... Nebraska Always," and "Solid as Nebraska." In his reelection campaign in 2006, prominent conservative groups had endorsed him, including the National Rifle Association, Nebraska Right-to-Life, and the U.S. Chamber of Commerce. His mother had headed up a local anti-tax group, and he had adopted her conservative views of taxes and spending.

Nelson also had close ties to the insurance industry. His first job out of law school was for the Central National Insurance Group of Omaha. He became an industry-friendly Nebraska state insurance director and then returned to the insurance company, where he became president, before he was elected governor.

But as Saul Shorr, who did the ads for Nelson's first campaign for governor, told me, there was a reason that Nelson became a Democrat. He cared about people who needed help. He had almost become a minister. As governor, he championed the establishment of the State Child Health Insurance Program. He was sincerely concerned about low-income families and rural communities. His longtime chief of staff and closest political confidante, Tim Becker, was widely considered to be a progressive.

Nelson was known for liking to be the last one to make a deal. In politics, legislators with centrist politics often maximize their power and influence by holding their vote in abeyance to the last minute, angling to cut a deal. Nelson had a reputation of being a master of waiting until the last possible moment to maximize his clout.

The HCAN field partner in Nebraska was an advocacy group on low-income issues called Appleseed. The organization created a small HCAN coalition and hired an organizer to start recruiting people to advocate for health reform.

Fortunately for HCAN, SEIU had decided to make a major investment in Nebraska by setting up a Change That Works (CTW) organization, run by Jane Kleeb. She had a powerful personal motivation to fight for health reform. "When I was a junior in high school in Fort Lauderdale, Florida, I struggled with life-threatening anorexia. My heart stopped. I was in and out of treatment facilities. My grandmother used her life savings to keep me alive. Insurance wouldn't cover the treatment. If my grandmother didn't have savings, I would have died. But I saw that others were being treated for only days, because insurance companies wouldn't cover any more. It's completely unfair that some insurance company person miles away can make a decision that would determine people's lives."

She concluded that the best way to demonstrate to Nelson the support of Nebraskans was with the same menu of tactics that HCAN was using around the country: generate lots of local press, including letters to the editor; flood him with letters and calls; bring people to meet him in person, including faith leaders and people with moving stories; and hold events with large numbers of people.

A crucial question for Nelson would be whether the campaign should be a bad cop, being critical of him for not supporting the campaign's position, as opposed to a good cop, accentuating the positives while gently asking him to do better. Kleeb's research concluded that Nelson's staff viewed attacks from liberal groups as an endorsement of Nelson's independent image, which helped them politically with the majority of voters in Nebraska. She also concluded that Nelson welcomed "the tearing down of the Republican brand so that Nelson looks good."

Working with the HCAN coalition that Appleseed had assembled, Change That Works started the campaign by holding some eighty educational forums in early 2009 around Nebraska, mostly in small towns, at which the organizers collected names of local people. The forums garnered local press and the organizers made sure that each forum was followed by letters to the editor of the local papers from local supporters of reform. In May, to increase the visibility of the effort, they organized an event called 24/7, in which every hour for a full day and night, a video was released on YouTube and sent to the press and the staff of the Nebraska congressional delegation, showing a succession of Nebraskans telling personal stories about their troubles with the health system. Kleeb told me, "We got tons of media. For the first time, members of Congress and the press were really seeing the stories of people in Nebraska."

In the spring, the coalition activities in Nebraska took on a new form, unique to the state. In D.C., SEIU had begun working with several large health advocacy groups that were not part of HCAN, including AARP, Families USA, and the American Cancer Society. To take advantage of that network in Nebraska, Kleeb formed the Nebraska Alliance, which included AARP, the Cancer Society, the Center for Rural Affairs, along with Change That Works and Appleseed. This group became the center for planning coalition activities on health care.

When the August tea parties erupted, the coalition recruited people to cover all ten of the town hall meetings Nelson held in a two-week period. Kleeb told me that the coalition strategy was to be respectful, in order to create a contrast with the tea partiers. They even handed out water at the town hall meetings. They also recruited people to attend the town halls held by Nebraska's Republican Senator, Mike Johanns. At the Johanns' meetings, Kleeb told me, "We really threw Johanns off. People would stand up and tell their stories and then ask a question. We had 80 percent of the questions."

The coalition also regularly brought people to meet with Nelson and with Tim Becker, his chief of staff. At one of those meetings, Nelson was almost brought to tears.

Janet Banks introduced herself as "a pastor and a nurse, a former underground coal miner and a recent breast cancer survivor." After working for four years in a coal mine, she got her nursing degree. "I worked as a nurse in Southern Indiana. I learned to be patient and compassionate. I loved working with families, being able to reassure them in any way possible concerning their loved ones. I also saw how much care depended on whether the families had insurance. Legally, we had to do enough to stabilize a patient, but if they weren't insured, they were out of luck in terms of getting continued care."

In 1994, Banks moved to Lincoln, Nebraska, to marry her high school sweetheart, who had become the senior pastor at a non-denominational church in Lincoln. She entered the ministry herself in 2006 and became ordained in November 2008, the same month that she discovered that she had cancer. A year earlier, Banks had purchased health insurance through Nebraska's high-risk pool for people with preexisting conditions, which had been established while Nelson was governor. The plan had a $5,000 deductible and premiums of $400 a month, a lot of money for a working family. Banks told me:

> For the cancer, I needed surgery and chemotherapy. The treatment was hard mentally and financially. We were living from paycheck to paycheck but still getting by. But the cost of the premiums and deductibles almost bankrupted us; we got behind in paying our mortgage. We're still making monthly payments on the deductible. I got hit with tons of prescriptions. My husband is still uninsured; he has preexisting conditions.

At the end of August, Banks joined a group of a dozen clergy at a meeting with Nelson at his Omaha office. Banks was the last of the group to tell Nelson her story. After relating what she had gone through, Banks told Nelson that he had to be a Good Samaritan, who didn't let people die in the streets. "I started crying. There were a lot of tearful people in the room. I could see that Nelson was really moved. He patted me on my shoulder before he left. Afterward, his staff called me and asked me to keep in touch. I brought a clean mammogram to Tim Becker in October."

A few days after meeting with Nelson, Banks — wearing a long silver robe — and several other ministers joined more than 800 people at a rally on the steps of the State Capitol in Lincoln, in front of a tall bronze statue of Abraham Lincoln. It was the biggest rally that people could recall being staged in Lincoln in years. Among the demonstrators was a large contingent of AARP volunteers, who joined the rally wearing T-shirts that read "Vote Yes on Healthcare Reform."

One of the speakers at the August rally in Lincoln was Nick Rathod, a Nebraskan native who had been appointed by President Obama as the director of the White House Office of Intergovernmental Affairs. Rathod led a chant of "Yes we can!" at the rally, complementing the chant that echoed through the rally, a message to the Nebraska congressional delegation, "Vote Yes!"

Rathod connected with another speaker at the rally, physician Dr. Amanda McKinney, who had grown up in Nebraska. After doing her residency in California, McKinney moved to Beatrice, Nebraska, a town of 13,000. "I wanted to give back to my community, since I was treated so well growing up, so I came home. Sometimes we have problems finding doctors, particularly specialists to serve."

A few weeks after the rally, Rathod invited McKinney to the White House to join a public meeting planned for October 5 between Obama and doctors from around the country who supported health reform. The group made an impressive picture in the Rose Garden, wearing their white medical coats. But McKinney was one of only four doctors — each from states represented by swing senators — who were asked to stand behind Obama when he made his speech.

Back home, McKinney found out from the CEO of the hospital where she practiced in Nebraska that Glenn Beck, the right-wing Fox News host, was watching. When someone said that Beck told his listeners that those really weren't doctors at the White House, the CEO proudly responded, "I can prove it — one of them works for me."

The rally speakers included small business people too, and one of the most active was Rick Poore, who grew up in

McCook, Nebraska, Nelson's hometown. Poore's grandmother used to baby-sit Senator Nelson, and his uncle dated Nelson's mother before she was married. When Poore first met Nelson, the Senator immediately said, "Hey, you're a Poore. All you Poores have the same noses."

Poore had built up a business designing and printing custom t-shirts. It now had thirty employees and sold T-shirts all around the country, including at 300 college campuses. Poore, who provided health coverage for his employees, said that he'd become "frustrated that it's my job in the first place to be the conduit for my employees to access the insurance system. It's a fluke of history after World War II. Rates went up thirty percent each year for no reason I could see. Insurance companies are like potato chip manufacturers — they put less in the bag and charge more. That's why I'm a national health care supporter — I don't want to have anything to do with it."

Poore told the Senator, "I was really hoping that regardless of what you hear from the Chamber of Commerce, that's not me. They don't speak for lots of small businesses."

Poore brought his business acumen to organizing turnout for the big rally in Lincoln. "I printed up T-shirts for the rally. One was "Beer drinkers for health care reform" and I did a Facebook group for it. I talked to two bars in downtown Lincoln, who agreed to give out free beers to people who got a ticket at the rally."

The Nebraska coalition kept plugging away with their strategy. During the fall, Change That Works joined Planned Parenthood in a canvass that knocked on 50,000 doors. The coalition rented an ambulance and took it on a tour of small towns throughout the state, collecting letters to Nelson. CTW organized nightly phone banks so that Democratic voters could leave a message with Nelson's office supporting reform. In September, AARP held a tele-town hall with Nelson, and more than 6,000 AARP members participated.

Throughout this process Jane Kleeb would meet regularly with Nelson's chief of staff, Tim Becker, updating him on the coalition's activities. Kleeb told me, "There were moments when Tim would look across the table and say, 'It doesn't look good.' He'd say we were getting outnumbered by calls, two to one. That the Senator is convinced his constituents don't want it. I had moments when I'd go back to my car and cry."

Jane Kleeb wasn't the only person with whom Becker was sharing his pessimistic appraisal. We had our own back channel to Becker in Mike Lux, who had worked on health care reform in the Clinton White House and was now a strategic adviser to HCAN. Mike had grown up in Nebraska and became good friends with Becker in high school. They had kept in touch, two Nebraska boys who had achieved stature in national politics. Throughout the next several weeks Lux would patiently make the strongest political arguments he could to Becker as to why his boss should vote for reform.

Becker told Lux that he was increasingly doubtful that his boss would follow Lux's advice. As *The Hill* reported, "Nelson had bucked his party more than any Senate Democrat on procedural votes in 2009." Nelson was personally responsible for thirty-two of the sixty Democratic defections on procedural votes.[57]

We had increasing doubts that the Nebraska strategy was working. During the previous spring we had seen some evidence that a more negative tactic could work. The Progressive Change Campaign and Democracy for America ran an ad in which a Nebraska small businessman, facing a 42 percent hike in insurance rates, attacked Nelson for taking $2 million from the insurance industry and opposing the public option. Nelson had responded by publicly backing away from his strong opposition to the public option.

The SEIU and Change That Works staff in Washington had prolonged arguments with Jane Kleeb, pushing her to be more aggressive with Nelson, but she refused. HCAN also sent our experienced Oregon organizer, Betsy Dillner, to Nebraska to work with Appleseed in the hope that she could get them to take a harder line with Nelson, all to no avail. MoveOn did stage protests at Nelson's offices, so there was some critical grassroots pressure in the state.

Meanwhile, the Nebraska health care coalition continued its busy pace of organizing activities, as it would until the final

Senate votes before Christmas, all the while keeping a positive tone.

We reinforced the organizing in Nebraska by running a television ad in the state that encouraged Nelson and his Republican counterpart Johanns to stand up to the insurance industry and allow the Senate to begin debate.

On November 21, Nelson joined all sixty Democrats and voted to allow debate to proceed. We had gotten him on round one. In keeping with the strategy that Jane Kleeb recommended, we promptly ran another TV ad in Nebraska that criticized the state's Republican Senator, Mike Johanns, for voting to prevent debate. The voice-over in the ad said:

> The first job of the U.S. Senate is to debate important legislation. But Nebraska Senator Mike Johanns must think that's not part of his job. Because Johanns voted to stop the debate on health insurance reform from even taking place. So who's he really working for? The health insurance industry. They're spending millions to stop health care reform, and they know they can count on Mike Johanns.

We heard that Nelson's office liked the ad, but that still didn't mean we had his vote to break a Republican filibuster on round two. The real test would come on a "manager's amendment," which would be a proposal by Reid that included all the changes he needed to make, and deals that he needed to cut, to secure the votes of all sixty Democrats.

From November 21 to December 19, the action in the Senate took place on two fronts. Publicly, Senators offered amendments, including many by Republicans that were only offered to embarrass Democrats, such as a proposal to prohibit giving prisoners drugs like Viagra that treated erectile dysfunction. The Republicans focused an enormous amount of their time attacking the $500 billion in reductions in Medicare over a decade, with a clear eye toward scaring seniors, who would vote heavily in the 2010 elections. It didn't matter that the savings were entirely from trimming costs to providers and that the legislation expanded Medicare benefits. I summarized our reaction in a *Huffington Post* column, which pointed out that Republicans had a long history of proposing cuts in Medicare benefits. My post began, "A sense of irony is clearly a luxury that politicians can't afford. So was the irony totally lost on Republican senators that after months and months of relentless attacks on a 'government takeover of health care,' they spent most of the week stomping their feet 'defending' Medicare, our national government health insurance program for seniors and people with serious disabilities?"[58]

Another debate filled with irony was started when North Dakota Senator Byron Dorgan proposed an amendment that would allow the importation of lower-cost prescription drugs, a position that both Republicans and Democrats had long supported, and had been endorsed by both Obama and McCain in the 2008 election campaign. But approving such a law would have blown up the White House deal with the drug industry, which was spending tens of millions of dollars to support reform. Obama and Reid convinced twenty-four Democratic Senators who had voted for the drug importation legislation earlier to reverse their votes, so the amendment received only fifty-one votes, short of the sixty votes needed for any amendment to pass.

While some Democrats were not willing to attack the drug industry, most had no such compunctions with the health insurance companies. The main Democratic theme was how their legislation would stop health insurance companies from delaying and denying care to patients. Democratic senators frequently told stories of victims of the health insurance industry in their Senate floor speeches, including many people who they had met through the HCAN coalition and Main Street Alliance. In addition, the HCAN research on the monopoly-like concentration of the health insurance industry and the high salaries of its CEOs peppered the talking points of Democratic senators.

Senator Reid added a major set of consumer protections to his bill, incorporating most of the Patients Bill of Rights legislation that had been heavily debated by Congress in the mid-1990s but never passed. As a result, the Reid bill included a comprehensive set of federal laws dictating how health insurance plans were to provide information to consumers and handle complaints and appeals about access to care.

Meanwhile, behind the scenes, Reid was negotiating with Democratic senators on the changes that would be included in the manager's amendment. They had a lot to discuss, but before anything could be settled, they had to decide on the biggest issue of all: what to do about the public option.

18

Lieberman's Revenge

Thanksgiving was over. Christmas Eve was less than a month away. Time was running out for Reid to make a deal. The war over the public option between the handful of its conservative Democratic opponents and the majority of moderate and liberal Democrats had to be ended. So in the first week of December, Reid put ten Democratic senators in a room with instructions to find a compromise. The liberal team included Sherrod Brown, Jay Rockefeller, Chuck Schumer, Wisconsin's Russ Feingold, and Iowa's Tom Harkin, who had taken over as the chair of the HELP Committee.

The conservatives included the two senators we most worried about — Nelson and Arkansas Senator Blanche Lincoln — as well as Louisiana's Mary Landrieu, who continued to voice concerns about the public option. In addition, Reid invited Delaware Senator Tom Carper, who had been floating compromises on the public option for months. Also included was Arkansas' Mark Pryor, a moderate who had been supportive of reform, to help reassure Lincoln. There was one notable absence. Connecticut Senator Joseph Lieberman refused an invitation to participate, sending an aide to observe instead.

When word of the negotiations got out, we set up a meeting with Sherrod Brown, who had been our chief organizer in the Senate. We urged him to hold fast and not make any further compromises. Brown was sympathetic. He had been protesting publicly that numerous compromises had already been made. But Brown also encapsulated the entire dilemma that advocates for reform — both in and out of Congress — shared. "The problem is that they are willing to kill reform, to walk away.

We are not. We're doing our best and I'm as frustrated as you are. The problem is, the negotiating table isn't even."

News from the closed negotiations soon began to leak. Instead of a new national health insurance plan run by the government, the federal agency that administers the Federal Employees Health Benefits Plan (FEHBP) would take bids from private insurance companies to establish health insurance plans that would be available across the country, at least one of which had to be a non-profit. If no such plans were established — but of course they would be since insurers were eager to serve a national market — then a public option would be triggered. In addition, the negotiators agreed to some tougher limits on how much insurance companies could spend on administration and profits.

The reaction across the progressive community to such a compromise was uniformly negative. As HCAN pointed out in a press release, half of privately insured Americans already were covered by non-profits — and that was the inadequate coverage we were fighting. As for the trigger, the idea that it would ever lead to a public option was so laughable that we didn't even dignify it with a response.

An email from "an insurance company insider" leaked to *Politico's* Ben Smith summarized it best, ""We WIN. Administered by private insurance companies. No government funding. No government insurance competitor."[59]

But one other provision in the compromise had great appeal to progressives. The Medicare program would be extended to people age fifty-five to sixty-four, starting in 2011. That meant a well-established, very robust public plan would be newly available to millions of people, including four million in that age group who were uninsured and faced the highest prices for private insurance because of their age.

The champion of the Medicare expansion was Howard Dean, the physician and former Democratic Party national chairman who had served twelve years as governor of Vermont. I was one of many people whom Dean had called to push the idea, so I knew firsthand what he had been urging liberal Democratic senators to demand in return for dropping the public option. Dean was deeply worried that the health reform plan did not contain enough tangible benefits to appeal to voters by the 2010 or 2012 elections. He was particularly concerned about older voters, who turned out to the polls reliably. And he was dismissive of the value of the compromised public option in the Reid bill. By offering Medicare to people in that ten-year age bracket, starting in 2011, Dean offered a solution that met both of his concerns. The Medicare "buy-in" would provide immediate benefit to the "older" voters who were eligible, and by expanding the nation's existing national health insurance program, it could pave the way for expanding Medicare to people of other ages in the future. While I disagreed with Dean about the efficacy of even the weakened public option, I thought his other points were on the money.

Over the next few days, progressives started to embrace the Medicare buy-in as a concrete achievement. New York Congressman Anthony Weiner, who had become one of the most visible public option proponents through frequent appearances on MSNBC's evening news lineup, commented that it "would perhaps get us on the path to a single-payer model. In a debate that hasn't focused enough on how to genuinely contain costs and deliver affordable health care, this is one idea I like a lot."[60]

At the same time, hospitals, doctors, and the insurance industry started to lobby hard against the proposal. Insurers didn't want the competition, and hospitals and doctors opposed expanding Medicare because it had proven to be much more effective than private insurance in limiting payments to providers. But the White House was thrilled to see a potential agreement, and the two Senate leaders who were most involved in the deal, Reid and Schumer, expressed confidence that the tentative agreement would hold. What they didn't count on was the opposition of a Senator who had publicly endorsed the idea of a Medicare buy-in only three months earlier. It was time for Lieberman to exact his pound of flesh from the liberals who, he believed, had denied him a chance to be president and who had almost ended his career in the U.S. Senate.

* * * *

Joseph Lieberman had been a major thorn in the side of progressive health care advocates ever since he first was elected to the Senate in 1988. He was the only Democratic Senator north of the Mason-Dixon Line who did not endorse a universal health reform bill in 1993 and 1994, when President Clinton attempted to move health reform. When national Citizen Action organized civil disobedience in June 1994 to try to rescue health reform, the one Democratic Senator whose office was a target for resistance was Lieberman, who had been defending the interests of the insurance industry, which had major companies headquartered in Hartford, Connecticut.

One of those who was arrested at Lieberman's office, sitting in front of the main doors to prevent them from being shut on his fellow demonstrators, was Tom Swan, the executive director of the Connecticut Citizen Action Group (CCAG). In 2004, when Lieberman ran for president, CCAG endorsed Howard Dean's candidacy, an affront to its home-state senator. Lieberman dropped out of the primaries early and blamed his poor showing on opposition from the left.

In 2006, Swan took a leave from CCAG to run the campaign of Ned Lamont, who was challenging Lieberman in the Democratic primary for Senate. Lieberman was vehemently opposed by the left in Connecticut because of his years of defending corporate interests plus his hawkish stance on the war in Iraq. Several labor unions and MoveOn joined CCAG in working to defeat Lieberman. By combining the traditional electoral tools of labor and community groups with the new web-based fund raising and volunteer recruitment pioneered during the Dean campaign, the Lamont campaign channeled the years of frustration with Lieberman among the Democratic base and beat him in the August primary. But Lieberman won reelection in that November election as an independent, with the support of Republicans, conservative Democrats, and a share of independent voters.

Returning to the Senate as an independent, Lieberman chose to continue to caucus with the Democrats in the Senate. But in 2008 he campaigned aggressively for John McCain.

When Senate Democrats returned to Washington after Obama's election, many were clamoring that Lieberman be denied his prized chairmanship of the Homeland Security Committee. But with the backing of Obama and Reid, Lieberman was allowed to remain as committee chair, with his full seniority intact. The presumption was that he owed Reid and Obama a deep debt of gratitude.

Gratitude wasn't a Lieberman character trait. As Swan told me, "Joe is a very vindictive person. For example, he would not endorse [Connecticut Senator Chris] Dodd when he ran in the Democratic primary for president, because Dodd had endorsed Lamont after Lieberman lost the primary. With so many progressives invested in the public option, it seemed to be a no-brainer for him to find the right time to maximize the potential to kill it. And on top of that, to help his friends in the insurance industry."

During the first months of 2009 Lieberman had not given us any reason to worry. We presumed that he would fall in line behind Obama and Reid. But in an appearance on CNN in August, Lieberman argued that there was no reason to spend money to cover the uninsured until the recession was over.[61] Then at the end of October, the day after Reid announced that he would introduce the "opt-out" public option, Lieberman announced that he would filibuster the final bill if it included any public insurance plan, even with an opt-out.[62]

Lieberman's filibuster threat prompted the progressive media watchdog group Media Matters to report that Lieberman had received more than $1.1 million in campaign donations from the health care industry during the 2010 campaign cycle, when he wasn't even up for reelection, and $2 million during his 2006 campaign for Senate. Media Matters also reported that Lieberman's wife, Hadassah, worked as a senior counselor in a lobbying firm's health care and pharmaceuticals practice.[63]

The following week, Lieberman appeared on *Fox News Sunday*. Lieberman, an Orthodox Jew who often expressed his political views in moral terms, stated, "If the public option plan is in there, as a matter of conscience, I will not allow this bill to come to a final vote."

That was the final straw. Up to this time the HCAN coalition in Connecticut, which was coordinated by CCAG, had decided to ignore any negative comments from Lieberman. The consensus was that organizing against Lieberman might backfire, because he craved public attention. We also believed that it was Obama's and Reid's responsibility to deliver Lieberman's vote. But as Swan told me, "we had a very engaged activist base getting increasingly frustrated with him." With time running out, and Lieberman threatening to filibuster, the HCAN coalition in Connecticut decided to hold a demonstration meant to focus on the morality of health care reform, challenging Lieberman's notion of conscience.[64]

On Sunday, November 15, more than 500 people filled the auditorium at Stamford High School, where — as Stamford Mayor Dan Malloy told the crowd — Lieberman went to high school, held his first public event after being chosen as the Democratic nominee for vice-president in 2000, and announced his candidacy for president in 2004. Rabbi Ron Fish read to the crowd from a letter that had been sent to Lieberman by more than seventy Connecticut clergy:

> The moral imperative for our time is clear. Anyone whose guide in public policy is conscience, anyone who argues that faith and religious traditions should direct our actions, such a person must stand for universal health care in America. It happens we are all also citizens of Connecticut. That fact leads us to ask you, Senator Lieberman, what is it that you stand for?

Another Connecticut rabbi, Stephen Fuchs, quoted scripture: "You shall not stand idly by the blood of your neighbors. It is with a heavy heart that I proclaim to you, Senator Lieberman, that that is exactly what you seem to be doing at this time."

The rabbis, joined by clergy of other faiths, then led the audience to hold a candlelight vigil across the street from the high school, at the apartment building where Lieberman lived. Other residents in the building appeared on the terraces to light candles in support of the demonstrators below. When the doorman would not allow a few people to enter the building in order to place a flyer under the residents' door, a well-dressed woman who lived in the upscale building said that she would distribute the literature to her neighbors.

If ignoring Lieberman hadn't worked, flaying him publicly was no more successful. Lieberman would exact revenge on the left and reward the insurance industry, in one vitriolic step. On the Sunday after the Medicare buy-in had replaced the public option, Lieberman appeared one more time on national TV. Speaking on CBS's *Face the Nation*, he said that he would filibuster the legislation if it included the Medicare buy-in. As an unnamed Democratic Senate staffer told *The New York Times*, "It was a total flip-flop, and leaves us in a predicament as to what to do."[65]

Just three months earlier Lieberman had told editors at Hearst newspapers that instead of a public option, he supported expanding "the existing, successful public health insurance programs, Medicare and Medicaid," a proposal he had first made when he ran for president. Lieberman said:

> When it came to Medicare, I was very focused on a group, post-50, maybe more like post-55, people who have retired early or unfortunately have been laid off early, who lose their health insurance, and they're too young to qualify for Medicare. And what I was proposing was they have an option to buy into Medicare early and, again, on the premise that would be less expensive than the enormous cost of obtaining private insurance at that age.

Harry Reid later told *The New York Times Magazine* that he had been "double-crossed" by Lieberman and was so angry he was willing to let the bill "go down." But Rahm Emanuel convinced him to keep pushing ahead even without the Medicare buy-in. In response, MoveOn scheduled an emergency vigil at the White House to protest that "the White House is pressuring Democrats to cave to Joe Lieberman."[66]

The anger on the left was deep and threatened support for the overall bill. The left blogosphere was enraged. Under the headline, "Liberal Revolt on Health Care Stings White House," *The New York Times* reporter Sheryl Gay Stolberg wrote on December 18, "Grass-roots groups are balking, liberal commentators are becoming more critical of the president, some unions are threatening to withhold support and Howard Dean, the former Democratic Party chief, is urging the Senate to kill its health bill."

The *Times* ran a picture of an angry, animated Vermont Senator Bernie Sanders, who told the newspaper, "I don't sleep well. I am struggling with this issue very hard, trying to sort out what is positive in this bill, what is negative in the bill, what it means for our country if there is no health insurance legislation, when we will come back to it. And I have to combine that with the fact that I absolutely know that the insurance companies and the drug companies will be laughing all the way to the bank the day after this is passed."

I was angry and depressed, a feeling that I'm sure was shared by countless progressives around the country. The rejection for me was even more personal. After all, I'd been one of the people who had first come up with the public option idea. I'd spent these past years developing the message to sell it to the American public. I'd led a campaign that had proved that my original vision was correct: the public option could unify the left, appeal to the majority of Americans, and had a good chance of becoming law. In spite of a massive attack from the right and the insurance industry, the idea had survived numerous premature obituaries and come further than almost anyone in Washington thought possible.

However, unlike Sanders and many on the left, I didn't have to struggle with whether to support health reform overall. As the HCAN Steering Committee had known all along, we had to focus on the overall picture. As I had argued with those who were single-payer die-hards, the fundamental moral question was whether the legislation would expand access to good health insurance. In personal terms, my wife is alive today because of the care she received for her Hodgkin's lymphoma from doctors and hospitals, care that was financed through a private health insurance company. The fact that I had spent countless hours sorting through and hassling with the maze of insurance claims, rejections, and resubmissions didn't change the fact that because she had good insurance coverage, she got the care she needed and most of it was paid for. As long as the health reform bill met that test, HCAN would still put our full force behind its passage.

19

Christmas Eve

With the public option gone, Reid rushed to close the deal on a manager's amendment that would command the vote of all sixty Democrats. Time was running out to complete the Senate's work by Christmas Eve, since the procedural rules required two votes to break filibusters and then a final vote — by a simple majority — to pass the actual bill.

Predictably, Reid's amendment included some deals that were made to help particular industries or states. But many important pro-consumer measures were also included, both to strengthen the bill's support with the public and compensate liberal senators for the loss of the public option. The amended legislation prohibited insurance companies from imposing annual or lifetime caps on what they paid for covered services. For the first time a national law would give consumers who were denied care by an insurance company the right to have an outside authority conduct an "external review" of the denial. The bill required that emergency care be covered without needing approval from an insurance company and prohibited insurers from charging consumers higher costs if they got emergency care outside of the approved network of hospitals. The amendment also further restricted the amount that insurance companies could spend on administration and profit.

Reid's amended bill also added additional funding for the State Child Health Insurance Program and included a number of provisions improving access to care for women and children. It included a long-sought major improvement in the woefully underfunded and outdated Indian Health Service, which provides health care to Native Americans. It also included measures aimed at reducing racial disparities in access to health coverage.

But first Reid needed to close the deal with Ben Nelson. Everyone else was on board. Some of the jockeying with Nelson played out publicly. On December 16, a headline in the *Lincoln Journal Star* read, "Nelson sounds conflicted on health reform." In the article he expressed unhappiness with aspects of the bill while at the same talking sympathetically about the four thousand Nebraskans that went bankrupt each year due to medical costs.[67] Nelson's mention of the bankruptcy statistic was evidence that he'd been impressed by another TV ad that HCAN had just run in Nebraska. The ad made the case for reform in plain terms. The script read:

> What's the real cause of rising health care costs? Lack of competition in the health insurance industry. In Nebraska, just two health insurance companies control 67 percent of the market. No wonder premiums have gone up almost three times faster than wages. In fact, nearly 4,000 Nebraska families go bankrupt every year as a result of medical bills. We need lower health care costs now. Tell Senators Nelson and Johanns, it's time to make health care affordable for our businesses and families.

The President was working on Nelson too. Nelson had been one of Obama's earliest supporters when he ran for President, and the two of them had a good relationship. On December 15, Nelson had spent a half hour with Obama in the Oval Office. While everyone was wondering what the price of Nelson's vote would be, he told the *Lincoln Journal Star* reporter: "My vote is not for sale. Period."

With time running out, we decided to run a more pointed ad in Nebraska. Unlike our other ads, which asked voters to contact both Nelson and Johanns, this focused on Nelson alone. It was designed to build Nelson up, looking at the beginning like an ad he might run in his own campaign, in order to establish the expectation that he would do the right thing. The script read:

Nebraska's Ben Nelson. As State Insurance Commissioner, Governor and U.S. Senator we've come to respect him for doing the right thing. Now Ben Nelson will help decide whether the health care debate in Washington will receive a final up or down vote. Last year Senator Nelson said, "I do not support procedural gimmicks that prevent a bill from getting an up or down vote." He's right. Tell Senator Nelson, we deserve a vote. It's the American Way.

In the end, Nelson's vote came down to two qualifications. Despite the Senator's declaration that his vote wasn't for sale, he insisted that Nebraska be given special treatment by being spared the additional cost of covering more people through Medicaid. Republicans quickly made a huge issue of the provision, labeling it the "Cornhusker kickback." The press leaped on the story, because, unlike complicated policy issues, it was easy to understand. The resultant furor further poisoned public opinion of the bill and would soon lead Nelson to abandon the special treatment.

The other issue involved both a matter of principle and politics for Nelson. As with the House, the last issue to close in the Senate was abortion. Nelson was personally opposed to abortion and counted the support of Nebraska's politically active right-to-life community as part of his base. Nelson had to find some way to resolve the abortion issue that he could live with. Pennsylvania Democratic Senator Bob Casey, a champion of health reform who was also anti-abortion, had been trying to find a compromise. Casey proposed that insurance companies set up separate funds for abortion coverage, segregating private payments for abortion from public funding. The compromise was swiftly rejected by the U.S. Conference of Catholic Bishops, who wanted nothing less than what the House passed, a strict prohibition on abortions, regardless of who paid for the insurance. However, Casey's proposal had the support of Sister Carol Keehan, president of the Catholic Health Association, the association of Catholic hospitals.

With some Democratic senators publicly saying that maybe the vote could wait until next year, and many groups — including the AFL-CIO and SEIU — publicly expressing their unhappiness with the Senate's legislation, the bill looked ready to fall apart. If the legislation failed to get out of the Senate in 2009, the loss of momentum could be fatal. In a last attempt to save the bill, Reid and the White House set up shuttle diplomacy between Nelson and California Senator Barbara Boxer, a champion of reproductive rights. Together Boxer and Washington Senator Patty Murray stated that they would not vote for a Stupak prohibition on abortion in the Senate.

After thirteen hours of negotiations, a compromise was reached. The heart of the compromise was that if an insurer covered abortion services, then the insurer would have to collect a separate premium payment for abortion coverage. In this way, private funding for abortions would be segregated from public funds. In addition, the legislation would allow states to vote to prohibit any insurance plans from offering abortion coverage in their state exchanges. The bishops were not happy, but the concession was enough for Nelson. The Nebraska health coalition helped to reinforce his decision by organizing a letter from two dozen Nebraska clergy, including several Catholics, supporting the compromise.

On December 21, the Senate broke the second Republican filibuster. On Christmas Eve, it passed the Patient Protection and Affordable Care Act, by a vote of 60 to 39.

It was done, and no one was happier than the health care activists in Nebraska. Tim Becker told his friend Mike Lux that the people who influenced his boss the most were: Jane Kleeb, Chuck Schumer, White House lobbyist Pete Rouse, and Lux. Becker told Jane Kleeb that he would often tell Nelson, when he was leaning against reform, that, "Jane is still hopeful. She believes you'll do the right thing."

But the jubilation was not shared by most of the HCAN coalition and the health reform community more broadly. The public option was lost. The legislation still included the so-called Cadillac tax, the excise tax on employer-provided coverage. The subsidies were still too little to make health insurance truly affordable to many middle-income people. And the employer responsibility and insurance regulations were much weaker than in the House bill. Richard Trumka, the new president of the AFL-CIO, declared that the labor federation would not support the Senate bill unless it was changed in negotiations with the House. SEIU's Andy Stern wrote a letter to the members of his union, in which he said:

> President Obama must remember his own words from the campaign. His call of "Yes We Can" was not just to us, not just to the millions of people who voted for him, but to himself. We all stood shoulder to shoulder with the President during his hard-fought campaign. And we will continue to stand with him, but he must fight for the reform we all know is possible.

The feeling I shared with almost everybody else — most deeply the Senate staff and members — was relief. The Senate floor debate had taken over twenty-five days in a row, the longest that the Senate had been in continuous session since 1917. It had consumed 229 hours and eight seconds.[68]

HCAN did not endorse the Senate bill. Instead we urged Senators to vote against a filibuster and improve the bill in final negotiations with the House. In the week before Christmas we held rallies in thirty states, including some round-the-clock vigils, under the theme, "Get It Right." Working America canvassers delivered 15,000 handwritten letters from constituents to Senate office in support of reform. We also braced ourselves for the final fight. Negotiations among the White House, Senate, and House were expected to begin right after the New Year, with the goal of passing a final bill before the President's State of the Union Address. January would witness further battles, but the conclusion seemed inevitable; we were about to make history.

* * * *

Amid all the stirring battles, we did not lose sight of more prosaic concerns. The year was ending and the health care legislation still had not been passed. That presented HCAN with another challenge. We were running out of money. We had planned a budget that lasted only through 2009, but we had to keep fighting for at least a few more weeks, with no guarantee of an end date.

During the past year and a half we had spent $43 million, not counting another million dollars of union funding for HCAN ads. The biggest chunk of our budget had been spent on our field campaign, followed by almost an equal amount on paid advertising. We had kept our central staff and operations lean.

Our biggest source of funds had been the Atlantic Philanthropies, which had made grants of $25 million. Atlantic had also helped us raise another $7 million, including $5 million from financier George Soros and $1 million each from two other foundations. As promised, The California Endowment had made grants totaling $4 million.

The members of our Steering Committee had added about $6.5 million. The rest, less than $1 million, had come mostly from a handful of large donors. That amount was much less than we had counted on in our original plan. We had spent a lot of money and time trying to raise money from wealthy individuals. Our fund-raising team, led by Kerry Greeley with the assistance of three well-established fund-raising consultants, had arranged for numerous trips to California and New York. The highlight was a private event with President Clinton, organized with the assistance of Erica Payne, but only the hosts, Anne and Vincent Mai, and two other donors of the dozen who came contributed.

The Clinton event was typical of the large donors' response. For the most part, major Democratic donors didn't care about health reform. I would hear over and over again, "I know what you are saying is important, and I really respect what you are doing and see why it would matter to the President, but it's just not a priority for me." I was disappointed, but not really surprised. In my experience, wealthy people don't care about economic justice issues. If you are rich, you don't have to worry about paying for good health care. The few exceptions included George Soros and another handful of very generous people who contributed, who did really care about the injustice of our health system.

Still, even if the individual fund raising had fallen short of our hopes, the funds we had raised still added up to enough money to run an ambitious nationwide campaign. With the campaign now expected to last into 2010, Atlantic was the first to step into the breach. In December 2009, the Atlantic Board made an additional grant of $1.5 million.

The rest of the money came from HCAN member organizations, demonstrating the wisdom of the initial depth of commitment we had asked of our partners. In early February we asked the members of the Steering Committee to make additional contributions. Within two weeks, based on nothing more than requests by email, the Steering Committee members contributed almost $1 million.

Our field partners came through too. We had already cut funding for a handful of states, where our partners were not able to deliver adequately or the political conditions did not warrant continued funding. Now we asked the remaining thirty-nine partners to continue organizing for half of what we had been paying them. If, in forming HCAN, we had chosen the D.C. election-style strategy of parachuting in staff instead of contracting with state organizations, that would have been impossible; campaign operatives don't keep working for half the pay. But our field partner organizations figured out how to make the dollars stretch. As Northwest Federation of Community Organizations' Executive Director LeeAnn Hall said to me, "These organizations are working twice as hard for half the pay."

In January, the Steering Committee made another decision, which I hadn't anticipated. I had always assumed that the campaign would end after the bill became law. But they decided that HCAN should start planning for continued operation, to ensure that the law was implemented properly. Someone else would have to take charge of that effort. Claudia moved back to our upstate New York home in January, to resume teaching at the University of Albany. I was going home to join her as soon as I could.

Despite the delay, we thought we were on the home stretch, with just a few more weeks to go before a White House bill signing ceremony.

Almost nobody was thinking about the Massachusetts special election to fill Ted Kennedy's seat, scheduled for January 19. Why would we? Massachusetts was a solidly Democratic state.

20

Not Again!

Four days into the New Year, negotiations began among the House, Senate, and White House to hammer out a final bill. The Republicans would not be included, since they had denied themselves any voice in the process by obstructing the legislation at every turn. Instead, the White House and Democratic Congressional leadership charged their staffs to merge the Senate and House bills as quickly as possible. The goal was approval of the legislation before the State of the Union address in late January.

The negotiators used the legislation passed by the Senate as their framework for the sections of the legislation expanding coverage, not because it was better written but because keeping together all sixty Democratic Senators was the biggest challenge to the process. Senators would be more willing to accept changes if the basic structure of the bill that they had passed remained intact.

During the summer and fall months, whenever progressives had complained to the White House about the Baucus bill, the administration's refrain had been, "We will fix it in conference." Now that we had reached that stage, we were wondering whether the Administration would make good on its promise. While the staff negotiations took place behind closed doors, with very few leaks, we soon realized that the White House was deferring to the Senate on most of the big issues, while incorporating House language that improved the legislation on a host of issues that were important, but less likely to be lightning rods for opponents.

HCAN used this brief window for a campaign we called, "Finish the Job Right," in which we advocated a handful of major changes to the Senate bill. To provide support for the campaign, we ran a new ad called "Marathon," which — against a background of a mass of runners — pushed for the major provisions in the House bill. Predictably, the White House objected to the ad, wanting HCAN to refrain from making any public attempt to defend principles that the President had endorsed. We also planned country-wide grassroots events for the third weekend in January to demonstrate popular support for our priorities.

A key issue was making health coverage more affordable for low-and moderate-income people who would buy insurance through the exchanges. The faith network PICO, along with two HCAN partners (SEIU and the Campaign for Community Change) and a health advocacy group called Community Catalyst, held an "Affordability Summit" on January 13 with 300 people on Capitol Hill to bring greater attention to the issue. We encouraged our state HCAN partners to participate in local events that week, and people delivered giant keys to Congressional offices, with the message that increasing subsidies to families was the key to affordability. The negotiators agreed on some small improvements to the Senate bill, but not nearly as much as we wanted.

The issue that cast a pall over the whole negotiations was the excise tax on employer-provided coverage. Labor unions would oppose the final bill if major changes in the tax were not agreed upon. The unions were organizing aggressively at the local level, and they scheduled a national call-in day on January 13. They had backed up their resolve with a letter that Connecticut Representative Joe Courtney circulated to his House colleagues, strongly opposing the tax. Courtney, with the backing of labor, secured the signatures of 193 House members. *The New York Times* summarized labor's message in an article that quoted an Ohio steelworker who had campaigned for Obama, "The president would be going back on his word. If he goes ahead and passes a bill with the excise tax, I won't be able to support him again."[69]

Obama met with a group of union presidents in the Roosevelt Room in the White House on January 11. They discussed multiple issues, but the central question was how to resolve the excise tax impasse. As National Education Association President Dennis Van Roekel told me, "On the one hand, we wanted health care very badly. On the other hand, we didn't want to settle for just anything."

The next day, the union presidents returned with their staffs for what proved to be a twelve-hour negotiating session with the White House. They were well prepared, providing figures on how many workers the Senate proposal would affect, roughly thirty million employees. Most of these people were not even union members. Although their health plans were more expensive than average, this was a far cry from the "Cadillac tax" that was supposed to affect gold-plated health plans that covered Wall Street executives. They also marshaled arguments that demonstrated that factors like the gender and age of workers, and their exposure to harmful working conditions, had a huge impact on the cost of benefits. These factors often mattered more than whether the health plan included comprehensive benefits, which the tax was meant to discourage.

When the negotiations began, the union staffers were kicked out of the room, leaving them to hope that their presidents had paid attention to the briefings. The presidents did well. After the day of marathon negotiations, they reached an agreement that delayed the start date of the tax, raised the value of the plans that would be subject to the tax, eliminated dental and vision benefits from the tax, and accounted for the cost of employee groups that had larger numbers of women, older workers (including early retirees), and employees in high-risk professions. The agreement also gave unions time to renegotiate health plans before the tax took effect and, starting in 2017, allowed unions to seek coverage for their employees through the exchanges. While the agreement still was far from ideal, it mitigated some of the most egregious effects of the excise tax and provided time for the system to adjust.

One advantage of the union presidents negotiating the deal is that they had significant ownership of it, putting them in a better position to sell it to their own membership and also to convince members of the House of Representatives that they would not suffer politically by voting for legislation that included the watered-down excise tax. Newly elected AFL-CIO President Richard Trumka spent hours personally talking with the presidents of the Federation's unions to ease their doubts about why they should support reform that still might adversely affect some of their members. Still, another month would pass before labor lined up behind the legislation. What made Trumka's task much harder was the confusion created by the Massachusetts special election, a stroke that threatened to destroy everything we'd accomplished during the past two years.

* * * *

Two days after Republican Scott Brown secured his surprise victory to fill Ted Kennedy's former seat in the U.S., we held a regularly scheduled meeting of the HCAN Steering Committee. Just before the meeting I had a conversation with HCAN's paid ad guru, Saul Shorr, who was advising several Democratic senators on their reelection campaigns. From his perspective, the game was up; the Massachusetts election meant that Democrats would have to retreat from health care. I entered the crowded conference room with a heavy heart. And I did something totally out of character. Instead of my usual role of being a cheerleader, I told the Steering Committee that the outlook looked bleak. I asked them how we would get out of this mess. Several people made some suggestions but I pushed back, saying that their ideas didn't seem to be convincing.

That forced SEIU's Bruce Colburn to step out of character too. Colburn had always played the role of the doubting Thomas, raising warnings when I and others were being positive. But hearing my dour tone, Colburn responded by taking the opposite view. He pointed out a number of ways that we could recover from this setback.

Mike Lux, the progressive strategist who had been so helpful with Ben Nelson, spoke up next. He almost berated me for losing hope and said that this was no time to give up. Mike wrote me a follow-up email, which expressed what he said at the meeting: "The odds are not good for us. It's an uphill fight. A lot of folks are on the verge of giving up. Fine, all true. But your job is to keep fighting until this thing has been declared dead, not by pundits or pessimistic insiders, but by the leaders of Congress. Because who knows, we might still catch a break, the tide could turn.... But if the leader of HCAN is telling everyone we're dead, then we might well be. Get your game on, for Christ's sake."

That quickly turned me around. I returned to character, working with the group to plan our next steps. But the situation did not look good and everyone knew it. Once again, after a century of failure, it looked like the Grail might slip out of reach.

As we had already planned "Finish the Job Right" actions, we were well prepared to show grassroots support around the country for Congress moving ahead despite Massachusetts. MoveOn also asked their members to hold Emergency Rallies for Health Care on the Tuesday following the Massachusetts election, and their members came through by turning out for 140 small events. We also decided to plan major events for the Presidents' Day week-long Congressional recess, which would begin in three weeks.

At the Steering Committee meeting, we decided that we should bring our grassroots energy to Washington, for Congress and the national press corps to see. We planned a demonstration for a few days later, to be held outside the United States Chamber of Commerce Building, right across from the White House.

USAction's Jeff Blum set to work recruiting some prominent individuals and asked them if they would be willing to participate in civil disobedience at the demonstration if we decided to do that. The reaction was very encouraging. Blum recruited three former members of Congress who had gone on to head progressive organizations: Bob Edgar, Tom Andrews, and David Bonior. Ben Jealous, the recently elected president of the NAACP, also agreed to attend. We also found several people who had powerful stories illustrating the horrors of the health care system. It was good to see people rallying around the crisis we faced. What I found most encouraging was that 250 people showed up on a cold January morning, with only two days' notice. Most of them came in response to emails we sent out, rather than being recruited by organizations. It was a strong indication that people were willing to fight for the legislation even in its weakened state.

In the House, Speaker Nancy Pelosi was trying to overcome the resistance among her members to passing the Senate bill. In the legislative solution that emerged, the House would pass both the Senate bill and another bill that corrected some of the Senate bill's biggest problems. The Senate would then, using the reconciliation process, which required only fifty votes, pass that corrections bill. The barrier to enacting this solution was that the House would have to pass the Senate bill first, with no guarantee that the Senate would ever pass the corrections bill. House Democrats harbored a reservoir of mistrust because the Senate had bottled up literally hundreds of House bills in the current Congress alone. However, the House had no choice but to trust the Senate. To save reform, we needed a big enough change in momentum to compel the House to act, and to assure that the Senate would follow.

Finally, Barack Obama fought back. With his back to the wall, the President engaged in a two-prong strategy designed to isolate Republicans and create an enemy: the insurance companies. Obama opened his offensive on the Republicans on their own turf. On January 29, the President spent ninety minutes at a House Republican retreat in Baltimore. Here's how *The Huffington Post*'s Sam Stein described the President's appearance, under the headline, "Obama Goes to GOP Lions' Den — and Mauls the Lions."

> President Obama traveled to a House Republican retreat in Baltimore on Friday and delivered a performance that was at once defiant, substantive and engaging. For roughly an hour and a half, Obama lectured GOP leaders and, in a protracted, nationally-televised question-and-answer session, deflected their policy critiques, corrected their misstatements and scolded them for playing petty politics. White House officials told the *Huffington Post* they were absolutely ecstatic.

HCAN was standing right outside. The Maryland HCAN coalition, led by USAction affiliate Progressive Maryland, AFSCME, and SEIU, held a rally in a blinding snowstorm outside the hotel where the President addressed the Republicans. Seventy-five demonstrators risked their lives to travel in the blizzard and represent our cause.

A week later, in an interview nationally televised by CBS during the Super Bowl pre-game show, the President invited the Republican Congressional leadership to join him and Congressional Democrats at a White House summit. As *The New York Times'* Jeff Zeleny put it, "He set out a plan that would put Republicans on the spot to offer their own ideas on health care and show whether both sides are willing to work together." The February 24 meeting, which would be televised, was scheduled for the Blair House, which was used to house visiting dignitaries.[70]

To create more public urgency for reform, the Obama administration seized on a big rate hike by Anthem Blue Cross of California. On February 1, the health insurer announced that on the first of March, premiums for the 800,000 people who bought coverage from the company directly (rather than through employers) would go up as much as 39 percent. The rate hike created a furor in California, and the White House pounced. On February 8, HHS Secretary Sebelius sent a letter to the company complaining about the increase. Obama upped the ante at a White House press conference on February 9 by citing the rate hike as a reason to pass reform. The following day, Henry Waxman, the California Congressman who chaired the House Energy and Commerce Committee, announced that he would hold Congressional hearings on the rate increase. Senate Majority Leader Harry Reid called the hike reckless, adding, "We don't have to let greedy health-insurance executives drag down our future."

At HCAN, we were thrilled to see the people who ran the country finally adopting the message we had been using for two years. HCAN in California held a protest outside of Anthem's California headquarters. We added fuel to the fire by releasing a report on February 11 that listed the 2009 profits of the nation's biggest health insurance companies.[71] The report found that the profits of the five largest for-profit health insurers increased by $12.2 billion at the same time the companies dropped coverage for 2.7 million Americans. *The New York Times* gave extensive coverage to the report in an article that summarized how the issue was playing in Washington: "Anthem's rate increases, set to take effect March 1, have galvanized some Democrats in Washington, including President Obama, who say they provide an example of why Congress needs to break its political logjam and pass legislation to overhaul the health care system."[72]

By contrasting the soaring industry profits with the decreasing ranks of the insured, the HCAN report neatly summarized the story we wanted to tell. I knew that the report had a big impact when, at a Congressional hearing that HCAN organized on March 10, a parade of members of Congress cited the report's main conclusion, unaware that we were the source of the talking point.

Many observers have blamed Anthem's clumsiness in announcing such a big rate increase at such an inopportune time as one of the big reasons that the movement for reform was saved. But the data that HHS released on February 18, as part of its continuing campaign to highlight the rate hike issue, demonstrated that the California hike was far from unique. HHS reported that in 2009, Blue Cross/Blue Shield of Michigan requested approval for premium increases of 56 percent for plans sold on the individual market, Regency Blue Cross Blue Shield of Oregon requested a 20 percent premium, Anthem in Connecticut requested a 24 percent rate increase, and some individual health plans in Washington increased by up to 40 percent.[73] Big rate increases had long been a regular occurrence. What had changed was the Obama administration's dropping its previous reluctance to demonize the health insurance industry.

Another reason for the administration's change of heart stemmed from news reports that detailed the scope of the industry's effort to defeat reform. On January 12, *National Journal* reporter Peter Stone finally broke the story that we knew was waiting to be uncovered. Under the headline, "Health Insurers Funded Chamber Attack," Stone reported:

> Just as dealings with the Obama administration and congressional Democrats soured last summer, six of the nation's biggest health insurers began quietly pumping big money into third-party television ads aimed at killing or significantly modifying the major health reform bills moving through Congress. That money, between $10 million and $20 million, came from Aetna, Cigna, Humana, Kaiser Foundation Health Plans, UnitedHealth Group and Well-Point, according to two health care lobbyists familiar with the transactions. The companies are all members of the powerful trade group America's Health Insurance Plans. The funds were solicited by AHIP and funneled to the U.S. Chamber of Commerce to help underwrite tens of millions of dollars of television ads by two business coalitions set up and subsidized by the chamber. Each insurer kicked in at least $1 million and some gave multimillion-dollar donations.[74]

Two weeks later the *National Journal* headlined an article, "U.S. Chamber Dwarfs Other Groups for Health Care Lobbying." Reporter Beth Sussman wrote, "All in all, the Chamber spent $123 million on lobbying in 2009, double what they spent in 2008, and most of it likely insurance industry money."[75] When the full story came out in the fall of 2010, the total amount of health insurance industry money laundered through the U.S. Chamber of Commerce in 2009 proved to be $86 million.

Much of the Chamber money was spent running saturation TV campaigns against vulnerable Democrats in nine states. While we couldn't hope to match the industry on the air, we continued to organize aggressively on the ground, taking advantage of the Congressional recess over President's Day. In Minnesota, 500 HCAN activists joined Senator Al Franken at a standing-room-only rally at the Minneapolis Regional Labor Federation. Organizing for America, the President's grassroots operation, helped recruit people to the Minneapolis event, as they did to other HCAN-organized demonstrations that week. The event organizers reported, "The crowd was more than fired up; they were at times, downright angry. This was our most emotionally charged event since the August town halls." In New York, more than 700 people marched across the Brooklyn Bridge. In Olympia, Washington, a rally that drew 5,000 people to the State Capitol to address state budget issues added national health reform to its theme. All in all, HCAN partners in more than thirty-five states organized events during the recess.

On February 23, the day before the Blair House Summit, a group of intrepid marchers brought our energy to D.C.

21

Stop Big Insurance — Congress Listens to Us

One month after the Massachusetts election, facing a full bank of TV cameras and reporters, Senate Majority Leader Harry Reid walked up to the podium and greeted the chanting crowd of 600 health care supporters who were celebrating the completion of Melanie's March, a 138-mile trek from Philadelphia to Washington to press Congress to finish health care reform. Behind Reid were a small group of determined marchers who had walked every one of those miles.

Reid was joined at the podium by Steve Hart and Romona Williams, two close friends of Melanie Shouse, a Missouri health care activist who had died earlier in the month, losing a battle with breast cancer that was made much harder because she had inadequate health insurance. Steve and Ramona presented Reid with a book of 10,000 condolences sent in memory of Melanie, including many people who told their own stories about the health care system. They asked the Senator to bring the book to the bipartisan health care summit that President Obama had organized the next day at Blair House.

The idea to march from Philadelphia to Washington had come from Antoinette Kraus, a twenty-eight-year-old community organizer who was working for the Pennsylvania Health Access Network, a key member of Pennsylvania HCAN. Early in February, Antoinette had been talking with her supervisor, HCAN's Pennsylvania Director Marc Stier.

Kraus recalls, "I said to him, we've tried everything else. Why don't we walk from Philadelphia to Washington?"

Stier loved the idea and so Melanie's March was born. The HCAN coalition in Pennsylvania began recruiting people who would be willing to walk the distance, particularly people who had personally experienced some of the horrors of our health care system.

Amy Fitzpatrick had been laid off two years before from her job as a legal receptionist. Working as a concierge, Amy did not have health insurance as she suffered from two separate medical conditions, making it impossible for her to find affordable coverage.

Bill West was marching for his son Ben, who has Crohn's disease, a serious, chronic disorder. Ben and his wife worried that if Ben were to lose his job, he would not be able to get the medical care he needed. Bill found out the hard way; he was laid off at the age of sixty-two by the insurance giant Cigna.

Twenty-six-year-old Athena Ford put all the personal angst of her family in a few short sentences: "I wonder if people really understand all the hidden costs faced by American families like mine: Moms are forced to fight insurance companies for the life-saving surgery their newborn needs instead of devoting that energy to their sick child. Dads are forced to work eighty hours a week to pay off medical bills, instead of spending that extra time with their young family. Grandpas are forced to risk their health by working too hard against doctors' orders. Young people resist going to the ER because they don't have insurance. And small family businesses can't hire another employee because they have to find a way to pay for health care coverage."

The march kicked off in Pennsylvania and scheduled small events and larger rallies along the way. Delaware ACORN and Progressive Maryland, our lead partners in those states, helped pick venues, organize people to greet and join the marchers and notify local press. SEIU and Families USA also lent resources to promote the march.

In Washington, we decided to name it "Melanie's March" because President Obama had discussed Melanie Shouse at a Democratic National Committee fund raiser on February 4. Melanie had been a health care activist with the HCAN coalition in Missouri and an Obama campaign volunteer. The President recounted:

> I got a note today from one of my staff — they for-warded it to me — from a woman in St. Louis who had been part of our campaign, very active, who had passed away from breast cancer. She didn't have insurance. She couldn't afford it, so she had put off having the kind of exams that she needed. And she had fought a tough battle for four years. All through the campaign she was fighting it, but fi-nally she succumbed to it. And she insisted she's going to be buried in an Obama T-shirt. (Laughter.)
>
> But think about this: She was fighting that whole time not just to get me elected, not even to get herself health in-surance, but because she understood that there were others coming behind her who were going to find themselves in the same situation and she didn't want somebody else go-ing through that same thing. (Applause.) How can I say to her, "You know what? We're giving up"? How can I say to her family, "This is too hard"? How can Democrats on the Hill say, "This is politically too risky"? How can Republi-cans on the Hill say, "We're better off just blocking any-thing from happening?"[76]

We timed the march to culminate on February 23, the day before President Obama's Blair House health care summit. The march would also have an online component. Several major progressive bloggers were holding a massive call-in day in support of reform that day. MoveOn teamed up with them to conduct a virtual march, which generated 1.2 million commu-nications with Congress — by phone, fax, tweets, and Facebook messages.

When we asked both Speaker Pelosi and Majority Leader Reid to greet the marchers when they arrived in Washington, the Majority Leader readily agreed. For Reid, who unlike Pelosi had been very quiet after the Massachusetts election, greeting the marchers was his way of publicly demonstrating his strong support for moving ahead with reform.

Working with Reid's office, we planned a rally in the Dirksen Senate Office Building, where several senators would meet the small group of marchers and the larger mass of supporters who met the marchers at Union Station in Washington, joining them for the last short leg of the hike to Capitol Hill. It was a boisterous bunch that poured into the large ceremonial room in the Dirksen Office Building. While we waited for the senators and press to arrive, I led the crowd in chants and called out the many organizations that had recruited people to the rally: unions, senior groups, an organization representing doctors, community organizations, health care advocate groups, and others. In the front of the crowd, 102-year-old Lillian Allen dozed in her wheelchair, oblivious to the raucous crowd around her.

Senator Reid promised to take the book of condolences for Melanie to Blair House and vowed to press on to pass reform, saying, "Health care is about people fighting for their lives.… This book is brimming with condolences for Melanie, which I'll bring to the White House tomorrow."

When Reid finished, the crowd started chanting, "Get it done! Get it done!"

Connecticut Senator Chris Dodd promised to do just that. "The last couple months have been difficult.… After that meeting tomorrow at the White House you [Republicans] can either join us or get out of the way."

Reid was also joined by both Pennsylvania senators, Arlen Specter and Bob Casey, Ohio's Sherrod Brown, and Iowa Senator Tom Harkin, who told the crowd, "I'm quite touched by the eight people here who walked all the way.… This is what energizes us. I lost my only two sisters to breast cancer at an early age. They didn't have good health insurance coverage either.… By the time Easter comes we will fulfill Ted Kennedy's dream that health care is a right and not a privilege."

It felt like a movement that afternoon in the Dirksen Senate Office Building. The energy in the room was electric, fed by the powerful stories of the marchers whose blistered feet belied their glowing cheeks. The senators responded to the crowd's enthusiasm and the marchers' aura, clearly moved. Each of them had braved political attacks for supporting reform. They'd endured the tension of intense internal fights between Democrats over items like the public option and slogged through endless hours of acrimonious debate during multiple Republican filibusters. After the Massachusetts election they had seen hope seem to slip away. To be in a room full of supporters cheering them on to cross the finish line clearly lifted their spirits. Later that afternoon I got an email from Michael Meyers, a longtime top aide to Senator Kennedy and staff director of the HELP Committee. "The health rally this afternoon was great. Really fired up our members."

It's a Crime to Deny Our Care

What next? We had to keep up the pressure. Luckily, AHIP — the big insurance company lobbying group — presented an opportunity to us. AHIP had scheduled a major conference at the Washington, D.C., Ritz Carlton for March 9. Tom Swan, the Connecticut Citizen Action Group executive director, envisioned a protest at the AHIP conference as a culminating campaign event, just days before the House was expected to vote on reform.

The HCAN Steering Committee did not immediately endorse a giant protest aimed at the insurance industry. As MoveOn argued, our problem was with the Democrats in Congress, who had to find a way to pass reform; shouldn't they be the targets of any actions? Others worried that we wouldn't draw enough people to Washington to make a real splash. Even if we did, the press had a history of ignoring protests. As evidence, they only needed to point out how the 10,000-person rally we had held the previous June 25 had been ignored.

The HCAN staff, backed by several Steering Committee members, argued that the best way to pressure Congress was to accentuate the President's campaign to target the insurance companies. We could emphasize that point by using the rally to call on Congress to "Stop Big Insurance." We also believed that "if you build it, they will come." We had seen the burst of energy around the country to save reform and felt in our organizer bones that people would answer the call, particularly if we used the event to channel their anger. We didn't want just another rally. We wanted a demonstration that would allow people to shout out their frustrations and demand that Congress stand up to the insurance lobby and all the powerful forces that were standing in our way.

We also wanted to express the moral force of our position. USAction's Jeff Blum, with the help of AFSCME's Suzanne Haviland, began to recruit progressive leaders to see if they would be willing to participate in civil disobedience at the protest. Within a week, more than forty heads of organizations and clergy members had agreed to risk arrest at the demonstration.

To make the protest a powerful moment for those who came, we looked for a way to involve every demonstrator in an edgy action. Swan turned to his friends at Agit-Pop, who had staged the surprise musical number at AHIP's last Washington conference in October. They proposed to turn around the idea of civil disobedience: the HCAN protestors would engage in a mass citizens' arrest of the leaders of the health insurance industry.

March 9 was a glorious late winter day in the South; sixty degrees and not a cloud in the sky. Five thousand demonstrators — some of whom had taken buses from as far away as Minnesota and Maine — assembled at two points, each a half mile from the Ritz Carlton. One column met at the AFL-CIO headquarters, where they were led by the federation's president Rich Trumka, AFSCME President Gerald McEntee and American Federation of Teachers President Randi Weingarten. The other column gathered at DuPont Circle, across from the SEIU building, where I joined SEIU Secretary-Treasurer Anna Burger and Governor Howard Dean.

The marchers carried bright red stop signs that read, "Stop Big Insurance — Tell Congress to Listen to Us." They also carried wanted posters, which brandished the names and mug shots of the CEO's of the big health insurance companies. The wanted poster listed the criminal record of the CEOs:

> ➤ 45,000 COUNTS OF INVOLUNTARY
>   MANSLAUGHTER

> — deaths incurred in the process of pursuing
>   insurance industry profit

Title 18 US Code § 1112

➢ BREACH OF CONTRACT & FRAUD

— denial of promised coverage paid for by
working Americans

Title 25 US Code § 3116

➢ MONEY LAUNDERING

— clandestinely transferred $10-20 million
dollars to fund attacks designed to deny health
coverage

Title 18 US Code § 1956

➢ BRIBERY OF PUBLIC OFFICIALS

Title 18 US Code § 201

Above the crowd assembled in front of the hotel, long yellow banners read "Corporate Crime Scene." From an improvised stage on the top of an elevated flatbed truck, USAction President William McNary deputized the crowd, who together took the oath of office. They charged themselves to arrest the CEOs, "whose greed, corporate abuses, and craven lobbying pose a mortal threat to our democracy and the health and well-being of our people."

Marcus Grimes stood on the flatbed, waving his white cane, and told the crowd, "I'm mad as hell and I'm not going to take it any more." Marcus had a reason to be angry. The Virginia schoolteacher had lost his vision because he was uninsured and could not afford the $3,000 procedure that would have saved his eyesight. Marcus spoke as a representative of a group of twenty-six survivors of insurance company abuses who had come to D.C. for the rally.

The demonstrators filled the street in front of the Ritz Carlton, where mounted policemen tried to keep them away from the hotel entrance. A column of protestors filled the tunnel leading to the parking garage under the hotel until the police on horseback cleared them out. When several leaders tried to enter the Hilton, the police dragged them away. There were no actual arrests; the D.C. police prefer to escort protestors away rather than put both the protestors and police through the travails of the District's legal system. But the drama of the confrontations was captured for the crowd and the TV cameras.

The demonstration succeeded in garnering extensive press coverage, some of which provided another telling example of how the national press is both a prisoner and creator of a group narrative. For an interview I had later that afternoon with CNN's Rick Sanchez, he introduced the segment by saying, "There is a development in the health care debate. And it has to do with a new group, a new group that rallied today in Washington, D.C., not against President Obama's health care reform, but for it."[77]

We had brought 10,000 people to rally in Washington ten months before. We had held several thousand rallies with several hundred thousand participants around the country during the previous twenty months. Yet now it was "news" that people were fighting for reform, not against it. Now health reform looked like it was the next "comeback kid." That was the story that Sanchez and other reporters were eager to tell.

The day after the rally, I finally engaged in a televised debate that had eluded us since we launched the campaign. Every single time that a TV news show had asked AHIP to debate me, the insurance lobby had refused. Their persistent unwillingness had become a joke between HCAN's Communications Director Jacki Schechner and me. But with their backs to the wall, AHIP finally agreed to engage. I took a cab out to the PBS *NewsHour with Jim Lehrer's* Virginia studio, where Lehrer interviewed AHIP Vice President Mike Tuffin and me.

The next morning, Chris Frates wrote in *Politico Pulse*: "CLIP OF THE MONTH — KIRSCH VS. TUFFIN: HCAN's Richard Kirsch and AHIP's Mike Tuffin go head-to-head on 'NewsHour.' This instant classic boils down an entire year of debate into a neat 11-minute package."

Surviving Big Insurance

Earlier that morning, we had brought the moral energy of the rally to Capitol Hill through the personal testimony of the two dozen insurance company "survivors" who marched with us. The HCAN staff, working with the Campaign for Community Change, had spent the two weeks before the rally recruiting a group of people who had suffered egregiously at the hands of our health insurance system. Throughout the morning of October 10, members of the House of Representatives joined the survivors in a conference room in the Rayburn House Office Building, which had been secured for us by House Judiciary Committee Chair John Conyers. Insurance company whistleblower Wendell Potter moderated a series of panels at which a group of survivors told their stories to members of Congress, who responded to what they had just heard. MSNBC host Ed Schultz attended the hearing and that evening invited Marcelas and Gina Owens on his show to tell their story to his national audience.

There were many moving stories told that morning, including some from people I've introduced to you: Nebraska Rev. Janet Banks, school teacher Marcus Grimes, Stacie Ritter (who knocked on the door of the Cigna CEO), and Dan Sherry, the Illinois small businessman who became uninsured when he missed one bill payment. Each of the people who shared their stories had become an activist. Most of them had not been "political" before becoming involved, but their personal experiences were powerfully transformative, revealing to them and their family members, friends, and neighbors how corporations can so callously determine people's destiny. They each had acquired a gritty determination to fight back and they were willing to share their stories in this national arena.

Kelly Arellanes, from Arkansas, had recovered from a life-threatening head injury sustained in a horseback riding accident. Her family was left with $200,000 in medical bills after United Health refused to cover the claim because the hospital she went to was out of network. Arellanes, now too disabled to resume her work, was forced to declare bankruptcy.

The son of Leslie Boyd of Ashville, North Carolina, died at the age of thirty-three. Uninsured, he could not afford the regular tests he needed after surgery for a birth defect left him at high risk for colon cancer as an adult.

Matt Masterson of Virginia Beach, Virginia, was forced into bankruptcy in order to pay for the care of his diabetic son. Matt was unable to find health coverage for the "preexisting condition" that was diagnosed when his son was two years old.

Story after story broke our hearts. They inspired everyone listening, including the members of Congress, to keep fighting. One story, involving Alaya Windham-Price, from Portland, Oregon, did a great job of summarizing so much of the work and passion that drove HCAN volunteers throughout the nation:

> I went to college in Portland and then took a job as a sommelier and did event planning, which I loved. It was exciting to get to meet people from all over the world. And by running my own business, I also learned to handle a high-pressure environment. After the 2008 election, I organized an Inauguration party for MoveOn, with whom I'd done a little volunteering. Seventy-five people came and, lo and behold, I started a MoveOn Council in Portland. We started to have regular meetings about once a month. When health care came along, it became clear that's what people wanted to focus on.
>
> Portland is hugely invested in health care reform, with most of us being for single-payer. It was a lot of work to get people to agree to support the public option. We explained what it was and that politically it could pass as opposed to what we most want, but won't fly. Most people were OK, knowing that it would be a lot better than what we had.
>
> At that point I didn't know about my medical condition. I didn't have a personal investment in health care. But then I found out, in April 2009, that I had a serious condition. I started shaking a lot and it gradually got worse. I'd been seeing a naturopath and we thought it might be stress. But it got worse over a six-month period. Then I had what felt like a seizure. My limbs were flapping, I couldn't control them, even though I was conscious. I went to the emergency room and they couldn't find anything. And then I went to a neurologist and got an MRI. They found a tumor about an inch in diameter on the vagus nerve, which controls your heart, lung, digestion.

> I had limited insurance. Being young — twenty-seven
> — and healthy and stupid I bought the $400 a month policy
> instead of the $800 a month. I had trained for half-mara-
> thons, had a good diet. My insurance capped at $20,000 a
> year and one MRI and one angiogram later, that was almost
> used up.
>
> They still don't know what kind of tumor it is. They
> haven't removed the tumor and I'm still having the symp-
> toms. And they can't explain how the tumor would be caus-
> ing the symptoms. I left my job and lost my insurance — I
> get pretty sick at times. It's been a slow process of getting
> the tests and working with a specialist. I paid for a lot of it
> out of pocket — by the end of the year my bills were
> $50,000, and the insurance covered $20,000.

Still, she persevered with her political activism. MoveOn
hosted one or more rallies a week during the summer of 2009.
She helped collect petitions addressed to Senator Jeff Merkley
and Senator Ron Wyden. They wrapped crime tape outside
Blue Cross's downtown office building at a rally where
Wendell Potter spoke.

At a round table with Senator Merkley in September, Alaya
spoke publicly about health care. She was featured on all of the
major news channels and on their websites and Merkley's
website. He took a personal interest in her, and she talked with
him after the round table about pressuring Senator Wyden to
get on board with the public option.

After one rally outside Wyden's office they met with his
staff. They asked, "Why isn't Wyden taking a position? Why
won't he support the public option?" Groups of people in her
MoveOn council regularly visited his office over several
months. They developed relationships with his staff.

For the March 9 rally she flew to D.C., and she related how
an activist's persistence can finally pay off:

> At the rally I was on the front of the line the whole time.
> It was awesome. I stood behind Howard Dean. It was a real
> rally, a way to express the passion that I was feeling. I was
> willing to get arrested.

The following week, I met Wyden in D.C., which was a victory for Portland MoveOn. We'd been trying to make contact with Wyden for years. He's not publicly available and I had trouble with that. He claims to be a progressive champion, but over the years he's been hiding. When we met with him, he got really fired up. He was passionate. It was funny because he hadn't been out there. But I believed him. He took a lot of time with us, a good half-hour. I also met with Merkley again, which was good. He remembered me and asked how I was doing.

We were in D.C. when the bill passed. It was spectacular timing. Afterward, [Oregon Representative Earl] Blumenauer told the other MoveOn Portland Council coordinator that he felt that it was our persistent focus on winning over Wyden that got him finally on board with the public option and with the bill that was being proposed.

I now have a new job with really good insurance. Yahoo!

* * * *

The day after our Congressional hearing, Seattle's Marcelas Owens became a national figure and an immediate target of the right-wing propaganda machine. Marcelas leapt to fame when Senator Patty Murray invited him to speak at a press conference with the Senate Democratic leadership.

Marcelas had turned eleven the day before the press conference. He had grown up a lot in the ten months since he first met Murray at the big rally in Seattle; he'd added a few inches and lost his little boy look. But he still was quiet and shy. After Harry Reid introduced him, Marcelas, wearing a maroon sweatshirt, told his story to the national press corps. His grandmother, Gina, stood at his side. Marcelas described how his mother died and he said that he wanted to continue in her footsteps as an activist. He concluded by saying, "I don't want any other kids to go through the pain that my family has gone through."

As hoped, Marcelas' appearance grabbed the mainstream media's attention. He also became the target of the right wing. But rather than going after Marcelas himself, they attacked his grandmother, the Democrats, and HCAN. Rush Limbaugh sneered, "Your mom would have still died, because Obamacare doesn't kick in until 2014." Blogger Michelle Malkin headlined her post, "Harry Reid hides behind 11-year old kiddie shield." Fox's Glenn Beck filled out the attack, as MediaMatters reported:

> Glenn Beck attacked Marcelas' grandmother — who appeared with Marcelas at the health care event — for her work with the organization Washington Community Action Network. Beck said the group was "all about economic, racial, gender, and social justice for all" — "pesky phrases" Beck then tied to "the Soviet Union" and the "democratic socialist republic in China." Beck said of Marcelas' appearance on Capitol Hill: "The trip was paid for by Health Care for America Now — that's the George Soros-funded, Barack Obama-approved group fighting for health care. Since all of these groups are so concerned and so involved now, may I ask, where were you when Marcelas' mother was vomiting blood?" Beck continued: "Wasn't this the perfect opportunity to help provide a decent quality of life for all — at least, for one? You had somebody in your own ranks that knew — her mother knew. Dare I ask: Where was Grandma?"[78]

Such a scurrilous attack set off a counter response. MSNBC's Lawrence O'Donnell did a nine-minute segment on his show, rebuking Beck and his cohorts. *Time* blogger Kate Pickert asked, "Aren't there better and tougher targets for Rush Limbaugh and Glenn Beck than an 11-year-old boy without a mother?"[79]

But the best response of all came from Marcelas, who told me, "I brushed it off my shoulder like getting sand out of my flip-flops. I remember that I came home from school one day. Some kids had been mean to me and tripped me in the mud. Mom said, 'If you respond, it's like leaving a trail of gasoline through the forest.'" When Beck and the others went after him, the young man remembered his mother's advice and told the press, "My mother always taught me they can have their own opinion, but that doesn't mean they are right."

Reconciliation Takes Some of the Sting Out of Baucus

The President and the Democratic leadership continued to make the case to House members that they had come too far now to turn back; failing to act now would be a political disaster. In order to provide some assurance to House members who didn't trust the Senate to pass the corrections bill, Reid garnered the support of more than fifty Democratic Senators for reconciliation.

The two chambers of Congress also reached an agreement on what the reconciliation measure would include. Because reconciliation is technically a budget process, the bill could only include provisions that the Senate parliamentarian agreed had an impact on revenue and spending. As a result, many of the important improvements in wording to the Senate bill that had been previously agreed upon could not be incorporated. However, the reconciliation measure did include several significant changes.

The measure incorporated the deal on the excise tax worked out between the White House and the unions in January. It also totally eliminated — over a decade — the Medicare "donut hole," a provision in the Medicare prescription drug program that required seniors to continue to pay premiums for prescription drug coverage while having to pay the full cost of the drugs out of their own pockets.

The bill eliminated the "Cornhusker Kickback" that Senator Nelson had received, while increasing the amount of federal funding that all states would get for Medicaid. The legislation made health care more affordable to lower-income families in the exchange and made some small, positive changes made in the employer responsibility provisions.

The reconciliation bill also included two changes that helped assuage the deep unhappiness among immigration advocates with the Senate bill's prohibition on undocumented immigrants using their own money to purchase coverage in the exchanges — the Joe Wilson provision, which remained in the bill. With these last-minute changes, the National Council of La Raza agreed to endorse the legislation, which meant that every member of the HCAN Steering Committee supported the final legislation.

The reconciliation bill also included an important measure that had no relationship to health care, but would raise revenue while at the same time meeting another important social need. The legislation included reforms in the federal student loan program, opposed by the banking industry, which would save the government $61 billion over a decade. The reconciliation bill used $36 million of this to increase Pell grants to low- and moderate-income students and the balance of the savings to help pay for expanding health coverage.

The Phoenix Gasps

If politics really were a science, and not a frail, very human art, then the public option would now be law. On paper, at least, reconciliation reopened the door to the public option, since it only required fifty votes in the Senate. The Progressive Change Congress Campaign (PCCC) and Democracy for America (DFA) teamed up in a valiant last effort to push through the public option this way. Working with champions in both Houses of Congress, they garnered a letter of support from 120 House members and twenty-seven Senators. Another thirteen Senators also voiced support.

But it was too late. Pelosi and the White House were twisting every arm in the House to find the 216 votes needed to pass the bill, and, with the exception of Ohio Representative Dennis Kucinich, the resistance was not coming from the left. Pelosi feared that adding the public option would make her negotiations too complicated. So did Reid, who was eager to keep the remaining process as simple as possible.

At HCAN, we too had moved on. While we supported the public option, we were well aware of the hard numbers faced by the leaders in Congress. We were focused instead on removing the last two obstacles that stood in the way. One was the fear of some Democratic members that a vote for reform would cost them reelection. The other — once again — was abortion.

22

Fighting for Our Health

Ever since the House had voted for reform in November, our legislative team had kept close watch on House members whose votes would be in question the next time around. The list included a group of pro-choice members who had voted against the bill the first time but might be persuaded to switch, as well as some who had voted for the bill but were in highly vulnerable districts. We also prioritized anti-abortion members who had voted for the bill but might be lost if the Stupak anti-abortion language were not included in the final legislation.

Of course, the opposition had the same list, as well as the resources on the air to pummel vulnerable members with ads opposed to reform. With the prospect of a final vote in the next ten days, *The Wall Street Journal* ran this headline on March 10: "Business Buys Ads vs. Health Overhaul." The *Journal* reported that the U.S. Chamber of Commerce would spend between $4 million and $10 million (money raised from health insurance companies) to target "several dozen Democratic lawmakers." The *Journal* also reported that, separately, health insurance companies and two conservative groups were launching smaller ad campaigns.[80]

While we didn't have nearly as much money, HCAN, AFSCME, SEIU, and MoveOn raised $2 million to run ads in twenty districts. Several of the ads were sponsored by Catholics United, a group that was organizing support among Catholics for reform, despite the opposition of the U.S. Conference of Bishops. The message of our ads was the same one that we had been projecting since the beginning of the campaign, only now we had the President of the United States delivering the same point. The script in Representative Bill Foster's Illinois District read:

> It's happening everywhere. Health insurance compa-
> nies jacking up premiums. Crushing small businesses and
> working families across America. Right here in Illinois,
> we've seen our rates go up by 30, 40, even 60 percent in just
> the past few weeks. *Remember, if the insurance companies win,*
> *we lose.* Tell Congressman Bill Foster to keep standing up
> for us, not the insurance companies. Pass health insurance
> reform now.

But while the ads helped give wavering members of Congress cover, the real battle — the one that we could win — was, as usual, on the ground.

Markey Mondays

Let's return to the districts of the three pro-choice members of Congress whom I profiled when they voted against the bill in November: Betsy Markey of Colorado; Susan Kosmas of Florida; and my own member of Congress, New York Representative Scott Murphy.

The HCAN coalition in Colorado, along with Markey's supporters in the Democratic Party, continued to keep up the pressure on the Congresswoman. Publicly, we delivered our message fairly gently: we are disappointed in you and next time we expect you do the right thing. Privately, key labor unions told her that their continued support would turn on how she voted on the final bill. Before New Year's Eve, constituents with personal stories about health care delivered waves of handwritten holiday cards to her Colorado offices. In January, they started a weekly program called "Markey Monday," so that she'd be guaranteed to get a large volume of calls in support of reform at least once a week. As the end neared, Markey was telling people privately that she would vote for the bill, but she still hadn't made a public statement.

On March 17, HCAN organized a big rally at Markey's Fort Collins office. As Tricia Smith, the woman who had to live with horrifying pain for eight years before she qualified for Medicare, told me, "We marched down the street to Markey's office. As we were headed south we saw people with signs heading north to the office and we thought uh-oh, here comes the tea partiers. But it was another group supporting reform. Markey's staff brought in a few of us to talk with them. The phones were ringing constantly when we were in there with calls calling for support of health care. The next day she came out in support of the bill."

Kosmas Comes Around

The HCAN coalition had kept up the pressure on Florida's Susan Kosmas too. After sending out her cell phone number when she voted against the bill, pulling all labor funding, and demonstrating at her office, they did not let up. The AFSCME union president in Florida wrote a letter to Kosmas in January that accused her of lying to AFSCME's national president, Gerald McEntee, before the first vote in November. ACORN had people dressed in death costumes deliver petitions to her door, and organized people to hold up giant banners outside Kosmas' office displaying the number of people who died every day because of their lack of health insurance. By mid-winter, members of the Florida HCAN coalition began to hear that Kosmas had assured people she would vote for reform, but they remained skeptical until March 19 when, two days before the scheduled vote, she told the *Orlando Sentinel* that she would vote yes.

Power Concedes

Despite an aggressive campaign, New York's Scott Murphy was proving to be a tougher sell. Ironically, the way the HCAN coalition in New York reacted to the defection of a neighboring Congressman who had voted yes the first time around finally scared Murphy into doing the right thing.

The week after he voted against the bill in November, Citizen Action of New York organized a demonstration outside one of Murphy's district offices. The Congressman had already received a cascade of angry calls, emails, and visits to his office, so he changed his schedule and met with the HCAN protestors. But he said nothing that indicated he was changing his mind.

To highlight the point that Murphy had received crucial support of labor and community activists during his special election campaign, Citizen Action put up a website called StandupScott.org. It showed a video of Murphy making a firm pledge to work with Obama and the Congress to pass health reform. A petition on the website called on Murphy to "Keep your promise." Al Ormsby, a Citizen Action leader who like many others had spent hours volunteering for Murphy's campaign, collected signatures on a petition from campaign volunteers that listed the number of hours they had volunteered on Murphy's campaign, hours they told him he would lose in his 2010 campaign for reelection if he voted no again.

In late January, HCAN volunteers were collecting petition signatures in Saratoga, New York, when they spotted the Congressman having pizza with his daughter at a local restaurant. Showing surprising politeness for an organizer, Chris Scoville, the Citizen Action staff person, called Murphy's chief of staff on his cell phone and asked if it was okay to talk with the Congressman when his lunch was over. Permission granted, the group of some thirty HCAN volunteers cornered the Congressman, who left the impromptu meeting wearing an HCAN sticker.

You may remember my anger with Murphy, when he ignored the personal story I told about how the Massachusetts health plan provided coverage for my daughter. I wasn't alone in having the impression that the Congressman was insensitive and uncaring. Scoville told me that his volunteer leaders thought that for Murphy, "It always came down to cost." So on March 9, a delegation of thirty HCAN activists who had travelled to Washington for the AHIP protest met with Murphy's chief of staff and kept hammering the point that the issue was not cost, but human lives.

Meanwhile, a Democratic congressman in an adjoining district who had voted for the bill in November was heading in the opposite direction. HCAN had held two big thank-you events for Representative Michael Arcuri, but the Congressman had become convinced that another vote for reform would be a political mistake.

Citizen Action of New York organizer Mary Clark, who had helped Arcuri get elected in 2006, was paying close attention to the wavering congressman. In December, Arcuri began to complain about the bill publicly, saying that it would hurt hospitals in his district and that many provisions needed to be fixed. In response, Clark bombarded Arcuri's office with calls and organized "Grinch" events outside his offices before Christmas. In January, Clark cornered Arcuri at a fund raiser. The Congressman complained about not being allowed to eat in peace, but Clark told him that people were counting on him to vote his conscience rather than follow the political advice of staffers who thought to enhance his chances of being reelected. On March 9, a big group of New Yorkers descended on Arcuri's Washington office after the D.C. demonstration. Clark recalls that it was "a contentious meeting" in which Arcuri's chief of staff "almost proudly told us, 'Well, my mother doesn't have health insurance.'"

After the meeting at Arcuri's office, Clark attended a meeting of most of the New York House Congressional delegation, which had been organized by Speaker Pelosi. Pelosi had invited key New York advocates of reform to meet with the New York members. When Clark made her presentation at the meeting, she looked right at Arcuri. "I was very impassioned. I said that we need you to be telling people while there are problems with the bill, here are the good things and I'm working to make it better. You can't be feeding into fear; that's a losing message. Arcuri was clearly pissed; there was no love lost there. He knew I was talking about him."

A few days later Clark circulated an online petition that soon garnered 5,000 signatures. Then she organized a caravan of health reform supporters, driving through the Congressional district to deliver the petitions to Arcuri's Cortland office, in front of the press. Yet when she arrived in Cortland, a reporter called her to inform her that Arcuri had publicly announced that he would vote no.

After Arcuri's announcement, the next step was clear: Arcuri had to be swiftly punished. Together, we took a number of steps, but it was a brilliant maneuver by New York's Working Families Party (WFP), with the backing of New York's powerful SEIU, that made the difference. They announced that they would field a third-party challenger against the Utica congressman. Third-party candidates are a longstanding tradition in New York state, and WFP made the threat even more credible by having a progressive, who had run for Congress before Arcuri entered the 2006 race, floated as a possible challenger.

Arcuri wouldn't change his mind, but the example was enough for Murphy. In what was my favorite email of the entire health care campaign, WFP's executive director, Dan Cantor, passed on a note to me from Murphy's chief of staff, Todd Schulte after the party announced they would not endorse Arcuri because of his betrayal on health care. Schulte's note read simply: "I cannot stress enough how incredibly unhelpful this all has been." Eleven minutes before Schulte sent Cantor his complaint, the Albany *Times Union* reported that Murphy would vote for reform.

Unhelpful? As Frederick Douglass said, "Power concedes nothing without demand. It never did and it never will."

Reforming the Ranks

The last-minute scramble for votes continued. The one Congressman on the left who had voted against the health bill in November, Ohio Representative Dennis Kucinich, announced that he would support the bill on March 17. Helping to change his mind was a push from the left. Markos Moulitsas, the founder of the prominent leftist blog *Daily Kos*, appeared on MSNBC and urged Kucinich to vote for the bill.

Moulitsas' support demonstrates how almost the entire progressive community recovered from their bitter disappointment after Lieberman killed the public option. Now he and others were arguing that the health care reform bill was an important social achievement that could be improved on over time.

MoveOn, the biggest group of progressive activists organized under one umbrella in the nation, had also reached the same conclusion. MoveOn surveyed their five million members on March 9 to ask them whether MoveOn should support the final reform plan proposed by Obama at the Blair House Summit, which did not include the public option. The response was an overwhelming yes from 83 percent of the members who answered the survey.

All that remained was the contentious hurdle of abortion. The U.S. Conference of Catholic Bishops continued to strenuously oppose the legislation, but on March 11, the Catholic Health Association announced that the Senate bill satisfied their concerns that federal funds would not be used for abortion. A week later, the heads of sixty orders of nuns endorsed a letter that supported passing the bill with the Senate language. Sister Simone Campbell, the head of Network, a group that lobbied on social justice issues on behalf of nuns, said, "From our reading of the bill, there isn't any federal funding of abortion.... For us, first of all, tens of thousands of people are dying each year because they don't have access to healthcare, so that is a life issue."[81]

The courageous support of the nuns and the Catholic Health Association satisfied the qualms of most of the Democratic House members who had voted for the Stupak amendment in the fall. But Stupak and a handful of other anti-abortion Congress members were still holding out for a separate vote on his amendment.

Catholics United, an online organization with 45,000 members, had also been supporting the legislation; the group shared the same belief of the nuns: Access to affordable health care is a pro-life issue. The organization ran TV ads in Congressional districts of eight of the Stupak-aligned members to endorse the reform bill.

One of the hold-out members was West Virginia Congressman Nick Rahall. On the Friday before the vote, Gary Zuckett, the executive director of the Mountain State's lead HCAN partner, West Virginia Citizen Action Group, learned that Rahall was a problem. He got in his car with a video camera and his eleven-year old daughter, Kathryn, and made the three-and-a-half-hour drive to Rahall's office in Beckley, West Virginia. There he joined thirty-five local leaders and activists who had turned out on a day's notice. Among the group were the head of the local AFL-CIO council; a former West Virginia state Senator, Billy Wayne Bailey, who said he'd had six heart bypass surgeries; an organizer for SEIU who was also a nurse and said she had once been uninsured for years; the head of West Virginians for Affordable Health Care; and a doctor who said, "My patients need health care reform now... and if you want to vote pro-life, consider the lives of West Virginians who will die without health care coverage."

Stupak kept pushing Pelosi to agree to a vote on his amendment, but this time she told him that allowing the amendment to be put forward would lose the votes of pro-choice members. Finally, a compromise emerged. On the day of the vote, Stupak appeared on TV with four other members to announce that they would accept an offer by President Obama to sign an executive order that clearly forbade the use of federal funds for abortion in any provisions of the health reform law.

The House Votes

Sunday, March 21, was the kind of electric spring day that was perfect for making history. As I walked to the Capital Hilton, where reformers were meeting to go over last-minute vote counts, I realized that I had felt this way only one time before in my life. On the day our first child was born, I had felt an enormous burst of energy, a buzzing through my limbs, and headed home. Claudia hadn't called me yet to say that she was in labor, but I knew it in my bones. On this morning in Washington, even though we had not yet heard that the Stupak deal was closed and that the votes were in hand, I knew that we had crossed the finish line. I felt it in my heart and my soul and in the smile that I couldn't suppress.

At eight o'clock that evening, I arrived at the House entrance of the Capitol and was escorted to an area in the House gallery reserved for guests of the Speaker. I would not have missed this occasion for anything in the world. I remember a few points about the debate that evening. One was how many Democrats spoke about how the legislation would cover thirty-two million Americans and save thousands of lives each year. This had not been the Democrats' main talking point, nor was it ours. The main message from the President and Democratic leaders in Congress had been aimed at the 85 percent of people who have insurance, not those who lacked it. But that night many Democratic members showed how much they were moved by a fundamental injustice that they were about to go a long way to correct.

Another memorable moment was when the Republicans used their right to propose one amendment to introduce the Stupak language on abortion. Stupak rose to speak against it, saying that "this motion does not promote life "and would "deprive thirty-two million people of coverage." From the floor Texas Representative Randy Neugebauer shouted, "Baby killer!" Again, the tea party's hatred and hostility had come to the House floor. The Republican amendment failed, as had the tea partiers' campaign to defeat the bill

For me the highlight of the evening was Pelosi's speech. I had met with her a few weeks earlier, and she was intensely focused on the enormity of what she was about to accomplish. At our meeting, she told the group of advocates who had gathered around the shining inlaid table in the ornate Speaker's Conference Room in the Capitol that she had been reading the biography of Frances Perkins. She was Roosevelt's pioneering Secretary of Labor — a woman who had championed Social Security and a host of other historic New Deal reforms, but who had fallen short on health care.

Perhaps with Perkins in mind, Pelosi delivered the final remarks before the vote was to take place. "It is with great humility and with great pride that we tonight will make history for our country and progress for the American people. Just think — we will be joining those who established Social Security, Medicare, and now tonight, health care for all Americans."

Pelosi transformed the famous line of a previous Democratic House Speaker, Tip O'Neill, that "All politics is local" into a succinct declaration of what HCAN had been proving to

Congress over and over again. "I say to you tonight that when it comes to health care for all Americans, 'All politics is personal.' It's personal for the family that wrote to me who had to choose between buying groceries and seeing a doctor. It's personal to the family who was refused coverage because their child had a preexisting condition.... It's personal for women — after we pass this bill, being a woman will no longer be a preexisting medical condition."

The Speaker reminded everyone of the words written by Senator Ted Kennedy in his letter to President Obama just before his death: "Access to health care is the great unfinished business of our society," and "At stake are not just the details of policy but ... the character of our country."

When the standing ovation of her Democratic colleagues was over, the House began to vote. Cleverly hidden in the brocade wallpaper above the gallery, a huge tote board appeared, with the names listed alphabetically of all 433 current House members. When the vote was closed, history had indeed been made, by a tally of 219–212. The next day the Speaker used a number of pens to sign her name to the bill before sending it to the White House. One of those pens hangs in a frame on my office wall.

As I left the House chamber, I felt an incredible sense of peace and serenity. I ran into Lauren Aronson, a White House aide who had worked tirelessly on the legislation, and we gave each other a jubilant hug. Outside, in the balmy air of the first day of spring, more than a hundred health reform supporters had waited to cheer on the House members who had just made history, by righting what Dr. King had called that most "shocking and inhumane" injustice, inequality in health care.

The President Signs

Two days later I stood in a packed auditorium in the Interior Department, waiting for a telecast of the bill-signing ceremony from the East Room of the White House to begin. Members of Congress were invited to the live bill signing, while supporters of the bill were assembled at the Interior Department. The

President and Vice President were to join us after the formal White House ceremony.

It was a festive atmosphere, smiles and hugs all around. It had the feeling of a giant reunion of people who had lived through a battle. People were so glad to join with others who understood what they'd been through, who were all amazed they'd lived to see the day. For many of these people, the day was not just two years in the making but went back seventeen years, to the Clinton health care fight in 1993. Some had been waiting since the days of the dueling proposals by President Nixon and Ted Kennedy.

What I'll always most remember was people coming up to me and saying "thank you." Looking me right in the eye, a real heartfelt *"thank you."* Not people I'd worked with day in and day out on the campaign, but people I hardly knew. Many, many folks, over and over again. I understood the thanks weren't for me personally. It was because of what we had built at HCAN.

Surprisingly, given all the tension with the White House, Patrick Dillon, the deputy director of political affairs told me, "We couldn't have done it without you." Two days earlier, as the House was about to vote, I had also received a brief, gracious note from White House Political Director Patrick Gaspard: "Awesome. Bloody awesome. Thank you for staying on the horse."

It was hard to focus on the President's words on the television monitors in the Interior Department auditorium. When he finished speaking, he sat down at a small table that bore the Seal of the President of the United States and began using twenty-two pens to sign the Patient Protection and Affordable Care Act into law. Right behind him were Speaker Nancy Pelosi and Majority Leader Harry Reid. The three of them had done what no President or Congressional leader had ever done before: piloted legislation that made affordable health care a right in the United States, through the giant shoals of the American legislative process, facing gale-force winds from corporate America and an enraged right wing. They were joined by Vice President Biden, other Congressional leaders and the chairs of the Senate and House Committees that had passed reform bills. Ted Kennedy's son Patrick and niece Caroline Kennedy also were in attendance.

On the President's left sat eighty-three-year-old Representative John Dingell Jr., who had first introduced a national health care bill in 1955. On the President's right stood a young boy from Seattle.

On the Monday after the House passed the legislation, Marcelas Owens was home with his grandmother Gina. He wondered out loud to his grandmother if the President would call him. Not five minutes later the phone rang and he picked it up. The voice on the other end said it was the White House, and he was invited to come to Washington.

Just before the signing ceremony, Marcelas met the President outside the East Room. Marcelas noticed that Obama was wearing the same solid baby-blue tie the White House staff had selected for Marcelas, after he left his own in Seattle. "I like your tie," the boy told the President. Obama answered, "I like yours too. It reminds me of someone, but I can't remember who."

During his remarks, Obama told the country: "I'm signing it for eleven-year-old Marcelas Owens, who's also here. (Applause.) Marcelas lost his mom to an illness, and she didn't have insurance and couldn't afford the care that she needed. So in her memory, he has told her story across America so that no other children have to go through what his family's experienced."

After the signing was over, Marcelas stood at the front of the room, waiting for his grandmother to join him. When she came up, he said to her, "I watched my Mom's legacy being signed today."

Marcelas Owens had witnessed the culmination of the legacy bequeathed to him by generations of activists who had proved that, as Barack Obama was fond of quoting, "The moral arc of the universe is long, but it bends toward justice."

Epilogue
The Fight Goes On

Rx for Success: Organizing and Organization

On the morning that President Obama signed the Affordable Care Act, I ran into Rob Andrews outside the Interior Department auditorium. Andrews is a Democratic congressman from New Jersey who chaired the Health Subcommittee of the House Education and Labor Committee, one of three committees responsible for writing the health care legislation.

"We could have never got the freshmen and sophomores without you," Rob volunteered when I introduced myself. He was referring to Democratic members of Congress who had been elected in the last two Congressional elections. Many of these members were elected in competitive, Republican-leaning districts and were deeply worried that voting for the health care bill would doom their reelection prospects.

When historians draw lessons about the passage of health reform in the Obama administration, I believe they will agree that Obama learned three lessons from past health reform failures. The first lesson was to prioritize health reform early in his first term and relentlessly push toward success. The second was to allow Congress to take the lead on the legislative process. The third was to placate enough potential industry opponents long enough so that they were not able to block reform.

Fighting for Our Health is the story of one more important lesson. After the campaign was over, I asked Paul Starr, the Pulitzer Prize–winning author of a history of American medicine, "Was there anything like Health Care for America Now before?" That is, was there ever a well-financed, strategic campaign that both brought together a large number of major organizations and ran a national campaign to mobilize Americans at the grassroots? Starr, who in 2011 published a history of health reform in the United States,[82] answered that none of the previous efforts employed the scope of grassroots activities generated by HCAN. "There have been coalitions before, which included many of the same groups, mainly unions. But there wasn't the field operation. That was a big difference."

If there is one lesson that I'm hoping will be learned from the campaign that HCAN ran, it is that grassroots organizing is essential to overcome the power that big corporations and wealthy elites wield. As people rose up to overthrow dictatorships in the Middle East, we witnessed that power. At home, when tens of thousands of people rallied in Wisconsin in the winter of 2011, and then translated that energy at the ballot box, we witnessed that power. But we don't have to wait until a breaking point is reached for strategically organized campaigns that harness the aspirations of ordinary Americans to make significant change.

That's the most important decision we made at Health Care for America Now. We focused our strategy outside the Beltway by organizing a grassroots campaign built on the existing infrastructure of organizations that have a mission of winning economic justice. As I related in Chapter 3, those decisions required departing from the norm of national issue campaigns, which typically have an Inside the Beltway focus and regard field activities through a Washington lens. A major focus of those campaigns is the D.C. press and elites, and most of the resources go into communication. "Field" in these campaigns consists largely of hiring consultants and communicators who try to create a veneer of organizing activity at the state level and then build that up nationally to look like a real effort. It's the left's version of Astroturf.

At Health Care for America Now we flipped the script. We assumed that the best we could do Inside the Beltway — against the army of corporate lobbyists and the bottomless war chest of corporate campaign contributors, the entrenched corporate connections of not only Republicans but of a great many

Democrats, a cynical press obsessed with the powerful and disdainful of the downtrodden — was to maintain a credible voice that could not be ignored. By using our relatively limited resources smartly, HCAN was widely quoted in the press, our television ads were seen in Washington, and we were recognized on the Hill. But if that were all we had done — along with the usual shallow investment in the field — the Affordable Care Act would not now be the law of the land.

Where we had a potential advantage over our opponents was outside the Beltway, where members of Congress and their staffs still meet face-to-face with constituents, and local press corps still report on civic action. If we organized people to raise their voices together, to tell their stories, to build relationships with Congress, and if we kept doing this over and over again and did it all over the country as part of a concerted strategic effort, we could accomplish what had been impossible for the past century. And we understood that doing so required investing money in organizers to do the day-to-day work of identifying, building relationships with, and empowering people.

Furthermore, we knew that the best way to find those organizers and potential activists was through working with established organizations within each state. We ran the field campaign through organizations that already had organizers, volunteer leaders, and coalition relationships and knew the politics in their communities and states. During the campaign, by working with our field partners, we modified our national strategy and tactics to meet local political conditions. That back-and-forth dialogue allowed the campaign to nimbly meld the best of national and local politics.

A key part of the field strategy was maximizing the potential of progressive membership organizations to engage their members. The foundation of the HCAN campaign comprised labor unions, community organizing networks, netroots, and constituency groups with memberships that had a history of multi-issue work for economic justice. One of the most gratifying things I heard from the leadership of many of these groups — from the directors of local community groups to the presidents of national labor unions — was how much the HCAN campaign increased their own organizations' ability to mobilize their members. By working as part of a strategic effort that employed specific tactics for which organizations could hold themselves accountable, the HCAN campaign transformed the capacity of many groups to engage their members effectively in political change.

I am not claiming that even the best-run grassroots campaigns will guarantee success. The HCAN campaign demonstrated both the strengths and limitations of a grassroots campaign conducted on a canvas of broad, national politics. A stark contrast is the result of the campaigns directed at Ben Nelson and Olympia Snowe. At the end, each was swayed by the pressures of national partisan politics. An intense campaign in Maine could not convince Snowe to resist enormous pressure from her Republican colleagues in the Senate. On the other hand, the work we did in Nebraska was a major factor in Nelson voting for reform, as his chief of staff acknowledged. As Rob Andrews said, HCAN's grassroots campaign was key to moving enough moderate Democrats in the House to assure that the legislation passed.

Jacob Hacker and Paul Pierson's book, *Winner-Take-All Politics: How Washington Made the Rich Richer — and Turned Its Back on the Middle Class,* is a trenchant analysis of how big corporations and the wealthy have captured American politics during the past three decades. The authors' prescription for how to reclaim American democracy — for no less is at stake — is to build up progressive organizational capacity. Hacker and Pierson write: "*Winner-Take-All Politics* also reveals *where* in our politics the central problems lie: in the fierce realities of organized combat. The foremost obstacle to sustainable reform is the enormous imbalance in organizational resources between the chief economic beneficiaries of the status quo and those who seek to strengthen middle-class democracy."[83]

Hacker and Pierson make three recommendations, saying that the most important and difficult of these "is the organized capacity to mobilize middle-class voters and monitor government and politics on their behalf."[84]

The biggest challenge in building an organization is raising enough resources. For decades, labor has been the biggest organized force for economic justice, both in mobilizing people and financing other efforts. That is why big corporations and the right wing continue to work so hard to weaken the right to collective bargaining.

The right-wing destruction of ACORN, the most effective organization in the nation at registering low-income people to vote, was another example of how the corporate elite is working to systematically defund the ability of progressives to organize.

During the health care campaign, SEIU demonstrated that an infusion of significant resources into organizing can quickly have a big impact. The Change That Works campaigns that SEIU built in a handful of states deployed a lot of organizers in each state. CTW hired just enough communication staff to ensure that the work of the many organizers became visible. Plus, each CTW organization partnered with the existing state progressive infrastructure. However, SEIU could not afford to keep up such a significant investment and closed the Change That Works operations in 2010. Progressives need sustained funding for state economic-justice organizations that work on multiple issues and elections. As HCAN proved, the funding should be invested in established groups and by creating new organizations in states where none now exist.

A bright spot in the hope for building progressive organizations with growing memberships and resources are netroots organizations, which are engaging millions of people to take political actions and contribute to progressive issues and electoral work. As the organizations have evolved, they are increasingly finding ways to move their membership from netroots to grassroots work. For example, as the HCAN campaign developed, MoveOn increasingly turned out its members to initiate and participate in rallies, vigils, and other actions. MoveOn now has a structure of local MoveOn councils, which train local leaders on community organizing.

Another important lesson was the role that philanthropy played in building HCAN. The Atlantic Philanthropies decided to invest in us because we were founded and backed by labor and community organizations. The foundation provided HCAN with the kind of substantial funding that allowed us to carry on a robust field campaign in more than forty states. If Atlantic, along with The California Endowment, had provided a much lower level of funding — or decided to favor policy, advocacy, and communications work rather than campaign-style organizing, as is so often done by foundations — health reform would have failed.

Another key virtue of HCAN's funders was their willingness to be nimble when opportunity presented itself, to act out of their traditional program areas and take risks. Each of these characteristics is essential to effecting major economic and social change, and they are rarely found in foundations. The Atlantic Philanthropies funded health reform even though no such program area existed at the foundation. The California Endowment recognized that the best chance of winning health reform in California was to win it nationally, so it was willing to spend millions on an effort that some might consider outside its California mission. An early grant to HCAN from the Arca Foundation was made simply because Arca recognized HCAN's promise and decided to step outside of its normal program areas. A handful of wealthy individual donors, notably George Soros, also understood the importance of extending beyond their usual areas of interest and seizing a rare moment when historic progress could be made.

Making Them Do It

Perhaps the most difficult point of tension in the HCAN campaign was the bridge with the Obama administration. While Jim Messina was particularly intolerant of any outside pressure from White House allies, the conflict goes much deeper than any one staff person and is inherent in our political system of competing interests.

Part of the issue is human, the difficulty and discomfort of disagreeing with friends. Making demands of people who you oppose because of conflicting values is easy. It is much harder to do that with people who you may know personally and with whom you share many common values. Those allies in power, besieged by a multitude of opponents, are likely to plead with their colleagues and friends to understand what they are facing and to trust that they are doing everything they can.

Part of the issue is one's view of how to exercise political power. If you view power as a fixed commodity, then you are reluctant to use it, since you may run out. As a result, there's always an excuse not to push too hard or confront someone, particularly if you'll want something else from him or her. On the other hand, if you view power as something that you create and often create more of by using it, then you will be more willing to use the power you have now. One of the advantages of my having worked for organizations that have had to create their own power is that I learned early on that power is a muscle that gets stronger through exercise.

The argument that the White House made most often to HCAN to discourage us from pushing for a stronger bill was that since health care was under such fierce attacks from the right, it could not survive any attacks from the left. As a result, we should trust them to do the best possible. Accepting this is tantamount to giving up, since by that logic the only pressure that the White House would need to respond to was from the right.

HCAN was very reluctant to put any pressure on an administration that was deeply committed to pass comprehensive health reform. We should have been not so timid. I'm not saying that we should have made major changes in almost all of what we did. We were right to concentrate most of our resources on fighting to lift the legislation and to focus our message on the attack on the insurance industry. Yet we should have directed more grassroots pressure on the administration and raised criticism in the press when the administration made concessions. The administration could have in turn used that pressure from the left to help resist the pressure from the right.

I'm reminded of a similar dilemma that we faced in New York when Governor Mario Cuomo had not committed to putting more money into the state's child health insurance program. In response, Citizen Action of New York organized families whose children were in the program to visit the office of the Governor's chief health care aide. I had a longstanding relationship with him, and I told him that we were coming. He could have screamed at me, asking me how could I embarrass the Governor, threatening to cut me off. He didn't, but unless the Governor had publicly promised to fund the program, we would have come anyway. After a few minutes of parents and children and TV cameras being crowded into the aide's office, we heard a knock on the door. I opened it and there was Mario Cuomo. He invited everyone down to his office and entertained the children in front of the press. And, of course, he supported the funding. We made him do it — and he looked like a hero.

It's not that easy to box in the President of the United States. But we certainly could have created a dynamic in which he could have used pressure from the left to stand up to pressure from the right.

Rx for Success: Other Lessons

In building the HCAN coalition, we overcame skepticism that we could keep it together in a divisive fight by building the coalition around a set of unifying principles. At the beginning, those principles kept groups out that did not share our values and vision. We further strengthened that unity through an arduous process of developing detailed policy positions on each of our principles. We had tough discussions about issues and trade-offs before we had to make actual decisions, and we learned to understand each other's priorities.

Another reason that the coalition stayed together is that we invested HCAN's decision making in organizations that made significant investments in HCAN and the health care fight. The HCAN staff also was acutely aware and respectful of the top priorities of each HCAN Steering Committee member. As a result, we understood what we needed to do to keep each group invested in the campaign.

Early, thorough preparation helped as well. Progressive health care groups engaged in an intense, innovative, and nuanced public opinion research project over several years, well before HCAN was founded. We developed the public option as a policy breakthrough that would help to both unify progressives and win the support of the public. We engaged in a collaborative planning process that brought to light possible strategic differences and resolved them. We wrote a highly detailed plan that forced us to think out every major pillar of the campaign in advance. We started the actual campaign early, months before we knew whether a Democrat would be elected president, taking the risk that the entire initial effort could have been for naught if a Republican had been elected to the White House in 2008.

In terms of the execution of the campaign plan, we could have broadened the narrative frame for our message. The message that we developed was too narrowly focused on health care and should have embraced the broader issues facing the American public. The crisis in health care is part of the larger crisis of growing income inequality in America. The strength of the American economy was built on shared prosperity and a large, thriving middle class. However, since the mid-1970s, economic growth has no longer been broadly shared. The problem is not that the nation hasn't generated wealth, it is that we've stopped sharing the wealth we've generated. If wages had kept up with productivity over the past thirty years, the median wage would be 60 percent higher than it is now.[85] If income had increased at the same rate for everyone from 1979 to 2006, the average family would make about $10,000 more a year, but the top 1 percent would make $700,000 less.[86] The failure to share the benefits of growth has led to the largest disparity between the rich and the rest of us in the United State since 1928.[87]

Health care is a very personal part of this story, involving the substantial rise in the number of uninsured and in the sums that people are paying out of their own income for health coverage. Our message would have been more powerful if we had told it as part of the broader story of the attack on the middle class and the concentration of wealth and power.

We also should have been clearer about the moral dimensions of the issue. A key part of our communications was revealing the stories of Americans who have been maimed and killed by the private insurance system. Instead of just telling these stories exclusively within the context of the insurance companies being greedy, we should have said forcefully that we have a moral responsibility to care for each other.

To protect the historic victory that will make affordable health care a right in the United States from the forces that are hell-bent on being sure the new law is not implemented, we will need to tell our story in terms of the larger narrative and do so with moral force. And we will need to do that through organizing.

The Fight Goes On

From the fall of 2009 through the Congressional elections of 2010, the political and corporate right spent gigantic sums to demonize health reform. Those same forces are continuing to press aggressively to defund and repeal the law before key provisions take effect in 2014.

In the 2010 Congressional elections, the Republicans combined the charge of a government takeover of health care with a relentless reminder that the bill "cut $500 billion from Medicare" to alarm senior citizens, who voted heavily Republican. The Republican tide defeated Democrats who voted for and against the health care legislation; it was the national mood that mattered, not how any one member of Congress had voted. The election results fueled the right-wing campaign to repeal the law.

The right understands that if the Affordable Care Act is implemented, it will create a bond between the American people and government, just as Social Security and Medicare have done. The last thing that the corporate and ideological right want is for a new health care pillar to be added the foundations of government social insurance.

The relentless, well-financed attacks on the Affordable Care Act have resulted in continued confusion among the

American public about the new law. Public opinion remains deeply divided. The main strategy to build support for the ACA since its passage has been to tout the new laws' initial benefits, such as making health insurance available to young adults and lowering the cost of prescriptions for seniors. But relying on this message as the core communications strategy can only get supporters so far. Continuing to rely on it exclusively would be a huge mistake at a time when opponents will accelerate their attacks.

The public will only start understanding and believing in the law's historic provisions, the ones that actually make health insurance widely available and affordable, when those provisions move from promise to reality in 2014. Until then the battle has to be fought as if the law's basic existence is in question, which it is.

To connect with people now, the Affordable Care Act has to be connected to the broader narrative on income inequality and the continued economic uncertainty facing American families. The message should be: "Instead of helping hard-pressed working families, Republicans want to keep the health insurance companies in charge and block the new health insurance law, which will guarantee affordable coverage even if you lose your job. If the insurance companies and the Republicans win, then our families will lose, and the promise that we will finally have a guarantee of good health care we can afford no matter what happens will be taken away."

The push to repeal the Affordable Care Act is part and parcel of a broader attack on the role of government overall and in particular in health care. The budget proposal enacted by the House of Representatives in April 2011 would turn Medicare from a public insurance system into a program that provided limited public funding to purchase private insurance. It would ruin Medicaid by replacing a program that now entitles low-income people to health coverage with a block grant to states to spend however they want on health care for the poor.

This dismantling of the nation's public health insurance programs and repeal of the Affordable Care Act is driven by ideologues who would eviscerate government and deny our responsibility to care for each other. Proposals to repeal the ACA, privatize Medicare, and slash Medicaid will kill people and make families destitute. Progressives should not shrink from the moral issues at stake.

HCAN has continued the fight. With many fewer resources, the coalition and grassroots partners have engaged in the regulatory battles on implementation, pressing for instance for the strongest regulations to defend consumers. The coalition has fought against the deep cuts and dismantling of Medicare and Medicaid proposed in the Republican budget proposals. HCAN's state partners, along with many other state groups, are fighting to win robust implementation of the law at the state level.

Here to Stay

As I write this epilogue in the summer of 2011, the Affordable Care Act faces two significant challenges to being fully implemented in 2014. The first major obstacle is the legal challenges to the constitutionality of the requirement that individuals purchase health coverage. The Supreme Court will almost certainly rule on those challenges by July 2012. While most legal scholars believe that the individual mandate is constitutional, the current Supreme Court has demonstrated a disdain for settled law, and so could well throw out that provision. If they do, it is still widely expected that they will leave the rest of the law in place.

What would it mean to have no individual mandate in the law? The ACA will still expand Medicaid to cover some sixteen million people who are now uninsured. But Congress would need to rewrite the rules for how health insurance coverage and subsidies work for people in the subsidized health insurance marketplaces. Even under the best-case scenario, under which a rational fix is agreed to by Congress and the President in 2013, the resulting changes will leave several million more people without health coverage than would be covered if the Court upheld the individual mandate.

Whether Congress would work with the President to patch the ACA or throw it out depends on the outcome of the second major obstacle, the 2012 election for president. The Republican candidate will certainly run on a pledge to repeal the ACA. If a Republican is elected and carries with him a Republican Congress, then the most important provisions of the law, those that expand Medicaid and provide government subsidies to people who cannot afford health coverage, will be in grave danger. However, repeal of those provisions will also require repeal of the single most popular part of the law, the prohibition against insurance companies denying people coverage for preexisting conditions. Repeal will also mean a loss of revenues for insurance companies and hospitals and other health providers who will benefit when thirty-two million more Americans are insured. All of which is to say that the politics of repeal will become much more complicated than the political gesture it is now with President Obama in the White House.

If President Obama is reelected, with or without Democratic majorities in Congress, I'm certain that he will veto any legislation that significantly guts the Affordable Care Act. As we saw over and over again during the campaign to pass the bill, while the President may have equivocated on some aspects of policy, he stood firm in his determination to pass a bill that established a framework for universal coverage. He won't allow his greatest legacy to be reversed.

In 2007, Massachusetts implemented a law that was the model for the ACA, including an individual mandate. The law is now very popular and 98 percent of the Bay State's residents are covered. Even if the Supreme Court overturns the individual mandate federally, it will continue under Massachusetts law.

The same will be true nationally; once the law takes effect and people see how much they benefit, it will become very popular and have a large constituency. This will be particularly true in states in which there is a favorable political climate for the law, as they will do the best job of implementation. Even if the Supreme Court overturns the individual mandate nationally, these states could require it as a matter of state law. The result would be a growing number of states that provide affordable coverage for most of their residents. Over time, even without a federal individual mandate, the ACA is likely to build popular strength across the country.

With or without a federal individual mandate, the ACA is likely here to stay. The question for future presidents and Congresses will not be whether the United States should establish a government promise of affordable health coverage, but how to change the system that is in place. Over time, both Social Security and Medicare have been expanded to cover more people with better benefits, despite opposition from conservatives to doing so. With the ACA in place, issues of changing and improving the law will become a regular part of the political debate in Congress and during elections.

The outcome of these debates will not be determined by reason. Political decisions are determined by power. The growing disparity of wealth in the United States threatens the foundations of our democracy. Plutarch observed, "An imbalance between rich and poor is the oldest and most fatal ailment of all Republics." Almost 2,000 years later, Supreme Court Justice Louis Brandeis echoed the Greek philosopher saying, "You can have wealth concentrated in the hands of a few, or democracy, but you cannot have both."

The greatest challenge to defending the Affordable Care Act is the fundamental challenge that faces the United States early in the twenty-first century, whether we will reverse the current course and move toward an economy based on shared prosperity. The implementation of the Affordable Care Act will help achieve that goal in itself. But the larger issue will be decided by whether everyday Americans will join a broader political movement to take back power from the elites that are wrecking our economy and ruining our democracy.

While the passage of the Affordable Care Act required many compromises with corporate power it was ultimately a triumph of grassroots organizing for economic justice. That organizing was demonstrated in the grassroots movement that helped elect an African American to the presidency. That grassroots energy found another home in the campaign that the

Health Care for America Now coalition conducted in achieving another seemingly impossible goal, making health care a government guaranteed right. I continue to rest my hopes in the power of people to organize together to bend the United States, however slowly, toward justice.

Notes

A Note on Sources: Quotations from individuals for which there are not notes or other explanations of the source in the text are from personal interviews conducted by the author in the fall of 2010.

1   "Pelosi Pole Vault," video clip, [n.d.], http://www.youtube.com/watch?v=i5iUlXBenXM.

2   U.S. Bureau of the Census, "Money, Income of Families, Households and Persons in the United States: 1982," Series P-60, No.142, February 1984, http://www2.census.gov/prod2/popscan/p60-142.pdf.

3   Richard Kirsch, "Tax Revolt with a Twist: Saving Services in New Jersey," *Dollars and Sense*, July/August 1983.

4   Kimberly Green Weathers, "Fitting an Elephant through a Keyhole: America's Struggle with National Health Insurance in the Twentieth Century," PhD Dissertation, University of Houston, May 2004.

5   David Blumenthal and James Morone, *Heart of Power* (Berkeley, CA: University of California Press), p. 58.

6   Ibid, p. 172.

7   Theda Skocpol, *Boomerang: Health Care Reform and the Turn Against Government* (Princeton, NJ: Princeton University Press, 1995), p. 146.

8   Jacob S. Hacker, "Medicare Plus: Increasing Health Care Coverage by Expanding Medicare," in *Covering America: Real Remedies for the Uninsured*, ed. Elliot K. Wicks (Washington, DC: Economic and Social Research Institute, June 2001), pp. 75-100, http://www.esresearch.org/RWJ11PDF/full_document.pdf.

9   David Cutler, "Advisor Describes Obama Health Plan," OurFuture.org/blog, June 1, 2007.

10 Paul Krugman, "Health Care Hopes," *The New York Times*, September 21, 2007, http://www.nytimes.com/2007/09/21/opinion/21krugman.html.

11 Julie Bosman, "New Health Reform Group to Spend $40 Million," *The New York Times*, The Caucus Blog, July 3, 2008, http://thecaucus.blogs.nytimes.com/2008/07/03/new-health-reform-group-to-spend-40-million/#.

12 Chris Frates, "Insurance Industry Forming Activist Army," *Politico*, July 17, 2008, http://www.politico.com/news/stories/0708/11814.html.

13 Seeking Alpha, "WellPoint Inc. Q1 2008 Earnings Call Transcript," April 23, 2008, http://seekingalpha.com/article/73633-wellpoint-inc-q1-2008-earnings-c all-transcript.

14 Timothy Noah, "Astro Turf Watch," *Slate*, July 24, 2008, http://www.slate.com/id/2195957/.

15 Tom Daschle and David Nather, *Getting It Done: How Obama and Congress Finally Broke the Stalemate to Make Way for Health Care Reform* (New York: Thomas Dunne, 2010), p. 3.

16 Jonathan Alter, *The Promise: President Obama, Year One* (Simon and Schuster, 2010), p. 38

17 *Getting it Done*, p. 117

18 Robert Pear, "Insurers Seek Presence at Health Care Sessions," *The New York Times*, December 17, 2008, http://www.nytimes.com/2008/12/17/us/politics/17health.html?scp=1&s q=Insurers%20Seek%20Presence%20at%20Health%20Care%20Sessions &st=cse.

19 Robert Pear, "At House Party on Health Care, the Diagnosis Is It's Broken," *The New York Times*, December 22, 2008, http://www.nytimes.com/2008/12/23/health/23health.html?scp=1&sq=A t%20House%20Party%20on%20Health%20Care&st=Search.

20 Chris Frates, "GOP Slow to Respond to Dems' Health Plan," *Politico*, November 25, 2008, http://www.politico.com/news/stories/1108/15936.html.

21 Arthur Delaney, "Marcelas Owens, 11-Year-Old Whose Mother Died Without Health Insurance: 'Get The Health Care Bill Passed'," *The Huffington Post*, March 11, 2010, http://www.huffingtonpost.com/2010/03/11/marcelas-owens-11-year-ol _n_495207.html.

22 David Whalen, "Specter Switch Good News for Obamacare," *Forbes.com*, April 28, 2009, http://www.forbes.com/2009/04/28/arlen-specter-business-healthcare-o bamacare.html.

23 Sam Stein, "Specter Won't Back Public Health Care or Employee Free Choice," *The Huffington Post*, May 3, 2009, http://www.huffingtonpost.com/2009/05/03/specter-wont-back-public_ n_195325.html.

24   Robert Pear, "Health Care Leaders Say Obama Overstated Their Prom-
     ise to Control Costs," *The New York Times*, May 14, 2009,
     http://www.nytimes.com/2009/05/15/health/policy/15health.html?scp=1
     &sq=Hospitals%20and%20insurance%20companies%20said%20Thursd
     ay%20that%20President%20Obama%20had%20substantially%20overst
     ated%20their%20promise%20earlier%20this%20week%20to%20reduce
     %20the%20growth%20of%20health%20spending&st=cse.

25   David Kirkpatrick, "Obama is Taking an Active Part in Talks on Health
     Care Plan," *The New York Times*, August 12, 2009,
     http://www.nytimes.com/2009/08/13/health/policy/13health.html.

26   Igor Volsky, "Daschle: Public Option 'Taken Off the Table' in July Due
     to Understanding People had with Hospitals,'" *Think Progress Health*,
     October 5, 2010,
     http://thinkprogress.org/health/2010/10/05/171689/daschle-interview/.

27   Open Secrets, "Net Worth 2009," *OpenSecrets.org*, n.d.,
     http://www.opensecrets.org/pfds/overview.php?type=W&year=2009&f
     ilter=A.

28   Bob Geary, "A Face of the Uninsured, a State of Denial," *Indyweek*, July
     15, 2009,
     http://www.indyweek.com/indyweek/a-face-of-the-uninsured-a-state-o
     f-denial/Content?oid=1216589.

29   Pew Research Center's Project for Excellence in Journalism, "Health
     Care Tops the News," *Journalism*, June 21, 2010,
     http://www.journalism.org/analysis_report/health_care_tops_news.

30   Robert Pear, "House Committee Approves Health Care Bill," *The New
     York Times*, July 16, 2009,
     http://www.nytimes.com/2009/07/17/us/politics/17cbo.html?scp=1&sq=
     House%20Committee%20Approves%20Health%20Care%20Bill&st=cse

31   Ben Smith, "Health Reform Foes Plan Obama's 'Waterloo'" *Politico*,
     July 17, 2009,
     http://www.politico.com/blogs/bensmith/0709/Health_reform_foes_pla
     n_Obamas_Waterloo.html.

32   Rick Pearlstein, "Crazy Is a Preexisting Condition" (Online title:
     "Birthers, Health Care Hecklers and the Rise of Right-Wing Rage"),
     The Washington Post, August 16, 2009,
     http://www.washingtonpost.com/wp-dyn/content/article/2009/08/14/A
     R2009081401495.html?sid=ST2010031102527.

33   David Leonhardt, "Opposition to Health Law is Steeped in Tradition,"
     The New York Times, December 14, 2010,
     http://www.nytimes.com/2010/12/15/business/economy/15leonhardt.ht
     ml?scp=1&sq=Opposition%20to%20Health%20Law%20is%20Steeped%
     20in%20Tradition&st=Search.

34   Sean Wilentz, "Confounding Fathers: The Tea Party's Cold War Roots," *The New Yorker*, October 18, 2010, http://www.newyorker.com/reporting/2010/10/18/101018fa_fact_wilentz.

35   Brian Beutler, "Major Insurance Company Urges Employees to Attend Tea Parties," *Talking Points Memo.com*, August 19, 2009, http://tpmdc.talkingpointsmemo.com/2009/08/major-health-insurance-company-urges-employees-to-attend-tea-parties.php.

36   Michael Vitez, Michael Matza, and John Sullivan, "Sestak health-care meeting a spoonful of sugar," *Philadelphia Inquirer*, August 14, 2009, http://www.philaup.org/health/2009_0813Inquirer.html.

37   Robb Mandelbaum, "Small-Business Group Forges an Alliance for Health Care Reform," *The New York Times*, September 1, 2009, http://boss.blogs.nytimes.com/2009/09/01/small-business-group-forges-an-alliance-for-health-care-reform/?scp=1&sq=Small-Business%20Group%20Forges&st=cse.

38   Sam Stein, "Grassley Endorses 'Death Panel' Rumor: 'You Have Every Right to Fear,'" *The Huffington Post*, August 12, 2009, http://www.huffingtonpost.com/2009/08/12/grassley-endorses-death-p_n_257677.html.

39   David Helling, "Sen. McCaskill's town hall dominated by health care reform supporters," *The Kansas City Star*, August 25, 2009.

40   Jim Siegel and Jonathan Rifkind, "Health-Care Supporters Rally," *Columbus Dispatch*, September 2, 2009, http://www.dispatch.com/content/stories/local/2009/09/02/health_rally.ART_ART_09-02-09_A1_PNEUNJC.html.

41   E.J. Dionne, "The Real Town Hall Story," *The Washington Post*, September 3, 2009.

42   Michael D. Shear and Ceci Connolly, "Debate's Path Caught Obama by Surprise" (Online version: "White House Is Seeking to Repair Intraparty Rift About Public Option"), *The Washington Post*, August 19, 2009, http://www.washingtonpost.com/wp-dyn/content/article/2009/08/18/AR2009081803655.html.

43   Barack Obama, speech at Newport News, Virginia, October 4, 2008.

44   Richard Kirsch, "The 'Government Take-Over' Isn't About the Public Option," *The Huffington Post*, August 13, 2009, http://www.huffingtonpost.com/richard-kirsch/the-government-take-over_b_258532.html.

45   Jonathan Alter, *The Promise: President Obama, Year One* (New York: Simon & Schuster, 2011), p. 395.

46   Alexi Mostrous, "Obama Rallies Union Support for Health-Care Reform," *The Washington Post*, September 8, 2009, http://www.washingtonpost.com/wp-dyn/content/article/2009/09/07/A R2009090700225.html.

47   Reed Abelson, "President's Speech Allays Some Fears in the Health Insurance Industry," *The New York Times*, September 10, 2009, http://www.nytimes.com/2009/09/11/health/policy/11insure.html?scp=1 &sq=President%E2%80%99s%20Speech%20Allays%20Some%20Fears% 20in%20the%20Health%20Insurance%20Industry&st=cse.

48   Frank Luntz, "The Language of Health Care 2009: The 10 Rules for Stopping the *"Washington Takeover"* of Healthcare," linked in Igor Volsky, "Deconstructing Frank Luntz's Obstructionist Health Care Reform Memo, Think Progress Health, May 6, 2009, http://thinkprogress.org/health/2009/05/06/170766/luntz-memo/.

49   Wendell Potter, *Deadly Spin: An Insurance Company Insider Speaks Out on How Corporate PR Is Killing Health Care and Deceiving Americans* (New York: Bloomsbury, 2010), p. 69.

50   *Deadly Spin*, p. 201.

51   George Stephanopoulos, "Latino Lawmaker Rips Obama for Making it Harder for Illegals to Buy Private Insurance," George's Bottom Line, *ABC News*, September 15, 2009, http://abcnews.go.com/blogs/politics/2009/09/latino-lawmaker-rips-oba ma-for-making-it-harder-for-illegals-to-buy-private-insurance/.

52   Robert Pear and Jackie Calmes, "Obama's Health Care Plan Builds on Other Ideas," *The New York Times*, September 9, 2009, http://www.nytimes.com/2009/09/10/health/policy/10health.html?scp=1 &sq=Obama%E2%80%99s%20Health%20Care%20Plan%20Builds%20o n%20Other%20Ideas&st=cse.

53   Shailagh Murray and Lori Montgomery, "Senate Health-Care Bill Diverges from House on Key Provisions" (Online version: "Senate announces $848 billion health-care bill"), *The Washington Post*, November 19, 2009, http://www.washingtonpost.com/wp-dyn/content/article/2009/11/18/A R2009111802014.html?wpisrc=newsletter&wpisrc=newsletter&wpisrc= newsletter.

54   Peter Grier, "Would Health Care Premiums Go Up Under Senate Finance Bill?" *The Christian Science Monitor*, October 13, 2009, http://www.csmonitor.com/USA/Politics/2009/1013/would-healthcare-premiums-go-up-under-senate-finance-bill.

55   *The Promise*, p. 404.

56 Stephanie Condon, "Liberals Open Fire on Harry Reid," *CBS News*, October 22, 2009,
http://www.cbsnews.com/stories/2009/10/22/politics/main5408951.sht
ml.

57 J. Taylor Rushing and Steve Stoddard, "Ben Nelson: Don't Count on My Vote," *The Hill*, September 9, 2009,
http://thehill.com/homenews/senate/57795-ben-nelson-dont-count-on-my-vote.

58 Richard Kirsch, "Republicans Champion Government Health Insurance ... for Seniors," *The Huffington Post*, December 7, 2009,
http://www.huffingtonpost.com/richard-kirsch/republicans-champion-gove_b_382510.html.

59 Ben Smith, "Insurance Industry Insider: We Win," *Politico*, December 7, 2009,
http://www.politico.com/blogs/bensmith/1209/Insurance_industry_insi
der_We_win.html.

60 Rachel Slajda, "Weiner on Medicare Buy-In: 'This Is One Idea I Like a Lot'," Talking Points Memo, December 9, 2009,
http://tpmdc.talkingpointsmemo.com/2009/12/weiner-on-medicare-buy
-in-this-is-one-idea-i-like-a-lot.php.

61 Ben Armbruster, "Lieberman: 'There's No Reason' to Deal With the Uninsured Until after the Recession," *Think Progress*, August 23, 2009,
http://thinkprogress.org/politics/2009/08/23/57368/lieberman-uninsure
d-recession/.

62 Manu Raju, " Joe Lieberman: I'll Block Vote on Harry Reid's Plan," *Politico*, October 27, 2009,
http://www.politico.com/news/stories/1009/28788.html.

63 Political Correction, "Sen. Lieberman's Friendly Relationship With the Health Care Industry," *Media Matters*, October 28, 2009,
http://politicalcorrection.org/factcheck/200910280002.

64 Ezra Klein, "Lieberman Will Filibuster Health-Care Reform 'As a Matter of Conscience,'" *The Washington Post*, November 9, 2009,
http://voices.washingtonpost.com/ezra-klein/2009/11/lieberman_will_fi
libuster_heal.html.

65 Robert Pear and David M. Herszenhorn, "Lieberman Rules Out Voting for Health Bill," *The New York Times*, December 13, 2009,
http://www.nytimes.com/2009/12/14/health/policy/14health.html?scp=1
&sq=Lieberman%20Rules%20Out%20Voting%20for%20Health%20Bill
&st=cse.

66   Adam Nagourney, "Reid Faces Battle in Washington and at Home,"
     The New York Times, January 24, 2010,
     http://www.nytimes.com/2010/01/24/magazine/24reid-t.html?scp=1&sq
     =Reid%20Faces%20Battle%20in%20Washington%20and%20at%20Hom
     e&st=cse.

67   Don Walton, "Nelson sounds conflicted on health reform," *Lincoln
     Journal Star,* December 16, 2009.

68   Newsweek, "What Senators Talk About When They Talk About Health
     Care: A By the Numbers Guide to the Debate," *Newsweek Blogs,* Decem-
     ber 24, 2009,
     http://www.thedailybeast.com/newsweek/blogs/the-gaggle/2009/12/24/
     what-senators-talk-about-when-they-talk-about-health-care-a-by-the-n
     umbers-guide-to-the-debate.html.

69   Steven Greenhouse, "Unions Rally to Oppose a Tax on Health Insur-
     ance," *The New York Times,* January 9, 2010,
     http://www.nytimes.com/2010/01/09/business/09union.html?sq=Union
     s%20Rally%20to%20Oppose%20a%20Tax%20on%20Health%20Insuran
     ce&st=cse&adxnnl=1&scp=1&adxnnlx=1305641336-U0nzr22gtbsbUZqY
     JyLdAw.

70   Jeff Zeleny, "Obama Plans Bipartisan Summit on Health Care," *The
     New York Times,* February 8, 2010,
     http://www.nytimes.com/2010/02/08/us/politics/08webobama.html?scp
     =1&sq=Obama%20Plans%20Bipartisan%20Summit%20on%20Health%
     20Care&st=Search.

71   "Health Insurers Break Profit Records as 2.7 Million Americans Lose
     Coverage," HCAN, February 11,2010,
     http://hcfan.3cdn.net/a9ce29d3038ef8a1e1_dhm6b9q0l.pdf

72   Katharine Q. Seelye, "Administration Rejects Health Insurer's Defense
     of Huge Rate Increases," *The New York Times,* February 12, 2010,
     http://www.nytimes.com/2010/02/12/health/policy/12insure.html?scp=1
     &sq=Administration%20Rejects%20Health%20Insurer%92s%20Defense
     %20of%20Huge%20Rate%20Increases&st=Search.

73   U. S. Department of Health and Human Services, *Insurance Companies
     Prosper, Families Suffer: Our Broken Health Insurance System,* February 18,
     2010,
     http://www.healthreform.gov/reports/insuranceprospers/insurancepro
     fits.pdf.

74   Peter Stone, "Health Insurers Funded Chamber Attack Ads," *National
     Journal,* January 12, 2010,
     http://undertheinfluence.nationaljournal.com/2010/01/health-insurers-f
     unded-chamber.php

75 Beth Sussman, "U.S. Chamber Dwarfs Other Groups for Health Care Lobbying," *National Journal*, January 25, 2010, http://undertheinfluence.nationaljournal.com/2010/01/health-care-lobbying-in-fourth.php.

76 Barack Obama, "Remarks by the President and Q&A at Democratic National Committee Fundraising Reception," The White House, Office of the Press Secretary, February 4, 2010, http://www.whitehouse.gov/the-press-office/remarks-and-qa-president-dnc-fundraising-reception.

77 Rick Sanchez, "Rick's List," *CNN*, March 9, 2010, http://archives.cnn.com/TRANSCRIPTS/1003/09/rlst.02.html.

78 Media Matters, "Right-Wing Media Sets Sights on Family of 11-Year Old Who Spoke About His Mother's Death at Health Care Event," March 16, 2010, http://mediamatters.org/research/201003160023.

79 Kate Pickert, "The Worst of Conservative Talk Radio," *Time*, Swampland Blog, March 19, 2010, http://swampland.time.com/2010/03/19/the-worst-of-conservative-talk-radio/.

80 John D. McKinnon and Brody Mullins, "Business Buys Ads vs. Health Overhaul," *The Wall Street Journal*, March 10, 2010, http://online.wsj.com/article/SB10001424052748704145904575112103505931106.html.

81 Mitchell Landsberg, "Nuns in U.S. Back Health Care Bill Despite Catholic Bishops' Opposition," *Los Angeles Times*, March 18, 2010, http://articles.latimes.com/2010/mar/18/nation/la-na-healthcare-nuns18-2010mar18.

82 Paul Starr, *Remedy and Reaction: The Peculiar American Struggle over Health Care Reform* (New Haven, CT: Yale University Press, 2011).

83 Jacob Hacker and Paul Pierson, *Winner-Take-All Politics: How Washington Made the Rich Richer — and Turned Its Back on the Middle Class* (New York: Simon & Schuster, 2010), p. 291.

84 Ibid, p. 303.

85 Robert Reich, *Aftershock* (New York: Knopf, 2010), p. 19.

86 *Winner-Take-All Politics*, p. 25.

87 http://elsa.berkeley.edu/~saez/TabFig2007.xls.

Bibliography

History of Health Care Reform:

Blumenthal, David, and James A. Morone. *The Heart of Power: Health and Politics in the Oval Office*. Berkeley, CA: University of California Press, 2009.

Downey, Kirstin. *The Woman Behind the New Deal: The Life of Frances Perkins, FDR's Secretary of Labor and His Moral Conscience*. New York: Anchor Books, 2009.

Johnson, Haynes and David S. Broder. *The System: The American Way of Politics at the Breaking Point*. Boston, MA: Little Brown and Company, 1996.

Potter, Wendell. *Deadly Spin: An Insurance Company Insider Speaks Out on How Corporate PR Is Killing Health Care and Deceiving Americans*. New York: Bloombury Press, 2010.

Starr, Paul. *The Social Transformation of American Medicine: The rise of a soverign profession and the making of a vast industry*. New York: Basic Books, 1982.

——. *Remedy and Reaction: The Peculiar American Struggle over Health Care Reform*. New Haven, CT: Yale University Press, 2011.

Skocpol, Theda. *Boomerang: Health Care Reform and the Turn Against Government*. New York: W.W. Norton and Company, 1997.

Weathers, Kimberley Green. "Fitting an Elephant through a Keyhole: America's Struggle with National Health Insurance in the Twentieth Century."PhD diss., University of Houston, 2004.

Health Care Reform 2008-2010:

Alter, Jonathan. *The Promise: President Obama, Year One*. New York: Simon and Schuster, 2010.

Daschle, Senator Tom, with David Nather, *Getting It Done: How Obama and Congress Finally Broke the Stalemate to Make Way for Health Care Reform*. New York: Thomas Dunne, 2010.

McDonough, John E. *Inside National Health Reform*. Berkeley, CA: University of California Press, 2011.

Potter, Wendell. *Deadly Spin: An Insurance Company Insider Speaks Out on How Corporate PR Is Killing Health Care and Deceiving Americans*. New York: Bloombury Press, 2010.

Staff of *The Washington Post*. *Landmark: The Inside Story of America's New Health Care Law and What it Means for Us All*. New York: Public Affairs, 2010.

Starr, Paul. *Remedy and Reaction: The Peculiar American Struggle over Health Care Reform*. New Haven, CT: Yale University Press, 2011.

Current Politics and Community Organizing:

Alinsky, Saul D. *Rules for Radicals: A Practical Primer for Realistic Radicals*. New York: Random House, 1971.

Atlas, John. *Seeds of Change: The Story of ACORN, America's Most Controversial Antipoverty Community Organizing Group*. Nashville, TN: Vanderbilt University Press, 2010.

Bobo, Kim, Jackie Kendall, and Steve Max. *Organizing for Social Change: Midwest Academy Manual for Activists*, 4th ed. Santa Ana, CA: The Forum Press, 2010.

Greider, William. *Come Home, America: The Rise and Fall (and Redeeming Promise) of our Country*. Emmaus, PA, 2009.

Hacker, Jacob S. and Paul Pierson. *Winner-Take-All Politics: How Washington Made the Rich Richer—and Turned Its Back on the Middle Class*. New York: Simon & Schuster, 2010.

Kahn, Si. *Creative Community Organizing: A Guide for Rabble-Rousers, Activists, and Quiet Lovers of Justice*. San Francisco, CA: Berrett-Koehler, 2010.

Krugman, Paul. *The Conscience of a Liberal*. New York: W.W. Norton, 2009.

Reich, Robert B. *Supercapitalism: The Transformation of Business, Democracy, and Everyday Life*. New York: Vintage, 2007.

Sen, Rinku. *Stir It Up: Lessons in Community Organizing and Advocacy*. Hoboken, NJ: Jossey-Bass, 2003.

Index

AARP, 269–70, 295

Abelson, Reed, 223

abortion, 202
House of Representatives bill on, 165, 272–74, 277
pro-choice representatives voting against health care reform, 346–50
in reconciliation bill, 343, 351–53
Senate bill on, 313–14
votes in House of Representatives tied to, 345

Abram, Katy, 192

ACORN (Association of Community Organizations for Reform Now), 279, 361

advertising
against insurance companies, 225–26, 228–29, 235
against public option, 150
in Congressional election of 2008, 95–96
by drug companies, 90, 135–36
after election of 2008, 106–7, 111
funded by insurance companies, 237, 327
Harry and Louise ads, 28, 32–33, 134
Magic 8 Ball ads, 68–70
in Maine, 254
"Marathon" ad, 320
in Nebraska, 296, 297, 312–13
in Nevada, 287, 288
by Obama campaign, 100–101
for Obama's health care plan, 152
for public option, 131, 220–21
targeting conservative Democrats, 278
thank you ads, 175, 276, 277
by unions in election of 2008, 101
before votes on reconciliation bills, 345–46, 351

Aetna (insurance company), 226

Affordable Health Care for America Act (ACA; U.S., 2010)
challenges to, 368–69
Democratic representatives opposed to, 278–83

in House of Representatives, 272–75
individual mandate under, 369–70
Pelosi on, 267
See also Patient Protection and Affordable Care Act

Agit-Pop (guerilla theater group), 236, 334

Alinsky, Saul, 145

Allen, Lillian, 332

Alter, Jonathan, 103, 106, 252

American Cancer Society, 269

American Environics (firm), 40

American Federation of Labor - Congress of Industrial Organizations (AFL-CIO)
in launching of HCAN, 49
on single-payer health insurance, 79–80
Trumka elected president of, 257
Working America and, 93

American Federation of State County and Municipal Employees (AFSCME), 36
on Baucus bill, 257
calls to Congress organized by, 268
Highway to Healthcare tour organized by, 209
in launching of HCAN, 47–49
on single-payer insurance, 78–79

American Hospital Association (AHA)
on Clinton's health care proposal, 28
on public option, 113

American Medical Association (AMA)
on Clinton's health care proposal, 28
on House of Representatives bill, 167
national health insurance opposed by, 26

American Medical Students Association (AMSA), 131

Americans for Prosperity, 189

Americans United for Change, 48, 50

Americans United to Protect Social Security (AUPSS), 48

America's Health Insurance Plans, debate between HCAN and, 336

383